New England Federalists

New England Federalists

Widening the Sectional Divide in Jeffersonian America

Dr. Dinah Mayo-Bobee

Fairleigh Dickinson University Press Series in American History and Culture

Series Editor: Dr. Kalman Goldstein (Professor Emeritus of History)

FAIRLEIGH DICKINSON UNIVERSITY PRESS
Madison • Teaneck

Published by Fairleigh Dickinson University Press
Copublished by The Rowman & Littlefield Publishing Group, Inc.
4501 Forbes Boulevard, Suite 200, Lanham, Maryland 20706
www.rowman.com

Unit A, Whitacre Mews, 26-34 Stannary Street, London SE11 4AB

Copyright © 2017 by Dinah Mayo-Bobee, Ph.D.

All rights reserved. No part of this book may be reproduced in any form or by any electronic or mechanical means, including information storage and retrieval systems, without written permission from the publisher, except by a reviewer who may quote passages in a review.

British Library Cataloguing in Publication Information Available

Library of Congress Cataloging-in-Publication Data
The hardback edition of this book was previously catalogued by the Library of Congress as follows:

Names: Mayo-Bobee, Dinah, 1957- author.
Title: New England Federalists : widening the sectional divide in Jeffersonian America / Dinah Mayo-Bobee.
Description: Lanham : Lexington Books, 2017. | Series: Fairleigh Dickinson University Press series in American history and culture | Includes bibliographical references and index.
Identifiers: LCCN 2016054227 (print) | LCCN 2017002316 (ebook)
Subjects: LCSH: Federal Party (U.S.) | United States—Politics and government—1801–1809. | New England—Politics and government—1775–1865. | Sectionalism (United States)
Classification: LCC E331 .M45 2017 (print) | LCC E331 (ebook) | DDC 324.2732/2—dc23 LC record available at http://lccn.loc.gov/2016054227

ISBN 978-1-61147-985-0 (cloth : alk. paper)
ISBN 978-1-61147-987-4 (pbk. : alk. paper)
ISBN 978-1-61147-986-7 (electronic)

∞™ The paper used in this publication meets the minimum requirements of American National Standard for Information Sciences Permanence of Paper for Printed Library Materials, ANSI/NISO Z39.48-1992.

Printed in the United States of America

To my father

Contents

Image Captions	ix
List of Abbreviations	xiii
Acknowledgments	xv
Introduction: The "Gloomy Night of Democracy"—Federalist Opposition to the Three-Fifths Clause	1
1 "Have these Haytians no rights?": Restricting Maritime Commerce to Safeguard Slavery (1805–1806)	23
2 "Indissolubly Connected with Commerce": Nonimportation, Southern Sectionalism, and the Defense of New England	51
3 "Squabbles in Madam Liberty's Family": Jefferson's Embargo and the Causes of Federalist Extremism (1807–1808)	83
4 "O Grab Me!": The Justification for Disunion (1808–1809)	119
5 "Sincere Neutrality": War, Moderates, and the Federalist Party's Decline (1810–1820)	155
Epilogue: Old Romans—Federalist Activism and Their Antislavery Legacy (1820–1865)	195
Bibliography	207
Index	223
About the Author	231

Image Captions

FIGURE 1

John Quincy Adams (1767–1848). Artist: Pieter Van Huffel, 1815. Oil on canvas. National Portrait Gallery, Smithsonian Institution; gift of Mary Louisa Adams Clement in memory of her mother, Louisa Catherine Adams Clement.

Adams broke away from the Federalist Party over the Embargo of 1807 and was replaced by the Massachusetts Legislature before the end of his Senate term. He joined Democratic-Republicans, was appointed ambassador to Russia by James Madison and served as James Monroe's secretary of state. In 1825, he became the nation's sixth president, but served only one term. Adams was elected to the House of Representatives in 1831 and became an avid opponent of slavery. A few years before his death in 1848, Adams forced repeal of the House gag rule prohibiting debates over slavery, successfully defended the illegally imported Africans from the schooner *L'Amistad* before the Supreme Court, and fought the annexation of Texas and the Mexican War as machinations to increase the power of slave states by extending slavery.

FIGURE 2

Fisher Ames (1758–1808). Artist: Gilbert Stuart, c. 1807. Oil on wood. National Portrait Gallery, Smithsonian Institution; gift of George Cabot Lodge.

Contemporaries viewed Ames as a leading voice in the Federalist Party and most historians agree. Ames championed ratification of the Constitution and was largely a nationalist until he saw the need to reject anti–New England commercial policies. He said little to oppose slavery, but after retiring from Congress, Ames praised France's former slaves and defended their right to declare independence and rule over the conquered territory that they established as Haiti in 1804. After denouncing U.S. policy toward Haiti, he published essays opposing what he saw as the Jefferson administration's Francophile, anti–New England policies that Ames urged Federalists to vigorously oppose Democratic-Republicans and their restrictive maritime policies. His sometimes mercurial writings can most likely be attributed to his long battle with a respiratory illness that ended his career and claimed his life at a young age.

FIGURE 3

Rufus King (1755–1827). Artist: Gilbert Stuart, 1819–1820. Oil on panel. National Portrait Gallery, Smithsonian Institution; this acquisition was made possible by a generous contribution from the James Smithson Society.

King was able to keep slavery out of the Northwest in the Ordinance of 1787, but he supported the three-fifths clause and moratorium on ending the slave trade at the Massachusetts Ratifying Convention in 1788. King served as a diplomat and was the last Federalist to run for president. He lost handily to James Monroe in 1816. By the mid 1820s he was a major opponent of slavery in Missouri, but also advocated compensated emancipation and the colonization of freed African Americans outside of the United States.

FIGURE 4

Timothy Pickering (1745–1829). Commissioned by Secretary of War William W. Belknap when assembling a War Department Gallery, the Army acquired the portrait of Secretary Pickering by Walter M. Brackett, 1873, reproduction of a painting by Gilbert Stuart, donated to the United States Military Academy.

George Washington appointed Pickering Postmaster General, Secretary of War, and Secretary of State. Pickering opposed the spread of slavery into the Northwest Territories, and after Jefferson's reelection in 1804, hatched a stillborn plan for a Northern Confederacy because of the three-fifths clause. In the Senate, he opposed commercial restrictions and criticized Democratic-Republicans for their racist policy toward Haiti. They would later consider Pickering's opposition to Jefferson's Embargo (1807) a central cause of the policy's failure.

FIGURE 5

Josiah Quincy (1772–1864). Reproduction of a painting by Gilbert Stuart, c. 1898. Image, courtesy of the Library of Congress Prints and Photographs Division Washington, D.C.

Quincy entered Congress as debates over the Haitian trade began. In Congress he extolled the superiority of the North's free labor force, threatened disunion, and later opposed the entry of slavery into Missouri along with Daniel Webster. Quincy opposed the separation of Maine from Massachusetts but remained active in state and local politics. After leaving Congress, he became a mayor of Boston and president of Harvard University. While he refused to formally join abolitionists, Quincy criticized former allies for compromising over slavery. He lived long enough to congratulate Abraham Lincoln for issuing the Emancipation Proclamation, which he compared to the efforts of leading Federalists, such as Pickering and Rufus King.

FIGURE 6

Daniel Webster (1782–1852). Artist: Frances Alexander, 1800–1880 (Black Dan, Class of 1801, 1835). Oil on canvas, courtesy of the Hood Museum of Art, Dartmouth College, Hanover, New Hampshire. Gift of Dr. George Shattuck, Class of 1803.

Early in his career Webster was an ardent opponent of the Embargo (1807–1809), spoke against the South's growing power through slave representation, and publically condemned the spread of slavery into Missouri. Later in his career, Webster became a Whig, was appointed secretary of state by three presidents, and supported compromises over the spread of slavery, which invoked the consternation of New Englanders and former Federalist colleagues such as Josiah Quincy.

List of Abbreviations

AAS	American Antiquarian Society
BA	Boston Athenaeum
BPL	Boston Public Library
BLYU	Beinecke Rare Book & Manuscript Library, Yale University
LC	Library of Congress
MHS	Massachusetts Historical Society
NYPL	New York Public Library
PEM	Phillips Library, Peabody Essex Museum
SCUA	Special Collections University of Massachusetts Amherst Libraries
UVA	University of Virginia Library, Special Collections

Acknowledgments

Meaningful engagement with any historical topic requires travel, delving into records, researching manuscript collections, making copious notes, and perusing scholarly literature. All of this takes time and reliance on the expertise of others. My process was no different. Reconstructing the history covered in the following pages involved poring over congressional records, diplomatic communiqués, broadsides, pamphlets, statutes, and transcribing handwritten correspondence. Undertaking this type of work is never a solitary venture and like all other historians, I incurred a debt to several people to whom it is my pleasure to express appreciation.

First, I wish to acknowledge the guidance of Professors Bruce Laurie, Barry Levy, and Leonard Richards, who worked closely with me to complete my dissertation, which is how this project began. I am also grateful for the assistance that I received at the University of Massachusetts Amherst from the History Department, the Commonwealth Honors College, and the Center for Teaching. In addition, I need to convey my gratitude and deepest respect to the research librarians and staff at the W. E. B. DuBois Library, who graciously exceeded their job descriptions to make collections available to me in various mediums.

Broadening the context of my work to encompass the Federalists' defense of maritime commerce, subsequent impact on sectional relations, and their contribution to the genesis of antislavery politics required researching an array of collections located in several repositories. For granting me access to these important sources I thank the American Antiquarian Society, especially Philip Lampi who generously shared boxes of the typed and handwritten election returns that he was compiling for the "First Democracy Project," which is now the online database, *A New Nation Votes: American Election Returns, 1787–1824*. I am also beholden to the staff and directors of the Boston Athenaeum and Boston Public Library, and extend a special thanks to the Peabody Essex Museum in Salem, Massachusetts. Through their Frances E. Malamy Research Fellowship, I was able to research several important collections at the Phillips Library. In addition, I wish to thank my colleagues in the History Department at East Tennessee University, especially Dale Schmitt, Daryl Carter, Dorothy Drinkard-Hawkshawe, Brian Maxson, and my faculty mentor Elwood Watson, for their support. It is also a privilege to extend appreciation to the editors of Fairleigh Dickinson University Press and their publishing partner Rowman & Littlefield. For his contributions, special recognition must go to Dr. F. Evan Nooe who unconditionally contributed his considerable and unique talents toward the preparation of this work for publication.

At every step of the way I received encouragement from peers and friends to whom I will always be indebted. First among these are my peer advisors Dr. Christoph Strobel and Dr. Carolyn Powell, for their friendship and mentoring which helped me to complete my doctorate work in a timely fashion and let me know what to expect as I tread the waters of academia. My warmest appreciation goes to professor Dr. Carlin Barton, whose tutelage, friendship, and advice continues to raise my spirits. But Carlin, I still love the Greeks! Another former professor who became a friend to whom I owe much both personally and professionally is Joseph J. Ellis. He remains a true mentor and someone I can always turn to for advice. Thank you so much for all of your time, guidance, and friendship, Professor Ellis.

I reserve special thanks, gratitude, and love for the Bobee family, especially Anita and Joe Sr. Through their unconditional love and friendship I received a steady stream of encouragement and moral support that sustained me through more than one academic and personal milestone. Their genuine affection made the fourteen years that I lived in New England the most memorable, happy, and fulfilling of my life.

The most important note of appreciation that I can provide must go to my parents James and Olivia Mayo, who from a very young age indulged my love of the past and encouraged my interest in history. They have provided love and encouragement my entire life, so my obligation to them is too profound to describe here. The best I can do is to thank them for everything. Finally, my undying love to my youngest sister Lora for her friendship and spiritual example, special thanks to my late sister Leslie Walker who always encouraged me to write, and to my brother and partner in crime, the late James Mayo III. He was always encouraging and taught me how to press on with humor and laughter no matter what life throws my way.

Introduction

The "Gloomy Night of Democracy" — Federalist Opposition to the Three-Fifths Clause

On January 2, 1809, an oration delivered before members and guests of the Wilberforce Philanthropic Association in New York commemorated the first anniversary of the United States' prohibition of the African slave trade. The association, which was named after the British abolitionist and parliamentarian William Wilberforce (1759–1833), was established by African Americans in the early 1800s. Among other things it provided economic relief to those in need and sponsored public activities for New York's free black population. Along with celebrating the government's prohibition on slave importations, the speaker honored those engaged in the ongoing fight to abolish slavery.[1]

He gave the New England states accolades for taking steps to ease the "hard condition" of his "unfortunate countrymen." But although most New Englanders demonstrated "humanity and justice" by fighting to end slavery, the speaker insisted that only members of the Federalist Party, particularly John Adams, Rufus King, and Timothy Pickering, merited praise by name for protecting the rights of black Americans. Members of the region's Democratic-Republicans, especially those in Congress, did not. Instead of fighting to stop the spread of slavery or abolish it altogether, these northerners regularly voted with southern slaveholders, "the very people who hold our African brethren in bondage."[2]

Wilberforce Association members considered Jeffersonians a threat to the freedom and "rights" of free African Americans. Nevertheless, as the Democratic-Republican Party's influence continued to grow nationwide, by 1824 the Federalist Party would cease to exist. Afterward, for over half of the nineteenth century, the presidency, Congress, and many state legislatures would operate under Democratic-Republican (and then Democratic Party) control. As members of the Wilberforce Association likely feared, proslavery southerners with help from their Northern cohorts would consistently gain enough congressional votes to diminish the rights of free African Americans, protect slavery where it already existed, and expand slave labor into new territories.[3]

This book looks at the emergence of radical Federalists in the wake of key events, policy enactment, and controversies that took shape during

Thomas Jefferson's presidency. Whereas Federalists had once championed a strong central government to protect the republic against civil unrest, after 1805 they questioned federal authority and even encouraged noncompliance with federal laws. Chiefly responsible for transforming the party's position would be the series of restrictions placed on maritime commerce. Once these policies were debated and passed, Federalists championed New England's causes in a way that would have an important effect on the sectional climate in politics for decades to come. Contemporaries and historians alike consider the Federalists, whose views are central to this study, radical or extreme due to their appeals to regional protectionism, opposition to the Constitution's three-fifths clause (which counted slaves into the number of congressional representatives and electoral votes), opposition to the War of 1812, and a willingness to abandon the Union that they helped to create. This work argues that Federalist radicalism began to crystallize when Congress disarmed merchant vessels and prohibited U.S. citizens from trading with the black leaders of Haiti (1805–1806). The Haitian embargo would be the first of several laws eventually constituted the Jefferson administration's "restrictive system."

First, Congress deprived merchantmen (commercial ships) of the right to arm for protection, and then, in what seemed like the passage of trade restrictions in rapid succession, the body placed a prohibition on the Haitian trade, passed the Nonimportation Act of 1806 against Britain, and then enacted the highly controversial embargo of 1807–1809, and several supplements thereafter. Embargo proponents explained that they appended new penalties and expanded the range of vessels covered under the original embargo in response to petitions for help from mariners victimized by the French and British. Unfortunately, the federal government's policies had a more negative impact on the nation's merchant fleet than on the warring European nations. Federalists questioned the motives behind each policy and tapped into the discontent and uncertainty escalating among New Englanders. Voters slowly returned them to Congress, but Federalists remained the minority in a hostile legislature, still unwilling to repeal the policies that had cost them northerners' support. It was in this climate that Federalists in and outside of Congress began to inspire violations of the law and threaten disunion to force the Jefferson administration to repeal the acts on maritime commerce. Yet, through their opposition rhetoric Federalists often transcended the immediate crisis. Some promoted northern nationalism while others extolled the maritime North's economic culture and its free labor force in language later used by antislavery politicians.

For twelve years before Jefferson and his party ascended to power Federalists dominated national politics. This comparatively short period of Federalist Party leadership was plagued by the formation of the Democratic-Republican Party. The latter vehemently opposed the Federalists' domestic programs and foreign policy. At the same time, divisive infighting and the lack of a coherent platform seemed to doom the Federalist Party to extinction. In addition, a range of controversies in the 1790s exaggerated, or in some cases fabricated by a growing partisan press, diminished the nation's economic and national security apparatus established under Federalist rule. The list of infractions that damaged the Federalist Party's credibility included elitism, military expenditures and taxes, objections to slave representation, affinity for Great Britain, and willingness to trade with the former slaves of Haiti. The final two positions alone raised the ire of southern Democratic-Republicans who regarded both relationships as dangerous to their economic survival.[4]

Jefferson's victory in the presidential election of 1800 transposed the parties' roles and Federalists became a jaundiced but innocuous opposition party. Even though criticisms of Democratic-Republicans did not start with the passage of trade restrictions of 1805–1806, their vitriol and intensity of Federalists' attacks escalated thereafter. The rhetoric underpinning each new bill played no small part in heightening resistance to the constraints placed on foreign trade. Calls to repeal the three-fifths clause, which Federalists deemed responsible for Jefferson's electoral victory and national influence, also grew more caustic and provocative. Federalists began to argue that the party in power was treating New Englanders with more disdain than the British or French who attacked them on the high seas.

Each commercial law fostered doubts about the federal government's impartiality, a view that the Democratic-Republican majority in Congress reinforced each time it dismissed memorials and reports describing the economic devastation that their policies caused in New England. More than one Jeffersonian representing northern and southern states questioned the sincerity of citizens' complaints. The language congressmen used when repudiating petitioners' claims merely accelerated New Englanders' resistance. In response to protests, criticism of slave representation, and charges that southerners passed laws out of an anti-northern bias, the party in power drafted an enduring narrative that depicted Federalists as partisan opportunists who condoned lawbreaking and promoted sectional hostility merely to reclaim political power or go so far as to destroy the Union.[5]

For the most part, the Democratic-Republicans' propaganda was successful. Regardless of how much the Wilberforce Association, New Englanders, or black voters supported Federalists, the party and its influence withered outside of New England. Negative characterizations in the press convinced many Americans that the Federalists' objections to maritime restrictions were not only obstructionist but also self-serving while their attacks on slave representation was neither principled nor humanitarian. Federalists lost support throughout the nation and, for a time, even in parts of maritime New England.

Democratic-Republicans attracted voters because they advocated expanded white male suffrage, economic opportunity, westward migration, and rapid immigrant participation in the political process. They became increasingly popular in New England as younger, outlying, and disgruntled voters found an alternative to the Federalists' elitism, cliquishness, and resistance to westward expansion. Many residents in the interior districts of Massachusetts, New Hampshire, and Vermont welcomed Jefferson's party. It would therefore take a serious crisis to create the level of disenchantment needed for Federalists to recapture and hold on to support throughout New England. This crucial development began to take shape in 1805.

The upheavals that recaptured New England voters and elevated radicals to the forefront of Federalist Party politics is the focus of *New England Federalists*. Between 1805 and 1815, congressional Federalists touched upon a growing malaise in maritime New England that resulted from federal prohibitions. In addition to denouncing the policies as efforts to destroy the region's economic viability, the radical voices in Congress defended their maritime interests with descriptions of northern superiority that touched upon free soil concepts and free labor ideals. Even though they could only eat away at the edges of the Democratic-Republican control of Congress, Federalists maintained control of New England's congressional seats through the War of 1812 and provided an enduring perspective of New England's role in the Union. Some Federalists later spun nascent threads of antislavery rhetoric into politics that outlived their party. For this reason a younger generation of northerners was able to combine the spirit and elements of the radical Federalists' arguments into an influential movement against the spread of slavery.

To outraged Federalists, commercial restrictions signaled greater problems than attacks on Americans' ships. Disputes in Congress that preceded the final vote on each act demonstrated southern antipathy toward the nonagricultural pursuits of northerners, which compelled Federalists to fight for economic independence and the preservation of employment opportunities available to the North's free labor force. Congressional Federalists stood alone in their efforts to repeal unpopular legislation and, through their protests, sanctioned civil disobedience when the legislative process failed. Though both parties played an active part in the region's politics, in these instances northern Democratic-Republicans usually toed the party line and voted against New England's interests. Although many believed that the restrictions would protect commerce, they still failed to support their region in the face of hostile criticism. New Englanders recognized and scholars have demonstrated that northern Jeffersonians endorsed pro-southern legislation more frequently than their Federalist counterparts. This political reality—more pronounced after hastily passed statutes threatened New England's economic stability—accentuated the need to promote the dynamic prospects in free northern economies.[6]

At the center of the crises affecting international commerce was the war between France and Britain, which gave both nations an excuse to attack American shipping in the West Indies and Atlantic. However, the partisan climate in Washington compounded the problems caused by foreign interference with U.S. shipping. Although he famously stated in his 1801 inaugural, "We are all republicans: we are all federalists," Jefferson intensified party rancor by removing large numbers of Federalists from government offices. Enmity between the parties deepened further when it appeared that Democratic-Republicans consistently ignored mariners' pleas for help simply to spurn Federalists.[7]

In a short time, the venomous atmosphere in Congress helped to modify the nationalism Federalists advocated in the 1780s and 1790s. They felt free to undertake a course of action inimical to the one they displayed while in power. One explanation many provided for this transformation was that southerners had ascended to power through slaveholding and were, with the complicity of likeminded northerners, undercutting New Englanders' political influence and way of life. Thus, a way to curtail the marginalization they were already experiencing was to repeal the three-fifths clause, which provided political rewards for slaveholding.

Democratic-Republicans attempted to counter Federalist opposition to slave representation by dismissing them as insincere. During the 1780s however, high-ranking Federalists had contributed to the North's abolition of slavery. Theodore Sedgwick, who served as Speaker of the House in the Sixth Congress (1799–1801), participated in the trials that ended slavery in Massachusetts. Similarly, New Yorker Alexander Hamilton, the nation's first treasury secretary who immigrated from the West Indies and at one time owned slaves, belonged to New York's antislavery association. Hamilton along with Secretary of State Timothy Pickering from Massachusetts drafted a new government for the self-liberated black leaders of Haiti.[8] Rufus King from Massachusetts (later residing in New York), a delegate to the Constitutional Convention of 1787 and the Federalists' last presidential candidate (1816), fought the westward extension of slavery and contributed to the creation of the nation's first free-soil territory under the Northwest Ordinance of 1787, which he helped to pass before ratification of the established Constitution.[9]

Still, King and other Federalists undercut their antislavery record when they promoted a constitution that sanctioned slave representation along with a twenty-year moratorium on ending U.S. participation in the African slave trade. The federal government was weak under the Articles of Confederation (1781–1788), but taking power away from the states involved making concessions to southerners who feared northern intervention with slavery. Northerners anticipated compromises but some were reluctant to yield ground over slavery. Sedgwick, for one, complained that the alliance between the northern and southern states was already unbalanced. He noted that slaveholders relied on the North for protection from foreign invasion and slave revolts but provided nothing in return. Southerners, he also contended, were hostile to the North's maritime industry and not satisfactorily employing northern merchants to ship their produce. In his mind that was the only compensation the South could offer and as it stood, the Union was not at all beneficial for the North. In 1786, Sedgwick suggested to Federalist Caleb Strong, a delegate to the Constitutional Convention the next year, that secession was an attractive alternative to sacrificing "everything" just to "perpetuate our connection with [the southern states]" under a stronger central government. He concluded that even "the appearance of a union cannot in the way we are long be preserved."[10]

Other Federalists shared Sedgwick's apprehensions about sectional incompatibility, but while debating features of the new government at the State Ratifying Conventions (1787–1788) some were more accommodating. King, for example, had opposed the three-fifths clause and twenty-year moratorium on ending the slave trade while at the Philadelphia Convention, and argued that northerners would never accept both. Yet at the Massachusetts Ratifying Convention he urged delegates to accept both clauses in a "spirit of accommodation." Hence, based on the disagreements that he and others had with southerners over inserting protections for slavery in the national framework, neither King nor anyone else involved with framing the Constitution should have been surprised when northern representatives called for repeal of the three-fifths clause almost as soon as the new government went into operation.[11]

Congress passed the Northwest Ordinance before the Constitution was ratified, but the question over expanding slavery resurfaced when the legislature began to organize the Southwest. In 1798 George Thatcher, a representative from one of Massachusetts' Maine districts, introduced a motion to keep slavery out of the Mississippi Territory. Similar to the black and white abolitionists of the era, Thatcher invoked the "rights of man," and added that slavery was hostile to republican government and "the greatest of evils." He proposed that Congress apply the Northwest Ordinance's antislavery provision to all newly ceded territories. Other New Englanders, including Democratic-Republican Joseph Varnum of Massachusetts agreed. But Federalists did not unite behind Thatcher's proposal. Another Bay State (Massachusetts) representative Harrison Gray Otis said that he did not wish "to interfere with the Southern States as to the species of property in question" merely to satisfy Thatcher's "philanthropy." Thatcher refused to back down, but his proposal failed. Had it succeeded, some, if not all, of the Southwest could have joined the Northwest as free territory.[12]

Historians have suggested that Congress was powerless when it came to keeping slavery out of the Southwest. Objections to banning slavery, some argue, came from slaveholders already residing in the territory, an early example of popular sovereignty. But there were slaveholders living in the Northwest when the Ordinance banned slavery. At various intervals the Territory's slaveholders and those who migrated into the area repeatedly petitioned Congress to repeal the prohibition. Following several unsuccessful attempts to suspend the ban permanently or temporarily, resolute legislators compelled the territory's slaveholders to honor the Ordinance. At times Congress did consider granting requests to lift the prohibition on slavery. On one occasion, a select committee voted to temporarily allow slavery into the territory only to have the Committee of the Whole reject the recommendation.[13]

Not only did Congress exercise its authority under the Constitution to organize new territories without slavery, its responses to northwestern petitioners showed that the federal government was capable of standing firm against slaveholders. Granted, the Ordinance upheld the rendition clause that appeared in the Articles of Confederation (Art. 4) and the Constitution (Art. 4, sec. 2) thereby strengthening slavery in the Southwest, but despite finding creative ways to circumvent the ban on slavery, inhabitants could not carve slave states out of the Northwest Territory. Congress would never again take such a firm stand against the spread of slavery. Proposals to keep involuntary servitude out of the Southwest failed, not because of the territory's inhabitants, but because legislators possessed the prerogative but lacked the will to impose a ban or test southern threats of disunion. In addition, because the three-fifths ratio amplified slaveholders' political clout, extending slavery into new territory was economically beneficial and politically advantageous.

Slavery's expansion became one of the reasons that Federalists accelerated their efforts to repeal the three-fifths clause. Another was their loss in the presidential race of 1800. Even though New York's twelve electoral votes gave Jefferson and Burr victory over John Adams, their calculations of the slave votes convinced Federalists that counting slaves helped Jefferson win the presidency. Before the contest, Adams recognized Burr's ability to turn his state's electoral votes "against the Federalists." Even with New York thrown in, Federalists argued, the Virginian could not have won without help from slaves. By the time Jefferson won reelection in 1804, Federalists were alarmed by the possibility that several slave states could be carved out of the vast Louisiana Purchase Territory acquired in 1803.[14] After the election of 1804, Massachusetts Federalist Leverett Saltonstall conveyed the angst that gripped his party as it braced for a "gloomy night of democracy" with "fear and trembling . . . confusion and misery."[15]

When Congress began to organize the Louisiana Purchase Territory in 1804, Connecticut Senator James Hillhouse, a Federalist, proposed a partial ban on slavery to outlaw the importation of foreign slaves, penalize lawbreakers, and grant freedom to illegally imported Africans. Hillhouse was a Revolutionary War veteran and state legislator who attended the 1787 Constitutional Convention before he entered Congress in 1791. While in Washington, he roomed with Pickering at Coyle's boardinghouse and agreed with his roommate that New England should separate from the Union. Pickering's plans to create a Northern Confederacy never reached fruition, but Hillhouse opposed slavery's entry into the new territory.[16]

On January 28, Stephen Row Bradley, a Jeffersonian from Vermont, proposed an amendment to permanently prohibit the importation of slaves into the Louisiana Purchase Territory and eventually emancipate every slave residing in the area. This time partisan rancor and apathy kept Federalists from rallying behind Bradley. Federalist John Quincy Adams called the proposal excessive and unrealistic. Adams voted against the amendment, convinced that Bradley's only objective was to use his "abhorrence of all slavery" as an excuse to oppose Hillhouse. Yet, in spite of opposition from leading Federalists, including Adams and Pickering, Bradley's proposal was defeated by only six votes (17–11).[17]

The Senate soon resumed the debate over the Hillhouse partial ban. Kentuckian John Breckinridge supported the proposal because he felt that limiting the importation of slaves to domestic traders would dilute slavery, "weaken that race—& free the southern states from a part of its black population, & of its danger." Senators approved Hillhouse's motion with the stipulation that only the slaves of bona fide U.S. citizens could be transported into the territory. His proposal became section 10 of the act that organized the Louisiana Territory; but it really did nothing to arrest the entry or spread of slavery throughout the vast, fertile land. Federalists voted inconsistently but when the final vote was taken on February 18, 1804, Hillhouse, Adams, and William Plumer of New Hampshire opposed the final draft. Adams said that the bill was "placed upon wrong foundations" and that time would substantiate his suspicion that the law could not prevent a massive influx of slaves. He was correct. The prohibition placed on the importation of slaves by foreigners was short-lived. After attaining territorial status, residents had the ban lifted. New Orleans became a major entrepôt for the foreign slave trade until it was outlawed in 1808, and an important depot for domestic slave traders thereafter.[18]

Because of the three-fifths clause, the admission of more slave states into the Union meant further marginalization for Federalists. They had already lost the ability to shape federal policy and Jefferson removed 146 Federalists from government posts at the beginning of his first term. That was not enough for northern Democratic-Republicans like Jacob Crowninshield, who after wresting the Essex South District seat away from Timothy Pickering in 1802, wanted the president to "replace every *federal* officer in Massachusetts." Although they no longer dominated national or state politics, Crowninshield and others feared Federalists because they remained "vigilant, as well as powerful" in New England. Federalists still controlled certain districts in Massachusetts and stayed in control of Connecticut state politics for some time.[19]

Nevertheless, Federalists watched helplessly as Democratic-Republicans gained solid support in the southern and western states.[20] New England had become their sole orbit of influence and many may have thought that their decline was inextricably linked to the region's failing political sway in the expanding nation. Actually, Federalists' frequent attempts to repeal the three-fifths clause and preempt the spread of slavery had caused the party's support to atrophy in the South. Efforts to limit voting rights, extend the time frame for naturalization, and decelerate settlement of the West ensured the loss or absence of constituents almost everywhere else.[21]

While losing the presidency and seats in Congress was disheartening, Federalists did not necessarily retreat from national politics *en masse*. John Adams, the last Federalist to win a presidential election, was nearly sixty-five years old when his reelection bid failed in 1800. Frequent traveling had taken a toll on his health and Adams often worked out of his home in Quincy, Massachusetts. He may have suffered from attacks of thyrotoxicosis due to hyperthyroidism. This recurring illness, sometimes induced by stress, would affect Adams physically and emotionally. His wife Abigail, who had rheumatoid arthritis, also found the long trips to Washington difficult. Her illness gave the president another reason to work from home. Though the loss to Jefferson was bitter, by the time they left Washington in 1801, John and Abigail had helped the thirteen colonies win independence, created international alliances for the fledgling republic, and established the executive's residence in the new capital. Leaving politics voluntarily would have been less traumatic, but they retired with honor.[22]

Other leading Federalists also retired from public life. Theodore Sedgwick and Harrison Gray Otis left politics believing that they would be replaced by younger Federalists. When this did not occur and voters sent Democratic-Republicans to Congress instead, Otis reentered politics.[23] A debilitating respiratory illness forced young Fisher Ames of Massachusetts, who was instrumental in his state's ratification of the Constitution, to leave Congress in 1796. At the time that his congressional career ended, Ames and his wife were expecting their second child and had a new home under construction. He apparently contracted pneumonia or an acute upper respiratory infection complicated by asthma and never recovered.[24] His optimism that the Federalist Party would "rise again" often fluctuated, but in the years before his untimely death in 1808, Ames played a major role in orchestrating the extreme responses adopted by several Federalists.

Maine voters, however, continued to send George Thatcher, an outspoken critic of slavery, to Congress. Thatcher's antislavery arguments were sometimes humanitarian but always sincere. In 1800, when the House took up the "Petition of Free Blacks," who were asking that they not be returned to slavery in North Carolina, Thatcher stood alone. He cast the only vote against a proposal to table the petitioners' request, which in addition to avoiding re-enslavement due to a repealed law, asked Congress to end the slave trade, amend the Fugitive Slave Act of 1793, and abolish slavery altogether.[25] Shortly after winning reelection in 1800, Thatcher accepted an appointment to the Massachusetts Supreme Court and relinquished his congressional seat. He returned to his district as an associate justice and held onto that post until Maine separated from Massachusetts in 1820. It was only after he resigned from Congress, however, that a Democratic-Republican, in this case Richard Cutts, won an election to fill Thatcher's seat.[26]

A few seasoned Federalists, including Hillhouse, Pickering, and John Quincy Adams, remained active in politics. They were joined by younger Federalists such as Martin Chittenden and James Elliot of Vermont, Abiel Foster of New Hampshire, as well as Josiah Quincy, William Ely, and James Lloyd of Massachusetts. Most would add their voices to the veterans' swelling criticism of the three-fifths clause, sectionally biased commercial restrictions, and the increase of Southern power in the federal government.

After Jefferson's reelection in 1804, one Federalist suggested that the North and South follow the biblical example of Abraham and Lot, and go their separate ways.[27] Pickering agreed. He believed that it was in New England's best interest to separate from the Slave South. Convinced that slavery rendered the North and the South innately discordant he concluded that New England had nothing in place to "countervail the power and influence arising from the Negro representation."[28] His solution was secession and the creation of a Northern Confederation. With Massachusetts taking the lead, Pickering predicted that the other New England states followed by New York, New Jersey, and Pennsylvania, would also secede to join a confederation of Free States. Neither slavery nor slave representation would mar their economic progress or threaten political equity in their new splinter Republic.[29]

Though his plan received scant support, Pickering's sentiments were not isolated. Others shared his contempt for the three-fifths clause, but considered disunion too drastic. Americans who survived the Revolution were acutely apprehensive about separatist plots, which they understandably associated with Britain's efforts to reclaim its former colonies. More practical and in line with general sentiment was the Massachusetts Legislature's resolution in 1804 requesting that the state's delegates in Congress propose a constitutional amendment to eliminate the three-fifths ratio. Federalists circulated the resolution to other New England states for support. Rumors of disunion quickly tainted the effort and while political leaders such as Isaac Tichenor, the Governor of Vermont and U.S. Senator at various times in his career, agreed that it was unjust for slaves to factor into southerners' political power, they refused to join Massachusetts because it seemed like a step toward secession.[30]

Other Federalists, including the aforementioned Harrison Gray Otis, were either apathetic toward slavery or outright proslavery, while a few Democratic-Republicans were critical of slavery. One who straddled party lines and vocally denounced slavery was Vermont Congressman James Elliot. As a noncommissioned militia officer during the Indian Wars of the 1790s, Elliot toured the nation's western boundaries. He witnessed slaveholding on the frontier but reported that slaves were not used as widely in the areas he visited as in the South. About Kentucky he wrote *"blacks* are not treated here as slaves, but as human beings." Elliot denounced slavery as an unprecedented evil but feared that immediate abolition might be more dangerous than the institution itself. Nevertheless, even if abolition destabilized certain areas of the country Elliot declared that no one more ardently anticipated its eradication than he.[31]

Vermonters sent Elliot to Congress as both a Federalist and a Democratic-Republican. He regularly attacked the three-fifths clause in his hometown press and defended New England's free-labor force during debates over impressments.[32] Elliot renounced any scheme that threatened the Union but boldly singled out slave representation for condemnation. He called the policy of counting slaves for seats in Congress "objectionable" and defended northerners' rights to speak out against it. It was not treasonous, asserted Elliot, to educate New Englanders about the fact that they were at a huge disadvantage in the Union and rapidly losing political influence because owning slaves gave southerners the numbers to control every branch of the federal government.[33]

William Ely of Massachusetts, a future representative in Congress, also proposed amending the Constitution to repeal the three-fifths clause. He predicted that the Union would not survive unless the central government functioned in a way that treated each state equally. As he offered his proposal to the state legislature Ely asked Pickering to present it as a constitutional amendment in the Senate. On December 7, 1804, Pickering introduced his resolution that congressional representation be based only on the number of free persons in a state. The Senate tabled Pickering's resolution and Democratic-Republicans in Massachusetts killed Ely's proposal. It was soon after these efforts failed, according to historian Leonard Richards, that Federalists concluded that a "Slave Power" controlled the federal government.[34]

After 1805, Federalists' respect for central authority declined even further. The former advocates of a strong federal government found themselves outside the circles of power and unable to correct a serious flaw in the government that they created. On the other hand, Democratic-Republicans who were once suspicious of centralized power now utilized the full weight of the federal government. Not only was slave representation a boon to their party's southern leadership, but northern Jeffersonians also benefited from the ratio and rushed to its defense.[35]

Providing detailed assessments of the obstacles that they faced in Congress, this book exposes the combination of factors beginning with the restrictive system that forced Federalists to abandon their nationalist posture and challenge federal authority. When their attempts to introduce alternatives to trade restrictions were rebuffed with indifference or disdain, Federalists came to believe that New England could only combat the machinations of an apathetic legislature, and president who rose to power on the backs of slaves with noncompliance, protests, and rejection of the Union if necessary.[36]

Of course, nowhere does this study make the case that as a group Federalists advocated abolition or that the motive for their tactics was always magnanimous. Instead, one of the main arguments that this work presents is that Federalists who pursued a decidedly radical course of action after 1805 did so in response to what they perceived as overt efforts to subdue New England to the Slave South by altering its maritime economy. Secondly, this study maintains that the Federalists' opposition message, which combined objections to commercial restrictions and opposition to the three-fifths clause, set the stage for the organized antislavery politics that came of age in the 1820s and 1830s. Finally, by emphasizing the Federalists' viewpoint, the discussions that follow add a perspective different from the orthodox interpretation of early national politics that paints Federalists in a very different light.

Federalist clamor over slave representation was not always linked to concern for the well-being of slaves, but nor were their challenges to the three-fifths clause and the expansion of slavery entirely detached from the antislavery sentiment of their generation. This connection was later comprehended by those who formed the nation's first antislavery political party. Liberty Party founders combined the Federalists' political objections to the three-fifths clause with abolitionist humanitarian opposition to slavery. In their tract, *The Slave Power* (1840), party leaders explained that it was because of the three-fifths clause that slaveholders had "wielded an enormous political force" and cost the North $22 million under the embargo of 1807 alone. Based on this clause in the Constitution, slavery had become an aggressive political system for which northerners, the tract itemized, had paid over $1 billion through lost property at sea, the Louisiana Purchase, and the reduction of maritime commerce for twenty-eight years.[37] The tract did not mention that the Liberty Party's major arguments had been raised by Federalists thirty-four years earlier, but it does demonstrate that the Federalists' cause formed a vital part of the philosophical basis for antislavery politics in antebellum America.

Along with dissecting battles in the legislature, a majority of the chapters herein emphasize the plight of merchants and seamen whose experiential accounts instigated the contentious debates and controversial policies that so deeply divided the nation. As attacks on New Englanders' property and persons played out before the nation, Democratic-Republicans transformed pleas for protection into reasons to interdict the nation's foreign trade. More problematic was the fact that many in Congress cited the immorality of maritime pursuits to justify their policies.[38]

To Federalists, condemnations of the wartime-carrying trade conveyed in criticism of northern mariners and commercial cultures in general gave credence to the notion that southerners were attempting to destroy New England through legislation. Verbal browbeating and contempt for merchants nourished these suspicions even further. Soon, newspapers and broadsides reported that the Democratic-Republicans' real objective was the subjugation of the Free North to slaveholders.

When casting themselves as the defenders of economic forces superior to agricultural economies driven by slave laborers, Federalists emphasized the North's dynamic society. Free laborers in the maritime trades enjoyed a good, steadily improving quality of life. They deserved federal protection equal to, if not greater than, slavern slaveholders, a message that eventually convinced an impressive number of New Englanders to vote Jeffersonians out of office. Thus, in the short run Federalists had a level of success, but could not avert a second war with Britain in 1812, or preserve New England's old maritime economy. In the long run their rabid regionalism inspired Northern unity, the fight to protect new territory for free labor, and coordinated political and humanitarian efforts to extend free soil and confine slavery to where it already existed.[39]

Despite the Federalists efforts, nearly a decade of protracted trade restrictions before and during the War of 1812 did transform New England's economy. Maritime commerce still existed but manufacturing became dominant and established New England markets for raw materials produced by slaves. Postwar improvements in transportation and communication also helped slaveholders transport produce to new markets—foreign and domestic—with greater speed. New England soon became part of a national economy with strong ties to the South that increased westward migration, immigration, and the spread of slavery. The Federalist Party's days were numbered.[40]

While interregional political and economic relations contributed to the Union's wealth and growth, anti-Southern, antislavery sentiment continued to deepen in New England. The region's congressional representatives extracted a comprehensive antislavery philosophy out of the ideas expressed by Federalists during their opposition to the embargo and other trade policies. Only slight variations existed between the Federalists' condemnation of the three-fifths clause and challenges to the spread of slavery that emerged between the War of 1812 and the 1820s. These similarities explain why proslavery southerners and ambivalent northerners attributed the rise of abolitionism to the Federalist Party. Had the congressional debates over New England's maritime culture not taken place, the antislavery politics that helped to precipitate the Civil War might have looked quite different or emerged much later, if at all.

Important insights into Federalist politics clarify the ways that generational changes and demographics altered their party's character and politicking practices in the 1790s and early 1800s, even after the presidency remained beyond arm's length. Yet, as a result of internal dissension, westward expansion, and the circulation of unfavorable propaganda, the party lasted less than a decade after the second war with Great Britain ended in 1815.[41] Scholars have emphasized various aspects of the Federalist Party's political culture, defense policies, involvement with civic organizations, and voluntary associations. Equally important was the language Federalists employed to set the limits of dissentient democratic practices and shape national development in the 1780s and 1790s. An important branch of scholarship also emphasizes the impetus for Federalists' antislavery sermons during the War of 1812, which chronicles their contributions to antislavery politics at a much earlier period than previously argued. Collectively, this scholarship integrates Federalists into the scholarly synthesis of nineteenth-century cultural, social, and political history previously dominated by studies focused exclusively on Jeffersonian politics.[42]

New England Federalists endeavors to add another layer to this body of literature by offering a fresh perspective on a crucial period in Federalist Party politics before the War of 1812. The Wilberforce Association's juxtaposition of the Federalists' defense of commerce and efforts to end the spread of slavery was no accident.[43] Newspapers repeatedly printed and circulated transcripts of congressional debates throughout the nation. This enabled Americans to make a connection between commercial restrictions and Federalist efforts to repeal slave representation (the Constitution's three-fifths clause). Opinion pieces linked New England's maritime woes to the extra votes and power that counting slaves gave to southerners. By the time that the Wilberforce Association speech was delivered in 1808, the intense sectionalism and partisanship chronicled in this study had been underway in Congress for three years.

Weaving the diverse historical developments covered in this work into a coherent narrative involved identifying the philosophies and political theories that surfaced often during congressional debates. Therefore, it is necessary to briefly discuss concepts pertaining to republicanism and other philosophies that found their way into several congressional speeches. Most of the time, when politicians conjured up ancient theorists or Enlightenment philosophers, they did so to lend credence to controversial statements or otherwise questionable positions. Yet seldom did such lofty, erudite appeals provide satisfactory answers or sway the opposition. Therefore, this book places more emphasis on the events, debates, and politics that informed legislation and sparked Federalist radicalism in and outside of Congress.[44]

Merchants, seamen, and other citizens who relied on the government to protect their property and personal safety found small comfort in philosophical reasoning. Even when Federalists complained that Jefferson was destroying commerce to test his commercial theories, that argument did little to help those in the maritime industry. Their lives and livelihoods were disrupted by French and British privateers, and finally their own government.[45] If Federalists had placed their political choices on philosophies when in power, they soon began to deal more with the realities facing their region and constituents between 1805 and the War of 1812.[46]

Because events in Congress form the nucleus of this study, readers are introduced to political actors who operated within the circles of power. Whichever side of the aisle they represented, these politicians either reflected cultural trends or influenced public opinion. Representatives, senators, diplomats, presidents, and their administrations drafted the legislation and enforced the federal laws featured so prominently in this book.

Needless to say, Americans' everyday experiences enrich our political history and tell us much about the relationship between U.S. citizens and their elected officials.[47] For this reason this book describes details of several ship seizures recounted by mariners who petitioned Congress or wrote narratives about their experiences. The same is true of town meeting resolutions, protests, and newspaper editorials that often revealed public opinion. All of these accounts demonstrate the crucial role that average citizens played in steering the course of early national politics.

In states where they could vote, free black men generally supported the Federalist Party. Information pertaining to their patronage adds another dimension to this work. Indeed historians have been demonstrating ways that diverse segments of the population participated in early national politics.[48] Understandably, the Federalists' persistent calls to end the three-fifths clause and arrest the spread of slavery played no small part in earning this constituency's support. In the years to come, their endorsement of Federalists was one reason that Democratic-Republicans would strive to disenfranchise black voters while simultaneously broadening the franchise for white males.[49]

The events covered in the following pages are arranged chronologically, which allows diverse themes to come together in interconnecting chapters. Segments from congressional debates, diplomatic and personal correspondence, speeches, newspaper articles, and other period publications are featured throughout. Wherever possible, the chapters feature the direct statements of congressmen, senators, diplomats, presidents, and cabinet members. This establishes familiarity with historical characters and facilitates immersion in the partisan struggles over the future of maritime commerce and the nation's character.

Chapter 1 looks at congressional efforts to deal with problems involving the Haitian trade between 1805 and 1806. In a reversal of policies implemented by Federalists, Democratic-Republicans disarmed merchant ships and ended trade with the former slaves who governed Haiti. The Haitian policy, which followed several contentious debates in the House and Senate, initiates the restrictive system. What begins as merchants' requests for protection and a diplomatic dispute involving France and Britain soon erupts into a debate over the protection of slavery as a reason to end the trade. Southern and northern Jeffersonians agree that any interaction with the island's self-emancipated black leaders threatens the South's economic well-being and security. In both houses Federalists fight unsuccessfully to keep the trade open. The policy and supporting rhetoric, often racist, has implications for maritime New England that begins to play on the fears of northerners who decry the Jeffersonians' racial discrimination and eagerness to suspend a profitable branch of commerce.

Chapter 2 chronicles the debates over nonimportation that take place shortly after the Haitian embargo is passed in 1806. Deliberations include proposals to end French and British attacks on the transatlantic trade, stop Britain's impressment of U.S. citizens, fortify the nation's coasts, and end the Atlantic slave trade. Northern Jeffersonians support sanctions against Britain, but sectional divisions are exposed as several southerners berate the North's merchants and seamen as they question the value of foreign trade instead. In response to these attacks, Federalists describe and defend a uniquely northern labor force that is averse to agriculture and the constraints of slave economies. The threat of disunion surfaces as a warning should the party in power continue to pass legislation biased against New England. Federalists also attempt to safeguard illegally imported Africans during deliberations over legislation ending the slave trade. By the end of the year, Federalists differentiated themselves from northern Democratic-Republicans by challenging southerners and defending commerce.

Chapter 3 focuses on the events leading to passage of an embargo in 1807. Following an attack on the U.S. frigate *Chesapeake* in June 1807, Jefferson, though receiving a level of bipartisan support to act against Britain, does not call for war. When Congress assembles for an early session, the majority hastily passes an embargo on all shipping. The policy immediately sparks protests from New Englanders, and Congress passes supplemental legislation to impose harsh enforcement measures in response to petitions for relief and Federalist proposals to repeal the embargo. Greater enforcement seemingly leads to greater resistance and violations of the law throughout the year. Federalists depict the legislation as an attempt by the slave interest to destroy New England's economy and gain more seats in Congress in the congressional elections of 1808.

New Englanders' call for disunion and repeal of the embargo are the focus of chapter 4. Hostility to the embargo deepens the sectional divide in Congress and across the nation after a year without exports and limited imports. Economic woes plague New England but the congressional majority rejects Federalist motions to repeal the policy and continue to stiffen enforcement and increase fines. Even though they wish to repeal the embargo, northern Democratic-Republicans claim that James Madison's 1808 presidential victory was a pro-embargo mandate and refuse to support repeal efforts. Instead, they pass the highly controversial Enforcement or Force Act of 1809. New Englanders then reject federal authority and call on their state governments to nullify the law or take steps toward disunion. At the height of the crisis, grassroots organizations prepare for possible armed conflict with federal agents, but Congress votes to repeal the law before any confrontation can take place and plans for a convention of New England states can be finalized.

Chapter 5 looks at developments from repeal of the embargo through the dissolution of the Federalist Party in 1824. President Madison inherits a disgruntled New England and has few alternatives after diplomatic efforts to end French and British attacks on U.S. trade fail. The federal government abandons neutrality and offers to join whichever nation ends its attacks on U.S. shipping. France claims to comply but continues to target American trade. Britain does not accede to U.S. demands and Federalists are unable to block a congressional declaration of war in June 1812. As they protest the conflict as unjust and argue that the war has nothing to do with commerce, some New England states refuse to contribute to the war effort. To assuage riotous New Englanders, Federalist leaders at the state level opt to organize a convention in Hartford, Connecticut. More radical Federalists are not invited to participate and the Convention proves anticlimactic. Under more moderate leadership and the weight the Federalist Party begins to disintegrate.

The epilogue reviews Federalist activities after the Federalist Party disbands around 1824, with a primary focus on those who were most vocal during the fight against Jefferson's commercial policies. This includes Timothy Pickering, Josiah Quincy, John Quincy Adams, and other Federalists contribute to the antislavery cause. As sectional hostilities over slavery escalate and abolitionists form social and political organizations in the North, growing contentions are ascribed to the defunct Federalist Party. Those still active in Congress—in particular the erstwhile Federalist John Quincy Adams in the House of Representatives—return to their roots and fight vehemently to arrest the spread of slavery. Others become associated with the Whig Party. One-time agitator Josiah Quincy, who lives long enough to witness southern secession, the Civil War, and the Emancipation Proclamation, assures President Lincoln that the eradication of slavery, however late, is in fact a Federalist Party victory.

During the commotion over their restrictive system, Democratic-Republican anxiety over losing ground to Federalists resurfaced during every congressional election in New England. "Federalists (notwithstanding their present depression)," wrote one Massachusetts Jeffersonian, "will not give up the whole ground without one more violent struggle."[50] He was correct about the struggle, but could not know that in spite of whatever progress they made, Federalists never became as politically astute as Democratic-Republicans, nor do they produce a leader with Jefferson's influence and ability to articulate a cogent vision for his party and the republic. On the other hand, Federalists did have an uncanny understanding of their opponents' shortcomings and the ability to forecast the effects that restrictive policies would have in New England. As soon as merchants trading with Haiti petitioned the government for help, Federalists correctly predicted that the Democratic-Republican response would be a turning point for commercial New England and the party. One of them correctly opined, "The cause of Federalism . . . will shortly be succeeded by a flood, which will overwhelm its enemies."[51]

NOTES

1. Joseph Sidney, *An Oration Commemorative of the Abolition of the Slave Trade: Delivered before the Wilberforce Phila nthropic Association in the City of New York on the Second of January, 1809*, (New York: Seymour, 1809), 6. Collection of the Boston Athenaeum, hereafter BA.

2. Sidney, *An Oration*, 6, 9, 13, 14 (emphasis in original), BA. See Leslie M. Alexander, *African or American?: Black Identity and Political Activism in New York City, 1784–1861* (Urbana: University of Illinois Press, 2008), 17, 49–51.

3. Some examples appear in Sean Wilentz, *The Rise of American Democracy: Jefferson to Lincoln* (New York: W. W. Norton and Company, 2005); John Ferling, *Adams vs. Jefferson: The Tumultuous Election of 1800* (New York, Oxford University Press, 2004); and James J. Horn, Jan Ellen Lewis and Peter S. Onuf, Eds., *The Revolution of 1800: Democracy, Race, and the New Republic* (Charlottesville: University of Virginia Press, 2002).

4. For examples of the turmoil associated with Federalist Party politics from 1789 onward see: Gordon S. Wood, *Empire of Liberty: A History of the Early Republic, 1789–1815*, reprinted ed. (New York: Oxford University Press, 2011); Doron S. Ben-Atar and Barbara B. Oberg eds. *Federalists Reconsidered* (Charlottesville: University of Virginia Press, 1998); Stanley Elkins and Eric McKitrick, *The Age of Federalism: The Early American Republic, 1788–1800* (New York: Oxford University Press, 1993); Lance Banning, *The Jeffersonian Persuasion: Evolution of a Party's Ideology* (Ithaca, NY: Cornell University Press, 1980).

5. *Pittsfield* (MA) *Sun, or Republican Monitor*, January 6, 1806, and March 17, 1806; George William Van Cleve, *A Slaveholders' Union: Slavery, Politics, and the Constitution in the Early American Republic* (Chicago: The University of Chicago Press, 2010), 139–42; James Roger Sharp, *America Politics in the Early Republic: The New Nation in Crisis* (New Haven, CT: Yale University Press, 1993), 247–48; Egan L. Clifford, *Neither Peace nor War: Franco-American Relations, 1803–1812* (Baton Rouge: Louisiana State University Press, 1983), 44–49. Also see, Richard Buel Jr., *America on the Brink: How the Political Struggle over the War of 1812 Almost Destroyed the Young Republic* (New York: Palgrave Macmillan, 2005), 36–42.

Introduction 19

6. Leonard L. Richards, *The Slave Power: The Free North and Southern Domination, 1780–1860* (Baton Rouge: Louisiana State University Press, 2000), 54, 58, 60–64; John Craig Hammond and Mathew Mason, eds., *Contesting Slavery: The Politics of Bondage and Freedom in the New American Nation* (Charlottesville: University of Virginia Press, 2011), 21?–13.

7. T. B. Wait, ed., *State Papers and Publick Documents of the United States: From the Accession of Thomas Jefferson to the Presidency, Exhibiting a Complete View of Our Foreign Relations since That Time*, 3 vols. (Boston: T. B. Wait and Sons, 1814), 1:10.

8. Rachel Hope Cleves, "'Hurtful to the State:' The Political Morality of Federalist Antislavery," in Hammond and Mason, *Contesting Slavery*, 212.

9. Rufus King to Timothy Pickering, April 15, 1785, in *Letters to Delegates to Congress, 1774–89*, ed. Paul H. Smith et al., 26 vols. (Washington, DC: U.S. Government Printing Office, 1979), 22:342. Different interpretations of the Northwest Ordinance appear in, Elizabeth Cobbs Hoffman, *American Umpire* (Cambridge, MA: Harvard University Press, 2013), 119, 120; James Oakes, *Freedom National: The Destruction of Slavery in the United States, 1861–1865* (New York: W.W. Norton & Company, 2013), 12–13, 440–42; Paul Finkelman, *Slavery and the Founders: Race and Liberty in the Age of Jefferson* (Armonk: M.E. Sharpe, 1998), 34–56; and "Slavery and the Northwest Ordinance: A Study in Ambiguity," in *Journal of the Early Republic*, 6: (Winter, 1986), 343–70.

10. Theodore Sedgwick to Caleb Strong, August 6, 1786; in *Letters of Delegates*, 23: 437, LC; also quoted in Robinson, *Slavery in the Structure of American Politics*, 171; Kerber, *Federalists in Dissent*, 39.

11. Max Farrand, ed., *The Records of the Federal Convention of 1787*, 4 vols. (New Haven, CT: Yale University Press, 1966), 1: 206, 2: 220–22, 632–33; Richards, *Slave Power*, 32–39; Don E. Fehrenbacher, *The Slaveholding Republic: An Account of the United States Government's Relations to Slavery* (New York: Oxford University Press, 2001), 33; Jonathan Elliot, ed. *The Debates in the Several State Conventions, on the Adoption of the Federal Constitution, As Recommended by the General Convention at Philadelphia in 1787*, 5 vols. (Philadelphia: J. B. Lippincott & Co., 1876), 2:36; *Worcester Magazine*, January 24, 1788; *Telescope or American Herald* (Leominster, MA), February 12, 1801 (emphasis in original); Van Cleve, *Slaveholders' Union*, 139, 216–17; Sharp, *American Politics*, 278; Elizabeth R. Veron, *Disunion! The Coming of the American Civil War, 1789–1859* (Chapel Hill: University of North Carolina Press, 2008), 25–27.

12. *Annals of Congress*, 5th Cong., 2nd sess., 1306–13; Adam Rothman, *Slave Country: American Expansion and the Origins of the Deep South* (Cambridge, MA: Harvard University Press, 2005), 24–35; Samuel Eliot Morison, *Harrison Gray Otis, 1795–1848: The Urbane Federalist* (Boston: Houghton Mifflin, 1969), 425; Finkelman, *Slavery and the Founders*, 58–63; Richards, *Slave Power*, 43; cf. John Craig Hammond, *Slavery, Freedom, and Expansion in the Early American West* (Charlottesville: University of Virginia Press, 2007), 5, 13, 14, 24.

13. *Annals of Congress*, 8th Cong., 1st sess., 1023, 1024; 9th Cong., 2nd sess., 482, 483; 10th Cong., 1st sess., 25–27; *American State Papers, Miscellaneous*, 1:9, 10, 484–85; Van Cleve, *Slaveholders' Union*, 211–13; Finkelman, *Slavery and the Founders*, 67–80; Richards, *Slave Power*, 43; Hammond, *Slavery, Freedom, and Expansion*, 5, 13, 14, 24.

14. John Adams, John Adams Autobiography, Part 1, sheet 25" Adams Family Papers, MHS; *Statutes at Large*, 1:123; Van Cleve, *Slaveholders' Union*, 214; Hammond, *Slavery, Freedom, and Expansion*, 10, 11.

15. Leverett Saltonstall, March 12, 1804, and Saltonstall to William Minot, April 17, 1806, in Robert E. Moody, ed., *The Saltonstall Papers, 1607–1815*, 3 vols. (Boston: Massachusetts Historical Society, 1974), 2:185, 302.

16. Kevin M. Gannon, "Escaping 'Mr. Jefferson's Plan of Destruction': New England Federalists and the Idea of a Northern Confederacy, 1803–1804," in *Journal of the Early Republic*, 21, 3 (Autumn, 2001): 413–43; Buel, *America on the Brink*, 62; Richards, *Slave Power*, 43; Robert A. McCaughey, *Josiah Quincy, 1772–1864: The Last Federalist* (Cambridge, MA: Harvard University Press, 1974), 33.

17. *Annals of Congress*, 8th Cong., 1st sess., 240, 241; John Quincy Adams, *Memoirs of John Quincy Adams, Comprising Portions of His Diary from 1795 to 1848*, ed. Charles Francis Adams (Philadelphia: J. B. Lippincott and Co., 1874), 1:292, 293, 295; Van Cleve, *Slaveholders' Union*, 218–23; Hammond, *Slavery, Freedom, and Expansion*, 37.

18. *Statutes at Large* (1845): 2:286; John Quincy Adams, *Memoirs*, 295; David F. Ericson, *Slavery in the American Republic: Developing the Federal Government, 1791–1861* (Lawrence: United Press of Kansas, 2011), 33; Hammond, *Slavery, Freedom and Expansion*, 53; Rothman, *Slave Country*, 29–35; Richards, *Slave Power*, 43.

19. Democratic Party Mass, *Massachusetts, Sir, Agreeably to a Previous Notice a Convention of Delegates was held at Danvers . . . to Nominate a Republican Candidate for Essex South District . . .* (Salem, 1802), Broadsides, AAS; Carl E. Prince, "The Passing of the Aristocracy: Jefferson's Removal of the Federalists, 1801–1805," in *Journal of American History* 57, no. 3 (December 1970): 565–73; Jacob to John Crowninshield, April 6, 1802, MSS 4, Box 4, Folder 2, Barnabus Bidwell to Jacob Crowninshield, September 2, 1805, MHS 15, Box 3, Folder 1, Crowninshield Family Papers, PEM (emphasis in original).

20. Richards, *Slave Power*, 41, 42; Andrew R. L. Cayton, "'Radicals in the 'Western World': The Federalist Conquest of Trans-Appalachian North America," in Ben-Atar and Oberg, *Federalists Reconsidered*, 93–95.

21. See Sharp, *American Politics*, 288; Morison, *Harrison Gray Otis*, 425.

22. Bowling and Kennon, *Neither Separate nor Equal: Congress in the 1790s* (Athens: Ohio University Press, 2000), 310–13; Gordon S. Wood, *Empire of Liberty: A History of the Early Republic, 1789–1815* (New York: Oxford University Press, 2009), 272.

23. Fischer, *Revolution of American Conservatism*, 26; Banner, *Hartford Convention*, 48–49, 218.

24. Bernhard, *Fisher Ames*, 252–54.

25. For example see, *Annals of Congress*, 6th Cong., 1st Sess., 229, 232, 236–37, 240–41, 244–45.

26. Bowling and Kennon, *Neither Separate nor Equal*, 179–80; *Eastern Herald and Maine Gazette* (Portland, ME), June 8 and 15, 1801.

27. Genesis 13: 5–11.

28. Timothy Pickering to George Cabot, January 29, 1804, Timothy Pickering Papers, MHS.

29. *Annals of Congress*, 8th Cong., 2nd sess., 21; Kevin M. Gannon, "Escaping "Mr. Jefferson's Plan of Destruction": New England Federalists and the Idea of a Northern Confederacy, 1803–1804," in *Journal of the Early Republic*, 21, 3 (Autumn, 2001): 413–43; Buel, *America on the Brink*, 23.

30. Massachusetts General Court, *Resolves of the General Court of the Commonwealth of Massachusetts, Together with the Governor's Communication to the Court, Begun and held at Boston in the County of Suffolk, on Wednesday, The Thirtieth Day of May, Anno Domini MDCCIV* (Boston: Young & Minns, 1804), 28, 29, 31; Vermont Assembly, *Journals of the General Assembly of the State of Vermont at Their Session, Begun and Holden at Rutland, on Thursday, October 11, 1804* (Bennington, VT: Haswell and Smead, 1805), 25, 26; see also Pennsylvania Senate, *Journal of the Senate of the Commonwealth of Pennsylvania. . . .* (Lancaster, PA: McDowell and Greear, 1804); *National Aegis* (Worcester, MA), February 8, 1804; *Albany* (NY) *Centinel*, November 2, 1804; *New-England Palladium* (Boston), November 13, 1804.

31. Eugene L. Huddleston, "Indians and Literature of the Federalist Era: The Case of James Elliot," in *The New England Quarterly* 44:2 (June 1971): 221, 222; James Elliot, *The Poetical and Miscellaneous Works of James Elliot . . .* (Greenfield, MA: Dickman, 1798), 161, 182.

32. *Vermont Gazette* (Bennington), December 6, 1802; *Weekly Wanderer* (Randolph, VT), May 27, 1805; *Post-Boy and Vermont & New-Hampshire Federal Courier* (Windsor, VT), June 11, 1805; *Rutland* (VT) *Herald*, June 8, 1805; *The World* (Bennington, VT), January 25, 1808; *Middlebury* (VT) *Mercury*, February 17, 1808.

33. "Mr. Elliot to His Constituents Letter IX," in *Post-Boy and Vermont & New-Hampshire Federal Courier* (Windsor, VT), June 11, 1805.

34. *U.S. Senate Journal*, 8th Cong., 2nd sess., December 7, 1804, 422; Kerber, *Federalists in Dissent*, 36; Richards, *Slave Power*, 43–45.

35. Robinson, *Slavery in the Structure of American Politics*, 270, 271: Richards, *Slave Power*, 46, 49–51.

36. McCoy, *Elusive Republic*, 252.

37. Liberty Party, *The Slave Power. Political Tracts, No. 1.* (Hartford: Christian Freeman, c. 1844), 2–4; Boston (MA) Citizens, [Daniel Webster, Josiah Quincy, et al., *A Memorial to the Congress of the United States, on the Subject of Restraining the Increase of Slavery in New States to Be Admitted into the Union* . . . (Boston: Sewell Phelps, Printer, 1819), Antislavery Collection, 1725–1911 (RB 003) SCUA.

38. Pickering to Jefferson, February 24, 1806, *Jefferson Papers*, LC; Samuel Taggart to John Taylor, February 26, 1806, Samuel Taggart Letterbook; AAS.

39. Eva Sheppard Wolf, "Early Free-Labor Thought and the Contest over Slavery in the Early Republic," in John Craig Hammond and Matthew Mason, eds., *Contesting Slavery: The Politics of Bondage and Freedom in the New American Nation* (Charlottesville: University of Virginia Press, 2011), 32–33, 40–41; Jonathan H. Earle, *Jacksonian Antislavery and the Politics of Free Soil, 1824–1854* (Chapel Hill: University of North Carolina Press, 2004), 5–7; Eric Foner, *Free Soil, Free Labor, Free Men: The Ideology of the Republican Party before the Civil War* (New York: Oxford University Press, 1995), 9–16, 124–25.

40. Alan Taylor, *The Civil War of 1812: American Citizens, British Subjects, Irish Rebels, & Indian Allies* (New York: Vintage Books, 2010), 120; Daniel Walker Howe, *What Hath God Wrought: The Transformation of America, 1815–1848* (New York: Oxford University Press, 2007), 95, 169.

41. David H. Fischer, *The Revolution of American Conservatism: The Federalist Party in the Era of Jeffersonian Democracy* (New York: Harper and Row, 1965); Banner, *Hartford Convention*; Linda K. Kerber, *Federalists in Dissent: Imagery and Ideology in Jeffersonian America* (Ithaca, NY: Cornell University Press, 1970); James H. Broussard, *The Southern Federalists, 1800–1816* (Baton Rouge: Louisiana State University Press, 1978); Shaw Livermore, *The Twilight of Federalism: The Disintegration of the Federalist Party, 1815–1830* (Princeton, NJ: Princeton University Press, 1962).

42. Nicole Eustace, *1812: War and the Passions of Patriotism* (Philadelphia: University of Pennsylvania Press, 2012); Alan Taylor, *The Civil War of 1812: American Citizens, British Subjects, Irish Rebels, & Indian Allies* (Vintage Books, 2010); Donald R. Hickey, *The War of 1812: A Forgotten Conflict* (Urbana: University of Illinois Press, 1989); Mathew Mason, "Federalists, Abolitionists, and the Problem of Influence," in *American Nineteenth Century History*, 10, No. 1 (March 2009): 1–27; Hammond and Mason eds., *Contesting Slavery*; Rachel Hope Cleves, *The Reign of Terror in America: Visions of Violence from Anti-Jacobinism to Antislavery* (New York: Cambridge University Press, 2009); Robert W. T. Martin, *Government by Dissent: Protest, Resistance, & Radical Democratic Thought in the Early American Republic* (New York: New York University Press, 2013). Ben-Atar and Oberg, *Federalists Reconsidered*; Garry Wills, *"Negro President": Jefferson and the Slave Power* (Boston: Houghton Mifflin, 2003); Richards, *Slave Power*; Jeffrey L. Pasley et al., *Beyond the Founders: New Approaches to the Political History of the Early American Republic* (Chapel Hill: University of North Carolina Press, 2004); Joshua Michael Zeitz, "The Missouri Compromise Reconsidered: Antislavery Rhetoric and the Emergence of the Free Labor Synthesis," in *Journal of the Early Republic* 20 No. 3 (Autumn 2000): 447–85. Eliga H. Gould, *Among the Powers of the Earth: The American Revolution and the Making of a New World Empire* (Cambridge, MA: Harvard University Press, 2012); David F. Ericson, *Slavery in the American Republic: Developing the Federal Government, 1791–1861* (Lawrence: University Press of Kansas, 2011); George William Van Cleve, *A Slaveholders' Union: Slavery, Politics, and the Constitution in the Early Republic* (Chicago: The University of Chicago Press, 2010); Hammond, *Slavery, Freedom, and Expansion*; Matthew Mason, *Slavery and Politics in the Early American Republic* (Chapel Hill: University of North Carolina Press, 2006); Richards, *Slave Power*; Don E. Fehrenbacher, *The Slaveholding Republic: An Account of the United States Government's Relations to Slavery* (New York: Oxford University Press, 2001); Reinhard O. Johnson, *The Liberty*

Party, 1840–1848 (Baton Rouge: Louisiana State University Press, 2009); Jonathan H. Earle, *Jacksonian Antislavery & The Politics of Free Soil, 1824–1854* (Chapel Hill: The University of North Carolina Press, 2004).

43. Joseph Sidney, *Oration of Slavery*, 9, 10. BA.

44. See Hammond and Mason, *Contesting Slavery*, 2, 41–43; Ben-Atar and Oberg. *Federalists Reconsidered*, 135–75, 246–53; Donald Hickey, "Federalist Defense Policy in the Age of Jefferson, 1801–1812," in *Military Affairs* 45, no. 2 (April 1981): 63–70.

45. Wood, *Empire of Liberty*, 654.

46. Ashli White, *Encountering Revolution: Haiti and the Making of the Early Republic* (Baltimore: The Johns Hopkins University Press, 2010), 163–65.

47. Pasley et al, *Beyond the Founders*, 2–9; Hammond, *Slavery, Freedom, and Expansion*, 5.

48. See, Omar H. Ali, *In the Balance of Power: Independent Black Politics and Third-Party Movements in the United States* (Athens: Ohio University Press 2008), 11–14, 28–29; Wood, *Empire of Liberty*, 521.

49. Ibid., 497; Wilentz, *Rise of American Democracy*, 192–93; Richards, *Slave Power*, 116–20.

50. Richards, *Slave Power*, 85, 86; Jacob Crowninshield to George W. Prescott, November 15, 1803; Thomas Kittredge to Jacob Crowninshield, December 10, 1804; Aaron Hill to Jacob Crowninshield, December 22, 1804 MH 15, Box 2, Folder 9; N. Dearborn to Jacob Crowninshield, July 10, 1805, MH 15, Box 3, Folder 1, Crowninshield Family Papers, PEM.

51. Thomas Green Fessenden, *Democracy Unveiled; or Tyranny Stripped of the Garb of Patriotism* (Boston: D. Carlisle, Printer, 1805), 122, American Culture Series, Microfilm Reel 412.1, SCUA.

ONE

"Have these Haytians no rights?"

Restricting Maritime Commerce to Safeguard Slavery (1805–1806)

While returning to Newburyport, Massachusetts, from a commercial voyage in the West Indies, the French privateer *Adet* captured the *Joseph*, an American-owned schooner. Upon seizing the schooner, John Saverneau, captain of the *Adet*, forced the *Joseph* along with its cargo and crew into a Cuban port. After French authorities destroyed the *Joseph*, the doomed ship's captain, John Lurney, lodged protests with Spain and the U.S. government. He reported that the French had robbed him of clothes and other personal belongings before leaving him stranded in a foreign port "without a dollar on which to subsist." When the six owners of the *Joseph* tallied the damages, they had lost £19,734–£2,500 for the ship and £17,234 for its cargo. In 1805 they joined several other merchants and submitted records of their losses to the Jefferson administration in order to demonstrate the urgent need for the government to help them get "compensation" and "that protection which a regard to the honour of our country . . . dictate and require."[1]

Similar reports began to pour into Congress from merchants, ship captains, and seamen as early as 1803 when the Napoleonic Wars resumed in Europe. Many of the mariners affected in British and French attacks hailed from the maritime districts of New England, so by the time the Ninth Congress convened for its first session on December 2, 1805, providing protection for the nation's merchant fleet had become a pressing issue. Captains watched helplessly as the French seized their ships and other property, or members of the British Navy boarded their vessels and impressed crew members. Along with individual accounts of seizures and impressments, Congress also considered petitions from various merchant organizations seeking redress. At the core of the nation's dilemma lay a profitable wartime trade and neutrality which began during the Washington administration. Another issue was the cost of building a naval force large enough to protect the merchant fleet in the Atlantic and Caribbean at the same time. Expanding the naval fleet was difficult since President Jefferson had already cut taxes and downsized the military.

For these and other reasons, the congressional response to piracy, property loss, and the loss of life soon involved questioning the wisdom of protecting New Englanders' maritime pursuits at the nation's expense. The question first surfaced in 1805 when problems with France and Britain arose over U.S. trade with Haiti. Several ships suffered the same fate as the *Joseph* and were taken, sometimes destroyed, and at other times seized as war prizes. As Congress sought solutions for these problems, during the debates that took place from 1805 through 1806, several members of Congress, primarily Democratic-Republicans, advocated outlawing armed merchant ships in the Caribbean and then ending the nation's trade with the black people of Haiti to avoid conflicts with foreign nations.

At first the Federalists' major objection to prohibiting trade with the self-liberated black people of Haiti was that the government was considering ending a branch of commerce to appease France. Soon the fact that Americans were trading with former slaves became the issue. During debates over the best way to protect merchants trading in the Caribbean, several legislators from the southern states expressed more interest in the trade's ramifications for slavery than the lives and property of fellow Americans. Their objections to the trade added a sectional dimension to the debates that raised questions over whether—with Democratic-Republicans in power—maritime New England and the rest of the seaboard states could rely on the federal government to protect their economic interests. As the following discussion will show, the decision to deprive merchantmen of their weapons and prohibit trade with Haiti initiated the Democratic-Republicans' restrictive system and an increasingly acerbic critique from Federalists. Consequently, decisions affecting trade spearheaded a radical response to the government and divided the nation along sectional lines. The Federalists' reaction involved placing the Haitian Act and other acts in the context of southern power and undisclosed, but dubious, motives for passing trade restrictions. Without possessing the ability to keep Congress from passing restrictive legislation, Federalists finally evaluated the cost of remaining in a Union dominated by slaveholders.

In most studies, the Haitian Act of 1806 is not connected to the major political battles over the Democratic-Republicans' restrictive system.[2] Recent scholarship dealing with prohibitions against the Haitian trade (also

Saint Domingue or St. Domingo) tends to look closely at the relationship forged between the United States and the areas of Hispaniola governed by African Caribbeans during John Adams's presidency.[3] But for the most part, the collapse of commercial ties with France's former slaves remains a central theme because of what the policy reveals about proslavery sentiment in the United States and the spread of antislavery sentiment in the Atlantic world.[4] Understanding this policy's role in the string of commercial policies that led to New England Federalists' extreme sectionalism and opposition to federal authority requires taking a new look at the context in which Congress and the Jefferson administration prohibited the Haitian trade. The policy gave many northerners reason to fear that the central government, while dominated by slaveholders, would not hesitate to sacrifice the well-being of northern maritime economies in order to protect slavery in the South. Indeed, shortly after the Haitian Act went into effect, many Federalists and others in the region started to believe that Democratic-Republicans intended to destroy New England's economy altogether.[5]

Trade with the French colony that became Haiti in 1804 antedated the Republic. New Englanders traded fish, salt meat, provisions, and slaves for large amounts of the colony's sugar and molasses through the port at Môle-Saint-Nicolas, which France opened to Britain's North American colonies in 1767. With federal support U.S. merchants maintained this mutually advantageous relationship with French portions of the island after the American Revolution. In the 1790s, a new trade agreement opened ports in Cap François, Port-au-Prince, and Cayes-Saint-Louis to U.S. trade and Americans exported coal, salt beef, salt fish, rice, corn, and vegetables into these ports and imported tons of the colony's sugar and coffee into the United States and elsewhere. By the late 1790s Federalists extended goods and other support to former slaves who rebelled against French rule and gained control over much of France's former colony.[6]

The first serious problem pertaining to U.S. relations with Haiti developed after France declared war on Great Britain in February 1793. The war, which was a byproduct of the French Revolution, affected all Caribbean and transatlantic trade, but as citizens of a neutral nation Americans were able to ship products from the Europeans' West Indian colonies to both belligerents and profit greatly. While most of Europe was engaged in or distracted by warfare, revenue from the carrying trade skyrocketed. Europeans and their colonists needed foodstuffs and supplies that neutral Americans were happy to provide. From 1793 to 1797 alone, the amount of Massachusetts' foreign exports grew from $3.7 to $7.5 million.[7]

France and Britain coveted a share in these profits, and also hoped to cut off supply lines to the enemy by attacking and seizing American ships. To avoid entering the war on either side President Washington declared the United States neutral, and worked out several points of contention with the British through the Jay Treaty. Once the Senate ratified the treaty in 1796, however, the French Directory authorized the seizure of all neutral vessels and initiated a policy of treating Americans with the same hostility that they showed the British.[8] This policy impaired U.S. trade in the Caribbean and from 1798 to 1799, according to one estimate, the value of goods traded in affected areas of the West Indies declined from $8 to $2.7 million.[9]

France justified its actions by claiming that the Jay Treaty violated the Franco-American Treaty of Amity and Commerce of 1778. Yet according to one historian, "From the start of the war in Europe in 1793 the French tried to bully the United States into a more pro-French alignment with threats, periodic harassment of commerce, and interference in American domestic politics."[10] Of course the British compounded the kerfuffle. Britain was still America's largest trading partner and although U.S. merchants were opening new markets around the world, a majority still traded along the routes established under the navigation system of the seventeenth and eighteenth centuries.[11] Some New England merchants also maintained personal and professional ties in London that allowed them to dispose of goods rapidly through lines of credit that they could use for everything from ship repairs to compensation for losses in foreign ports. Others also had support from or trade with Loyalist relatives, friends, and associates who helped them establish new trade routes and open new markets.[12]

In response to more amicable Anglo-American relations under the Jay Treaty, France invoked a previously unenforced provision of its treaty with the U.S. and demanded that ship captains produce a *rôle d'équipage* listing the names and nationalities of their crews. But French agents did not give Americans time to prepare and began to seize ships for even the slightest irregularity. In 1797 President Adams, at Congress's urging, compiled a report of all impressments and seizures that occurred after October 1796. Secretary of State Timothy Pickering listed hundreds of ships seized by the French, Spanish, and British, but placed special emphasis on French spoliations (ship seizures) in the West Indies, where "the most lamentable scenes of depredation" occurred. French tribunals condemned ships (deemed them a lawful prize for confiscation) and often denied U.S. citizens the right to present a defense in court. Mariners complained that they were "beaten, insulted, and cruelly imprisoned" while in French custody. There were also reports that France's agents seized U.S. ships and cargo "without any pretence or [for] no other [reason] than that they wanted [them]." According to some accounts, French corsairs burned ships and committed depredations against U.S. citizens on a daily basis.[13]

Pickering's report held Britain primarily accountable for impressing U.S. citizens, which involved seizing and then forcing seamen to work on British naval vessels under harsh circumstances, but he insisted that such incidents had "not been numerous." Although Pickering listed scores of impressed Americans in his report, the secretary commended the British for handling impressment cases judiciously. On occasion, there were reports that the Royal Navy even protected U.S. vessels from French attacks. In December 1796, for example, a French privateer pursued the *Commerce*, a New England ship bound for Jamaica, until a British ship of war forced the privateer to abandon the chase. While several merchantmen reportedly escaped capture by French privateers (privately owned ships sanctioned by warring governments to attack and capture an enemy's vessels) under similar circumstances, the United States could not rely on Britain to protect its citizens or their property. It was the federal government's job to address the plight of Americans trading in West Indian waters, "swarm[ing] with privateers and gun boats" under French authority.[14]

Pickering was decidedly pro-British, but some eyewitness reports indicate that Britain did at times follow legal protocol regarding war prizes while the French did not. The Boston firm J. & T. H. Perkins received a letter in March 1794 regarding their schooner and its cargo of coffee, sugar, and indigo that the British seized as the ship departed Port-de-Paix, on the northern tip of Saint Domingue. James Carter, a passenger on the ship, described the fate of crew and cargo at the hands of the French and British. Carter called both nations' treatment of Americans "really insufferable," but in a subsequent letter explained that the British had "stop'd libeling American property," although the French continued to do so. The details of this account were commensurate with conclusions drawn in Pickering's report.[15]

In reply to the report Adams prohibited trade with all French colonies in the West Indies.[16] On June 25, 1798, he signed an act that allowed merchants to arm their vessels for protection. In addition to firing on French privateers, under the new law Americans could recover stolen property, intervene in seizure attempts, and pursue and capture any French ship suspected of seizing or in the process of capturing any vessels owned by a U.S. citizen. To ensure that they were not violating laws governing neutral trade by selling weapons that should be used to protect their ships, the act required merchants or captains to post bonds double the value of vessels and munitions before they could clear to travel. Captains of armed vessel also had to account for every weapon when their ships returned. As written, the policy was in effect for one year or until France agreed to stop attacking American ships.[17]

Adams also signed an act creating the Department of the Navy on April 30, 1798, and Congress authorized deployment of the newly built frigates *United States* 44 and *Constitution* 36 to patrol problem areas and act as escorts to protect commercial vessels. Encounters between French privateers and the U.S. Navy became the nation's first undeclared military engagement against a foreign power. Usually called the Quasi War

(1798–1800), the navy fought largely in the Caribbean under the first Secretary of the Navy, Benjamin Stoddert (1751–1813). The U.S. Navy received help from the British but also from France's former slaves, who were leading a revolt against colonial rule. Conflict between the slaves and their former owners allowed the U.S. to establish its first foreign naval base at Cap-Français (Cap Haïtien) in Haiti. Americans were able to reduce French spoliations and Adams reopened trade with areas of Hispaniola under the Haitians' control.[18]

François Dominique Toussaint Louverture had been leading the slave rebellion for about four years when Adams became president. At first Adams was uncertain of how an independent nation governed by black men would affect the United States and speculated that it might be dangerous. He soon dropped these apprehensions and opened communications and trade with the black leaders of Haiti, cautioning that if the United States intervened, it "had better leave the independence of the island complete and total, in commerce as well as legislation, to the people who assert it, the inhabitants of the island."[19] Adams was referring specifically to places under Louverture's control, such as Cape François and Port-au-Prince.[20]

The Quasi War and reopened trade with Haiti were so successful that Adams could boast, "Since the renewal of this intercourse, our citizens trading to those ports, with their property, have been duly respected, and privateering from those parts has ceased." Adams's policies also fostered interaction among the Haitians, British, and U.S. government (although unofficial), guaranteeing Americans safe passage to and from ports under Louverture's authority. The United States treated the island's former slaves as the official government of St. Domingue.[21]

Through these policies Adams did much to promote national prosperity. Despite the fact that the U.S. government did not formally acknowledge the African Caribbeans' independence, and the former slaves did not declare independence from France until 1804, Adams did generate congenial commercial relations and political accord with the Haitians. From 1797–1800, the Federalist-dominated Fifth and Sixth Congresses passed several laws to protect the nation's merchant fleet and its personnel. The government even empowered some armed vessels to profit from the capture of French privateers.[22] Merchants publicly praised these policies and pledged continued support for the federal government because Adams made their protection a priority.[23]

While he expressed concerns over whether trading with the Haitians threatened southern slavery, under Adams the nation's merchants exported provisions, and sometimes guns and ammunition to help the rebellious slaves continue their fight for independence. Americans captured ships trading with the rebels' enemies, which helped expand black rule into other areas of Hispaniola previously under French control. Federalists Timothy Pickering and Alexander Hamilton even outlined a new government, albeit a military dictatorship, for the former slaves.[24] Historian Ronald Angelo Johnson agrees that U.S.–Haitian relations at this time were consequential for the U.S. and the Atlantic World. Indeed, Haitian independence, the founding of a new republic, and the Louisiana Purchase were some of these consequences. More importantly, Adams's Haitian policy marked, "the first U.S. diplomatic engagement with a black-led government."[25]

A few months before losing reelection to Democratic-Republican leader Thomas Jefferson in 1800, Adams engineered the Treaty of Môrtefontaine with France, which ended the Quasi War and the U.S. naval presence in Haiti. Even though he leaned toward recognition and commercial partnership with Haiti, and several Federalists, including future chief justice of the Supreme Court John Marshall sought to expand U.S.-Haitian relations, in a final proclamation, Adams announced that the federal government would continue to deal with Haitian leaders in certain matters but officially consider the former slaves French colonists. The United States had come close, but was now retreating from granting Haitians recognition of their independence. However, the defense of slavery in the United States was not the guiding principle in Adams's treatment of the former slaves or his foreign policy.[26]

When he entered office in March 1801, Jefferson had no problem denying the Haitians recognition or even nominal acknowledgment. He was a Virginia slaveholder who withheld all courtesies that the federal government had extended to Haitian leaders during Adams's presidency. Jefferson's treatment or mistreatment of the rebels sent a signal to France that his administration's policies toward Haiti would differ radically from those of his predecessor.[27]

Following ratification of the Franco-American treaty in 1800, the first round of wars between France and Britain ended under the Treaty of Amiens (1802). The end of hostilities in Europe eased tensions surrounding the Haitian trade, yet they soon resumed when Napoleon launched a military campaign to reclaim the colony and reestablish slavery. By the end of 1802 French forces had failed to defeat the Haitians and Napoleon lost a good portion of the large expeditionary force led by his brother-in-law General Charles Victor Emmanuel Leclerc. Napoleon compensated for his losses in 1803 by relinquishing his country's North American territory to Jefferson in what became known as the Louisiana Purchase. That same year the war between France and Britain resumed.[28]

Napoleon had not been able to subdue France's former slaves and began to attack American vessels trading with the Haitian rebels instead. Under its new emperor, Jean Jacque Dessalines, Haiti declared independence from France in 1804. American merchants considered Haiti an independent nation, continued to trade with the new republic, and sailed armed vessels into the West Indies. When France ignored its recent loss to the rebels, as well as Haiti's declaration of independence, to seize

American ships they resumed attacks on merchantmen, which forced merchants and seamen to turn to the federal government for protection—again.[29]

Although the rebels received no formal recognition from other countries, Haiti's leaders assumed the privileges of a sovereign nation, including the right to trade freely without interference, especially from their former colonial leaders in France. Before issuing Haiti's declaration of independence Dessalines contacted Jefferson to establish a dialogue, but the president ignored his request.[30] France, aware of the hostility that slaveholders would likely have toward interacting with a government run by rebellious, independent black men, exploited racial attitudes in the U.S. to sanction renewed assaults on merchantmen in the West Indies.[31]

As in the 1790s, merchants armed their ships for protection from privateers, but the presence of armed merchant vessels trading in a theater of war prompted the French and British to lodge complaints with the Jefferson administration. In a letter dated May 7, 1804, the French chargé d'affaires carped that U.S. merchants were dealing arms with the black rebels in violation of neutrality laws. Commercial interaction with colonists in the midst of revolution constituted a "private and piratical war" against France. On August 31 the British also complained that Americans were violating laws of neutrality because they were trading "contraband of war . . . to the enemies' possessions in the East as well as West Indies."[32] Both nations objected to the Haitian trade, but the major substance of their complaints differed. While France primarily opposed trade with their former slaves, the British were disturbed that armed vessels and weapons were falling into the enemy's hands.[33]

At the same time, the Jefferson administration received a wave of petitions from merchants and seamen pleading for protection and compensation for their losses. In February, Vincent Gray at the U.S. Consulate in Havana, Cuba, notified Secretary of State Madison that French privateers had seized several U.S. commercial vessels. Among these was the brig *Dove*, which belonged to Bostonians James and Thomas H. Perkins. After its capture the French escorted the *Dove* to Cuba, where someone stole its cargo during the night. Gray feared that the French would scuttle (sink) the ship, which was "the way they clear of the Vessels after robbing them of their cargoes." He prevailed upon Madison to intervene since French agents in Cuba had received authorization to seize any U.S. ship entering or exiting a Haitian port.[34]

Secretary of State Madison also heard complaints from Spanish diplomats regarding the Haitian trade. Spain, France's ally, was also seizing and destroying U.S. ships and requested that the administration end U.S. commercial ties with Haiti. In his letter to Carlos Fernando Martinez de Yrujo, Spanish minister to the United States, Madison appeared annoyed over Spain's attempt to insert itself into an already prickly situation.

Spain had no right to demand that the United States "control the commerce of their citizens" with "[the] Negroes of St. Domingo." If France had a problem, they might have a legitimate reason to make demands, but Spain had no standing and could not assume the status or rights of a belligerent nation.[35]

Though he recognized that the alliance system in Europe was complicating problems in the West Indies, Madison remained adamant. He held to the position that U.S. relations with France would have nothing to do with Spain. An exasperated Madison wrote Robert Livingston, U.S. minister to France, "It is the more important that something should be done in this case and done soon, as the pretext founded on the supposed illegality of any trade whatever with the Negroes in St. Domingo is multiplying the depredations on our Commerce." He found the situation "highly irritating" and included a number of claims and complaints from U.S. merchants with his communiqué. He suggested that if Livingston told the French that the U.S. would place limited prohibitions on the Haitian trade, even though it was not obligated to do so, that might ease French aggressions and "put an end to the evil" that they were inflicting on U.S. shipping.[36]

But France was not disposed to correct the evil in response to hypothetical proposals. Congress would need to address the problem legislatively. First, in December 1804, the House considered a bill regulating the clearance of armed trading vessels. Democratic-Republican Jacob Crowninshield of Massachusetts, chairman of the Committee on Commerce and Manufacturing, applauded merchants' efforts to protect themselves from seizures and objected to any policy that would leave them defenseless. However, Crowninshield did not receive support from southern members of his party. John Wayles Eppes of Virginia, one of President Jefferson's sons-in-laws, said he "did not approve of allowing merchant vessels to arm at all." Eppes wanted the federal government to completely destroy the "Negro government." His primary reason for disarming merchantmen was to terminate trade with the black leaders of Haiti, "a class of people it is in the interest of the United States to depress and keep down."[37]

Thomas Lowndes, a Federalist from South Carolina, was more direct and said that Congress should have the courage to agree that trading with Haiti was illegal and end commercial ties with the black republic, or protect the country's merchants. William Eustis, a Massachusetts Democratic-Republican who had just lost his seat to Federalist Josiah Quincy in the 1804 election, cautioned that disarming commercial vessels would damage Haiti and jeopardize the lives and property of Americans trading in the West Indies. Eustis admitted that mariners had committed a few "irregularities" while engaging in the Haitian trade, but believed that merchants should arm themselves to protect their ships, cargo, and crews. A representative from Pennsylvania said that the bill needlessly punished Americans while benefitting the merchants of other nations. And then several southern congressmen began to censure mariners after Eppes added, "American merchants are not fit to be trusted with arms, [any] more than *highwaymen* are with pistols."[38]

The Senate was also dealing with the issue, and on January 28, 1805, senators requested documentation regarding complaints against armed merchantmen. Jefferson forwarded letters from the French and British governments, a report from Secretary Madison, and several authenticated accounts of French seizures. One document involved the ships *Hopewell* and *Rockland*. A French privateer fired on the *Rockland*, killing two and wounding several Americans. The captain was also wounded in the struggle and later died while under detention in Guadeloupe. The privateer then attacked the *Hopewell*, and in the ensuing gunfight wounded six Americans and killed three. Once French authorities learned that one of the ship's passengers was a black general and that the ship was transporting mail addressed to various locations in Haiti, they condemned the ship and claimed it as a prize of war. Similar attacks followed the French government's directive that any U.S.-owned ship and crew "bound to St. Domingo, if taken, shall be treated as pirates."[39]

Instead of formulating a plan utilizing military escorts to protect the merchant fleet, the Senate majority agreed to regulate armed merchant vessels, and disagreed only over the wording in sections of the bill related to penalties and bonds. Federalists rejected proposals requiring shipmasters or merchants to pay bonds double the value of their property. They also opposed trying cases related to unlawful acts on the seas as if they had been committed in the United States. Federalists were in the minority and had little input when Congress passed the bill regulating the clearance of armed commercial vessels beginning March 3, 1805.[40]

The law contained several provisions that New Englanders had opposed during the debates, particularly the language pertaining to ships headed to the West Indies. For instance, to ensure that no armed vessels traveled to Haiti, captains had to swear under oath that the black republic was not their destination.[41] The law was in effect for one year, but it was soon apparent that Democratic-Republicans planned to prohibit the Haitian trade altogether. On February 23, Pennsylvania Senator George Logan, a Democratic-Republican, announced his intention to present a bill that would place an embargo on U.S. trade with Haiti.[42]

Federalists recognized the direction that government's trade policies were taking and strenuously defended the legality of trading with Haiti. "If the blacks of St. Domingo are slaves, who are the masters, and in whom is the lawful property?" asked one Massachusetts editorial. Others insisted that Americans had the right to trade with any nation that welcomed their business, especially when the trade was legal, which was, they argued, the case with Haiti, a free republic.[43]

The Jefferson administration viewed the situation quite differently. Treasury Secretary Albert Gallatin advised New York Senator Samuel Mitchill that the Haitian trade was illicit "in toto." France, he continued, had a right to search and seize any vessel trading with its former slaves.[44] Only a day before Gallatin's letter, the Federalist press had called the Haitian trade, "the most lucrative which our country enjoys," and condemned the impending legislation.[45]

Federalists maintained that southerners' hostility to maritime economies actually drove the policy.[46] They mocked Jefferson's assertion that commerce thrived "when left most free to individual enterprise." Democratic-Republicans in Congress had actually decided that Americans trading with Haiti would not be free to engage in a profitable commercial enterprise because it involved persons of African descent. Many northerners were also peeved that their government would allow foreign nations to charge U.S. citizens with piracy and then prosecute mariners in the United States for trading in Haiti. Frustrated merchants were already complaining that federal laws unjustly banning armed merchant vessels "exposed and shackled" the Haitian trade.[47]

On December 20, 1805, Logan pressed the Senate to take up his bill, which would completely suspend commercial intercourse with Haiti. As senators parsed complaints from merchants and seamen about French atrocities, these became less important than France's grumbling over trade with its former slaves, who they deemed "colonists." Logan then resubmitted the British and French missives dated May 7 and August 31, 1804, as evidence that Congress had an obligation to stop the Haitian trade immediately.[48]

In addition to armed vessels violating laws governing neutrality by traveling to Haiti, Logan pointed out that the trade jeopardized southern slavery. He asked if it was "sound policy to cherish the black population of St. Domingo whilst we have a similar population in our Southern States, in which should an insurrection take place, the Government of the United States is bound to render effectual aid to our fellow-citizens in that part of the Union?" He justified his proposal as an effort to "preserve the immediate honor and future peace of the United States." Logan already had a history of intervening in diplomacy to ameliorate tensions between the U.S. and France. In the late 1790s without permission from the Adams administration, Logan traveled to France to strike a citizens' accord with a hostile nation. The government deemed the senator a threat to national security and in 1799 a Federalist Congress passed Logan's Act. That law, which imposes fines and imprisonment on anyone negotiating with a foreign power without federal authorization, remains in effect today.[49]

John Quincy Adams, a Federalist from Massachusetts, objected to Logan's bill, arguing that its only purpose was to prohibit "a branch of our commerce, which . . . proved to be of great importance to the country."

Adams implored the Senate to reject any measure that would unfavorably impact "the commercial interest," or "affect individual merchants, in the course of their affairs." He was also against taking drastic steps because the letters Logan presented were the same ones that the Senate had already considered. Mitchill, who was not yet persuaded by Gallatin's reasoning, concurred with Adams and added that Congress had already complied with France "in the true spirit of good neighborhood" by restricting armed vessels. Legislators had already done everything that they "politically could or ... honorably ought."[50]

Federalists called ending the Haitian trade a gross overreaction to a problem that Congress had already solved. More than one of them asserted that it was wrong to cut off relations with the independent people of Haiti based on old complaints from foreign nations at war with each other, or because of slaveholders' racism. A New York senator warned prophetically, "If we agree to interdict this intercourse, we may, at the next session, be informed that we ought to withdraw from some other important port or region." James Hillhouse of Connecticut agreed and called the bill "ill-timed." He said Americans expected Congress to do "something energetic and spirited" to protect their rights and property. "How great will be the surprise," he added, "if the first step taken by the Senate of the United States is found to be a further restriction, or a total restriction of a lawful and lucrative branch of our commerce?" Along with other Federalists, Hillhouse believed it more dignified to "send armed ships into those seas, to capture or demolish those bucaniers [sic] and pirates, who rob us of our property, and insult and murder our citizens" than prohibit trade with Haiti.[51]

The Democratic-Republican proponents of Logan's bill ignored all of these objections, and John G. Jackson of Virginia criticized Adams for complaining that the letters were old and the arguments for ending the trade trite. He reminded Adams and others that southerners had been forced to listen to arguments from antislavery groups and Quakers since the Constitution was ratified and "not a new one had been produced." If slaveholders had to put up with stale, redundant antislavery petitions, Jackson said northerners would just have to grin and bear old evidence when Congress wanted to protect slavery.[52]

It was true that the letters on which Logan relied were nearly two years old, but instead of dropping the issue as Adams and opponents of the bill suggested, the Senate asked for updated documentation before proceeding. On January 10, 1806, Logan submitted letters that France's Minister Plenipotentiary Louis Turreau and Minister of Foreign Affairs Charles Talleyrand issued in 1805 and 1806. The more recent communiqués repeated the complaints of 1804 but placed even more emphasis on the degradation that white merchants brought on the United States by trading with former slaves, black persons who were "the reproach, and the refuse of nature."[53] When Logan resubmitted his bill on January 17,

1806, it called for the suspension of all U.S. commercial interactions with Haiti for one year and gave the president power to extend the prohibition when it expired.[54] Based on their responses, Federalists could not avoid the conclusion that Congress had prohibited a branch of maritime commerce to protect slavery and appease the French. Few accepted the act as a suitable response to citizens' requests for protection.

Federalist Samuel White of Delaware, who later published a pamphlet criticizing the policy, interjected that keeping the trade status quo would confine the former slaves to their sphere of control. Continuing trade with Haiti, he insisted, would actually avert the threat of slave revolts that southern congressmen "seem so much to apprehend." Neither White's rationalization nor similar appeals to southern sensibilities from others dissuaded the bill's proponents. On February 20, 1806, amid sharp criticism, the Senate passed the final version of the Haitian bill 21–8.[55]

The House received the bill on February 21 and began deliberations three days later. As soon as James Sloan of New Jersey asked for a third reading of a proposed tax on imported slaves, Democratic-Republican Peter Early of Georgia, a transplanted Virginian who unapologetically defended slavery and the slave trade, insisted that the House postpone consideration of the tax, because in his opinion, ending the trade with Haiti was an emergency. Early, who often threatened civil war over any northern proposal affecting slavery, was quite annoyed that the measure had already taken so long to pass. When House debates resumed the next day, Jacob Crowninshield unexpectedly broke with his party and opposed the bill. He had predicted that France would not be able to conquer Haiti and argued that merchants would find prohibiting the trade "extremely burdensome." Crowninshield had reservations about offending the Haitians, but the gist of his argument was that U.S. merchants had the right to engage in the trade.[56]

Before the Salem Congressman could finish his next sentence, Early interrupted and asked the Speaker if Crowninshield was out of order. He was not out of order, but the disruption seemed to interrupt Crowninshield's train of thought. When he resumed, Crowninshield questioned the wisdom of ending the trade and said he doubted that a Democratic-Republican Congress would prohibit trade to appease England if the black population of Jamaica or those in the East Indies revolted against their colonial rulers. He maintained opposition to the bill and implored the House not to sacrifice commerce in this manner.[57] Early almost certainly tried to disrupt Crowninshield, whose opinion in commercial matters was highly respected. If allowed to speak extensively Crowninshield might have persuaded other northerners in his party to vote against Logan's bill. After all, in the Eighth Congress he had convinced several of them to oppose restrictions on armed merchantmen. Neither Early nor any other southerner wanted to risk losing the vote over Haiti.

It was obvious that the bill's proponents were making an effort to hasten its passage. Massachusetts Federalist Josiah Quincy, who just began his first term in the House, admitted that the law would only have a mild effect on Boston merchants, but objected to the fact that Democratic-Republicans' were trying to rush the bill through the House. Due to "the magnitude of its principles and consequences," the proposal certainly merited further deliberation, said Quincy. He then recommended that the House restrict the shipment of arms and "military apparatus" but not food or the other "necessities and conveniences of life" that the United States also shipped to Haiti.[58]

Quincy, who former president Adams described as "a rare instance of hereditary eloquence and ingenuity," had learned politics in his youth. He was the scion of seventeenth-century British colonists who with each generation increased their participation in state and local politics. At the same time, his family also amassed wealth and status through various economic ventures including privateering. After starting a law practice in the 1790s Quincy sat on town committees and became town orator. Finally, following an unsuccessful run for Congress in 1800, he won the Suffolk District's congressional election in 1804 and represented the District from the Ninth through the Twelfth Congresses. Before he declined reelection in 1812, Quincy had earned a reputation for being an outspoken agitator, especially if he considered legislation inimical to New England's prosperity.[59]

Depending on their political persuasion, representatives found Quincy's aggressiveness commendable or distressing. Fisher Ames encouraged Quincy to divide House Jeffersonians and diminish "their power to destroy." Though most attempts to do this were unsuccessful, Quincy made the most of his rhetorical skills in disputes over commerce and national defense. He took advantage of almost every opportunity to confront Democratic-Republicans. Though Ames may have believed that these efforts checked the majority, Quincy grated on opponents like future Supreme Court associate justice Joseph Story. Like others, Story, who served a brief term in the House, complained that Quincy never stopped debating and though talented was "ridiculous."[60]

No amount of reasoning or confrontation could dampen the majority's determination to end the Haitian trade, but Federalists hardened their resolve to oppose the bill. Massachusetts Federalist William Ely, who had frequently opposed the three-fifths clause and the spread of slavery, said that the language used by the bill's supporters during debates gave him even more reason to oppose it. "Have these Haytians no rights?" he asked as the bill's proponents insisted that a slaveholding republic like the United States could neither acknowledge Haiti nor offend France. The House passed the bill 93–26, in one of the rare instances in which a Democratic-Republican (Crowninshield) joined Federalists in their opposition to restricting foreign trade. Ely then added his regrets that American traders would suffer while coffee and other Haitian produce found their "way to the different ports in Great Britain."[61]

Based on trends already apparent in Congress, John Quincy Adams informed his father well before the bill's passage that the prohibition was a *fait accompli*. He wrote, "The general tendency of opinions and passions which govern our administration has always been such that this course might have been expected from the commencement of our session."[62] The Federalist press also kept a close watch on the bill's progress and had much to say before and after Congress passed the act. By defending slavery and liberally expressing racist sentiments during congressional debates, southerners gratuitously gave the Federalist press tons of material.[63]

Historian Henry Adams later asserted, "The whole body of Federalists, who hated the South and the power which rested on the dumb vote of slaves, were exasperated . . . in regard to their trade with St. Domingo."[64] Southerners had demanded and then hastily passed legislation injurious to northerners' commercial endeavors. For many Federalists this action confirmed the influence of a powerful proslavery bloc in Congress.[65] Passage of the bill also underscored the Federalists' powerlessness. Confirming their fears was the new law, which stipulated U.S. merchants could only legally trade in areas of Hispaniola still under France's control. To prevent ships from sailing to "Negro parts of the islands," owners or ship masters had to pay heavy bonds and swear under oath that Haiti was not their destination. If a French privateer seized Americans and their property during an illegal trading venture with the Haitians, the lawbreakers could expect no help from the federal government.[66]

The irony of the situation was not lost on mariners. The government that they had turned to for help was now dictating that they could only conduct business with France, the nation that had been confiscating their property and harassing seamen without letup. The shipbuilders, sailors, ship owners, and merchants of New England who expected relief and support had lost legal access to a profitable market and continued to read about French atrocities on the high seas. Many of the accounts reported physical abuse inflicted on U.S. citizens in addition to the unbridled torture of black men and women.[67]

The federal government had not reacted to their petitions as merchants had hoped. According to one newspaper, the government's response to France's attacks evoked neither pride nor national honor. Maritime commerce, as one Federalist paper reported, was about to suffer because of "feeble and ruinous" legislation.[68] As Hillhouse said at the beginning of the debates, Americans expected Congress to protect their property, not criminalize their actions or deprive them of an important source of revenue. The *Hampshire Federalist* reiterated this sentiment in an article stating that the Haitian prohibition did nothing but "embarrass all our foreign commerce" and ruin a "valuable part of our trade."[69]

Federalists exclaimed that the government's plan was to destroy New England's prosperity and political influence. The legislation that outlawed trade to appease slaveholders and satisfy the designs of a foreign nation laid the foundation for their allegations. To them the Haitian prohibition confirmed suspicions that southerners had never fully absorbed the ideals of the American Revolution. Otherwise, they would not have expressed such hostility toward Haitians who, as the *Salem Gazette* insisted, were "men standing in the same relative situation as the colonists of the United States stood in 1775, when *Great Britain* was endeavoring to enslave them!"[70]

Another unacceptable reason for ending trade relations with Haiti was southerners' "peculiar aversion," as Samuel Taggart of Massachusetts observed, to "considering any people with a black skin as free and independent." Thus, the Haitian legislation indulged France, catered to racism, and demonstrated the influence of slavery which many of the legislation's supporters communicated while expressing condemnations for maritime commerce. One newspaper writer commented, "Split my timbers, but ain't [Haiti] an independent nation!" and another suggested somberly that Democratic-Republicans had now found a way to condone "monarchy and slavery."[71] Most also realized that through this law the government avoided taking steps that actually protected Americans trading in the West Indies.

Retired Congressman Fisher Ames who tussled with southerners over tariffs and export duties during the 1790s had much to say about the policy. He was troubled that Congress completely ended the Haitian trade at U.S. mariners' expense. Ames concluded that Democratic-Republicans would "hang the traders or permit the French to do it," even though the people of Haiti had earned their freedom and founded a nation "already *de facto* and of course *de jure*, independent."[72] Utilizing a combination political acumen and awareness of the challenges facing his region, Ames was able to articulate the fears bubbling just below the surface in New England.[73] While he said little about slavery, Ames insisted that the former slaves who founded Haiti clearly merited recognition and the right to trade with autonomy.

According to Ames, the congressional majority had acted like "knaves, who happen to be in a situation to do more than ordinary mischief." He grumbled that Jefferson, who while famous for writing the Declaration of Independence, had "done more than any other man living to undo it." To expel any doubts, Ames and other Federalists pointed to the Haitian policy. The U.S. had made itself complicit with Napoleon's efforts to impose "a degree of servile condescension" over the self-emancipated black people who now ruled Haiti.[74] A few Federalists still urged the government to enter into a treaty with the Haitians; others recognized that the prohibition could likely be the first of many trade restrictions to come.[75]

Federalist denunciations prompted Democratic-Republican Orchard Cook of Massachusetts to defend the Haitian prohibition. Before entering Congress, Cook had held several municipal and state appointments before running in a primary to represent Maine's First Eastern District as a Federalist. During the primary, Cook received newspaper endorsements touting his "integrity, active habits, commercial knowledge, and general respectability."[76] Cook had been a judge of the Court of Common Pleas, a member of the Wiscasset and Augusta Turnpike Corporation, and was the front-runner in the district caucus. He led the race but lacked a majority and in November rumors surfaced that a coterie of Federalists were protracting the caucus process because they preferred Nathaniel Dummer to Cook.[77]

Federalists provided only vague statements about Cook's influence over the press to explain why they "disown[ed] him as a federalist, and are ashamed of him as a man." Jeffersonians countered that the problem stemmed from Cook's disagreements with Federalists over issues such as a standing army. Cook pulled out of the Federalist race in the spring of 1802 and resurfaced in the election of 1804 as a Democratic-Republican. They were happy to have him.[78] Esteemed for his rapport with farmers, mechanics, merchants, and shipowners, Cook won the election to Congress despite Federalist charges that Jeffersonian support was the best proof that they had been right to have rejected him.[79]

In Congress, Cook generally voted with his party, but felt the need to explain why he supported the Haitian act even though it was primarily "calculated to have a favorable effect on the Southern States." He acknowledged the fact that the law would adversely affect Maine's merchants and economy, but said he was willing to sacrifice his constituents' interests for "the common good."[80] Jeffersonian newspapers in Maine defended the Haitian law as a protection for merchants, and called the Federalists' opposition disingenuous, partisan rancor. It was not because the policies were *"bad in themselves* that Federalists found fault with them," claimed the *Pittsfield Sun*, but that they were "the *measures of Mr. Jefferson and his friends."* Depicting their opposition in this way discredited Federalists by denying that they had valid philosophical or political objections to isolating the black republic.[81]

But the Federalists' record regarding Haiti contradicted the propaganda. Besides supporting the slave rebellion and outlining a government for Haiti, Federalists had authorized naval escorts to give U.S. merchants safe passage to and from areas controlled by the former slaves.[82] As late as 1805 William Bentley of Salem, Massachusetts, recorded in his diary that over "9 millions weight [of coffee]" had been imported into Salem from Haiti.[83] Several merchants including Joseph Peabody of Salem, whose schooner *Fishhawk* transported brown sugar, coffee, and molasses from Cape François on at least thirteen voyages between 1799 and 1804, were among those affected by the prohibition.[84]

For some Haiti was an important source of revenue, and the reason why they may have risked losing their investments by breaking the law. The penalty for violating the ban was the loss of ship and cargo, but the ruling in *United States v. The Penelope* (1806) encouraged circumvention of the Haitian prohibition. Authorities captured *The Penelope* while it was functioning as an intermediary between Haitian and American traders in a restricted area. Because *The Penelope* was not the property of a U.S. citizen or resident, the Pennsylvania district court determined that the law applied only to citizens or persons who had established permanent residence in the United States.[85] Following the court's decision, merchants were able to exploit the loophole and trade with Haitians through third parties without incurring penalties. Also luring merchants to the area were the Haitians' invitations to "come, then, with confidence, trade to our ports; exchange the fruits of your industry for our riches, and be assured that in trusting to our promises you will never find your confidence to have been misplaced."[86]

Secretary Madison even proposed that U.S. merchants continue to trade with Haiti surreptitiously. He never supported prohibiting the trade anyway, and suggested to Jefferson that Americans could interact with Haiti "thro' a Danish Island." He restated his position that the recent act went "beyond our legal obligations," and added that since "the trade will certainly go on indirectly thro' other merchants," U.S. merchants should also reap some of the profits.[87]

The frequency of violations did not mean that the law was a dead letter, however, and some Americans found themselves engaged in legal battles with unfavorable results. Judges tried cases in district courts from New England to South Carolina and in *United States v. The Schooner Betsey and Charlotte and Her Cargo* (1807), a lower court ruled against the owners of the ship and cargo that authorities confiscated for violating the prohibition. Besides the *Betsey* and *Charlotte*, they owned two other ships that authorities captured while they were trading illegally in Cape François. The higher court upheld the lower court's ruling against the ship owners on appeal.[88]

For some time historians endeavored to separate Jefferson from the proslavery overtones of the Haitian embargo, suggesting that he accepted black control of France's former colony. In some instances this interpretation is based on a letter to James Monroe in which Jefferson said that the former slaves had "established [themselves] into a sovereignty *de facto* and have organized themselves under regular laws and government."[89]

When the Adams administration opened trade with Haiti in 1799 however, Jefferson raised fears that the unregulated activities of "black crews, & supercargoes & missionaries thence into the southern states" would encourage slave insurrections in Virginia. In the event that there was a slave uprising, he feared that Virginia could not depend on other states for assistance and cautioned southerners to do something before the revolutionary spirit in Haiti could infect their slave population. If they failed to act, slaveholders would become the murderers of their own children.[90]

The racism that he espoused in his *Notes on the State of Virginia* (1781) also indicated that Jefferson would never accept persons of African descent as political or social equals to whites. Therefore, trading with and acknowledging an independent government under black rule was out of the question. Furthermore, Jefferson never published anything to recant or revise his opinions on black inferiority, which undoubtedly played a part in his initiation of the Haitian act. As one historian maintains that "Jefferson lost his philosophical bearings when he confronted the question of color or at any rate when he addressed its African aspect."[91]

Recognition of black rule in Haiti was never his administration's policy, nor did Jefferson seriously consider it. Unlike Adams who dealt openly with the Haitians, Jefferson refused even perfunctory dealings or communication with Haiti's leaders. Madison, Monroe, and Gallatin made it clear on several occasions that the administration considered Haiti a French colony and would never enter into any type of agreement with a black government. Long after Haitians declared independence, non-recognition remained the official U.S. policy.[92]

The idea that Jefferson agreed to end the Haitian trade in order to annex West Florida is also problematic. Well before he brokered the Louisiana Purchase, it became clear that Jefferson would never interact with black political leaders who presumed political equality. As soon as he took the oath of office, Jefferson began to dismantle the diplomatic and commercial apparatus left in place by the previous administration.[93] He certainly could have ended the trade to appease France, hoping that Napoleon might reciprocate by convincing Spain to relinquish claims to parts of Florida, but in correspondence with Robert Livingston, the U.S. diplomat in France, Madison offered to prohibit gun running to keep French privateers from harassing merchantmen, but did not suggest ending the trade as a bargaining chip for Florida.[94] The acquisition of Florida, while an important issue, was not included in the instructions to Livingston.

If the Haitian embargo was part of an attempt to annex West Florida, it was a lame sacrifice compared to Jefferson's Mobile Act of 1804 (an effort to claim the territories surreptitiously) or his request in 1806 for a $2 million appropriation to purchase the territory.[95] Federalists certainly could have used a connection between annexing Florida and the Haitian for propaganda and seized every opportunity to criticize the administration on those grounds, especially since everyone thought that the Louisiana Purchase already included the disputed parts of Florida. There were some hints of a connection, but Federalists did not press the conspiracy theory linking Florida to the ban on trade with Haiti.[96]

Instead, before the president signed Logan's bill into law, Timothy Pickering sent Jefferson a lengthy letter outlining his objections to the policy. If he signed Logan's bill instead of finding a way to protect commerce, Pickering predicted that Jefferson would "encounter the reproaches" of seamen, merchants, and anyone else who depended on the Haitian trade. He also correctly foretold that ending commercial relations with Haiti would be only the first of several maritime restrictions to come. Pickering cautioned, "One act of submission begets further unwarrantable demands," and if the federal government should pursue a similar course when responding to other attacks on commerce, it "further debases the nation."[97]

Pickering then begged the president to reconcile his support for the French Revolution with his abhorrence for the Haitians. Clearly, the Haitians' only infraction, he pointed out, was having "a skin not colored like our own."[98] Pickering understood that safeguarding slavery undergirded the policy and was concerned that southern interests would take priority and jeopardize New England. By the end of 1806 even the French architect of the Haitian policy, Turreau, regretted the prohibition. He reportedly confessed that he could not request that the United States repeal the law in his official capacity, but added that doing so "would not be displeasing to him or to his court." Turreau's change of heart came about because, as some of the bill's opponents had admonished, the Haitian trade had "almost entirely fallen into the hands of the British, who are, in general so well armed as to bid defiance to French Privateers."[99]

Federalists could now claim with some authority that Jeffersonians had no desire to protect commerce. Part of the reason Congress dismissed their proposals to use naval escorts to protect the merchant fleet was that Jefferson had reduced of the nation's naval power. He had allowed the number of commissioned vessels to decline from approximately forty-five in 1799 to fourteen by 1802. "Yet, when Mr. Jefferson came into office, the ships were scattered to the Four Winds of heaven. And what is the consequence? The plunder of our commerce . . . while the *coach* of the Southern planter is exempted," reported one Federalist.[100] Only a bias against maritime commerce could explain why Congress had disarmed merchant vessels and ended the Haitian trade, "the most lucrative which our country enjoys."[101]

Neither inside nor outside of Congress did northerners silently acquiesce to the Haitian policy. Crowninshield admitted that they rejected the policy "to a man." But back in New England, Federalists were freer in their condemnations than Democratic-Republicans could afford to be. The president of Yale University, Timothy Dwight, cautioned Virginians that for preserving slavery they would suffer the same "dreadful doom" as the slaveholders of Haiti. His younger brother Theodore Dwight, who briefly represented Connecticut in the Ninth Congress, also criticized the Slave South, called for abolition, and argued, "Justice must behold with a smile of approbation, the rapid progress of the slaves to triumph and independence."[102]

Some New England Jeffersonians voted with the South but supported antislavery legislation as well. Under the Democratic-Republican's caucus system, southerners influenced members' votes by controlling appointments to state and national offices. Patronage included cabinet and diplomat appointments, which were important posts for those who might lose congressional races, need to resign, or retire. For their own sakes, northern Jeffersonians "muffled whatever antislavery or anti-southern feelings they might have, voted with the South on crucial measures, and converted a southern minority in the House . . . into a majority political position," confirms historian Leonard Richards. New Yorkers would be among the first to break away from southern control of the party, but because no comparable rewards existed for Federalists, unless they were connected to the South financially or familially, most had no reason to support legislation that encouraged the perpetuation and spread of slavery.[103]

The Haitian policy also signaled a rejection of antislavery currents in the Atlantic world that exposed merchants and seamen to ideas that affected everything from industrialization and imperialism, to the abolition of slavery. Trading with the independent black merchants of Haiti was clearly a unique situation for every nation. But these ideas were anathema to slaveholders and others in the United States who could not countenance the implications of black persons achieving self-rule by defeating and ousting a major European nation, and expecting to be treated equally with whites.[104]

That black control of Haiti was foreboding for many Americans in government became apparent when congressmen dealt with a petition from a group of freed black men and women who asked Congress to amend the Fugitive Slave Law of 1793, end kidnapping, and take steps toward abolition. John Rutledge of South Carolina ably summarized southern sentiment and indicated the direction that federal policy would take when he condemned the French "philosophy of liberty and equality" that had infiltrated the nation. Rutledge argued that the Haitians began their revolt using the same phrases as the petitioners and feared that French abolitionists were in the country. He was appalled that northerners would even consider a petition that meddled with slavery. The House decided not to discuss any part of the petition and for years to come, the Haitian Revolution was an excuse that moved many to cater to slaveholders' demands.[105]

In less than a decade merchants that engaged in the Haitian trade went from having vigorous support and naval protection to being disarmed, under restriction, or facing legal action and a loss of revenue.[106]

With Democratic-Republicans in power, southerners were now in a position to manipulate northern economies, which is why Jeffersonians such as Barnabus Bidwell of Massachusetts constantly worried about the backlash. He cautioned Crowninshield that Federalists were still "vigilant, as well as powerful." Thus, surmised Bidwell, "a degree of regard ought to be had to the political situation of this important state."[107]

Drafting a congressional response to merchants' requests for protection against French and British attacks in the Atlantic was the next order of business and the solution could present even greater problems than Haiti. Even though it seemed unlikely, New Englanders like Orchard Cook, who rhapsodized over the interdependency of agriculture and commerce, might vote to impose restrictions on the transatlantic trade. Americans were still being attacked and their ships and cargo seized, but complaints from foreign nations appeared to carry more weight than their entreaties for protection. Would petitions asking for help move the government to pluck mariners out of the Atlantic world altogether? This was on the minds of maritime New Englanders, who in just a few days would find out how the Democratic-Republicans in Congress would address problems affecting trade with Europe.

NOTES

1. T. B. Wait, ed., *State Papers and Publick Documents of the United States from the Accession of Thomas Jefferson to the Presidency, Exhibiting a Complete View of Our Foreign Relations Since That Time*. 3 vols. (Boston: T. B. Wait and Sons, 1814–1815), 1:447, 448, 452.

2. Act to Suspend Commercial Intercourse between the United States and Certain Parts of the Island of St. Domingo, 1806, in *Statutes at Large of the United States of America*, 1789–1873, 17 vols. (Washington, DC: Government Printing Office, 1850–1873), 2:351.

3. Ronald Angelo Johnson, *Diplomacy in Black and White: John Adams, Toussaint Louverture, and the Atlantic World Alliance* (Athens: The University of Georgia Press, 2014); Eliga H. Gould, *Among the Powers of the Earth: The American Revolution and the Making of a New World Empire* (Cambridge, MA: Harvard University Press, 2012); Matthew J. Clavin, *Toussaint Louverture and the American Civil War: The Promise and Peril of a Second Haitian Revolution* (Philadelphia: University of Pennsylvania Press, 2010).

4. See Edward Bartlett Rugemer, *The Problem of Emancipation: The Caribbean Roots of the American Civil War* (Baton Rouge: Louisiana State University Press, 2008),42–53; Douglas R. Egerton, "The Empire of Liberty Reconsidered," in James Horn, Jan Ellen Lewis, and Peter S. Onuf, *The Revolution of 1800: Democracy, Race, and the New Republic* (Charlottesville: University of Virginia Press, 2002), 309–26; Don E. Fehrenbacher, *The Slaveholding Republic: An Account of the United States Government's Relations to Slavery* (New York: Oxford University Press, 2001), 111–18; Tim Matthewson, *A Proslavery Foreign Policy: Haitian-American Relations during the Early Republic* (Westport, CT: Praeger, 2003), 123–32; "Jefferson and the Nonrecognition of Haiti," in *Proceedings of the American Philosophical Society*, 140, no. 1 (March 1996): 29–35; "Jefferson and Haiti," in *Journal of Southern History* 61, no. 2 (May 1995): 235–41; Doron Ben-Atar, *The Origins of Jeffersonian Commercial Policy and Diplomacy* (New York: St. Martin's Press, 1993), 161–62; Stanley Elkins and Eric McKitrick, *The Age of Federalism: The Early American*

Republic, 1788–1800 (New York: Oxford University Press, 1993), 661–62; Michael Zuckerman, "The Power of Blackness," in Zuckerman, *Almost Chosen People: Oblique Biographies in the American Grain* (Los Angeles: University of California Press, 1993), 205–9; Robert W. Tucker and David C. Hendrickson, *Empire of Liberty: The Statecraft of Thomas Jefferson* (New York: Oxford University Press, 1990), 125–31, 184–87; Donald R. Hickey, "America's Response to the Slave Revolt in Haiti, 1791–1806," in *Journal of the Early Republic* 2, no. 4 (Winter 1982): 361–79; Adams, *Documents Relating to New-England Federalism*, 699–700; Ludwell Lee Montague, *Haiti and the United States, 1714–1938* (Durham, NC: Duke University Press, 1940), 45–46; Charles C. Tansill, *The United States and Santo Domingo, 1790–1873: A Chapter in Caribbean Diplomacy* (Baltimore: Johns Hopkins University Press, 1938), 97–109.

5. Tucker and Hendrickson, *Empire of Liberty*, 180; Ben-Atar, *Origins of Jeffersonian Commercial Policy and Diplomacy*, 161, 164–65.

6. Hickey, "America's Response to the Slave Revolt in Haiti," 362, 363; Tansill, *United States and Santo Domingo*, 1–2, 4; Samuel Eliot Morison, *Maritime History of Massachusetts, 1783–1860* (Boston: Houghton Mifflin, 1921), 160–67; Johnson, *Diplomacy in Black and White*, 14–19; Clavin, *Toussaint Louverture and the American Civil War*, 21; White, *Encountering Revolution*, 155–64; Rugemer, *The Problem of Emancipation*, 21, 42–43.

7. Timothy Pitkin, *A Statistical View of the Commerce of the United States of America* (Hartford: Charles Hosmer, 1816), 51, 397; cf. Adam Seybert, *Statistical Annals, Embracing Views of the Population, Commerce, Navigation, Fisheries, Public Lands, Post-Office Establishment, Revenues, Mint, Military and Naval Establishments, Expenditures, Public Debt, and Sinking Fund of the United States of America . . . 1789–1818* (New York: Burt Franklin, 1969 [1818]), 142; Rugemer, *The Problem of Emancipation*, 22, 25.

8. Ben-Atar, *Origins of Jeffersonian Commercial Policy and Diplomacy*, 122–41; Tansill, *United States and Santo Domingo*, 11–12; U.S. Congress, *American State Papers, 1789–1838: Documents, Legislative and Executive, of the Congress of the United States*, 38 vols. (Washington, DC: Gales and Seaton, 1832–61), 1:28.

9. White, *Encountering Revolution*, 120, 155, 156; Michael A. Palmer, *Stoddert's War: Naval Operations during the Quasi-War with France, 1798–1801* (Columbia: University of South Carolina Press, 1987), 74–75.

10. Palmer, *Stoddert's War*, 4; Johnson, *Diplomacy in Black and White*, 23; Richard Buel Jr., *America on the Brink: How the Political Struggle over the War of 1812 Almost Destroyed the Young Republic* (New York: Palgrave Macmillan, 2005), 14, 15.

11. Rugemer, *Problem of Emancipation*, 25.

12. Morison, *Maritime History*, 169, 180–83.

13. *American State Papers* 1, *Foreign Relations* 2: 126–30; quote from "Schooner Catherine," an undated letter in James Cocks (Cox) Papers, MH 64, Box 1, Folder 1, PEM; Thomas Parsons to Parents, March 14, 1797 and August 1, 1797, MH 175, Box 1, Folder 1, Parsons Family Papers, PEM.

14. *American State Papers* 1, *Foreign Relations* 2:15, 56–90, 315, 316, 593; Buel, *America on the Brink*, 14, 15.

15. James Carter to James and Thomas H. Perkins, March 31, 1794, Thomas Handasyd Perkins Papers, MHS.

16. Palmer, *Stoddert's War*, ix, 42.

17. Defense of Merchant Vessels Act of 1798, Pub. L. No. 5–60, 1 Stat. 572 (1798).

18. Department of the Navy Established Act of 1798, Pub. L. 5–34, 1 Stat. 553 (1798); Palmer, *Stoddert's War*, 4–6, 8, 16, 75; Gould, *Among the Powers of the Earth*, 202; Johnson, *Diplomacy in Black and White*, 144; Ada Ferrer, "Haiti, Free Soil, and Antislavery in the Revolutionary Atlantic," in *American Historical Review* 117, no. 1 (February 2012): 40; Joseph A. Fry, *Dixie Looks Abroad: The South and U.S. Foreign Relations, 1789–1973* (Baton Rouge: Louisiana State University Press, 2002), 27, 28, 78.

19. John Adams to Timothy Pickering, April 17, 1799, in *The Works of John Adams, Second President of the United States: With a Life of the Author*, ed. Charles Francis Adams

(Freeport, NY: Books for Libraries Press, 1969), 634; Johnson, *Diplomacy in Black and White*, 17.

20. Suspension of Trade with France Act of 1798, Pub. L. No. 5–88, 1 Stat. 611 (1798); Adams to Pickering, May 1, 1799, *Works of John Adams* 639 n2.

21. American State Papers 1, Foreign Relations 1:50–51; James H. Broussard, *Southern Federalists, 1800–1816* (Baton Rouge: Louisiana State University Press, 1978), 14–15.

22. See, Effectual Protection for Commerce and Coasts Act of 1798, Pub. L. No. 5–62, 1 Stat. 574 (1798); "Documents Relating to the Controversy over Neutral Rights between the United States and France, 1797–1800," in Carnegie Endowment for International Peace, Division of International Law, *Arbitrations and Diplomatic Settlements of the United States* (Washington, DC: The Endowment, 1914), 51–76.

23. U.S. House Journal, 5th Cong., 3rd sess., May 14, 1798, 292.

24. Tansill, *United States and Santo Domingo*, 73–75; Palmer, *Stoddert's War*, 160–62. See, Pickering to Hamilton, February 9, 1799, and Hamilton to Pickering, February 9, 1799, in *The Papers of Alexander Hamilton*, ed. Harold C. Syrett et al. 27 Vols. (New York: Columbia University Press, 1961–1987), 23:475.

25. Johnson, *Diplomacy in Black and White*, 3, 17, 41.

26. Johnson, *Diplomacy in Black and White*, 151–58; James D. Richardson, *Compilation of the Messages and Papers of the Presidents, 1789–1897*. 10 Vols. (Washington, DC: Government Printing Office, 1896–99), 6: 302–305.

27. Tansill, *United States and Santo Domingo*, 76–78; Fry, *Dixie Looks Abroad*, 28–29; Johnson, *Diplomacy in Black and White*, 164, 168.

28. For a contemporary discussion of France's efforts against Haiti, see Jacob Crowninshield to Nich Thiery, June 1, 1803, Crowninshield Family Papers, MH 15, Box 2, Folder 9, PEM.

29. Johnson, *Diplomacy in Black and White*, 180; *Senate Executive Journal*, 8th Cong., 1st sess., October 18, 1803, 57.

30. Clifford L. Egan, "Franco-American Relations, 1803–1814," PhD dissertation, University of Colorado, 1969, 44.

31. Fry, *Dixie Looks Abroad*, 28; Clifford L. Egan, *Neither Peace nor War: Franco-American Relations, 1803–1812* (Baton Rouge: Louisiana State University Press, 1983), 44–49; Tansill, *United States and Santo Domingo*, 97.

32. *Annals of Congress*, 9th Cong., 1st sess., 27, 28.

33. Wait, ed., *State Papers and Publick Documents*, 1:238.

34. Vincent Gray to James Madison, February 11, 1804, in James Madison, *Papers of James Madison: Secretary of State Series*, vol. 6, *November 1, 1803–March 31, 1804*, ed. Mary A. Hackett et al. (Charlottesville: University of Virginia Press, 2002), 466–67.

35. Madison to Carlos Martinez de Yrujo, March 1, 1804, in *Papers of James Madison: Secretary of State*, 6:522.

36. Madison to Robert Livingston, March 31, 1804, *Papers of James Madison: Secretary of State*, 6:641–44.

37. *Annals of Congress*, 8th Cong., 2nd sess., 812; Paul Finkelman, *Slavery and the Founders: Race and Liberty in the Age of Jefferson*, 2nd ed. (Armonk, NY: M. E. Sharpe, 2001), 127; Fry, *Dixie Looks Abroad*, 29; Jacob Crowninshield to Captain John N. Andrew, February 15, 1805, Crowninshield Family Papers, MH 15, Box 3, Folder 1, PEM.

38. *Annals of Congress*, 8th Cong., 2nd sess., 812–36; quoted in William Plumer, *William Plumer's Memorandum of Proceedings in the United States Senate, 1803–1807*, ed. Leverett Somerville Brown (New York: Macmillan, 1923), 242; Leonard W. Levy, *Jefferson and Civil Liberties: The Darker Side* (Chicago: Ivan R. Dee, 1989), 111.

39. Wait, ed., *State Papers and Publick Documents*, 1:236–43; see also, *Annals of Congress*, 8th Cong., 2nd sess., 1289–94.

40. *Senate Journal*, 8th Cong., 2nd sess., March 3, 1805, 474.

41. *Statutes at Large* (1845): 2:342–43.

42. *Annals of Congress*, 8th Congress, 2nd sess., 62–64.

43. *Hampshire Gazette* (Northampton, MA), November 12, 1804.

44. Albert Gallatin to Samuel L. Mitchill, January 3, 1805, in Albert Gallatin, *Writings of Albert Gallatin*, ed. Henry Adams (1879; New York: Antiquarian Press, 1960), 219–26.

45. *Hampshire Gazette* (Northampton, MA), January 2, 1805; Johnson, *Diplomacy in Black and White*, 144.

46. James M. Banner, To the Hartford Convention: The Federalists and the Origins of Party Politics in Massachusetts, 1789–1815 (New York: Alfred A. Knopf, 1970), 45.

47. *Salem* (MA) *Gazette*, March 3, 1805; November 5, 1805.

48. *Annals of Congress*, 9th Cong., 1st sess., 26.

49. *Annals*, 9th Cong., 1st sess., 28, 29; Plumer, *William Plumer's Memorandum*, 94–95, 250–51.

50. *Annals of Congress*, 9th Cong., 1st sess., 29–33.

51. Ibid., 34–36.

52. Ibid., 30.

53. Wait, ed., *State Papers and Publick Documents*, 1:360–66. See also, *Essex Register* (Salem, MA), January 27, 1806.

54. *Annals of Congress*, 9th Cong., 1st sess., 79.

55. Ibid., 117–38.

56. Jacob Crowninshield to William Bentley, December 14, 1805, Crowninshield Family Papers, MH 15, Box 3, Folder 4, PEM; *Annals of Congress*, 9th Cong., 1st sess., 276, 498–511; Fehrenbacher, *Slaveholding Republic*, 144; Robinson, *Slavery in the Structure of American Politics*, 332–33.

57. *Annals of Congress*, 9th Cong., 1st sess., 511.

58. Ibid., 514.

59. Robert A. McCaughey, *Josiah Quincy, 1772–1864: The Last Federalist* (Cambridge, MA: Harvard University Press, 1974), 17–23.

60. Fisher Ames to Josiah Quincy, December 16, 1805; February 3, 1807, in Ames, *Works of Fisher Ames*, 1:346, 392, 393; Joseph Story to Jacob Crowninshield, January 4, 1806, Crowninshield Family Papers, MH 15, Box 3, Folder 2, PEM; McCaughey, *Josiah Quincy*, 37–45; Buel, *America on the Brink*, 62–64.

61. *Annals of Congress*, 9th Cong. 1st sess., 515–16; Jacob Crowninshield to William Bentley, December 14, 1805, Crowninshield Family Papers MH 15, Box 3, Folder 4, PEM.

62. John Quincy Adams to John Adams, February 11, 1806, in *Writings of John Quincy Adams*, ed. Chauncey Ford Worthington, 7 vols. (New York: Macmillan, 1914), 3:134.

63. Jeffrey L. Pasley, *"The Tyranny of Printers": Newspaper Politics in the Early American Republic* (Charlottesville: University of Virginia Press, 2001), 235–36; Ronald P. Formisano, *the Transformation of Political Culture: Massachusetts Parties, 1790s–1840s* (New York: Oxford University Press, 1983), 16.

64. Henry Adams, *History of the United States During the Administrations of Thomas Jefferson*, 2 vols. (New York: Literary Classics of the United States distributed by Viking Press, 1986), 1:662.

65. *Salem* (MA) *Gazette*, March 7, 1806.

66. Suspension of Trade with parts of St. Domingo (Haiti) Act of 1806, Pub L. 9–9, 2 Stat. 351 (1806); *Newburyport* (MA) *Herald*, February 14, 1806.

67. *The Bee* (Hudson, NY), March 31, 1807; *Salem* (MA) *Gazette*, May 31, 1805; *National Intelligencer* (Washington, DC), February 3, 1806.

68. *Newburyport* (MA) *Herald*, March 21, 1806.

69. *Hampshire Federalist* (Springfield, MA), February 4, 1806.

70. *Salem* (MA) *Gazette*, March 7, 1806 (emphasis in original).

71. Samuel Taggart to John Taylor, February 26, 1806, Samuel Taggart Letterbook, AAS; Matthewson, *Proslavery Foreign Policy*, 63–64; *Columbian Centinel* (Boston), April 5, 1806; *New-England Palladium* (Boston), August 22, 1806.

72. Ames to Thomas Dwight, January 20, 1805; Ames to Pickering, January 28, 1806, in Ames, *Works*, 1:338, 351–54.

73. Fischer, Revolution of American Conservatism, 21.
74. Fisher Ames to Pickering, March 10, 1806, in Ames, *Works*, 1:368–71, 2:293. First published as "Dangerous Power of France No. 1" in the *Repertory* (Boston), May 1806; Ames to Pickering, June 4, 1798, in Ames, *Works of Fisher Ames*, 1:227; Leverett Saltonstall, March 12, 1804; Saltonstall to William Minot, April 17, 1806, in Robert E. Moody, ed., *The Saltonstall Papers, 1607–1815*, 3 vols. (Boston: Massachusetts Historical Society, 1974), 2:185, 302.
75. Ames, *Works*, 1:353; Elkins and McKitrick, *Age of Federalism*, 662; *Hampshire Federalist* (Springfield, MA), February 4 and 25, 1806.
76. *Eastern Herald and Maine Gazette* (Portland, ME), February 1, 1802; *Salem* (MA) *Gazette*, September 18, 1801.
77. Find election returns in the *Columbian Courier* (New Bedford, MA), December 18, 1801; and the *Eastern Herald and Maine Gazette* (Portland, ME) dated February 1, 1802.
78. *Columbian Courier* (New Bedford, MA), December 18, 1801; *Massachusetts General Court, Acts and Laws Passed by the General Court of Massachusetts at the Session Begun and Held at Boston, in the County of Suffolk, on Thursday the Thirteenth Day of January, Anno Domini, 1803* (Boston: Young and Minns, 1803), 114–15.
79. *Edes' Kennebec Gazette* (Augusta, ME), May 21, 1802; *Eastern Herald and Maine Gazette* (Portland, ME), May 31, 1802; *Eastern Argus* (Portland, ME), October 18 and 25, 1804; *Repertory* (Boston), November 13, 1804.
80. *Annals of Congress*, 9th Cong., 1st sess., 529.
81. *Pittsfield* (MA) *Sun*, or *Republican Monitor*, January 6, 1806; March 17, 1806 (emphasis in original). For a similar interpretation see Rugemer, *Problem of Emancipation*, 225.
82. Johnson, *Diplomacy in Black and White*, 15–17, 64, 65, 168–69.
83. See James M. Forbes to James and Thomas H. Perkins, February 5, 1801, *Thomas Handasyd Perkins Papers*, MHS; William Bentley, *Diary of William Bentley D.D.: Pastor of the East Church Salem, Massachusetts*, 4 vols. (Salem, MA: Essex Institute, 1905–14), May 25, 1805, 3:159.
84. Walter M. Whitehill, ed., *Captain Joseph Peabody: East India Merchant of Salem (1757–1844): A Record of His Ships and of His Family Compiled by William Crowninshield Endicott Edited and completed, with a sketch of Joseph Peabody's life, by Walter Muir Whitehill* (Salem, MA: Peabody Museum, 1962), 17, 92–94.
85. *United States v. The Penelope*; Case No. 16,024 District Court, D. Pennsylvania 1806 U.S. Dist. Lexis 5; 27 F. Case 486; 2 Pet. Adm. 438.
86. *New England Palladium* (Boston), October 14, 1806; January 9, 1807; February 27, 1807.
87. Madison to Jefferson, August 4, 1806, in James Morton Smith, ed., *Republic of Letters: The Correspondence between Thomas Jefferson and James Madison, 1776–1826* (New York: W. W. Norton and Company, Inc., 1995), 1433.
88. See *United States v. The Schooner Betsey and Charlotte and Her Cargo* 8 U.S. 443; 2 L. Ed. 673; U.S. Lexis 405; 4 Cranch 443 (1807); *Yeaton and Others, Claimants of the Schooner General Pinkney And Cargo*, v. United States; 9 Sup. Ct. 281; 3 L. Ed. 101; (1809) U.S. Lexis 431; 5 Cranch 281 March 7, 1809, Decided; *Young et al. v. Tavel*, 18,175 S.C. (1806) U.S. Dist. Lexis 4; 30 F. Case. 867, 1 Bee 228 (1806).
89. Thomas Jefferson to James Monroe, November 24, 1801, in *Jefferson Papers* LC; Merrill D. Peterson, *Thomas Jefferson and the New Nation: A Biography* (New York: Oxford University Press, 1970), 823–24; Matthewson, *Proslavery Foreign Policy*, 105–8, "Jefferson and Haiti," 225, and "Jefferson and the Nonrecognition of Haiti," 22. See also Rayford W. Logan, *Diplomatic Relations of the United States with Haiti, 1776–1891* (Chapel Hill: University of North Carolina Press, 1969), 153; and Tansill, *United States and Santo Domingo*, 109.
90. Jefferson to Madison, February 12, 1799, Jefferson to St. George Tucker, August 28, 1797, in *Jefferson Papers* LC.
91. Zuckerman, *Almost Chosen People*, 201; Rugemer, *Problem of Emancipation*, 43.

92. See James Madison to Robert Livingston, January 31, 1804, in James Madison Papers, Manuscript Division, LC; James Monroe to James Madison, July 1, 1804, in *Writings of James Monroe*, ed. Stanislaus Murray Hamilton (New York: AMS Press, 1969), 220–21; Johnson, *Diplomacy in Black and White*, 164, 167, 168.

93. For instance, see Johnson, *Diplomacy in Black and White*, 163–67.

94. Madison referred Livingston to earlier correspondence with Marquis D'Yrujo and added that the United States was bound to do nothing regarding the trade, but would prohibit "the export of contraband articles." "If for example," explained Madison, "France would agree to permit the Trade with St. Domingo in all other articles, on condition that we would agree to prohibit contraband articles . . . the arrangement would in itself be so reasonable on both sides, and so favorable even to the people of St. Domingo [Haiti], that the President authorizes you not to only make it . . . the subject of a frank conference with the French Government; but to put it into the form of a conventional regulation . . . which may lead to the regulations on each side respectively necessary." See Madison to Livingston, March 31, 1804, in *Papers of James Madison: Secretary of State*, 643.

95. Samuel Flagg Bemis, *Diplomatic History of the United States*, 5th ed. (New York: Henry Holt and Company, 1965), 182–86.

96. See *Massachusetts Spy, or Worcester Gazette*, May 7, 1806.

97. Timothy Pickering to Thomas Jefferson, February 24, 1806, Jefferson Papers LC; Johnson, *Diplomacy in Black and White*, 168.

98. Pickering to Jefferson, February 24, 1806, Jefferson Papers LC.

99. Plumer, *Memorandum*, 540–41.

100. *Newburyport* (MA) *Herald*, March 14, 1806 (emphasis in original).

101. *Newburyport* (MA) *Herald*, March 14, 1806; Donald R. Hickey, "Federalist Defense Policy in the Age of Jefferson, 1801–1812," in *Military Affairs* 45, no. 2 (April 1981): 66, 67; cf. Seybert, *Statistical Annals*, 644–45; *Hampshire Gazette* (Northampton, MA), January 2, 1805.

102. Matthewson, "Jefferson and Nonrecognition of Haiti," 34 and *Proslavery Foreign Policy*, 130; Jacob Crowninshield to William Bentley, December 24, 1804, Crowninshield Family Papers, MH 15, Box 3, Folder 4, PEM; Linda K. Kerber, *Federalists in Dissent: Imagery and Ideology in Jeffersonian America* (Ithaca, NY: Cornell University Press, 1970), 46, 49; David Hackett Fischer, *Revolution of American Conservatism: The Federalist Party in the Era of Jeffersonian Democracy* (New York: Harper and Row, 1965), 286, 287, 296, 297; *New-England Palladium* (Boston), January 6, 1801; Dwight quoted in Rachel Hope Cleves, *The Reign of Terror in America: Visions of Violence from Anti-Jacobinism to Antislavery* (New York: Cambridge University Press, 2009), 150.

103. Leonard L. Richards, *The Slave Power: The Free North and Southern Domination, 1780–1860* (Baton Rouge: Louisiana State University Press, 2000), 60–67; Kerber, *Federalists in Dissent*, 46 n61, 49; Jacob Crowninshield to Barnabas Bidwell, February 26, 1804, Crowninshield Family Papers, MH 15, Box 2, Folder 9, PEM; *New-England Palladium* (Boston), January 6, 1801.

104. Gould, *Among the Powers of the Earth*, 203.

105. *Annals of Congress*, 6th Cong., 1st Sess., 230, 235–36, 241–42, 244–45; Rugemer, *The Problem of Emancipation*, 43.

106. Thomas C. Cochran, ed., *The New American State Papers [1789–1860]; Social Policy*, 47 vols. (Wilmington, DE: Scholarly Resources, 1972–1973), 2:312; 3:29.

107. Barnabus Bidwell to Jacob Crowninshield, September 2, 1805, Crowninshield Family Papers, MH 15, Box 3, Folder 1, PEM.

TWO

"Indissolubly Connected with Commerce"

Nonimportation, Southern Sectionalism, and the Defense of New England

On December 2, 1805, notary public Michael Hodge recorded an incident dictated by William Morris, captain of the brigantine *Lucretia*. The brig left Massachusetts for the West Indies in August 1804. Its voyage was going smoothly and according to plan until 5:00 p.m. on September 20 when the British privateer *Andromeda* attacked the *Lucretia*. The British then boarded the *Lucretia*, held the crew at gunpoint, and stripped the vessel of its cargo and supplies including "canvas, candles, pump nails, and cabin stores." After taking away as many items as they could carry off of the *Lucretia*, the raiders returned to rob Morris and the crew of their personal belongings including shoes and clothing. Around midnight they released the ship and its personnel, but only after viciously pummeling the crew with clubs and striking Morris across the face with a tiller (a lever used to steer the ship) for asking them to leave.[1]

In dozens of reports and petitions, merchants recounted similar accounts of mistreatment and financial loss at the hands of the British. Mariners at every level appealed to the government to protect them from Britain's ship seizures and its impressment of U.S. citizens. They wanted protection just as the ship owners, captains, and seamen who sent complaints to Congress and complained about French spoliations in the Caribbean. In that case, however, instead of protecting merchantmen the government disarmed commercial vessels and then outlawed the Haitian trade. That policy, which southerners rammed through to protect slavery, left New England Federalists with the impression, as articulated by Senator William Plumer of New Hampshire, who wrote New Englanders "have an interest different from that of the southern[ers]," but the party in power was reluctant when it came to "supporting that interest."[2]

Unlike the policies implemented by Federalists in the late 1790s, the government's recent response to complaints that France confiscated Americans' property and mistreated U.S. citizens had not resulted in protective measures. If Congress adopted a similar policy to deal with problems in the Atlantic, the results could be catastrophic. Americans believed that as neutrals they had a right to uninhibited trade in any open port, even when transporting goods from a belligerent's colonies. Yet, though their ships flew the flag of a neutral nation, Americans were under constant attack. European privateers, primarily from France and Britain seized their property, and the British also impressed seamen into naval service.

As the House discussed the problems enumerated in merchants' petitions, several representatives expressed attitudes about the carrying trade that digressed into heated exchanges over whether maritime commerce and citizens engaged in foreign trade deserved federal protection. During the early months of 1806, the tone of these debates affected harmony within the Democratic-Republican Party. By the end of the year, Federalists had adjusted their approach to congressional debates, entered the sectional dispute that was already in progress, and intensified their opposition to commercial restrictions and what they regarded as the anti-New England, anti-maritime biases that preceded the passage of each restrictive policy.

In their responses to weeks of sectional chides and the denigration of northern mariners, a few Federalists came to describe seamen as a class of free, upwardly mobile laborers who rejected the constraints of southern agriculture and deserved the nation's protection. Through these speeches Federalists introduced key elements of free labor ideology into the nation's political discourse. Their arguments would be incorporated into northerners' opposition to the spread of slavery in antebellum political debates. It is undetermined whether their articulation of free-labor ideology reflected a growing consensus in New England, but the ideology did surface in response to southerners' criticisms of New England's commercial culture. In addition, the persistence of conflicting sentiments that undergirded public policy pushed Federalists closer to the periphery of the standard of political decorum that they once advocated.

Comparing free laborers to slaves had been part of abolitionists' critique since the 1700s. In 1784 James Phillips attempted to dispel the philosophical defenses and theories that used climate and harsh conditions to justify slavery. "There is not perhaps a climate on earth, where freemen may not be engaged to work," and "the hope of reward is a stronger incentive to industry, than the dread of punishment." Ending slavery would allow freed persons, Phillips continued, to "profit from the sweat of their brow." Noah Webster provided a world history in 1793 to demonstrate the harmful effects that slavery and other forms of oppression had on "agriculture, arts, commerce, and science." He insisted, "Men will not be industrious . . . without a well founded expectation of enjoying the fruits of their labor." Webster recommended "honest employments" as a remedy for a host of social ills and concluded, "Freed men are more profitable as hired men, than they were as slaves."[3] Free labor ideology also appeared in Benjamin Franklin's writings of the 1750s.[4]

In their responses to southerners' condemnations of mariners and the carrying trade, Federalists moved the defense of free-labor beyond the basic denunciations of slavery by indicating that northern commercial cultures were superior to the South's slave-based agricultural economies. In this way, they politicized the free labor concept and added it to the nation's political discourse as a means to defend the North's political economy. Webster also touched upon the moral supremacy of the Free North, which remained a part of abolitionist writings.[5] By the 1830s the defense of free laborers in politics was over twenty years old and became part of the composite message of antislavery politicians who also included abolitionism in their rhetoric. Along with the fact that they were hardly egalitarian, it is significant that the Federalists' defense of free labor derived as much from southerners' insolence as it did from their inability to shape public policy, repeal the three-fifths clause, or thwart the spread of slavery.[6]

Nevertheless, the free labor ideals espoused by Federalists had more to do with sectional particularism and the idea that mariners were engaging in a virtuous form of commerce, rather than building a shared class consciousness. The slave trade, which had formed a commercial bond between the regions, was now rejected by most New Englanders and Federalists lauded laborers in a system that escaped both the slave trade's stigma of immorality and the economic and cultural inertia of slave-based agriculture. Even though historians continue to debate the economic nature of southern slavery, Douglas R. Egerton argues, "agrarian capitalists of the South . . . found it impossible to come to terms with the industrial capitalists of the North, or to follow free labor advocates down their path to greater prosperity."[7] The South's lack of economic development for all of its residents was the gist of the Federalists' arguments and a basis for their appeal to the federal government to protect mariners and merchants. But their entreaties were eclipsed by partisan politics and the Jefferson administration's difficulties in Britain.

By the time the House began its debates over British seizures and impressments, the recently passed Haitian policy had already tarnished Anglo-American relations.[8] Haiti was not the primary problem in U.S. diplomacy but it did become a factor in Britain's response to American diplomats. Members of Parliament approached U.S. minister James Monroe as early as 1804 to discuss the U.S. response to French spoliations in the West Indies. At first Monroe replied that France would likely end its attacks once the United States confirmed that it would never enter into a trade agreement with the former slaves of Haiti. The British countered that France was just using the Haitian trade to manipulate the U.S. presence in the West Indies. If that were the case, suggested Monroe, frigates could be sent to the Caribbean to "coast it awhile thro' the Islands, tho' under secret orders to touch no vessel."[9]

An illusion of force against France did not appear to be a satisfactory solution. After the United States ended the Haitian trade but left merchants free to trade with areas under French control, James Stephen, a British publicist and abolitionist, accused the United States of replenishing France's resources and protracting the war. He called the Haitian prohibition anything but neutral, and argued that by trading in French West Indian ports and transporting those goods to France, the U.S. government was actually waging a war against Britain "in disguise." Stephen then established the intellectual framework for the *Essex* decision, described later in this chapter, when he asserted that Britain had a right to regulate neutral trade and intercept any ships suspected of furnishing supplies to its enemies. Even though he was sure that the British economy could survive without imports of raw material from America, Stephen was optimistic that amicable trade relations would soon be restored and that the English-speaking nations would join forces to enforce prohibitions on the African slave trade that Parliament was about to enact.[10]

Stephen provided an important perspective, but one of the main reasons that the British interfered with the wartime carrying trade was to grab a share of the profits. Revenue for the neutral carrying trade grew from $13.5 million to $60.2 million from 1803 to 1806 but because the Jay Treaty did not specifically define contraband of war, U.S. merchants were left vulnerable to the judicial and political fiat of foreign nations. The treaty's ambiguity became evident when the British Admiralty Court overturned its *Polly* ruling of 1800 through the *Essex* decision of 1805. The first ruling had been in effect since 1800 when the *Polly*, a ship owned by a Massachusetts merchant, was captured and taken to England because its cargo included Havana sugar and Caracas cocoa. Prior to being captured, the ship stopped in the United States—a neutral nation—and the court ruled that entering the port of a neutral nation neutralized all cargoes exported out of a belligerent's colony (except contraband of war). In practice, ships imported goods into the United States, unloaded their cargo, and paid a duty before reloading the same cargo and sailing on. On the ensuing voyage British inspectors considered the shipment neutral, which protected both ship and cargo from seizure.[11]

Sometime later the ship *Essex* was re-exporting goods that had been stored in Salem, Massachusetts, for nearly a month before the cargo was reloaded and the ship sailed for Havana, Cuba. British agents seized the

Essex while en route and escorted the ship into New Providence in the Bahamas. In 1805, after a trial and an appeal, the British reversed the *Polly* decision declaring that the transport of belligerent goods through a neutral port was an insufficient action for neutralization.[12] Thereafter any ship transporting cargo from an enemy's colony violated the law and was subject to confiscation. After the ruling, the British attacked ships that set sail before the court issued its decision. Captains, who had no idea that their cargo was now illegal, faced the loss of ships and goods considered neutral when their voyages began.[13]

In addition to reversing its policy, Britain escalated its impressments of U.S. citizens. The British did not recognize expatriation at this time, especially when wartime demands increased the need for able-bodied personnel. To staff its fleet, the Royal Navy employed press-gangs comprised of military companies or civilians who were paid to find deserters on foreign ships or in seaport towns. The practice of seizing and forcing men to work on naval vessels began during the Renaissance and was widespread by the time it was legalized by Parliament in 1650.[14]

Since the early 1790s the United States denounced Britain's method of recovering deserters because the press gangs frequently impressed U.S. citizens. Secretary of State Madison submitted an abstract to Congress listing about forty-three impressed seamen when the war resumed in 1803. By 1806 the number of documented impressed Americans had climbed to over two thousand.[15] The nations were unable to strike an agreement over impressments because of the large numbers of British subjects and deserters employed in the U.S. merchant fleet. Jefferson once considered banning British seamen from the merchant marine but found out that more than a third of its personnel, about nine thousand out of twenty-four thousand, were British subjects. Even though the United States welcomed many of these seamen as naturalized citizens, Jefferson abandoned the plan.[16]

Though they were unable to end British impressments when in power, Federalists portrayed the Jefferson administration as apathetic to the plight of impressed seamen. According to Federalists, Democratic-Republicans campaigned on assurances that they would stop impressments if elected, but that was nothing more than "a fine sounding promise." Neither the Jefferson administration nor the majority in Congress had done anything to solve the problems facing maritime trade although they had complained about it for nearly a decade. Federalist correspondents asked rhetorically, "How do the democrats protect American commerce and American seamen? . . . They dismantle our infant navy; they dismiss the best commanders, and turn adrift the sailors." Now that they had forbid the trade with Haiti, the president's "minions in Congress have begun a warfare against the British trade."[17]

In rebuttal, Democratic-Republicans claimed that the entire situation arose because mariners begged the government to protect them from

Britain's fluctuating laws involving neutral trade. The British exposed them to personal danger and economic ruin, and these merchants urged Congress to end impressments and the "plunderings of privateers" with "national force."[18] Though France and Spain had also assailed merchantmen in the West Indies, Britain's infractions, they insisted, were "more numerous and extensive." No matter where they sailed, Americans were attacked and mistreated by foreign nations, and the problem was not limited to the neutral trade. Merchants engaged in the direct trade of U.S. produce, they claimed, also risked losing their ships and cargoes. Jeffersonians consistently reminded colleagues on both sides of the aisle that along with great financial damage, the nation's commerce was being "checked and embarrassed" by foreign powers.[19]

On February 26, 1806, shortly after voting to end the Haitian trade, the House took up the matter of fortifying and defending the nation's ports and harbors. Jeffersonian Nathaniel Macon of North Carolina opened the discussion by suggesting that the United States lend its navy to another nation that could manage it better. Macon had recently become Speaker of the House in a sectional contest with Joseph Varnum of Massachusetts. During their battle over their speakership, Barnabus Bidwell of Massachusetts voiced concerns about his party's survival in New England and asked southerners to support Varnum. If they did, he assured them, Democratic-Republicans could present a united, multiregional front that would help defeat Federalists in New England's next congressional elections.[20]

Although Varnum lost the race for speaker, Bidwell and other northerners remained loyal to their party. According to New Hampshire Senator William Plumer, Federalists voted for John Cotton Smith of Connecticut and wasted twenty-seven votes that could have helped Varnum defeat Macon. In his opinion, their vote split the region's delegates which deepened partisan "bitterness" in New England even further.[21] Macon, who held the post beginning with the Seventh Congress, was still Speaker when the Ninth Congress began deliberations over its response to Britain's attacks. Debates over coastal fortifications and other defensive measures followed Macon's proposal regarding the navy, and disagreements among Democratic-Republicans' remained minor until Orchard Cook of Maine proposed that Congress use the navy to protect commerce. His suggestion changed the tone of the debate.

Cook advocated the use of naval escorts to protect commerce since the crisis began, and in reply to Macon's proposal to remove the navy from the United States' control said that his constituents in Maine were growing hostile to the federal government because of the recent commercial restrictions, which worked against their prosperity. One reason that "our merchants have suffered greatly; some half, and some wholly ruined," according to Cook, was the federal government's neglect of the navy. He reasoned that the only practical solution was to purchase "line-of-battle ships and frigates," rebuild the naval force, and use it to protect citizens and their property at sea. Cook hoped that southerners would respond favorably to his motion because, as he confessed for the record, he had voted to protect their interests (slavery) during the Haitian crisis, even though that policy was counterproductive to his supporters' livelihoods. Cook was probably not prepared for his colleagues' response when he asked, "Shall we or shall we not increase the navy to meet the exigency of our affairs?"[22]

Northern Democratic-Republicans were among the first to reject Cook's proposal in favor of a bill banning the importation of certain goods manufactured in Britain. Andrew Gregg of Pennsylvania, who introduced the nonimportation bill, was certain that British manufacturers relied too heavily on U.S. imports to endure the sanction for an indefinite period. Britain, he thought, would not allow the situation to deteriorate into warfare. Gregg then made it clear that he did not intend for the proposed law to protect "American merchants, engaging in that wild, extravagant carrying trade." Only mariners transporting produce or goods that originated in the United States deserved protection. He would never risk the nation's security over the carrying trade, which he deemed an illegitimate form of commerce.[23]

From February 28 to March 26, 1806, Jeffersonians argued over the wisdom of nonimportation among themselves. They exchanged insults and slung about charges of anti-commercialism and sectionalism. Early in March one northerner reminded southern representatives that the entire House "expressed a just abhorrence of slavery . . . [and] a commendable sympathy for the untutored sons of Africa, of a different color from ourselves stolen or forced from their families and all that is dear to them and shall we make no exertions to protect our citizens from a worse kind of slavery?" Northern Democratic-Republicans considered a ban on British imports the most rational way to protect commerce, but their southern colleagues remained adamantly opposed. Along with apprehensions over the effects that nonimportation could have on their export trade to Britain, southerners questioned the morality of the carrying trade and rejected Gregg's proposal because it threatened their economic stability.[24]

John Randolph of Virginia—a long-winded, flamboyant states' rights agrarian who clashed with Jefferson and attended congressional sessions with his dog and a riding whip—severely rebuked the supporters of nonimportation.[25] The bill's supporters, he scolded, deserved "a straight waistcoat, a dark room, water gruel, and depletion." He was especially hostile toward Jacob Crowninshield of Salem, Massachusetts, accusing the New Englander of attempting to start an Anglo-American war for profit. Randolph then snapped that the United States was an agricultural country and promised that he for one would never allow "Salem and Boston, New York and Philadelphia" or any other seaport town to dictate the nation's policies. Neither he nor any other southerner, asserted Randolph, could endorse measures to protect foreign commerce, especially the carrying trade, which was a "fungus of war." He adamantly opposed fighting a war to defend northerners' "circuitous" trade since it would destroy the Constitution.[26]

Southerners also objected to Gregg's bill on the grounds that Britain would likely retaliate by imposing restrictions on their cotton and tobacco exports, potentially costing planters about 80 percent of their revenue.[27] Most preferred suspending the carrying trade altogether instead of sacrificing the South's economic interests. South Carolinian David Rogerson Williams said that the memorials read in Congress did not represent the sentiments of all Americans and warned that if Congress listened to them, "The whole of agriculture would be sacrificed to the mercantile interest." Had he known that Crowninshield had assembled about 150 merchants to draft one of the Salem petitions, his accusations would have no doubt been even more damning. Yet even without such information southerners were not pleased with the prospect of sacrificing "good markets and high prices" to protect a wartime trade that most said should not exist.[28]

Through their arguments southerners were establishing the contours of what the nation should deem legitimate forms of capitalism. As long as the maritime industry confined itself to the direct trade of agricultural products, foreign commerce was valuable to the nation and worthy of federal protection. This was not the case with the wartime carrying trade. From their perspective, because it had nothing to do with southern prosperity and was purely a moneymaking enterprise primarily benefiting northerners, they felt that the federal government should not expend resources to protect the carrying trade.[29] As the representatives of southern agriculturalists these Jeffersonians eyed the capitalist impulse exhibited in the carrying trade with suspicion and portrayed mariners as immoral opportunists lacking ethics and republican virtue. The carrying trade, they argued, derived from greed and the love of money, which southerners insisted was directly responsible for endangering seamen and involving the United States in foreign conflicts.[30]

A few historians have also questioned the morality of the carrying trade because merchants were profiting from Europe's wars. Some argue that the United States lacked the moral authority to protest seizures related to the neutral trade or to take offense at impressments, because the carrying trade relied solely on conditions created by war. Even though one of the reasons that the British attacked the carrying trade was to reap some of the profits, many scholars conclude that it was immoral for "the United States to fatten on the follies of Europe."[31]

A more evenhanded assessment would take other factors into consideration. First, the fact that British subjects could naturalize according to U.S. policy flew in the face of international comity and antagonized the British.[32] More importantly, however, is the reality that the only economic system southern agriculturalists thought worthy of defending thrived on slave labor. Certainly, whenever domestic or foreign developments endangered slavery, as was the case with the Haitian trade, southerners assumed a constitutional, moral, and legal right to federal protection. Their denunciations of the wartime carrying trade had much more to do with sectional interests and an antagonism toward maritime activities—that were independent of slavery—than the morality of the trade itself.

The employment of free African Americans was another problem that southerners had with northern maritime operations. Free men of color with limited employment opportunities found work in the maritime industries and experienced a degree of egalitarian treatment not available to them in agriculture or most other occupations. Captains sometimes staffed their ships with all-black crews, and the number of black men working on shipping, whaling, and other vessels exceeded their percentage of the population. Many of these mariners were older family men who received wages equal to or, depending on their skills, higher than their white crewmates. Paul Cuffe of Westport, Massachusetts, capitalized on the state's shipping business and became the nation's wealthiest African American. Before his death in 1817, Cuffe also participated in efforts to end the slave trade.[33] Southerners did not abide this type of success for a black person or sanction any endeavor that condoned racial tolerance or equality. Therefore, during the nonimportation debates they criticized northern merchants for lacking the sophistication to practice racial discrimination. New Englanders would deal with "a white emperor or a black one—with Bonaparte or Dessalines—it is all one" to the merchant, according to one southern congressman.[34]

It is also worth noting that within a few years, the slave states would codify their anxieties over the presence of black seamen in their ports beginning with South Carolina's Negro Seamen's Act in 1822. Other slave states would soon follow. The purpose of these laws was to prevent free black mariners from gaining unrestricted access to slaves. Slaveholders feared that African Americans who had been free for some time or those recently freed would share news about slave revolts or entice their human property to run away to freedom. In fact, it was for the latter reason that Jefferson and slaveholders in Congress opposed the Haitian trade, which would allow free persons of African descent to trade in southern ports.[35]

Under the seamen acts, local sheriffs and other law enforcement agents arrested black seamen and ferried them to local jails. At a captain's or ship owner's expense, towns and cities detained these sailors for the entire time that a ship remained in port. If the fines related to the cost of imprisonment went unpaid, municipalities could and sometimes did sell these men into slavery. Sometimes, even when black sailors stayed aboard their ships, local authorities would have them arrested and confined on shore. New Englander Eleazer Graves, captain of the barque

Amelia, witnessed the forced removal of two black sailors from the *Edward*, a ship docked in a southern port. He deplored the infringement on the rights of black Americans "born free and in a land of liberty." Graves called the laws "an outrage on the liberties of the northern states."[36]

Well before this incident, on March 6, 1806, as Congress debated how to sanction Britain, Randolph assailed northern merchants for caring about nothing but monetary gain. He claimed that greed accounted for northerners' willingness to stoop so low as to conduct business with the black merchants of Haiti. Four days later Macon alleged that northern representatives only wanted to curtail British imports because a law of that type would be detrimental to the South, like the Federalists' Quasi War or "sort of half war," which he asserted had already damaged the South's economy by lowering the prices of certain commodities. If northern congressmen wanted to get serious, they would "cut off all intercourse" with Great Britain, but this was out of the question, concluded Macon, because cutting off all trade would have dire effects on the North and not just the South.[37]

George W. Campbell of Tennessee confessed that he had always thought it wrong for the government to protect any form of trade conducted "out of sight of our own territory, or beyond the reach of our cannon from our shores." He then advocated prohibiting all trade with Great Britain to send a stronger message than limiting importations, and joined other southerners in their censure of non-agrarian commercial economies. The United States, he continued, could only hope to escape the growth of poor and dependent laboring classes, as well as political decay by limiting commerce and expanding agriculture.[38] Campbell delivered one of several speeches reflecting southerners' aversion to northerners' independent maritime pursuits when he said, it "would have been well for us, sir, if the American flag had never floated on the ocean, under the authority of Government, to waft to this country the luxuries and vices of European nations, that effeminate and corrupt our people." If Congress allowed commerce to fend for itself added Campbell, the nation would not be so entangled in the affairs of the decaying, base nations of Europe.[39]

When the bill's supporters included impressments as another reason to ban British imports, similar criticisms entered into this new thread of the discussion. Impressing men into military service was always a nasty business, and New Englanders were no strangers to the process. Colonial New Englanders had accepted commissions to "search diligently for and impress into his Majesty's service . . . able bodied seamen." In 1745 William Shirley, governor of Massachusetts Bay, authorized an Essex County sheriff to hire several men to search Salem, Marblehead, Ipswich, Newbury, Gloucester, and Boston for men to impress into the military. The sheriff and his deputies did not limit their search to deserters, and the Crown paid them well for each man they impressed. After independence Britain did not sanction impressing U.S. citizens, but press-gangs forced thousands into the Royal Navy nonetheless.[40]

Under Washington and Adams, Federalists had attempted to limit impressments through citizenship certificates. These documents, commonly called "protections," required customs officers to register the names of seamen who were U.S. citizens. Secretary of State Pickering also made numerous requests to the British to free detained Americans and placed a U.S. agent in the British West Indies to help prevent further impressments. Issuing the certificates was left to the states, and while they varied in appearance and level of detail, all proclaimed the bearer a U.S. citizen.[41] Unfortunately, counterfeit certificates were easily printed and sold for about ten dollars. Due to the wide circulation of these fraudulent documents, protections quickly lost their value.[42]

Neither press-gangs, nor British officers were interested in verifying a seaman's nationality during the war. Captains attempted to fill quotas or impress men possessing certain skills. One ship captain admitted that he would not bother to examine protections when his ship was "in distress." This attitude was common based on an account provided by James Durand, an impressed sailor from Connecticut. Durand describes several instances of British naval officers blatantly disregarding his papers and the other valid certificates presented by U.S. citizens. One officer, he recalls, struck an impressed seaman and knocked him below deck just for referring to his citizenship papers.[43] Tales of cruelty toward impressed Americans and bungling by both British and American authorities exacerbated the problem, which had grown critical by 1806.

The U.S. government might have ameliorated the problem by imposing penalties on merchants who employed British subjects but the nation's liberal naturalization policies encouraged immigration.[44] Though exact data are not available, by some estimates the number of impressed Americans was minuscule compared to the number of British deserters working on U.S. vessels. On the other hand, because press-gangs were notoriously haphazard, it is likely that only one out of ten men taken from U.S. ships was actually a British subject.[45] Neither nation was blameless. Americans employed British deserters, and Royal naval officers intentionally ignored or were unwilling to verify the true nationalities of the seamen they forced into service. In support of Gregg's bill, along with comparing impressing seamen to slavery, congressmen noted that the only justification for this "sentence of condemnation to slavery" was that "a seaman speaks the English language or has become an American citizen." Opponents of the bill, most of them southerners, were right to argue that a sanction on imports would do nothing to end impressments, because as they noted, there were greater numbers of British subjects employed by Americans than the other way around.[46]

Maryland representative Joseph Nicholson accused nonimportation supporters of sneaking impressments into the debates to hide the fact that their chief concern was protecting the carrying trade. Nicholson said he had previously attempted to introduce legislation to end impressments but could not get the proposal through the House. He was sure that "strong measures were not then the order of the day, nor would they be now if impressing Americans was the only ground of complaint." For him, diplomacy was the only viable solution. Nonimportation would lead "headlong into war." If they caused a war, he promised that the present Congress would not be burdened with conducting it, because "the people will supply our places with other representatives, they will not so readily forgive us."[47]

In an attempt to persuade their southern counterparts to support the bill, northern Jeffersonians asserted that the carrying trade was inseparable from the direct shipping and by protecting one Congress protected both. In addition, agriculture and maritime commerce depended on each other. They also tried to appeal to southern sensibilities by comparing treatment under impressment to the horrors of slavery. Crowninshield reiterated his support for the carrying trade, adding that John Randolph would be right beside him if he were sent to an insane asylum. If Congress refused to "hold out [its] protecting arm" to mariners engaged in the carrying trade, foreign nations would ruin fellow Americans. The carrying trade was as legitimate as the direct trade in agricultural staples, and Congress should not forfeit either. Possibly referring to returning fugitive slaves and helping to quell rebellions, Crowninshield said that if southerners are not willing to give up their slaves, they needed to "afford a reasonable protection to Commerce."[48]

Bidwell chimed in and repeated the charge that being impressed was a fate worse than "African bondage." William Findley of Pennsylvania added, "if the planters of South Carolina, or any other state where slaves are employed, should forcibly take any of our sons," the outrage "would be horrid indeed, but not equal to the impressment of our citizens." Northern Jeffersonians expressed disdain for southern slavery, but tried to do so in a context that southerners considered inoffensive.[49]

Pennsylvanian John Smilie had previously stated that Americans would be happier had they "found themselves without commerce and had still remained so," after the American Revolution. He now found it disconcerting that southerners were insisting that Congress had no obligation to protect commerce. Joining the chorus of those claiming that impressing Americans into service was comparable to slavery, Smilie insisted that Congress had a duty to do something about it. Putting aside his earlier disdain for foreign commerce, including the carrying trade, he averred that the "Eastern States" would not have entered the Union had they known that "commerce was to receive no protection." He considered the language that southerners used during the debates inappropriate, and predicted that such rhetoric would give the impression that the "fate of the country" was in "irresponsible hands."[50]

Neither the analogy with slavery nor the link between commerce and agriculture proved persuasive. Nor did it help to describe the physical abuse heaped on impressed seamen such as "flogging through the fleet." For infractions such as striking an officer or attempting to escape, impressed seamen reportedly received hundreds of lashes administered from ship to ship until the sailor was flogged aboard every available ship in the fleet. Since the chances of survival were much higher than hanging, impressed seamen claimed that sailors generally preferred flogging through the fleet as an alternative.[51]

Macon asked if any of his colleagues honestly thought that Gregg's bill would end impressments. To him, the best way to alleviate sailors' suffering was to keep merchants from hiring British subjects. Gregg then remarked, "If the merchants really be the friends of the American sailors, they would willingly agree to such a regulation."[52] During the final days of the debate no southerner appeared convinced that nonimportation would protect seamen, but many agreed that the United States could survive with agriculture alone. Punishing Britain would only damage the South's economic prosperity and at this time southern representatives saw no reason to do so.

One northerner who did not attempt to reconcile protection of New England's maritime concerns with the survival of southern agriculture was James Elliot of Vermont. Elliot straddled the fence between the Federalist and Democratic-Republican parties, but his arguments often fell in the Federalist camp. After first winning election to Congress as a Federalist, Elliot was reelected as a Democratic-Republican with Federalist support. During the debates over nonimportation he attacked southerners for approaching impressments as a sectional problem because most of the "unfortunate men" taken by the British were from the "Northern and Middle States."[53]

After listening to hours of speeches delivered by southerners who gratuitously insulted northern mariners, Elliot used his time to defend New England's laborers. The mariners who needed help were not without "character or consequence—mere adventurers on the ocean, wandering beyond the limits and the powers of the national jurisdiction and protection." He explained further that these unfairly maligned mariners were citizens, businessmen, and laborers, "employed in an honest occupation; and surely the impressment of thousands of them . . . is of as much importance as the price of cotton and tobacco." Elliot cited "the principles advanced by" political economists to validate his assertion that a nation's wealth came from its labor force "upon the ocean as well as upon *terra firma*."[54]

In several public letters to his constituents Elliot intimated that New England's free culture was superior to that of the Slave South. Whereas southerners thrived only through the labor of persons in bondage, Elliot was proud that he cultivated his own farm and did not need to enslave other human beings. Slaveholders might be better republicans theoretically, but their republicanism is "not quite as practical as mine" boasted Elliot.[55] Elliot's pride in his region's free labor force was unmistakable.[56]

For the most part, disagreements over nonimportation were between southern and northern Democratic-Republicans. Federalists had been conspicuously silent. Thomas Newton of Virginia, a supporter of the sanction noticed their quiescence and applauded the quiet absence of their "steady opposition." Newton derided Federalists for incessantly attempting to obstruct the legislative process until the nation faced a crisis. Now that the legislature had to solve a serious problem, "The former champions of commerce have hung up their coats of mail—the helmet and the buckler, the sword and scabbard, are thrown aside—the prophetical finger no longer points to war. . . . From my heart I wish it an uninterrupted repose."[57] Even though he was correct, Newton's chiding did not embarrass Federalists into taking part in the debate or apologize for not doing so. For some reason they were missing an important opportunity to offer legislative solutions to ship seizures and impressments.

Not certain about what to do, Massachusetts Federalist Samuel Taggart nervously scribbled, "No Federalist has spoken on the subject [of nonimportation]. It seems to be their determination to let the majority manage all these affairs in their own way, without doing anything farther than give a simple vote." Taggart was not convinced that Federalists were taking the correct course of action and at one time considered joining the verbal fray. But before entering the debate he decided to yield "to what appeared to be the general opinion" of his party and kept quiet.[58]

Fisher Ames, who retired from Congress after 1796 because of an acute respiratory illness, was less forgiving. Conservatism was fine, said Ames, but Federalists were "carry[ing] their reserve to an extreme." He was looking for input from Federalists, especially junior congressman Josiah Quincy, but neither he nor others had said anything during the debates. Ames complained of being "quite in the dark" about where Quincy and other Federalists stood on nonimportation. Voters were naturally interested in how their representatives would handle the crisis and given the sectional divisions among Democratic-Republicans, Federalists were missing an opportunity to garner support. If they hoped to survive as a political party, Ames urged them to let "the nation know that they still exist." He knew they were the minority party and would likely lose the political battle, but asked why Federalists should "care what sexton happens to be in office at our funeral?"[59]

Federalists apparently stepped back knowing that the majority was uninterested in bipartisan solutions. They refused to let Democratic-Republicans hector them into another fruitless debate. At least this was the excuse that Timothy Pickering gave Ames. Anytime Federalists decided to sponsor bills or offer proposals, "their usual opponents" simply closed ranks and outflanked them.[60] But Crowninshield voiced greater suspicions than Newton and feared that Federalists were being taciturn in order to observe the debates and "do mischief" by "throw[ing] their votes where they do the most harm."[61]

Perhaps Crowninshield was right. Pickering explained to Ames that he and other Federalists thought it better to watch the majority self-destruct, and then vote wisely instead of wasting time battling both southern and northern Democratic-Republicans. More importantly, he was convinced that Jefferson's policies alone would lead New England's voters back to "their old friends and steady habits" in the 1806 congressional elections. Others agreed. The Federalist Central Committee of Boston explained, "We have reason to believe" that Democratic-Republicans' lack of "talents and efficiency," along with their "utter ignorance of the true interests of this country," would soon become apparent.[62] Regardless of Ames's frustrations over their disinterested approach, Pickering, Quincy, and other Federalists thought it prudent to let the majority "knock their heads one against another" rather than participate in another squabble.[63]

The strategy did not sit well with Ames, who argued that no aspect of the majority's opinion should have gone unchallenged. By remaining silent, Federalists gave Democratic-Republicans enough time to introduce several proposals that they should have made. Cook's suggestions, for example, reflected the Federalists' defense policy that included maintaining a robust military, increasing the nation's war readiness, and deploying naval escorts to protect the merchant fleet.[64] In addition to advocating naval assistance, Cook also defended merchants' rights, resolutely contending that the government was obliged to defend the foreign trade. He also adopted the Federalists line that the "power to wage war is the best security for peace."[65]

Ames reminded Quincy and Pickering that these were the arguments Federalists should have been making. Actually, Cook's thinking was so harmonious with Federalist policies that a friend wrote Pickering, "I see a good speech of one *Cook*. If we get into a serious broil, this would be a *Cook* very much to my palate. Who is this new *Cook*?"[66] Yet, the partisanship was still so thick that northerners from both parties might agree on many points, but none of them would praise the opposition publicly. A pamphleteer reminded readers that they may not "all [be] tyrants," but Democratic-Republicans were still under the supervision of "haughty and imperious demagogues ... slave-driving-nabobs of Virginia."[67]

A primary division among New England's congressmen according to some Federalists was northern Jeffersonians' subservience to the southern wing of their party. Most believed that the dynamics in that relationship would never change. "As New England has so long been in a practice of being the dupe of her southern neighbors, it is to be expected she will not soon change it," remarked Quincy. Unlike their northern adversaries, Federalists were opposed to any legislation restricting commerce under the guise of protecting it, even limiting British imports. When the opposition supported nonimportation they took the issue out of "the hands of southern men" and placed the onus for commercial restrictions on themselves.[68]

There was some merit to this assessment. Northern members of his party had rejected Cook's motion for military aid and vigorously promoted using trade as a weapon instead. Others, like future congressman and associate justice of the Supreme Court Joseph Story of Salem informed Crowninshield that he had doubts about "the policy of an *absolute non-intercourse*" with Great Britain. Another of Crowninshield's friends argued that sanctions "would cripple our commerce without giving us material advantage." Like most northern Jeffersonians Crowninshield stayed true to his convictions until it became clear that southerners would not acquiesce. On those occasions, he and others usually compromised just to placate their southern counterparts. Crowninshield later confessed that while he and other northern "Democrats" (which some contemporaries already called Democratic-Republicans), had fully supported Gregg's nonimportation bill, but submitted and passed a weaker act "with a view *to unite with the majority of our southern brethren*."[69]

The bill that Crowninshield and others settled for was sponsored by Joseph H. Nicholson of Maryland. It was a watered-down version of Gregg's bill that was signed into law on April 18, 1806. The policy prohibited the importation of certain manufactured articles from Great Britain, Ireland, and British colonies, beginning on November 15. Shipmasters, agents, importers, and consignees had to take an oath that they would not knowingly break the law, and would report anyone who did. Violators risked losing their cargo and faced fines up to three times the value of any confiscated merchandise. Anyone caught buying a banned item was penalized double the amount of the purchase, and once a government official seized the forbidden goods they remained impounded until the courts settled any claims.[70]

Federalist newspapers attacked the policy and assailed the act's authors for lacking the talent, wisdom, or determination to draft legislation "proper for extricating us from our present difficulties." All they needed to do to solve the problem was deploy "Frigates and armed vessels" to protect the nation's commerce. The Haitian prohibition had already humiliated the country enough, said one writer, and now Congress is getting ready to sacrifice all trade and start a war with Great Britain. Unlike their northern counterparts, who consistently sought sectional harmony, Federalists attributed southerners' irascibility to their habitual abuse of slaves. Virginians, according to one Federalist newspaper, were "so much in the pleasant habit of the rule and domination by managing her negro [sic] slaves that she ardently desires to consider the eastern states under the control of ancient dominion." Others claimed that the violence of slavery had spilled over into the halls of Congress and was manifest in bitter insults, duels, and southerners' obstinate refusal to even consider using the military to address the crisis.[71]

Unfortunately, during the March debates Federalist newspapers had scant input from their party's representatives and improvised by publishing any speech delivered against nonimportation. Many were from the garrulous and condescending John Randolph of Virginia. Fisher Ames chided, "It is certainly better that Randolph should expose the wretched policy of our Solomons, than that it should be left unnoticed." He continued to demand that Federalists pubically outline their own remedies for the crisis, and point out how their proposals differ from those offered by southern and northern Jeffersonians.[72]

Some agreed with some of the points made in his speeches, but Federalist papers still spurned Randolph and other southerners for insulting members of New England's congressional delegation. Newspaper writers took issue with attacks leveled against their representatives during debates, and the fact that all the victims were New Englanders regardless of party affiliation. Randolph always found a way to degrade their congressmen in his speeches, "particularly his old and very humble supporter Mr. Crowninshield." Crowninshield's wife Sarah (Sally) encouraged her husband to respond to Randolph, but for the sake of intraparty harmony she urged him to do so with "moderation and a command of . . . temper."[73] Such timorous responses to these frequent slights led Federalists to question New England's Jeffersonians' role in the party. Why, if southerners found them as contemptible as their remarks suggested, asked Federalists, did northerners continue to support the administration and acquiesce to southerners' demands? Obviously, they concluded, it was not because they were "loved or respected."[74]

After wasting an opportunity to exploit the internal disputes that surfaced among Democratic-Republicans that March, Federalists decided to weigh in on the sectional divisions shaping public policy when a coastal fortifications bill resurfaced for debate. Earlier in the year, William Ely introduced a bill to fortify the nation's coasts and harbors and proposed allocating $150,000 as a starting point. When northern representatives tried to increase that amount, several southerners staunchly disapproved of spending any more money on the coasts, and questioned maritime commerce's value to the nation. When the House revisited the topic in April, Josiah Quincy, who had unwisely sat out the nonimportation debates, took issue with southerners' objections to increasing the allocation for coastal defenses.[75]

Aggrieved by the unfavorable depictions of merchants and seamen, Quincy lashed out and rebuked southern congressmen for being "narrow, selfish, local," and "sectional." As for the anti-commercial statements made by Randolph and others, Quincy called it amazing that "men from the interior . . . in one breath tell you they know nothing about the subject, and in the next pass judgment against the adoption of measures of defense." He noted that increasing the public debt had not been an issue when southerners "wanted to purchase Louisiana," but then they audaciously opposed investing more money in coastal fortifications because the funds would protect northern states. Quincy continued, "two-fifths of your white population are commercial" and deserve the government's protection. In fact, "of the 5 millions which now constitute the white population of these states, two million are north and east of New Jersey." Furthermore, "this great mass is naturally and indissolubly connected with commerce." He added, that the maritime industry was comprised of two million "merchants, tradesmen, mechanics, seamen, and laborers" from New England. Now that southerners could shape federal policy, "Are such portions of the Union to be told that they are not to be defended, neither on the ocean, nor yet on land?" Like James Elliot had done earlier, Quincy praised northern laborers but went a step further. These citizens, he said, rejected southern culture and had no desire to become farmers because "they love a life of activity, of enterprise." This, he said, was a major difference between "the Southern and Eastern states" and the primary cause of "diversity of sentiment" over appropriate commercial and defense policies.[76]

Here, Quincy expressed another aspect of free-labor ideology when he associated the North's labor force exclusively with white Americans. This was significant because by omission his description of free laborers did not include the North's black workers even though black seamen made up over 15 percent of the maritime labor force. Although New England's African Americans were among those impressed, abused, and economically devastated under sweeping trade restrictions, Quincy identified white laborers as the laboring class that Congress needed to consider. Indeed, white workers in America already objected to the use of terms such as "master" or "servant" because these would connect them to persons of color, whether they were slaves, free African Americans, or Native Americans.[77]

The complexities of free labor ideology intersected with the Federalists' argument that commerce fostered economic independence and nurtured the type of useful ambitions that made men virtuous citizens. As for their participation in the development of modern capitalism, as Stephen Watts explains, Federalists were more than traditional, "antidemocratic reactionaries"; they played an important role in the early republic "promoting various innovations—commercial expansion, [and] entrepreneurial individualism."[78] For these reasons free labor ideology can be seen as a natural consequence of the Federalists' political economy.

When appealing to Congress on behalf of the nation's mariners, Quincy struck a sharp contrast between New England's free labor force and the slave laborers who kept southern agriculturalists afloat. Unlike slaves, free laborers north of New Jersey were enterprising and ambitious. Federalist Daniel Webster of New Hampshire, who in 1806 also criticized commercial restrictions and advocated the protection of commerce, later called "the whole North . . . the people who till their own farms with their own hands" the nation's most educated, enterprising, and independent citizens.[79]

Westward expansion, population growth, immigration, and the development of diverse economies in the North amplified these differences further as the free-labor ideology evolved in ensuing decades. The debates of 1806 demonstrated that Federalists were already making these comparisons and injecting free-labor ideology into the political debates over the preservation of northern interests. Elliot, for example, repeatedly commented on the political disparities that existed throughout the nation because as he saw it, the three-fifths clause nourished a parasitic system. "Laboring slaves consume nothing of consequence upon which a duty is paid . . . while the farmer and every man of business in the northern and middle states pays his taxes with the sweat of his own brow." He was afraid that in the not too distant future, "the southern and western states will have more representatives in Congress and electors of president *for slaves* only, than the northern will have *for all their free people!*"[80]

After lauding northern laborers Quincy issued a proposal similar to the one that Cook made during the nonimportation debates. He argued that building up and deploying the navy was the only logical way to stop attacks on the nation's merchant fleet. Along with the fact that Democratic-Republicans preferred restricting commerce rather than protecting seafaring citizens, what really bothered Quincy was the blatant pro-southern bias governing the use of public funds. Congress quibbled over exceeding $150,000 for coastal defenses at the same time that they planned to spend millions on "Southern land," the exploration of newly acquired western territories, and the purchase of Florida—all to protect the interests of slaveholders. Quincy found the disparity inexcusable. New Englanders were simply asking "for reciprocity . . . security of the North and East." But after funding every project that benefitted their interests, southerners were complaining that there was no money left. If the sectional bias in Congress continued, thundered Quincy, there would be a change in government or the Union would unravel.[81]

Democratic-Republicans dismissed Quincy's effusions and passed an act to fortify the ports and harbors on April 21, 1806, allocating only the $150,000 originally proposed. The law also supported more reductions of the navy and allowed the president at his discretion to sell any armed vessel he deemed unfit for service. Congress later increased this amount but Federalists had made a point about their perceptions of the sectional bias in Congress.[82] Federalists made sure that voters read or heard about any statements by southerners' that demonstrated disdain for commerce, along with evidence of northern Democratic-Republicans' deference to the South. Some thought that emphasizing the sectional, doctrinaire attitude underlying recent trade restrictions would move New Englanders to vote for Federalists in 1806. For this reason Ames urged Quincy to be more emotionally involved and avoid displaying "too much maiden modesty" about "causing your speeches to be carefully corrected and printed."[83]

The mid-term congressional elections were only months away and with little faith in voters' ability to see the dangers of the "Jacobin party" Ames continued to reprimand Federalists. Recent congressional debates had been no time to woolgather on the sidelines because the legislature's solutions would have a direct effect on New England. Shaping public opinion, Ames asserted, required constant "exhortation, consolation, and encouragement." Randolph's speeches had been popular because he was the only one making the type of objections to trade restrictions expected from Federalists but, Ames admonished, "it is true that you are a minority, and what you ask for will be refused . . . it will nevertheless remain a notorious fact that you ask, and you are not tongue-tied, but you can surely make the reasons why you ask universally known." If they again indulged in coy reserve, "Federalism will not only die, but all remembrance of it [will] be lost."[84]

Of course there is no way to confirm that the elections might have turned out differently had they challenged nonimportation, but as Ames said, at least voters would have learned that Federalists could offer an alternative to restricting imports. They also could have provided responses to southerners who insulted maritime commerce and New England's mariners. Providing a counter-narrative certainly would not have hurt Federalists in 1806, but because they did not, it apparently appeared to voters that northern Democratic-Republicans were the only ones sincerely interested in protecting commerce, while combating southern intransigence singlehandedly. Perhaps because of Ames's foreboding, Quincy admitted being anxious about the upcoming elections if "the last year was the turning point."[85]

When the votes were tallied in Massachusetts where Jeffersonians worried that they had lost voter confidence, it became apparent that Federalists probably should have participated in the debates as Ames advised.[86] Federalists did not see the turnaround they had hoped for and even lost a House seat when Democratic-Republicans won the Cumberland District in the wake of Federalist Peleg Wadsworth's decision not to seek reelection. On the other hand, the returns were promising in key areas. One was the Essex South District, which included the seaport towns Salem, Gloucester, and Marblehead. Jacob Crowninshield, who had defeated his chief opponent, Federalist Nathan Read, by 561 votes in 1804, won reelection by only 267 votes. Before entering Congress, Crowninshield had a career at sea, which began as a supercargo (an officer in charge of the care, purchase, and sale of cargo) before he became a ship captain, and headed the family firm George Crowninshield and Sons, in Salem. Crowninshield was a consistent defender of seamen's rights in

Congress, became chair of the Committee on Commerce and Manufacturing, and was Jefferson's choice for secretary of the navy in 1805. Though he had to decline the appointment, Jefferson and Madison consulted Crowninshield about commercial matters, and he was influential in shaping the administration's policies toward Britain. Crowninshield understood that Federalists could succeed if his party erred and kept a steady finger on the pulse of public sentiment in his district.[87]

In spite of Crowninshield's popularity, Federalists might have won the district or made a better showing had they not waited until the last minute to nominate Samuel Putnam and place him on the ballot only two days before the election. Once they saw that Crowninshield only won decisively in Marblehead, the *Salem Gazette* excitedly reported, "The federal vote was better than the best hopes and calculations could promise.... A few days of preparation might have given a different result; as it was Mr. C's majority is 300 less than in 1804."[88]

Other seaport districts in Massachusetts also revealed declining support for Democratic-Republicans. In Maine, still a part of Massachusetts, incumbents held onto their seats but with fewer votes than in the previous election. Similar to Crowninshield, Orchard Cook, who represented the Lincoln District, consistently demonstrated a personal commitment to maritime interests and frequently advocated military protections for commerce. He won reelection in 1806 by only 140 votes in a two-man race, 57 fewer votes than his victory in the three-way race of 1804. The same was true of the Kennebec candidate, John Chandler, who held on to his district with 263 fewer votes than he received in 1804.[89]

Signs of voter disenchantment in the northern districts of Massachusetts were important because before 1806 Maine had developed a solid Democratic-Republican base. An elite merchant class dominated district politics, as demonstrated by the York District campaign. In 1801 Democratic-Republican Richard Cutts won a special election to fill the seat left vacant when Federalist George Thatcher accepted an appointment to the state supreme court.[90] The Cutts family had shrewdly established economic and personal alliances with merchants, and after wresting control away from Federalists held on to their positions through patronage. Politician Joseph Bartlett enthusiastically supported Cutts's candidacy earlier, but the men became bitter enemies over time.[91] In the congressional race of 1806 Cutts faced Bartlett and Federalist Joseph Leland.

Bartlett charged Cutts with corruption, accusing him of stealing elections through bribes in the form of patronage, and voter intimidation. He claimed that deference to the wealthy Cutts family had become the only road to success in York District politics. Furthermore, his *"foreign attachments,"* which were mostly commercial partnerships in France, and ties to the Virginia gentry through his marriage to James Madison's sister, clearly influenced the policies Cutts supported in Congress. Bartlett urged voters to elect "New-England men who have attachments in uniform with those of their constituents." Cutts's record was nothing more than "a blank piece of paper, with perhaps, here and there a blot," chided Bartlett.[92] Bartlett's accusations about Cutts's dependence on patronage and southerners could be verified, but the incumbent still won in 1806 and defeated two opponents by 146 votes.[93] Cutts held on to his congressional seat until 1812.

It was clear that after 1800 Massachusetts voters simply replaced Federalist elites with Jeffersonian elites who fought as hard as their predecessors to maintain their hold on power in local, state, and national politics. Networks forged by family and professional ties, as well as wealth and patronage that once kept Federalists in power, and about which Democratic-Republicans vehemently complained, now operated in the latter's behalf.[94] For a long time before 1806 it was nearly impossible for Federalists to win elections in the Maine districts, but trade restrictions eventually showed that Jeffersonians' fears of losing support in New England were well founded.

Although some of the faces changed, Federalists did hold on to six Massachusetts districts. Edward St. Loe Livermore, who would serve three terms in Congress before becoming a justice in the New Hampshire supreme court, won the Essex North seat, and Jabez Upham captured the Worcester South District formerly held by Seth Hastings, who declined renomination in 1806.[95] As the November elections ended, each district began to answer the *New-England Palladium*'s call "that some person should represent us to Congress who is acquainted with our commercial interests, who is friendly to them, and who, by his habits and talents is able to . . . detect and oppose such measures as may injure them."[96]

Other matters—such as the impeachment of federal judges appointed by Adams and the removal of Federalists from government posts—most certainly influenced voters. But northerners were still enthralled with the Jeffersonians' message of democracy, increased voting rights, promotion of westward expansion, and the headiness of the Louisiana Purchase. Even if the impeachments or Jefferson's schemes for acquiring West Florida added to the Democratic-Republican's popularity in New England, the policies that affected commerce and the maritime industry would damage their popularity.

By the end of 1806 commercial restrictions couched in southerners' invectives leveled at the carrying trade forced New Englanders to take a second look at Federalist contentions that neither Jefferson nor his party had an interest in their economic well-being or protection.[97] By taking on the South instead of the northern Democratic-Republicans who verbally defended seamen and in some cases called for military action, Federalists entered congressional debates as the only supporters of New England who would not advocate restrictive policies or quietly submit to southerners' domination. Their approach conveyed a degree of solidarity with fellow New Englanders. Plus, Federalists had become aware that merchants "are pretty universally opposed and alarmed at Gregg's motion . . . for it will then be a state of commercial hostility."[98] The opportunity to regain congressional seats would come again and based on the way they soon began to conduct themselves in Congress, Quincy, Pickering, and other Federalists had decided that Ames was correct.

In December 1806, shortly after the November elections, President Jefferson recommended that Congress delay implementation of the Nonimportation Act to give James Monroe and William Pinkney a chance to settle Anglo-American differences through diplomacy. Congress complied by passing an act to postpone enforcement until July 1807 giving Jefferson authority to suspend the policy again should he see fit.[99] If the Monroe-Pinkney negotiations succeeded, Democratic-Republicans would win the war and the Federalist Party would be dead as Ames had predicted. If diplomacy failed, as they expected, Federalists could fight harder to defend New England's commerce and possibly win voter support in 1808.

With future election victories in mind, Federalists acted shrewdly and supported the bill suspending nonimportation, which was wise since disapproval of commercial restrictions was escalating. By December, John Randolph, the strongest non-Federalist opponent of nonimportation, had fallen from grace. Federalist organs turned against the verbose Virginian's diatribes and the Boston *Repertory* prefaced one of his speeches, "Mr. Randolph . . . Again."[100] Now that Federalists were criticizing Democratic-Republicans for failing to protect the merchant fleet and defend seamen against impressments, Randolph was no longer needed. Federalist began their own attacks calling the Nonimportation Act "that stupid offspring of democratick [sic] ignorance and obstinacy" that ought to be "knocked in the head."[101] As Crowninshield, Bidwell, and others in their party feared, Federalists were poised to capitalize on the unpopularity of their policies.[102]

Taking advantage of an opportunity to set themselves apart, Federalists participated in debates over ending U.S. participation in the African slave trade. Slaveholder influence in Congress was even more pronounced as the House discussed legislation to end the slave trade from December 1806 through February 1807. During this time, Federalists who would be deemed radical wrestled with southerners over several points including capital punishment for those breaking the law. Josiah Quincy became a major advocate for the protection of illegally imported Africans, proposing that the federal government take responsibility for their welfare.

Peter Early of Georgia wanted to leave the future of illegally imported Africans up to each state. He confessed that it was simply a "melancholy truth" that even if illegally imported Africans would be "sold as slaves" in the southern states. Quincy opposed Early's plan but admitted that he had no proposal to offer at that time. Jeffersonian Joseph Barker of Massachusetts disagreed with Early and said that the U.S. government had a right to free such persons. Barnabus Bidwell replied that releasing illegally imported Africans to state authorities was better than having the federal government take ownership of slaves. In his rebuttal Quincy said, "I think I now understand the plan . . . and I like it less than before." Leaving the fate of these Africans up to authorities in the southern states, he remarked, was just another way of saying that the government was "leaving them to be slaves." James Sloan of New Jersey concurred. Allowing illegally imported persons to become slaves would place "an everlasting stigma" on the government. He proposed granting automatic freedom to those brought into the North and a return trip to Africa for those illegally imported into the South. Southerners replied that the government could not force slave traders to forfeit their captives and lose money. Bidwell agreed, and Orchard Cook echoed the familiar excuse that freeing illegally imported Africans would "let loose a set of banditti in hostility to the whole country." Timothy Pitkin of Connecticut was baffled and asked how Congress could pass legislation to prevent the slave trade but declare that "unfortunate blacks, brought into this country . . . against their own will" and against the law could still be sold as slaves. If they had the right to prohibit the importation of slaves, Congress certainly could dictate that lawbreakers had "no right or claim whatever" when it came to deciding the fate of Africans imported into the United States against the law.[103]

Since all parties said they wanted to end the slave trade, Quincy encouraged the House to "unite more perfectly on the means" to do so. Bidwell and others who held similar positions needed to "descend from their high abstract ground" and deal with reality according to Quincy. Once the trade was illegal, traders had no right to claim humans as property because, he asserted, "These persons are free by law of nature—as free as any of us." Congress should do everything possible to prevent violations of the law, take steps to "grant that these persons have all the rights of man," and make provisions to ameliorate their condition. Just as impoverished children had rights and were cared for until they were able to take care of themselves, Quincy proposed a plan to care for illegally imported Africans that would have similar results. Once brought into the country Africans would have no knowledge of the language, laws, or culture. They would be here against their will and Congress had to provide the "means to make them useful members of society."[104]

As Quincy and others worked on provisions of the bill, Federalist William Ely, who regularly called for repeal of the three-fifths clause, suggested the death penalty as punishment for breaking the law. Benjamin Tallmadge of Connecticut supported the proposal and quoted the biblical exhortation at Exodus 21:16, which condemned "man stealers" to death. Some agreed with Ely, but a few representatives were uneasy over citing Mosaic Law in a congressional session. Others argued that the death penalty was too harsh for this particular crime, but Smilie said that seizing people to sell them into slavery was actually worse than murder. Tallmadge wondered aloud why representatives who said they wanted to end the slave trade refused to "unite with us in providing adequate punishment." Ely offered an explanation: "I will tell the truth. A large number of people in the Southern States do not consider slavery as even an evil." They would never consider it a crime, and based on their objections, "some gentlemen" in Congress were engaging in the process of ending the trade "for the sake of appearances" only.[105]

At certain junctures Quincy, Sloan, and Smilie refused to accept the bill because it authorized selling "persons of color" into slavery even if illegally transported into the country. In the end, however—after threatening disunion and attempting "to terrify the committee by making a dreadful picture of the people's rising *en masse*," as Sloan complained— southerners got their way. Section 4 of the bill prohibiting the slave trade left the fate of illegally imported Africans up to state governments and punishment for violating the law included a five-thousand-dollar fine and the possible loss of the ship that transported the slaves. The House debated the bill until February 26, and when the final version passed, 63–49, Quincy and several other Federalists refused to approve the legislation that was signed into law on March 2, 1807.[106]

As for the problems involving commerce, an end to the crisis seemed probable when on December 27, 1806, diplomats contacted Madison with news that they had signed a treaty with Britain.[107] Though the terms were still unknown to the president or the Senate, the year 1806 was ending on a positive note for the Jefferson administration. A treaty that would end seizures and impressments was signed, nonimportation would not need to be enforced, and even with its inconsistencies most Americans welcomed the passage of legislation ending the slave trade. If everything worked as planned, New Englanders could overlook the hostile rhetoric that southerners spewed that March and April. There would be no reason to listen to or vote for Federalists.

Not everyone expected positive outcomes, however. Based on the information they received from British Ambassador Anthony Merry, who met with Josiah Quincy and other Federalists at some point, his country would not agree to the administration's terms. Britain had been willing to limit impressments at one time, but according to Merry, Jefferson and Madison had become so inflexible in their demands that his government could not comply. The president appeared unwilling to make "any amicable adjustment, except on terms, which they very well knew, G.B. would never concede."[108] If Merry was right, the administration might reject the new treaty.

It was possible that he was still angry over Jefferson's lack of decorum during their first meeting when Merry was dressed in full diplomatic regalia and Jefferson appeared "standing in slippers," in his underclothes. Adding to his offenses, Jefferson ignored the conventional seating arrangements and then insulted Mrs. Merry. The British considered such conduct a snub, and it stoked anti-U.S. passions in England. Merry was convinced that Jefferson purposefully set out to insult the British with boorish behavior toward its envoys. He also informed Federalists that Virginians had been protecting British deserters and exacerbating tensions over impressments. Nor was Merry alone in perceptions that President Jefferson had acted boorishly. The president's slovenly appearance and perceived lack of manners also offended Irish poet Thomas Moore. Moore attacked Jeffersonians in his poetry. The president was amused, but Jefferson's family remained angry for some time.[109]

Federalists were familiar enough with Jefferson and members of his party to know that the diplomat's assertions found their basis in truth. Jefferson's hard line was encouraged by advisors such as Jacob Crowninshield, who believed that Britain had no right at all to search U.S. vessels for deserters. His advice was that "The search for British subjects should be done away," because the U.S. flag protects "the whole crew." Though Democratic-Republicans endorsed making some compromises to resolve the nations' disagreements, most of them were Anglophobes and agreed with Crowninshield that Britain should "fail in obtaining a single commercial advantage over us by any concession on our part."[110] There was good reason for Federalists to expect the administration to reject the treaty.

By the end of 1806, some Federalists had interjected key components of free-labor ideology into a sectional defense of maritime commerce.[111] They had also mounted challenges to southern power over coastal fortifications and the slave trade. Many expressed their ideas in the context of basic concern over the continuance of New England's economic freedom, defense, and influence within the federal government. Ensuring that the North's free laborers had protection under the law and that free states received equal consideration in Washington was central to the fight that Federalists began to see themselves waging. Their battle was against a government dominated by slaveholders who they felt were insensitive to the needs of maritime New England. By the beginning of 1807 the gap between the protections New Englanders expected and what their government was willing to provide was widening.

NOTES

1. T. B. Wait, ed., *State Papers and Publick Documents of the United States from the Accession of Thomas Jefferson to the Presidency, Exhibiting a Complete View of Our Foreign Relations Since That Time*, 3 vols. (Boston: T. B. Wait and Sons, 1814–1815), 2:455–57.

2. William Plumer, *William Plumer's Memorandum of Proceedings in the United States Senate, 1803–1807*, ed. Leverett Somerville Brown. (New York: Macmillan, 1923), 337.

3. James Phillips, *Thoughts on the Slavery of the Negroes* (London: George-Yard, 1784), 17–18, 32; and Noah Webster, *Effects of Slavery on Morals and Industry* (Hartford: Hudson and Goodwin, 1793), 10, 22, 49, Antislavery Collection, 1725–1911 (RB 003), SCUA.

4. Eva Sheppard Wolf, "Early Free-Labor Thought and the Contest over Slavery in the Early Republic," in John Craig Hammond and Matthew Mason eds., *Contesting Slavery: The Politics of Bondage and Freedom in the New American Nation* (Charlottesville: University of Virginia Press, 2011), 32–40.

5. See Webster, *Effects of Slavery*, 7, 12–20 and Elias Hicks, *Observations on the Slavery of the Africans and Their Descendants, and on the Use of the Produce of Their Labour* (New York: Samuel Wood, 1814), Antislavery Collection, 1725–1911 (RB 003), SCUA.

6. Jonathan Halperin Earle, *Jacksonian Antislavery and the Politics of Free Soil, 1824–1854* (Chapel Hill: University of North Carolina Press, 2004), 7; Eric Foner, *Free Soil, Free Labor, Free Men: The Ideology of the Republican Party before the Civil War* (New York: Oxford University Press, 1995), xiv, xv. Cf. Joshua Michael Zeitz, "The Missouri Compromise Reconsidered: Antislavery Rhetoric and the Emergence of the Free Labor Synthesis," in *Journal of the Early Republic*, 20, 3 (Autumn 2000):451–52.

7. Philip Gould, *Barbaric Traffic: Commerce and Antislavery in the 18th Century Atlantic World* (Cambridge, MA: Harvard University Press, 2003), 4; Douglas R. Egerton, "Markets Without a Market Revolution: Southern Planters and Capitalism," in Paul A. Gilje, ed., *Wages of Independence: Capitalism in the Early American Republic* (Lanham, MD: Rowman & Littlefield Publishers, Inc., 2006), 59.

8. Clifford L. Egan, *Neither Peace nor War: Franco-American Relations, 1803–1812* (Baton Rouge: Louisiana State University Press, 1983), 23; Elkins, Stanley, and Eric McKitrick. *The Age of Federalism: The Early American Republic, 1788–1800* (New York: Oxford University Press, 1993), 688, 689.

9. Monroe to Madison, July 1, 1804, in James Monroe, *Writings of James Monroe: Secretary*, ed. Stanislaus Murray Hamilton (New York: AMS Press, 1969), 220–21.

10. James Stephen, *War in Disguise, or, the Frauds of the Neutral Flags* (New York: Hopkins and Seymour, 1806), Pamphlets in American History (594 W21), SCUA; Samuel Flagg Bemis, *A Diplomatic History of the United States*, 5th ed. (New York: Henry Holt and Company, 1965), 141; James Stephen, *Observations on the Speech of the Hon. John Randolph, Representative for the State of Virginia . . .* (New York: S. Gould, Printer, 1806), 8, 10, 14–16, 22, 28–30, Pamphlets in American History (594 W21), SCUA; Burton Spivak, *Jefferson's English Crisis: Commerce, Embargo, and the Republican Revolution* (Charlottesville: University of Virginia Press, 1979), 10; Robert W. Tucker and David C. Hendrickson, *Empire of Liberty: The Statecraft of Thomas Jefferson* (New York: Oxford University Press, 1990), 190–91; David Brion Davis, *The Problem of Slavery in the Age of Revolution, 1770–1823* (New York: Oxford University Press, 1999), 310–466 passim. Davis provides a thorough examination of Stephen's work as an abolitionist and the success of his efforts to end Britain's participation in the Atlantic slave trade.

11. Paul A. Gilje, ed., *Wages of Independence: Capitalism in the Early American Republic* (Lanham, MD: Rowman & Littlefield, 2006), 10, 11; Spivak, *Jefferson's English Crisis*, 7–12, 15–16; George C. Herring, *From Colony to Superpower: U.S. Foreign Relations since 1776* (New York: Oxford University Press, 2008), 115; Tucker and Hendrickson, *Empire of Liberty*, 66; Drew R. McCoy, *The Elusive Republic: Political Economy in Jeffersonian America* (Chapel Hill: University of North Carolina Press, 1980), 166; Bemis, *Diplomatic History*, 140–42.

12. See *Annals of Congress*, 9th Cong., 1st sess., 896.

13. Bemis, *Diplomatic History*, 140–42; Spivak, *Jefferson's English Crisis*, 24.

14. "Business Papers," Joseph Bowditch Papers, MSS 156, Box 1, Folder 2, PEM.

15. See Wait, *State Papers and Publick Documents*, 1:212–18; *Annals of Congress*, 8th Cong., 2nd sess., 1260; James Fulton Zimmerman, *Impressment of American Seamen* (New York: Longmans, Green and Co., 1925), 25–26; John C. A. Stagg, *Mr. Madison's War : Politics, Diplomacy, and Warfare in the Early American Republic, 1783–1830* (Princeton, NJ: Princeton University Press, 1983), 305–9.

16. Daniel James Ennis, *Enter the Press-Gang: Naval Impressment in Eighteenth-Century British Literature*, (Newark: University of Delaware Press, 2002), 32; Wait, *State Papers and Publick Documents*, 2:23–34; *Annals of Congress*, 9th Cong., 1st sess., 635.

17. *Hampshire Federalist* (Springfield, MA), May 13, 1806; *Hampshire Gazette* (Northampton, MA), September 12, 1804.

18. Wait, ed., *State Papers and Publick Documents*, 2:73–87.

19. *Annals of Congress*, 9th Cong., 1st sess., 890–900.

20. Barnabus Bidwell to Jacob Crowninshield, October 28, 1805, Crowninshield Family Papers, MH 15, Box 9, Folder 3, PEM.

21. Plumer, *Memorandum*, 337.

22. *Eastern Herald and Maine Gazette* (Portland, ME), February 1, 1802; *Salem* (MA) *Gazette*, September 18, 1801; *Annals of Congress*, 9th Cong., 2nd sess., 52–30.

23. *Annals of Congress*, 9th Cong., 1st sess., 537–43; Richard Buel Jr., *America on the Brink: How the Political Struggle over the War of 1812 Almost Destroyed the Young Republic* (New York: Palgrave Macmillan, 2005), 31; Spivak, *Jefferson's English Crisis*, 32–36.

24. *Annals of Congress*, 9th Cong., 1st sess., 611; Spivak, *Jefferson's English Crisis*, 42, 43.

25. Robert A. McCaughey, *Josiah Quincy, 1772–1864: The Last Federalist* (Cambridge, MA: Harvard University Press, 1974), 39; Donald R. Hickey, *The War of 1812: A Forgotten Conflict* (Urbana: University of Illinois Press, 1989), 30; Elizabeth R. Varon, *Disunion! The Coming of the American Civil War, 1789–1859* (Chapel Hill: University of North Carolina Press, 2008), 36.

26. *Annals of Congress*, 9th Cong., 1st sess., 557–60.

27. Ibid., 624–25; Spivak, *Jefferson's English Crisis*, 41.

28. Benjamin Goodhue to Timothy Pickering, February 12, 1806, Timothy Pickering Papers, MHS. See also Jacob Crowninshield to Thomas Jefferson, January 30, 1806, Jefferson Papers, LC; *Annals of Congress*, 9th Cong., 1st sess., 624, 636, 644–47.

29. Spivak, *Jefferson's English Crisis*, 10, 28–30, 32, 42.

30. *Annals of Congress*, 9th Cong., 1st sess., 599; Spivak, *Jefferson's English Crisis*, 44, 45.

31. Tucker and Hendrickson, *Empire of Liberty*, 193–95; *Annals of Congress*, 9th Cong., 1st sess., 192–95.

32. Compare Alan Taylor, *The Civil War of 1812: American Citizens, British Subjects, Irish Rebels, & Indian Allies* (New York: Vintage Books, 2010), 102–4.

33. W. Jeffrey Bolster, "'To Feel Like a Man': Black Seamen in the Northern States, 1800–1860," in *Journal of American History* 76, no. 4 (March 1990): 1174, 1183; Ira Dye, "Early American Merchant Seafarers," in *Proceedings of the American Philosophical Society* 120, no. 5 (October 15, 1976): 353; Eliga H. Gould, *Among the Powers of the Earth: The American Revolution and the Making of a New World Empire* (Cambridge, MA: Harvard University Press, 2012), 145, 146.

34. *Annals of Congress*, 9th Cong., 1st sess., 592–99.

35. See Matthew E. Mason, *Slavery and Politics in the Early American Republic* (Chapel Hill: University of North Carolina Press, 2006), 223; Paul A. Gilje, *Liberty on the Waterfront: American Maritime Culture in the Age of Revolution* (Philadelphia: University of Pennsylvania Press, 2004), 139.

36. Eleazer Graves to Benjamin W. Crowninshield, February 4, 1825, Crowninshield Family Papers, MH 15, Box 15, Folder 2, PEM. Discussions of specific cases related to the Negro Seamen's Acts can be found in Paul Finkelman, *An Imperfect Union: Slavery, Federalism, and Comity* (Chapel Hill: University of North Carolina Press, 1981), 280.

37. *Annals of Congress*, 9th Cong., 1st sess., 592–99, 686–95.

38. McCoy, *Elusive Republic*, 37; Lance Banning, *The Jeffersonian Persuasion: Evolution of a Party Ideology* (Ithaca, NY: Cornell University Press, 1978), 187–206. For a description of merchants and virtue in revolutionary thought see Gordon S. Wood, *The Radicalism of the American Revolution*, Reprint, (New York: Vintage Books, 1993), 106–9.

39. *Annals of Congress*, 9th Cong., 1st sess., 706–7.

40. "Business Papers," Joseph Bowditch Papers, MSS 156, Box 1, Folder 2, PEM; Bemis, *Diplomatic History*, 145.

41. Dye, "Early American Merchant Seafarers," 331, 352; Gerald Clarfield, "Postscript to the Jay Treaty: Timothy Pickering and Anglo-American Relations, 1795–1797," in *William and Mary Quarterly* 3rd ser., 23, no. 1 (January 1966): 112–16; Zimmerman, *Impressment of American Seamen*, 48.

42. *Annals of Congress*, 9th Cong., 1st sess., 695; Bemis, *Diplomatic History*, 145.

43. Gilje, *Liberty on the Waterfront*, 160–61; James R. Durand, *The Life and Adventure of James Durand, During a Period of Fifteen Years from 1801 to 1816: In Which Time He Was Impressed on Board the British Fleet and Held in Detestable Bondage for More Than Seven Years* (Rochester, NY: E. Peck and Co., 1820), 109, 129.

44. Tucker and Hendrickson, *Empire of Liberty*, 195; cf. Spivak, *Jefferson's English Crisis*, 13, 14.

45. Spivak, *Jefferson's English Crisis*, 65; Bemis, *Diplomatic History*, 145.

46. *Annals of Congress*, 9th Cong., 1st sess., 611, 665.

47. Ibid., 673–76.

48. Spivak, *Jefferson's English Crisis*, 35; *Annals of Congress*, 9th Cong., 1st Sess., 706–7, 751–60.

49. *Annals of Congress*, 9th Cong., 1st sess., 750–60; see also 623–27 for calculations respecting the value of southerners' trade with Britain; Spivak, *Jefferson's English Crisis*, 41.

50. *Annals of Congress*, 9th Cong., 1st sess., 583, 584, 591.

51. Firsthand descriptions of flogging through the fleet appear in Durand, *Life and Adventure*, 102–3, and Joshua Davis, *A Narrative of Joshua Davis, An American Citizen, Who Was Pressed and Served On Board Six Ships of the British Navy . . . The Whole Being an Interesting and Faithful Narrative of the Discipline, Various Practices and Treatment of Pressed Seamen in the British Navy, etc.* (Boston: B. True, 1811), 8.

52. *Annals of Congress*, 9th Cong., 1st sess., 687–96, 781–82.

53. *Annals of Congress*, 9th Cong., 1st sess., 642.

54. *Annals of Congress*, 9th Cong., 1st sess., 642; On Elliot's party affiliation, see *Vermont Gazette* (Bennington), December 6, 1802; *Post-Boy, and Vermont & New-Hampshire Federal Courier* (Windsor, VT), May 21, 1805; *Weekly Wanderer* (Randolph, VT), May 27, 1805; and Philip J. Lampi, First Democracy Project, AAS.

55. James Elliot, *The Poetical and Miscellaneous Works of James Elliot, Citizens of Guilford, Vermont and Late a Noncommissioned Officer in the Legion of the United States, in Four Books [Thirteen Lines from Pope]* (Greenfield, MA: Dickman, 1798), 182; *Green Mountain Patriot* (Windsor, VT), June 11, 1805.

56. Foner, *Free Soil, Free Labor, Free Men*, xiv–xvii, 11.

57. *Annals of Congress*, 9th Cong., 1st sess., 871.

58. Taggart to John Taylor, March 12, 1806, Samuel Taggart Letterbook, AAS.

59. Fisher Ames to Josiah Quincy, March 19, 1806; Ames to Timothy Pickering, March 10 and 24, 1806, in Fisher Ames, *The Works of Fisher Ames: With a Selection from His Speeches and Correspondence*, ed. Seth Ames, 2 vols. (New York: Da Capo Press, 1969), 1:369, 371–72, 373–74.

60. Timothy Pickering to Fisher Ames, April 2, 1806, Timothy Pickering Papers, MHS.

61. Jacob Crowninshield to William Bentley, March 16, 1806, Crowninshield Family Papers, MH 15, Box 3, Folder 4, PEM; *Annals of Congress*, 9th Cong., 1st sess., 549–55.

62. Federal Party, *Central Committee, Boston, Feb. 1806: Sir, The Central Committee Have Taken Measures to Circulate Two Pamphlets, Calculated, as They Hope, to Produce a Favorable Effect at the Approaching Election* (Boston, 1806), Broadside Collection, AAS.

63. Timothy Pickering to Fisher Ames, April 2, 1806, Timothy Pickering Papers, MHS.

64. Donald Hickey, "Federalist Defense Policy in the Age of Jefferson, 1801–1812," in *Military Affairs* 45, no. 2 (April 1981): 64–68.

65. *Annals of Congress*, 9th Cong., 1st sess., 528.

66. Peters to Pickering, March 20, 1806 (emphasis in original), Timothy Pickering Papers, MHS).

67. Thomas Green Fessenden. *Democracy Unveiled; or Tyranny Stripped of the Garb of Patriotism* (Boston: D. Carlisle, Printer, 1805), 3n4, American Culture Series (Reel 412.1), SCUA.

68. Josiah Quincy, "Journals, 1805–1806," Quincy, Wendell, Holmes, and Upham Family Papers, MHS.

69. Joseph Story to Jacob Crowninshield, December 17, 1805, Crowninshield Family Papers, MH 15, Box 3, Folder 1; Jacob Crowninshield to William Bentley, March 16, 1806, MH 15, Box 3, Folder 4 (emphasis in originals), PEM. Democratic-Republicans were also called Democrats, Republicans, and even Federal Republicans in correspondence among themselves, in the press, and by Federalists.

70. *Annals of Congress*, 9th Cong., 1st sess., 1259–62; Nonimportation of items from Britain Act of 1806, Pub. L. 9–29, 2 Stat. 379 (1806); Spivak, *Jefferson's English Crisis*, 46; Bemis, *Diplomatic History*, 45, 46.

71. *Salem* (Mass.) *Gazette*, March 14, 1806; *Newburyport* (Mass.) *Herald*, January 27, 1809; Benjamin Goodhue to Timothy Pickering, February 12, 1806, Timothy Pickering Papers, MHS.

72. *Salem* (MA) *Gazette*, April 15, 1806; May 20, 1806; *Repertory* (Boston), April 15, 1806; April 22, 1806; Ames to Josiah Quincy, January 27, 1807, in Ames, *Works of Fisher Ames*, 1:391.

73. Sally Crowninshield to Jacob Crowninshield, March 20 and 27, 1806, Crowninshield Family Papers, MH 15, Box 2, Folder 8, PEM.

74. *Hampshire Gazette* (Northampton, MA), May 30, 1804; *Repertory* (Boston), April 4, 1806; see also April 8, 1806.

75. *Annals of Congress*, 9th Cong., 1st sess., 379–80.

76. *Annals of Congress*, 9th Cong., 1st sess., 1033, 1037, 1039–41.

77. W. Jeffrey Bolster, *Black Jacks: African American Seamen in the Age of Sail* (Cambridge, MA: Harvard University Press, 1997), 30–33; Gilje, *Liberty on the Waterfront*, 24–26; David R. Roediger, *The Wages of Whiteness: Race and the Making of the American Working Class, Revised Edition* (New York: Verso, 1991), 28, 47–50. Compare Wolf, "Early Free-Labor Thought and the Contest over Slavery in the Early Republic," 39–42 in Hammond and Mason, *Contesting Slavery*.

78. Steven Watts, "Ministers, Misanthropes, and Mandarins: The Federalists and the Culture of Capitalism, 1790–1820," in Doron S. Ben-Atar and Barbara Oberg, eds., *Federalists Reconsidered* (Charlottesville: University of Virginia Press, 1998), 158–62; cf. Wood, *Radicalism of the American Revolution*, 298; and Ronald Formisano's challenge of the "First Party thesis" in *Transformation of Political Culture: Massachusetts Parties, 1790s–1840s* (New York: Oxford University Press, 1983), 3, 7–10; Spivak, *Jefferson's English Crisis*, 44; and Ben-Atar, *The Origins of Jeffersonian Commercial Policy and Diplomacy* (New York: St. Martin's Press, 1993), 149.

79. Daniel Webster, *An Anniversary Address, Delivered before the Federal Gentlemen of Concord and Its Vicinity, July 4th 1806* (Concord, NH: George Hough, 1806), 11, 12, Collection of the BA; a quote from 1850 appears in Foner, *Free Soil*, 15.

80. "Mr. Elliot to His Constituents Letter IX," in *Post-boy and Vermont & New-Hampshire Federal Courier* (Windsor, VT), June 11, 1805; "Mr. Elliot to His Constituents, Letter VIII," in *Rutland* (VT) *Herald*, June 8, 1805 (emphasis in original); Foner, *Free Soil*, 18, 31–38, 43, 44.

81. *Annals of Congress*, 9th Cong., 1st sess., 1035–42.

82. Fortification of Ports and Harbors Act of 1806, Pub. L. No. 9–47, 2 Stat. 402 (1806); Fortification of Ports and Harbors Act of 1808, Pub. L. No. 10–7, 2 Stat. 453 (1808).

83. Federal Party, Central Committee, Boston; *Statutes at Large of the United States* 2:379–81; Ames to Quincy, January 27, 1807, in Ames, *Works of Fisher Ames*, 1:392.

84. Ames to Pickering, March 24, 1806 and Ames to Josiah Quincy, January 27, 1807; in Ames, *Works of Fisher Ames*, 1:373–74, 391–92.

85. Josiah Quincy to Fisher Ames, 1806, Quincy, Wendell Holmes, and Upham Family Papers, MHS.
86. James M. Banner, *To the Hartford Convention: The Federalists and the Origins of Party Politics in Massachusetts, 1789–1815* (New York: Alfred A. Knopf, 1970), 211, 361–67.
87. McCoy, *Elusive Republic*, 215; John H. Reinoehl, "Some Remarks on the American Trade: Jacob Crowninshield to James Madison 1806," in *William and Mary Quarterly* 3rd ser., 16, no. 1 (January 1959): 85–87; Spivak, *Jefferson's English Crisis*, 214–15; Paul Goodman, *The Democratic-Republicans of Massachusetts: Politics in a Young Republic* (Cambridge, MA: Harvard University Press, 1964), 109–15; *Repertory* (Boston), November 7, 1806. See Jacob Crowninshield to William Bentley, November 13, 1803 and March 16, 1806, MH 15, Box 3, Folder 4; Jacob Crowninshield to B. Lynde Oliver December 22, 1805 and Albert Smith, December 23, 1805, MH 15, Box 3, Folder 1; Jacob Crowninshield to Nathaniel Silsbee, December 29, 1805 and Thomas Jefferson, June 21, 1806, MH 15, Box 3, Folder 4, Crowninshield Family Papers, PEM.
88. *Salem (MA) Gazette*, November 7, 1806.
89. Election results and computations based on Lampi, First Democracy Project, AAS.
90. *Eastern Herald and Maine Gazette* (Portland), June 8 and 15, 1801; Kenneth R. Bowling and Donald R. Kennon, *Neither Separate nor Equal: Congress in the 1790s* (Athens: Ohio University Press, 2000), 179–80.
91. Goodman, *Democratic-Republicans of Massachusetts*, 121–24; *Independent Chronicle and the Universal Advertiser* (Boston), June 11, 1801; *Massachusetts Spy, or Worcester Gazette*, May 20 and June 3, 1801; *Columbian Minerva* (Dedham, MA), November 16, 1802.
92. "The Anti-Aristocrat, or Congressional Election for York District, November 1806" (Portland, 1806), 6–13, Books and Pamphlets, AAS; Noble E. Cunningham, "The Diary of Frances Few, 1808–1809," in *Journal of Southern History* 29, no. 3 (August 1963): 353. William Bentley briefly comments on the Cutts family's ownership of an eighteen-acre island and stately home on the Saco River, *The Diary of William Bentley D.D.: Pastor of the East Church Salem, Massachusetts*, 4 vols. (Salem, MA: Essex Institute, 1905–1914), 1:65–67.
93. Lampi, First Democracy Project, AAS.
94. Goodman, *Democratic-Republicans of Massachusetts*, 123; Banner, *Hartford Convention*, 170–73.
95. See Elizabeth F. Hoxie, "Harriet Livermore: 'Vixen and Devotee,'" in *New England Quarterly* 18, no. 1 (March 1945): 39, 43.
96. *New-England Palladium* (Boston), October 31, 1806.
97. *Hampshire Federalist* (Springfield, MA), October 21, 1806.
98. G. Goodhue to Timothy Pickering and James Hillhouse, February 12, 1806, Timothy Pickering Papers, MHS.
99. *Annals of Congress*, 9th Cong., 2nd sess., 1248; Spivak, *Jefferson's English Crisis*, 50.
100. *Repertory* (Boston), December 2, 1806.
101. Ibid., December 16, 1806.
102. David Waldstreicher, "The Styles of Politics, and the Politics of Style," in Ben-Atar and Oberg, eds., *Federalists Reconsidered*, 101–5, 107.
103. *Annals of Congress*, 9th Cong., 2nd sess., 167–69, 176, 177, 183.
104. Ibid., 221, 223.
105. Ibid., 184, 223–27, 232, 233, 236, 238, 239.
106. Prohibition on Slave Importations Act of 1807, Pub. L. No 9–22, 2 Stat. 426 (1807); Ibid., 242, 270–73, 636, 1266, 1267; *House Journal* (1817) 9th Cong., 2nd sess., 614–15; Don E. Fehrenbacher, *The Slaveholding Republic: An Account of the United States Government's Relations to Slavery* (New York: Oxford University Press, 2001), 144–46.
107. Wait, *State Papers and Publick Documents*, 3:173; *Vermont Gazette* (Bennington), May 19, 1806.

108. Josiah Quincy Jr., "Journals, 1805–1806," Quincy, Wendell, Holmes, and Upham Family Papers, MHS.

109. See Lucia Stanton, "Looking for Liberty: Thomas Jefferson and the British Lions," *Eighteenth-Century Studies* 26, no. 4 (Summer 1993): 649–50; Ben-Atar, *Origins of Jeffersonian Commercial Policy and Diplomacy*, 162.

110. Reinoehl, "Some Remarks on the American Trade," 117; Barnabus Bidwell to Jacob Crowninshield, June 9, 1806, Crowninshield Family Papers MH 15, Box 3, Folder 2; Jacob Crowninshield to Albert Smith, December 23, 1805, MH 15, Box 3, Folder 1, PEM.

111. Jonathan Halperin Earle, *Jacksonian Antislavery and the Politics of Free Soil, 1824–1854* (Chapel Hill: University of North Carolina Press, 2004), 4.

THREE

"Squabbles in Madam Liberty's Family"

Jefferson's Embargo and the Causes of Federalist Extremism (1807–1808)

The health of former congressman Fisher Ames of Dedham, Massachusetts, was failing and in 1808 he would succumb to a lingering respiratory illness. Yet, he took time during the last three years of his life to encourage Federalists to be more aggressive during congressional debates over foreign trade policies. Beginning in 1805, as the Democratic-Republicans in Congress passed legislation that would negatively impact New England's maritime industry, Ames advocated U.S. recognition of Haiti and decried Jeffersonian efforts to help France crush "the independent spirit of those blacks" before "waging war on the British trade." In letters to Timothy Pickering in the Senate and Josiah Quincy in the House of Representatives, Ames predicted that Federalists would never regain control of the federal government, but insisted that they not shrink back. Federalists needed to more forcefully oppose policies restricting maritime commerce. He chastised them for retreating from the nonimportation debates in 1806, stating, "What your party neglects to do and say seems to me very wrong, for it leaves us to the impression of the clumsy arts of your adversaries. They do what ought not to be done, they neglect what ought to be done, and all seems right to us, the people, so long as you good men in Congress forbear to expose the facts." Ames admonished Federalists to "cry 'fire' and 'stop thief,'" in order to keep the government from destroying their region's economic prosperity.[1]

Congress already demonstrated a preference for prohibiting commerce instead of taking steps to protect the merchant marine from French and British privateers. Ames was convinced that New England Federalists lost a seat in the 1806 midterm elections because they failed to give voters a policy alternative to the Nonimportation Act. Developments in Europe would lead Congress to impose other commercial restrictions more damaging than the Haitian embargo or nonimportation, but Federalists now realized that they would not automatically win the public's confidence when this happened. Ames urged Federalists to pursue a radical course of opposition. When they did it would entail unapologetic sectionalism and unrelenting criticism of the Jefferson administration's motives and policies. Federalists' implementation of what today we call a "scorched earth" policy began with a change in their deportment. It was not just Ames advice but southerners' incendiary statements and the partisan climate in Congress that contributed to the Federalists' radicalization. The combination of developments, which contributed greatly to the onset of so-called radical Federalists' leadership and the sectional, disunionist brand of politics with which they would be hereafter associated is the focus of this chapter.

When Congress began to draft new legislation to deal with Britain's escalation of hostilities against the United States in 1807, the Democratic-Republicans' rejection of bipartisan solutions continued. From the *Chesapeake* incident of that June through the months following passage of the embargo, Federalists would construct a multifaceted, often scathing critique of Democratic-Republicans and the rationale for their restrictive system.

Regional protectionism was the basis for the Federalists' sharpened invective. One issue they raised was the majority's competence and unwillingness to protect commerce. Another would be the majority's refusal to repeal or even relax the embargo. Due to what they deemed an to be an illogical intractableness on the part of Democratic-Republicans, Federalists accused them of implementing policies to subjugate New England with its advancing socioeconomic progress to the South's slave-centric agricultural economy. Subservience to France also became an important, albeit secondary critique of the imperfections in Jeffersonian foreign policy, which had become inseparable from their domestic agenda.

Federalists linked what they saw as the Democratic-Republicans' Francophile bias to their contrasting hawkishness when passing sanctions against Great Britain. The majority's course of action would lead to a war for which the nation was not prepared and New England would suffer most of the consequences. From late 1807 through 1808, positions taken by the majority in Congress agitated New Englanders and stoked disunionism. Federalists conflated repealing the embargo with ending the North's disadvantages due to slave representation. Securing a leading role for New England in the political and socioeconomic development of the republic was one of the Federalists' primary objectives.

Any attempt to explain this period in Federalist political strategy has to take the combative atmosphere in Congress into consideration. At the end of 1806, legislators had hoped that diplomacy would settle long-standing problems with Britain and bring an end to ship seizures and the impressment of U.S. citizens. Earlier that year, as Congress engaged in heated debates over restricting the importation of British goods, southerners questioned both the value of maritime commerce and the government's obligation to protect it. They also rejected the strong sanctions proposed by northern Jeffersonians, fearing that the British might retaliate by restricting their export trade, which would affect at least 80 percent of the South's revenue.[2]

The northern proponents of nonimportation yielded to southerners' desires and settled for the Nonimportation Act (1806), which limited the importation of fewer manufactured goods than they originally desired. Ironically, for all of the bickering and insults exchanged during those debates, nonimportation was suspended pending the outcome of Anglo-American negotiations. Should diplomacy fail, the sanction would go into effect in November 1807.

Diplomats James Monroe and William Pinkney faced the unenviable task of striking an accord with Britain while extracting the concessions that President Jefferson demanded. To their credit an agreement was reached and a treaty signed in December 1806. Unfortunately, Jefferson was more than slightly displeased. The Monroe-Pinkney Treaty did not include the provision that he coveted most, namely an agreement to end impressments. Based on his most recent experiences with Britain, the president should have expected to fail in this regard.[3]

By the time that Monroe and Pinkney completed their negotiations, the vector of Anglo-American relations had veered a good distance away from the spirit of compromise. In 1803, Britain agreed not to search U.S. merchantmen for deserters on the high seas. But they did insist on reserving the right to stop and inspect ships sailing the Narrow Seas, located between the English Channel and the North Sea, where Britain claimed sovereignty. U.S. Minister to Britain Rufus King, a Federalist, rejected the treaty largely because of the Narrow Seas clause. That was the last time that the British would agree to limit their right to search foreign vessels and impress deserters.[4]

Monroe and Pinkney still managed to hash out an agreement that all parties felt comfortable signing on December 31. The treaty contained several terms favorable to the United States, such as the suspension of impressments and seizures within five miles of the nation's coast. It also provided compensation to cover losses that might result from treaty violations. But Jefferson did not accept these terms as adequate concessions. Without presenting it to the Senate, he rejected the treaty and ordered the diplomats to renegotiate. In a letter dated May 20, 1807, Secretary of State Madison explained, "The President . . . laments more especially that the

British Government has not yielded to the just and cogent considerations which forbid the practice of its cruisers in visiting and impressing the crews of our vessels covered by an independent flag . . . which ought to be sacred with all neutrals." The first of six enumerated points to renegotiate specified that, "Without a provision against impressments . . . no treaty is to be concluded." And no treaty was concluded. When word of a probable settlement reached the states in the closing days of 1806, British Ambassador Anthony Merry informed a group of Federalists that they could link any failures in diplomacy to the administration's anti-British attitudes. Britain had once been willing to limit impressments, Merry confirmed, but the United States always made excessive demands and gave nothing in return. In his opinion, Jefferson and Madison had grown even more unreasonable over time.[5]

Another year passed before the public learned the terms of the rejected treaty, but the deterioration of U.S. relations with Britain would become evident much sooner. In his aforementioned conversation with Federalists, Merry complained that Virginia's laws shielded deserters and frustrated British ship captains, which intensified suspicions on both sides. Tensions finally exploded on June 22, 1807. As the U.S. warship *Chesapeake* departed Chesapeake Bay for Mediterranean ports, the British man-of-war *Leopard* stopped her near Cape Henry, a promontory at the bay's entrance. Captain Salusbury Pryce Humphrey of the *Leopard* announced his intentions to search the *Chesapeake* for deserters but the American captain, Commodore James Barron, refused to allow the search team onboard. The *Leopard* then fired on the *Chesapeake* killing three men, and wounding eighteen others. There was at least one more fatality from among the wounded, and the British escorted four seamen off of the *Chesapeake*. Of the four, only one was a British deserter, who was later hanged. The other three were native-born Americans, who had only recently escaped impressment. In response to the incident, Jefferson issued a proclamation, dated July 2, 1807, ordering armed British ships to vacate U.S. waters. Americans supported the president's decision and demanded an apology or an embargo on all trade with Britain in retaliation.[6]

Initially, some Federalists supported military action against the British. "We want and must ultimately have a sufficient armed force of *some kind*, and *if the government will not provide one for us*, why not, by *voluntary contribution* prepare it ourselves," asked the Federalist *Salem Gazette*. Finding any support from New England Federalists stunning, Jefferson reportedly exclaimed, "Lord, what have I done that the wicked should praise me!"[7] Upon hearing rumors that a call to mobilize state militias was forthcoming, Massachusetts Federalists proudly offered the services of eleven thousand volunteers who would gladly serve in the interest of national security. At the end of July, participants at a Boston town meeting selected a committee that included John Quincy Adams, Harrison

Gray Otis, and Christopher Gore to communicate the city's support to the president. The committee was to relay a resolution promising "full approbation of the course of policy adopted by the executive." But this time, according to Adams, few attended the meeting, and the majority of those present supported the administration before the *Chesapeake* was attacked.[8]

The summer of cooperation, though nominal at best, was ending. If Jefferson called Congress into an early session to draft embargo legislation immediately following the *Chesapeake* incident, he might have doubtlessly received strong bipartisan support. Indeed, several leading Federalists, such as those at the Boston meeting in July, had already showed a willingness to endorse any military response that the president might choose to adopt. Regardless of widespread expectations, however, Jefferson took no immediate steps to satisfy the public's call for an apology, atonement, or armed retaliation. His inaction gave Federalists time to regroup and analyze the president's handling of the crisis.

By August, Federalists were questioning the circumstances surrounding the *Chesapeake* and dissecting the administration's failure to act. Even though they did not know all of its provisions, Federalists also raised suspicions concerning Jefferson's unilateral rejection of the Monroe-Pinkney Treaty. If he was sincere about ending impressments, they asked, why had Jefferson not demanded the return of a single impressed American? If he had asked for the release of impressed seamen why was the public left in the dark? Finally, since the president was being so pacific, why was everyone else letting the attack whip them into frenzy? Federalists explained that they were not backing down from defending the nation, but the entire situation was shaping into a "*governmental peace and a citizen war.*" They chided those showing support for Jefferson, with reminders that before the *Chesapeake-Leopard* clash, the president and his party had rejected any serious efforts to end impressments or protect the neutral trade but, "now [that] a frigate has been attacked, and our seamen killed, the whole country . . . [is] going to war and marching militia to the sea shore to shoot porpoises."[9]

Just a few weeks earlier the *Salem Gazette*, a Federalist newspaper out of Salem, Massachusetts, swore fealty to the president and his administration. Two months later the same paper doubted that justification existed for hostilities toward Britain. The *Gazette* called for the administration to "Let the people see . . . in what *it is* that Great Britain refuses justice and where she is guilty of wrong." Because few details about the Monroe-Pinkney treaty were made public, Federalists posited the theory that Jefferson and his administration had intentionally created a crisis to lead the country into a war with Britain. "Be assured I am not sneaking out of a war," explained one correspondent, "I think it must happen." But if and when an Anglo-American war does take place, "it has been brought to us not by King George, but King Thomas."[10] Federalists went on record as opponents of the administration's secrecy in foreign relations and inaction after the *Chesapeake* attack, which they now insisted had been staged to provoke the very conflict that they spent the first decade under the Constitution trying to avoid.

Jefferson finally did convene a special session of Congress in October. His message stressed the seriousness of the *Chesapeake* attack and the legislature's obligation to draft the nation's response. He also provided a brief explanation for rejecting the treaty explaining that even though the diplomats thought Britain had compromised on several key points, "no sufficient provision was made against the principal source of irritations and collisions"—impressments. Since then, in addition to seizing Americans' property, impressing citizens, and attacking the *Chesapeake*, Britain refused to evacuate U.S. waters. The British also added to their list of offenses in January 1807 with an Order In Council that blockaded French ports and increased seizures of American merchantmen trading in Europe. France was also attacking the merchant fleet seizing, selling, or destroying American-owned ships and cargo. Federalists acknowledged the need to protect commerce from both nations. The nation's foreign trade was in danger of being "swept away" by the British just to get at France.[11]

In the Senate, Jefferson's message was relegated to a select committee, but the matter proceeded less smoothly in the House. On October 29 Democratic-Republicans proposed distributing responsibility for each of the points outlined in Jefferson's letter among several committees. The committees would consider aggressions by foreign nations, violations of neutral rights, military preparedness, and public safety as separate issues. Josiah Quincy, apparently taking Fisher Ames's advice to heart, positioned himself as one of the most outspoken and controversial Federalists in the House. He immediately objected to the plan and complained that the House was mistakenly treating spoliations in the Atlantic and Caribbean, the *Chesapeake* attack, and a possible military response for British actions as if they were unrelated.[12]

The president, Quincy explained, had been specific in his message, and because hostilities against the *Chesapeake* were committed by "a particular nation . . . all the other circumstances mentioned are stated merely as aggravations of this attack." He proposed assigning every issue raised in the letter to one committee, with specific instructions to make inquiries into the facts surrounding the *Chesapeake*. After all, he continued, the president had called the special session because the *Leopard* attacked the *Chesapeake*. That attack was the specific event that "stood most prominent in the public mind" and "had occasioned a great degree of irritation." Congress needed to launch an investigation and compile a report so that the "public would no longer remain ignorant of circumstances" surrounding the attack.[13] Quincy determined that the issues would not receive proper scrutiny if the House parsed and then diced the president's message into several pieces as if it dealt with several different, unrelated topics.

Opponents accused Quincy of trying to justify Britain's conduct and "cramp the operations of the committees by giving them special instructions." Quincy, they charged, misunderstood the resolution, and since the president did not give the House any additional information, a direct inquiry into the *Chesapeake* was "premature." Quincy snapped back that he was not defending Great Britain but wanted to "have the whole detail of the affair respecting the Chesapeake laid upon our tables." He claimed to have no reason to exonerate the British and said he was just as patriotic as any Democratic-Republican in Congress. He again contended that adequately addressing the president's message required the House to "fix on a single object, and not to extend our views over the whole horizon." Americans would soon demand to know details about the deaths of several Americans—and after all, Anglo-American relations were also on the line. For these reasons alone Congress should compile a comprehensive report.[14]

When debates resumed on November 5 Quincy renewed his call for an official inquiry. Newspapers had been printing erroneous information, he said, which Congress had a duty to rectify. But instead of launching an inquiry, the House had taken up the president's message, "cut it up into parts . . . and referred them" to different committees. Americans deserved to hear the facts from their elected officials and not be forced to rely on dubious information printed in newspapers or passed along by word of mouth.[15]

Federalist Samuel W. Dana of Connecticut, whom Fisher Ames called one of the brightest stars in Congress, defended Quincy's motion. "If there were any one subject which required the particular attention of Congress" and deserved an inquiry, it was the recent events involving the *Chesapeake*.[16] Along with an investigation, Dana also proposed forcibly removing British warships from U.S. waters. Nonetheless, Jeffersonians were unreceptive to either proposal and rejected Quincy's motion 93–24.[17]

This debate might have ended at that point, but four days later, a front-page article appeared in the *National Intelligencer*, a Democratic-Republican newspaper, gloating over the defeat of Quincy's motion. The paper congratulated the "five sixths" of Congress that united against their opponents, who would exploit any opportunity to bolster their image. The piece also called Federalists hypocrites for warming up to the administration immediately after the *Chesapeake* incident. The warm season of probable bipartisanship, as brief as it was, had been an unappreciated waste of time and effort. The *Intelligencer* then excused any Democratic-Republicans who might have voted for Quincy's proposal because "*their* motives undoubtedly were pure, though we differ from them as to the correction of one vote that they gave."[18]

When the final committee report regarding the *Chesapeake* was read on November 17, Quincy proposed that the House request copies of the president's proclamation banning British ships from U.S. harbors to distribute to each representative. He then cited parliamentary procedure to validate the motion. Democratic-Republicans first chastised Quincy for referencing a foreign nation's rules and then Jeffersonian Jacob Crowninshield of Massachusetts said that the demand for copies was unnecessary because the proclamation had been "published in almost all papers in the Union." Quincy replied that members of Congress should not need to lift presidential proclamations out of newspapers, and wondered aloud why the House had not requested official documents in the first place. Nor could he understand why a mere request for copies evoked such hostility. Was it possible, he asked, that the majority party opposed his motion because they had determined beforehand "to vote down at all events any question that might be moved, or any inquiry that might be requested" by Federalists?[19]

Quincy then produced the *National Intelligencer* article and read an excerpt urging Democratic-Republicans to continue defeating Federalist motions without letup, just as they did when they voted down his proposal for an inquiry into the *Chesapeake*. It appeared to him that a newspaper publisher was directing the House majority's actions. Otherwise there was no other way to account for their vehement opposition to a simple request for official copies. Crowninshield, who had arrived in Washington after publication of the *Intelligencer* article, rebuked Quincy for making blanket accusations. Gentlemen had "a means of satisfaction" when they felt personally slighted, Crowninshield said, before abruptly changing his tone. Perhaps he thought he had gone too far by hinting that Quincy resort to the code duello, but more likely, as events would bear out, Crowninshield's health was failing. The death and burial of his wife, Sarah, delayed his arrival in Washington and seemed to be taking a toll. Crowninshield tempered his reproof of Quincy and used his remaining time explaining that the president did not always forward official documents to the House. Exposing partisan tactics worked this time and Quincy's resolution passed 70 to 32. Following the vote, the House created a committee to retrieve an official copy of the proclamation from Jefferson. The audacious Quincy was placed on the committee.[20]

Historians generally admire his abilities, erudition, and eloquence, but usually criticize Quincy for his rambunctiousness in Congress. To his contemporaries and many scholars today, Quincy's constant opposition and sectionalism were insufferable. Distant relative John Quincy Adams tried at one time—unsuccessfully—to cure the congressman of this vigorous agitation. Contemporaneously, the Bostonian's outspokenness was savored by Sussex District voters, who continued to elect Quincy to Congress until he declined a nomination for reelection in 1812. Later in his life these qualities would endear Quincy to a generation of New Englanders who opposed southern power and the spread of slavery.[21]

The episode involving Quincy's proposal was indicative of the elevated level of bitter partisanship in the Tenth Congress. Most of the time major disagreements occurred amid divisive rhetoric and sectional antipathies that emerged during debates over public policy. Clashes occurred with even more frequency as Congress debated trade restrictions. In addition to newspapers circulating the ideas expressed by both parties, congressmen often published their own speeches. Insulting sectional language had surfaced during debates over the Nonimportation Act in 1806. Contrary to the problems that Federalists and merchants anticipated, when that law finally did go into effect it would be the least of their problems. The next legislation passed by Congress extended the verbal sparring over New England's economic interests into physical resistance to the law and the alienation of many in New England and in New York.

As the time for nonimportation to take effect approached, New England merchants petitioned Congress to delay implementation and Federalists introduced these requests in the House and Senate. Quincy alone presented twenty-two memorials signed by some nine hundred Bostonians asking Congress to modify, suspend, or repeal the Nonimportation Act. Yet, even though they had themselves opposed sanctions against Britain in 1806, southerners rejected consideration of the Boston petitions. The House should not even acknowledge the petitioners, according to some, because they could not consider repealing nonimportation based on complaints from only one section of the Union. Quincy championed the constitutional right to petition Congress and the House's obligation to listen. The petitions were even more significant, he added, because they pertained to a law that, although intended to punish a foreign nation, would actually result in "real and great evil" to New Englanders. Representatives from both parties supported and won a motion to hear the petitions in a 79–38 vote.[22]

While bipartisan support gave the petitioners a hearing in Congress, the ruling party would not grant their requests. As with the Haitian prohibition, those most immediately affected by a federal statute were powerless to change it. The *Newburyport Herald* criticized southerners' objections to the petition and their suggestions that maritime New Englanders be "patriotic and not complain." Furthermore, dismissing petitions because they represented concerns from only one section of the country discouraged sectional harmony. This was especially confusing since a majority of the petitions that led to the restrictive system came from New England. If the party in power sincerely wanted to promote "the necessity of union," they were going about it the wrong way, concluded the *Herald*. Unity was hardly promoted or strengthened when Congress refused "to hear and consider the petitions" of U.S. citizens based solely on geography.[23]

Federalists continued to introduce petitions and defend the rights and interests of their constituents nonetheless. A few of them, including Quincy, began to concur with the disunionist sentiment circulated by some New Englanders.[24] John Quincy Adams took a different course. Federalists expected Adams to present the Boston petitions in the Senate. He had previously opined that the administration should abandon nonimportation "and repeal it at once." When the time came however, Adams confessed that he only "barely presented the petition from Boston" and offered no "motion for its reference." It was only through the prompting of other Federalists that a Senate committee finally considered the Boston memorials. Adams decided not to back the Boston merchants or "countenance any thing [sic] that should attempt to weaken the Government by opposition."[25]

His nationalism and independence impressed many contemporaries and still has an impact on historians, but Adams's unwillingness to support the Massachusetts petitioners appeared derelict to his Federalist colleagues in 1807. He considered himself a "man of my whole country," but at this point they suspected that Adams's country excluded certain citizens from his state.[26] Members of the Massachusetts General Court, who had elected him to the Senate, now questioned Adams's value as their senator and reassessed his ability to objectively address their concerns.

Congress had not yet drafted legislation in response to the *Chesapeake* or the ongoing problems caused by France and Britain. Nevertheless, as previously mentioned, by the time nonimportation went into effect, it was the least of commercial New England's problems. In a message dated December 18, Jefferson informed Congress that dangers posed by the warring European nations had reached critical mass. U.S. sovereignty, merchant vessels, seafaring citizens, and national security were in jeopardy. Along with his message, the president included a copy of Napoleon's Berlin decree of November 21, 1806, which declared all British ports in a state of blockade. Napoleon's final word on the treatment of neutral vessels was pending, but under the decree it was possible that France would seize any U.S. ships "bound to or from England even those without English merchandise on board."[27]

Congress, initially under an injunction of secrecy, responded to the president's message with an embargo on all foreign trade to begin on December 22, 1807. The Senate passed the embargo bill 22–7, with John Quincy Adams voting for the measure along with Democratic-Republicans.[28] Back when Federalists needed to unite over legislation related to the Louisiana Territory, Adams urged Pickering to work with him for success. Pickering spurned him and Adams was disheartened. When the Senate discussed the *Chesapeake* incident that October, Adams had a change of heart. Before the vote he decided to attend each session regularly but "restrain rather than indulge the propensities to debate." By November 3 he was dining with the president and enjoying polite conversation with members of the opposing party, especially Secretary Madison. Adams called one soiree the most *"agreeable* dinners I have had at Mr. Jefferson's."[29] Casting a vote for the embargo confirmed that Adams had rejected the Federalist position, and the General Court decided that it was no longer getting the desired return on its investment.

As proceedings in the Senate played out before him, Pickering became chagrined over his party's inability to stop the bill. Federalists could not block passage of the embargo even if Adams had voted with them (there were only 8 Federalists and 34 Democratic-Republicans in the Senate). Federalists, including Adams, deemed the evidence upon which the embargo was supposedly based "inadequate to warrant such a measure." But the lack of data did not stop the "dead majority" in the Senate, from laying an embargo on all of the nation's trade, based on "two or three beggarly scraps of papers." Pickering anticipated that opponents in the House would block the bill, which would enable Federalists to win over enough "proselytes" to make significant amendments and provoke meaningful debate once the amended bill returned to the Senate.[30]

The House actually did spend more time in debate than the Senate, but Federalists converted few Democratic-Republicans to their position. Resigned to the fact that they were also powerless to stop the bill in the House, Quincy proposed an amendment to exempt fishing vessels from paying certain duties and restrictions. His amendment was defeated 82–45. When the House passed the embargo, the bill stipulated that only ships possessing presidential authorization could legally depart from U.S. ports. Passage of the bill was largely along party lines, with Federalists voting in opposition and hardly surprised by the outcome.[31] Even before voting for legislation that each of them knew would be controversial, New England's Democratic-Republicans refused to discuss how the embargo would affect their constituents. In fact, when they requested more information, Federalists were chastised and told that it was futile to object or attempt to delay passage of the bill.[32]

Why the president waited two months after calling Congress into session—and six months after the *Leopard* fired on the *Chesapeake*—before calling for an embargo is still a mystery. Some historians suggest that Jefferson did not declare war immediately because he expected an apology or a diplomatic solution. Others speculate that because Britain and France were escalating their attacks the embargo was laid in order to give merchants time to gather millions of dollars in ships and cargoes from the oceans before declaring war. But throughout its duration supporters promoted the embargo as an alternative and not a precursor to war. John Smilie of Pennsylvania, who once expressed regrets that Americans had not abandoned maritime pursuits after the Revolution, argued that the government had only three choices: "submit to all the injuries received, go to war, or lay an embargo." Few recalled this fact but southern Democratic-Republicans had argued that because their region alone would be damaged by nonimportation, Congress should lay an embargo on all trade, which would affect the North as well.[33]

Seaport towns felt the effects of the embargo immediately. When attempting to present a memorial from Philadelphia mariners on January 4, Democratic-Republican John Porter broached an issue that embargo drafters overlooked. The petitioner's ships had been loaded and cleared to disembark before the embargo was signed into law and a few that had already sailed were being detained. The mariners asked for permission to complete their voyages since the embargo was not in effect when they cleared; besides, they had obeyed all of the existing laws. The first response to Porter's motion to consider the petitions came from fellow Democratic-Republican Thomas Newton of Virginia. Newton opposed reading the memorial because even with the statute's imperfections, "the ink in which it was traced is scarcely cold" and representatives were already introducing petitions to ignore it. If the House considered these petitions Congress would look weak and so would the embargo. Porter saw any effort to dismiss the petitions without reading them a violation of citizens' constitutional rights nonetheless.[34]

Federalist William Milnor of Pennsylvania added that the petitioners had not broken any laws. He was not ready to say that they should receive exemptions, but these Pennsylvanians had already "endured more than their portion of inconvenience" and Congress should give them a hearing. At the very least the House needed to decide if enforcement would be *ex post facto*. Orchard Cook of Maine (Massachusetts) complained that the embargo had been passed with such rapidity that he must have overlooked any such provisions. He wanted the petitioners to have a hearing and for Congress to investigate such cases. John Taylor of South Carolina disagreed and alleged that the memorialists were under foreign influence and attempting to subvert the nation's laws. He called the Pennsylvania petitioners "the votaries of Mammon." Federalist Samuel Dana of Connecticut wondered out loud what those against reading the memorials were afraid of and why they would want to deprive any fellow citizen of the right to petition. Were they afraid to face disagreements from colleagues? Perhaps the House should create a select committee to look into the matter. These merchants already paid fees and would need to unload, reload, and pay fees again. Like Milnor, Dana did not see this as equitable treatment under the law.[35]

On January 9, 1808, a supplemental act added smaller vessels to the list of ships already affected by the original embargo. To gain clearance from customs agents, the law required shipmasters engaged in domestic trading to pay bonds double the value of their vessels and cargoes before sailing. Captains or the owners of fishing vessels had to pay bonds equal to four times the value of ships and merchandise. To recover a ship seized by authorities while violating the law, offenders might pay up to twenty thousand dollars in fines for each incident. Finally, to enforce the embargo more efficiently, the government awarded informers half of the fines paid by the lawbreakers who were captured with their help.[36] Because of the increased fees and time limits, fishermen and coastal traders now found it extremely difficult and expensive to conduct their business.

In March the House debated another supplement designed to stop northerners' overland trade with Canada.[37] South Carolinian David R. Williams, a cotton planter, wanted to exempt vessels weighing less than five tons from paying bonds so that his constituents could transport at least six hundred bales of cotton to Charleston without the added expense. Williams, who was responsible for building the first cottonseed oil mill in his state, promised that he did not intend for the exemption to weaken the embargo, which he said he would stick by to the death. If Congress wanted Americans to abide by the law, however, Williams recommended that it not be too harsh. On the other hand, when Quincy objected to voting on amendments without proper intelligence, southerners scolded him for persistently lodging complaints. None of his attempts to frustrate or amend the administration's policies ever worked, so Williams spoke for himself and other Democratic-Republicans when he recommended that Quincy just be quiet.[38]

New York Federalist Barent Gardenier then became even more caustic and disruptive than Quincy. "The more we legislate on this subject, the worse we legislate—the more we legislate the more we legislate to the destruction of the country," announced Gardenier. He could not fathom why Congress passed the embargo in the first place, and "God only knows" why they were passing supplements to "make the original evil more perfect and more universal." The embargo was not operating as intended. If its purpose was to keep the nation's resources safe, how would stopping Vermont farmers from selling pigs to Canadians "increase or diminish" these resources? He emphasized the fact that the latest supplement was a nonintercourse law and should rightly be identified as such.[39] Gardenier's verbal gymnastics evoked grumbles from some, applause from others, and various attempts to shout him down.

A cloud of complaints, mostly about Gardenier, wafted above the House chamber. Amid a cacophony of shouts, including accusations that embargo supporters were using the law to wreck the maritime states, someone yelled that the law's real purpose was the destruction of commerce. "Instead of ameliorating, we go on to make worse and worse the condition of our beloved country," Gardenier let fly. The embargo furnished proof that Democratic-Republicans were incapable of designing a foreign policy "unless everybody is destroyed." At any rate, there was no way for the embargo to prepare the country for war when federal laws treat American merchants as if they were the nation's real enemies. When the House finally came to order, embargo supporters—including Jeffersonian Ezekiel Bacon of Massachusetts, who called Gardenier's speech "melancholy madness"—censured the New Yorker.[40]

Tennessean George W. Campbell took the dispersions that Gardenier cast at embargo supporters personally and nearly killed the audacious New Yorker in a duel. After spending several weeks recovering from his wounds, Gardenier was able to return to Congress and continue to attack the policy.[41]

The supplemental act of March 12, over which Gardenier had provoked the ire of Democratic-Republicans, clamped down on overland commerce. Section 4 of the act attached wagons, sleighs, and other ground vehicles to the enumerated list of vessels that traders would forfeit if they were captured while violating the embargo. Anyone smuggling goods into Canada risked losing apparel, horses, mules, or oxen, and also faced fines up to ten thousand dollars for each offense. In an effort to prevent ships from clearing for domestic ports and then sailing to foreign markets, the law stipulated that after posting bond, captains, merchants, and crews had four months to reach their destinations and return to the port of origin. The penalty for exceeding the time limit was a forfeiture of property, which could only be recovered through legal proceedings. Captains and mates of fishing and whaling ships had to declare under oath that they had not sold any fish to foreign vessels during their voyages, or they risked paying a $100 fine.[42]

As mariners experienced economic problems because of the embargo, they continued to petition Congress for repeal. However, while northern Democratic-Republicans might vote to hear northerners' petitions, repealing the law was not on their agenda. From this point forward, Federalists were virtually alone when they began to attack the embargo and call for repeal without letup, and combating the majority in Congress while simultaneously waging a propaganda war was beneficial because 1808 was an election year. This fact did not escape Democratic-Republicans who countered by holding Federalists responsible for the embargo in several newspapers. Federalists, they claimed, created the crisis over foreign trade. Their support for Great Britain "encouraged the depredation of our commerce, and the capture of our seamen." Pro-British corruption had left the administration no choice but "to lay an embargo to prevent a continuance of the outrage . . . [and] if the produce of the farmer is lower, this faction must answer for it. If bankruptcies take place in our seaports, this faction must answer for them."[43]

The accusation was bold but incomplete. The president and Democratic-Republicans in Congress touted the policy as a response to French spoliations as well as British infractions. It was, however, necessary to establish a connection between Federalists and the British to keep the electoral landscape in New England and other northern states from changing overnight. Jeffersonians from the maritime mid-Atlantic and Upper South also understood the political problems that could be created by the embargo. Even though they knew this, protests from mariners, and the fact that the nation was dealing with domestic and international turmoil forced northern Democratic-Republicans to rush the embargo through Congress. They consciously ran the risk of "federalizing all the eastern States," as one woman in Philadelphia predicted.[44] This is eventually what happened.

Many of the New Englanders who at one time blamed Federalists for the controversy ended up opposing the embargo and rejecting many of the representatives who refused to support repeal. Northerners in the fishing industry were the first to feel the embargo's effects, but other businesses soon followed. In much of New England, seaport towns became the conduits through which outlying communities thrived. In Massachusetts, towns from Maine to Gloucester were shipbuilding or trading centers, and sometimes both. Maritime profits funded the toll bridges, turnpikes, and canals. These projects improved transportation and trade between the bustling coast and the interior. It was the maritime industries and not agriculture that funded the public works and building projects of the region. The laborers, artisans, and professionals thrown out of work by the embargo included sailors, captains, fishermen, shipbuilders, mechanics, bankers, insurance underwriters, seamstresses, artisans who made sails and other ship rigging, blacksmiths, carpenters, lumberyard workers, and shopkeepers. Even the farmers who provided food for the coastal towns and shipped their produce to other states and foreign markets suffered under the embargo. It would therefore be difficult, if not impossible, for New England's maritime economy to survive a prolonged embargo intact.[45]

Discriminatory enforcement of the law was also problematic in various municipalities. In Massachusetts for example, the government issued more federal bonds to those in Democratic-Republican than Federalist towns. Townspeople believed that the administration politicized shipping permits to intimidate communities that supported Federalists or opposed the embargo. On more than one occasion officials on the Penobscot River in Maine would not give schooners permission to deliver shipments of provisions and lumber to ports in Federalist-controlled areas nearby. Government agents also used the embargo to blockade entire towns if the inhabitants protested, or if they suspected that merchants planned to break or circumvent the law.[46] One Bostonian denounced the embargo as *"crooked* and *partial"* and expressed horror when he saw gunboats fire on coasting vessels, even those that had already received the proper clearances.[47]

Towns that heavily favored Democratic-Republicans fared better. Customs agents in Marblehead, a decidedly Jeffersonian town, issued a number of bonds during the embargo. Sometimes ships that cleared through such ports even sailed to the West Indies, but captains were still required to post bonds and swear under oath that they would not trade with Haiti. In nearby Salem, embargo opponents accused the Crowninshield family of profiting from the embargo. Based on a widely circulated rumor, authorities deliberately neglected inspections or permits for Crowninshield vessels loaded with approximately $300,000 worth of property. The allegations were never substantiated, but according to some sources, by the end of the embargo the family's wealth had increased by about $270,000. Whether the Crowninshield family profited from the embargo or not, they did establish soup kitchens and provide aid to those in Salem who found themselves in dire financial straits because of the embargo.[48]

Indeed, the law severely strained Salem merchants and the town's maritime industry was never fully restored. One reason for Salem's suffering was its strong Federalist leanings. Even though Jacob Crowninshield remained the town's favorite son until his death, many from his party, including Jefferson, considered Salem the nerve center of the elusive "Essex Junto." The town was, after all, the home of such noted Federalists as Timothy Pickering. In Newburyport, another Federalist-leaning town, citizens became furious over the preferential way that federal authorities enforced the embargo. One inhabitant vowed that he would never again "purchase a barrel of Flour" from "any known supporter of Mr. Jefferson's administration."[49]

Multiple components of the embargo fostered doubts over the true purpose of the legislation. Politically motivated enforcement was just one of several complaints that Federalists lodged against the embargo and its supporters. A more important objection was that the policy lacked an expiration date, which suggested a perpetual prohibition. Another significant issue raised by Federalists was that the embargo kept Americans from trading in Asia, the Near East, and other markets that had nothing to do with France, Britain, or the wars in Europe. Daniel Webster of New Hampshire, who would enter the House of Representatives in 1813, argued that the Constitution's commerce clause did not give Congress authority to place a total, never-ending prohibition on all exports amid a ban on imports. The commercial states, asserted Webster, "never would have consented" to the Constitution if they thought it gave Congress the authority to "force them to relinquish the ocean, and to cut them off from one of their great and leading pursuits."[50]

Even Treasury Secretary Albert Gallatin suggested that an embargo only remain in effect a *"limited time,"* but this view was neither public nor reflected in the legislation. As the policy progressed Democratic-Republicans did little to strengthen their image in New England. The normal time for ships to fit out and clear for foreign ports was March, but in 1808, because of the embargo, merchantmen either remained in port or were used for smuggling. There were some merchants who managed to circumvent the embargo through the legal system. Gallatin informed the president that under a "system adopted in Massachusetts" lawsuits and the threat of legal action intimidated government officials. For a time, the tactic allowed merchants to evade the embargo without reprisal. In order to counteract the defiance escalating in New England, Gallatin proposed harsher penalties for embargo violators.[51]

Increased penalties under new supplemental laws only led to more anxiety. Federalist Edward St. Loe Livermore, a freshman congressman from Massachusetts, called on Congress to repeal the embargo. The purpose of the March supplement, as he understood it, was to eviscerate the few remaining avenues of trade previously "saved from the fangs of the embargo." Because the law's pretext was the protection of Americans and their property on the high seas, Livermore asked how the government could protect ships by seizing sleighs, horses, and mules. Nor did he understand how placing limits on the paltry overland trade would have any affect at all on Britain or France. Orchard Cook agreed and added that while the embargo was already "intolerably oppressive" for the fisheries, his efforts to amend the supplements were always unsuccessful.[52]

When other representatives also objected to extending the embargo's reach, supporters tried to impose a gag on further debate. Matthew Lyon, a Democratic-Republican who represented Vermont before moving to Kentucky, confirmed what Federalists had been saying all along: the embargo was ill-conceived and rushed through Congress without sufficient debate. In the 1790s Lyon, an Irish immigrant, criticized the Adams administration and was convicted, fined, and imprisoned under the Sedition Act. He was also involved in the earliest physical altercation in Congress when he exchanged blows with Connecticut Federalist Roger Griswold in 1798. No love was lost between Lyon and the Federalists, but he agreed with them over the effects of the embargo. Americans suffered while Congress bungled its way through an increasingly oppressive, "anti-Republican" law. Speaker of the House Joseph Varnum of Massachusetts, also a Democratic-Republican, ruled Lyon out of order. Varnum said that the president had already signed the embargo into law, so it could no longer be a topic for debate. Others attempted to call Lyons to order after he charged Varnum with being arbitrary. Either way, Lyon retorted, because the word "embargo" appeared in the title of the supplemental bill, "it is in order to speak of the embargo" despite the speaker's ruling.[53]

Embargo proponents decided that representatives had to debate new restrictions without reexamining or challenging the intent of the original legislation. Lyon then denounced members of his own party for eroding the nation's economic and political climate through blind support for the embargo, adding, "Every addition you make to it renders it more abominable—worse and worse." As was always the case, the supplemental act passed despite strong objections from New Englanders from both parties. Livermore, as he had promised, again motioned for total repeal. The financial cost to Americans was staggering and Congress had enacted a species of law that nations did not impose on their citizens in peacetime. He emphasized the fact that, "Nations at war embargo each other as much as they can, as is now practiced in Europe, but to destroy our own commerce in order to injure our neighbor is certainly a novel invention." Livermore proposed reopening trade with Asia, Africa, Brazil, the Indies, the Baltic, and Haiti, and replacing the embargo with a nonintercourse policy directed specifically at ending trade with Britain and France. While a few Democratic-Republicans expressed doubts about continuing the embargo, most seemed uninterested in a bipartisan solution. Hence, the majority found nothing salvageable in Livermore's recommendations and defeated his motion by sixty votes.[54]

The major problem now facing the nation was not France or Britain whose policies and methods had changed little since the 1790s, but the political economy of the ruling party. More than a few Democratic-Republicans sincerely believed that depriving British manufacturers of America's raw materials would force that nation to rescind Orders in Council that sanctioned preying on U.S. ships. Nonetheless, just as they had during the nonimportation debates, advocates of the policy expressed contempt for maritime commerce, which further heightened hostility to the embargo. Either way, Americans considered passage of one supplement after another preposterous. As one correspondent wrote, "One would have thought that Congress with their 4 embargo laws had done enough toward the annihilation of commerce. . . . But it appears Mr. Jefferson is not content with the crippled and embarrassing state" of commerce and wants to "destroy it altogether."[55]

During his failed attempt to repeal the embargo, Livermore added, "Human laws may be obeyed until a large proportion of the people find them too grievous to be borne." Instead of easing the law's constraints, however, the administration responded to greater defiance with increased enforcement. When he learned that merchants in the Lake Champlain region of Vermont were still trading with Canadians, Jefferson issued a proclamation that the federal government deemed them in a state of insurrection. Determined "to crush every example of forcible opposition to the law," the president authorized collectors to look for volunteers to enforce the embargo "by force of arms." But federal forces did not reach the area in time to catch the smugglers. In the future, he planned to have governors call on state militias to stop insurrectionists from violating the embargo if necessary.[56]

Congress then passed another supplement to take effect on April 25. Under the revised law, collectors had authority to search and seize any vessels suspected of past violations, or of planning to break the law in the future.[57] Instead of calming tempers and easing lawbreaking by implementing more stringent methods of enforcement, greater fines, or giving collectors' virtually unchecked authority to search ships and seize private property, the supplement provoked greater resentment and led to more smuggling.

Resistance to the embargo resulted in more than 140 court cases in Massachusetts alone. For many of those prosecuted, financial necessity apparently outweighed the penalties. Various ports outside of the United States became popular smuggling depots. Impressed seaman Jacob Nagle reported that an area of Amelia Island off the Florida coast was a busy entrepôt for cotton smugglers. "The English came . . . for cotton . . . [and] there was several ships waiting for cargoes besides ourselves. In about three weeks we receiv'd cotton as fast as we could stow it away." Some Americans participated in illegal trading for the duration of the embargo and escaped penalties by departing from and then staying away from the United States while the law was in effect. Markets in Halifax, Nova Scotia, and other parts of Canada also welcomed smugglers throughout the embargo, and in some New England towns, mobs strong-armed collectors to help lawbreakers escape or reenter specific ports.[58]

Defenders of the legislation remained passionate, but neither Britain nor France eased their attacks. In the face of failure, excuses for continuing the embargo rang hollow and were sometimes sanctimonious. Thomas Newton chimed that fate chose Democratic-Republicans, not Federalists, "to rescue commerce from inevitable destruction" through the embargo. He then insisted, "The finger of Providence appears to have prepared a crisis for the operation of a measure the best calculated of all others to reestablish the relations of reciprocal justice and admonish despots that there is a just and controlling power that assigns to iniquity and oppression their limits."[59]

Understandably, few if any New Englanders accepted the notion that it was God's will for their families to go hungry or suffer bankruptcy at the hands of their elected officials. Perhaps, suggested one *Hampshire Gazette* writer, the president was keeping congressmen "in ignorance," about developments in foreign policy which is why they could offer no reason for supporting the embargo other than that they were ordered to do so by Jefferson, "the Grand Lama of their political Idolatry." Blind obedience was the explanation for legislators who knew they would face voters in a few months, to stand behind a policy of "cruel political fanaticism," that "sacrifice[d] a nation, rather than question the infallibility of their idol."[60]

Before the next election, opponents challenged the embargo's constitutionality in the Essex County federal district court in Massachusetts. In *United States v. The William* (1808), defense attorneys argued that the embargo was unconstitutional because it had no termination date. *The William* was a brigantine seized by the collector of Marblehead and Lynn as it was transferring cargo to other ships. The connecting vessels would then sell the goods in foreign markets. The defense also questioned the limits of congressional authority under the commerce clause and maintained that regulating trade did not include prohibiting it altogether. Judge John Davis, a Federalist appointee, shocked his party by ruling that the embargo, even without an expiration date, was constitutional. At the heart of his ruling was the decision that congressional power over commerce was not limited to regulation alone. Federalists did not try to take the case further, but future Supreme Court Justice Joseph Story, who worked with the prosecution in the case, said years later that Davis's ruling stretched the Constitution. The decision may have reflected the judiciary's unwillingness to tangle with Jefferson, who wrote that giving the Supreme Court the final word on legislation put U.S. citizens "under the despotism of an oligarchy." On several occasions during his presidency Jefferson challenged, undermined, or dismissed the Court's authority. Orchard Cook indicated that Democratic-Republicans even considered an amendment that empowered Congress to remove federal judges.[61]

An intriguing aspect of Davis's decision is that he ruled in the government's favor on the embargo's constitutionality, but decided that the plaintiff's evidence did not justify confiscating *The William*. He returned the brig to its owners. In a letter to Timothy Pickering, Chief Justice John Marshall mentioned the "inefficacy of the embargo" and said he was afraid that "the same spirit which so tenaciously maintains this measure" would provoke a war with Britain, "the only power which protects . . . the civilized world." Marshall did not discuss the embargo's constitutionality in this letter, but had recently clashed with Jefferson in the contentious *United States v. Aaron Burr* (1808). After his recent victory over Jefferson in that case, Marshall might not have been willing to take on another major fight with the president so soon. For similar reasons, Federalists familiar with Marshall may have thought it best not to pursue a Supreme Court case over the embargo.[62]

Losing in federal court did not dampen the Federalists' zeal. They continued to raise flags about the real purpose of the embargo and tell voters that Democratic-Republicans were "no longer worthy to be trusted with the interests and honor of a nation." A Newburyport committee sent a petition directly to Jefferson, asking for a partial suspension or repeal of the embargo. In his reply the president said that his administration had enacted the law to force Britain and France to change their policies. An attempt to relax the embargo before it achieved this objective, however, was out of the question. Jefferson told petitioners that he lacked the power to act alone, adding that only Congress had the authority to repeal or suspend the embargo. Yet, Congress did grant the president the ability to suspend the embargo, but it was a power he chose not to exercise.[63]

In the meantime, every day that the embargo remained in effect, doubts about its ultimate goal deepened. Pickering, among others, found it inconceivable "that Mr. Jefferson should so obstinately persevere in the odious measure of the embargo, which he cannot but see has impaired his popularity and hazards its destruction."[64] The policy grew more and more unpopular but neither the president nor majority leaders in Congress showed signs of rescinding the embargo. Federalists began to organize resistance in New England towns. One of their first actions was a campaign of memorials demanding repeal.[65] By November, several petitions had received no response from Congress or the president, so the petitioners redirected their pleas and resolutions to the Massachusetts legislature. One writer called the embargo "the deepest calamity and distress," because commerce "is without any reasonable pretext, wholly interdicted," trade and plunged "great numbers" of New Englanders "to poverty." Judging by the number of memorials that poured into the General Court it became clear that many in the region had lost patience with the embargo and the federal government.[66]

Losing trade due to the embargo also splintered New York Democratic-Republicans. The rift became evident when Vice President George Clinton criticized the administration. Clinton told his nephew DeWitt Clinton that the Virginians in power were only interested in maintaining a military force "sufficient to keep their slaves in awe & prevent their cutting their masters' throats." The idea that southern Jeffersonians cared nothing about protecting maritime New Yorkers divided New York's Democratic-Republican Party between the administration's supporters and the Clinton faction. Clintonites rejected the restrictive system as a threat to the state's welfare, and supported DeWitt Clinton's campaign to defeat Madison in the election of 1812.[67]

Pickering also publicly criticized the embargo and raised concerns over the reasons for its enactment. Because of his flirtation with disunion and creation of a Northern Confederacy, Pickering is generally depicted as a scoundrel. Often depicted as the perennial bad boy of early national politics to many historians, Pickering had few if any redeeming qualities.[68] Never tolerant of Jeffersonians or the South's slave culture, Pickering hoped to, but could not repeal the three-fifths clause. By 1804 he thought it best for New England to leave the Union. Pickering considered a union of northern states, free from slavery and slave representation, "the only means of maintaining our ancient institutions in morals and religion."[69]

Although he listed other reasons to separate from the South, the three-fifths clause was at the center of Pickering's frustration. Other Federalists wanted to end slave representation after the election of 1800, and some called Jefferson a hypocrite for holding slaves while preaching about liberty. Thomas Fessenden derided slaveholders' extra votes in Congress and the electoral college in a poem about Jefferson's sexual dalliances with his slave Sally Hemings. "Great men can never lack supporters / who manufacture their own voters / besides, 'tis plain as yonder steeple / they will be *fathers* to *the people*."[70] Jefferson was not the only slaveholder to procreate with his slaves, but according to Federalists he became president because he and other Virginians had enough slaves to swing a close election in his favor.

Although he could not rid the nation of the slave ratio Pickering calculated the consequences of Democratic-Republican policies and shaped public opinion. He had been correct in 1806 when he told Jefferson that ending the Haitian trade would be the first of many commercial restrictions to come, and now Pickering was predicting that the embargo would eventually lead to war with Great Britain. Even if Jeffersonians had "no intention to make war" they faced the danger of exasperating Americans and carrying diplomatic brinksmanship to a point from which "British pride will not and American pride cannot retreat."[71] He was definitely a partisan and certainly a frustrated secessionist, but Pickering also had a clear understanding of human nature and politics.

During the embargo he reacted to letters from constituents who complained of the hardships they were experiencing under the embargo. "I do not think Congress have ever passed an act which has caused so much uneasiness and irritation," wrote one supporter. And no one who this writer knew was "bearing the act with calmness and dignity." The embargo would eventually affect the wealthy, as with most policies it was already changing the lives of middle- and lower-class New Englanders, "those of small property—such are likely to be ruined."[72] Pickering called on his state to nullify the act and also lambasted the embargo in a highly publicized letter to Massachusetts Governor James Sullivan. In Salem, Pickering's hometown, a caucus resolution denounced the policy and the suffering it caused fishermen, seamen, and poor laborers.[73]

James Elliot of Vermont also supported an amendment to rescind the provision in Article 1 that allowed three-fifths of a state's total number of slaves to count toward the number of seats it held in the U.S. House of Representatives. Political enemies accused Elliot of advocating disunion because he frequently denounced the three-fifths clause as "objectionable." In letters to his constituents Elliot echoed Pickering's thinking when he complained that because slaves counted toward the South's congressional seats and also electoral votes, New England's "situation is indeed wretched as we have no compensation for the monstrous sacrifice." Even though he would never advocate disunion, Elliot reasoned, "It cannot be *treason, conspiracy, or a division of the Union* to contemplate our misfortunes" that resulted from slave representation. In a similar vein, during an oration delivered in 1805, Daniel Webster said that New Englanders had few protections due to the Constitution's slave ratio. Counting slaves created an "inequity" under which southerners would "forever be able to control all of the Country."[74]

Federalist William Ely of Massachusetts' Hampshire North District also published a letter in the *Hampshire Gazette* that questioned Jefferson's motives for laying an embargo on all trade and criticized Democratic-Republicans for defeating, with little debate and no explanation, every Federalist proposal to repeal or relax the embargo. In an opinion that others shared, Ely called the embargo an experiment intended to "change the whole country and especially the commercialists to the northward, into agriculturalists and manufacturers." The southern party's ultimate goal, per Ely, was to suppress commerce and force northern states to relinquish maritime occupations. If successful, the elimination of maritime pursuits would "suffer foreign nations to come and take off our surplus produce." Like Pickering and Webster, Ely, who previously sponsored amendments to repeal the three-fifths clause, believed that slave representation had given the agricultural barons of the South enough influence in the federal government to ruin commerce and remake New England in their image. To keep this from happening, he urged northerners to protest loudly. They were the only ones that could force Congress to lift the embargo.[75]

For some time Federalists maintained that the Democratic-Republican Party's southern leadership was hostile to commerce. Based on the statements of many in Congress, Federalists had enough evidence to cast the embargo as a plot to ruin New England's economy. Previously undecided voters joined with Federalists, fearing that "Southern leaders who have no affection for commerce" would continue the embargo until they succeeded in "putting a stop . . . to the coasting 'trade altogether.'"[76] The prospect was disconcerting to Federalist Leverett Saltonstall of Salem, who digested southerners' statements that it would be beneficial if the embargo was perpetual.[77]

Another reason that Federalists could believe that the embargo was a ploy to destroy commerce was the close proximity that engaging in foreign trade put merchants and seamen with the broader Atlantic world. Mariners came into contact with innovative forms of capitalism that delegitimized the South's growing reliance on slave labor. In a "Supposed Conversation" Federalists conflated what they considered the Democratic-Republicans' Anglophobia and anti–New England bias with the fact that the British "carried off some of their slaves" at the end of the American Revolution. Thus, to safeguard and perpetuate slavery, they deduced that the "administration have determined to cripple and crush commerce because they consider the New-England states as growing dangerously rich and powerful by it."[78]

This, they claimed, was why southerners insisted that if seamen suffered under the embargo, "It is their own fault there is land enough, let them take to the spade." Farming had not led to seizures, impressments, or damaged U.S. relations with France and Britain. Activities associated with maritime trade caused a litany of problems and if mariners became tillers of the soil the entire country would be safe.[79] Such statements appeared to substantiate Federalists' assertions regarding the sinister reasons for maintaining the embargo.

Jefferson had said all the right things about maritime commerce to win the presidency, but nothing in his conduct or policies showed that he cared for or wanted to sustain it. When rumors surfaced that southerners would secede from the Union because of New Englanders' criticism of slavery, one Federalist responded, "In the name of God let them go—we can do without them [!]"[80] Consciously or unconsciously, the embargo forced some northerners to agree with Pickering: The commercial states would fare better in a union without slavery.

The fact that France was often overlooked in Jeffersonian arguments regarding the embargo was another thread in the Federalists' opposition message. When Federalists opposed France in the 1790s, Democratic-Republicans had not shown the patriotism that they were now demanding of maritime New Englanders. At every turn they undermined Federalist efforts to protect the nation. Once they gained power, Jefferson and his surrogates in Congress were surreptitiously allying the United States with France and risking a war with Britain. These allegations gained even more traction after Napoleon issued the Bayonne Decree on April 17, 1808. It allowed French agents and privateers to "enforce" the embargo under the presumption that any U.S. ships at sea had violated the embargo or were British. The decree simply gave the French another reason to subject U.S. merchantmen to theft or destruction.[81]

In the broadside *American Commerce in Flames*, Federalists affirmed that if the "outrages" sanctioned under the Bayonne Decree "had been committed by British cruisers the whole nation would have been roused to arms." It was not the embargo, but "Mr. Jefferson's submission which does not *avert* but *invites* Insult . . . Perish Commerce and abandon the Ocean, says Bonaparte, and it is *echoed by the philosophic Jefferson*." Federalists complained that Congress kept the focus on Britain even though France's attacks were consistently "glossed over and excused." Instead of bottling up the maritime industry on false pretenses, Federalists maintained that the federal government should at least let merchants sail and be responsible for their own safety.[82]

When the problem of ship seizures intensified in the late 1790s, the Adams administration armed merchant vessels and waged a Quasi War naval with France. In a letter to Josiah Quincy, Adams explained why the nation was in a more complex and dangerous predicament in 1808. "If you continue the embargo the times will be hard. If you institute a total non-intercourse, the times will be not more cheerful. If you repeal the embargo, circumstances will occur of more animation, but perhaps not more profit or more comfort. If you arm our merchantmen that will be war." Adams agreed that the nation would be better prepared for an attack had Jefferson maintained the navy constructed under his administration. Unfortunately, the naval force that remained posed no challenge to France or Britain. Jeffersonians left the country without a military or diplomatic solution and according to Adams, the United States could "not probably, be in a worse [situation] whatever may happen."[83]

Though uneasy, Addams was still "fully convinced that the embargo must be removed." He never believed in embargoes or other trade restrictions and told Quincy that he only tolerated them during the revolution because they unified the colonies. Jefferson's policies, on the other hand, were dividing the nation and failing to intimidate either France or Great Britain. "If the shackles continue on our commerce, they will produce an animosity and a rancor which will give much uneasiness to Mr. Jefferson's successor and be very prejudicial to the public service." Still, as Democratic-Republicans lose support, "The Federal Party will increase daily. That you will say will be a blessing, but it may be obtained at too dear a rate."[84]

Even with public opinion turning against the embargo in the maritime North, Democratic-Republicans continued to deny that their policies were causing economic and civil unrest in New England. Salem diarist William Bentley reflected this frame of mind. After finding out that Federalists had arranged to riot and hang Jefferson in effigy, he noted in his diary that "Republicans suffered much from the . . . pains taken to make . . . [them] accountable for the Embargo, the loss of Free trade, and for war." He could not view the policy as a problem and helped to block a Federalist-led attempt to send the government a petition urging Congress to repeal the embargo.[85]

On the other end of the political spectrum, a "Fellow Sufferer" funneled all of the Federalists' objections into a pamphlet that excoriated Jefferson for making demands of Britain that it refused to make of France, even though the French also "plundered, sunk . . . seized, confiscated, and condemned our vessels." Federalists recalled that it was at France's insistence that the federal government had "abandoned the lucrative trade" with Haiti. Since then, "on a principle unwarrantable and unknown, our government punishes our citizens at home." What the embargo really demonstrated was southerners' *"deep rooted hostility"* to New England, which Congress and the administration were trying to decimate through legislation.[86]

Despite the claims of some historians, it is not at all clear that the embargo would have forced Britain to make the concessions that Jefferson demanded had Federalists not provoked resistance and violations of the law in New England.[87] When Saltonstall entered in his diary, "Our country never saw a more gloomy moment. Commerce is totally suspended and we know not how long it will continue so," he had no reason to exaggerate the embargo's effects. Moreover, results in the 1808 congressional elections indicated that Saltonstall was not alone. Like him others had decided, "Every days [sic] events convince me more and more of the correctness of Federal principles and that the country must be saved by them if it is to be saved."[88]

The embargo also affected the African American workers in seaport communities. Many found employment in the foreign and domestic trades at an early age and remained in the maritime industry years longer than the average white seamen. They had few other employment options.

Since they depended so heavily on commerce and supported the abolition of slavery and an independent Haiti, black voters in New England gravitated to the Federalist Party and would voice their displeasure with the ruling party in the upcoming congressional elections.[89]

Before then, two developments weakened support for the embargo in Congress. The first was the sudden illness and death of Jacob Crowninshield, who, except for his vote against the Haitian nonintercourse bill, had been loyal to the administration's restrictive system. In some instances he furnished or strengthened his party's intellectual framework for commercial coercion. On January 18, 1808, Crowninshield collapsed in the House chamber and clung to life for a few months. The House formed a committee and colleagues from both parties took turns sitting with the young congressman and attending to his needs. Federalist Samuel Taggart of Massachusetts thought that he saw signs of improvement and was hopeful that Crowninshield would recover. However, on April 15, after dictating his final will to his brothers and leaving instructions for his burial, Crowninshield, a recent widower and the father of four young children, died at age thirty-eight.[90]

The person elected to fill Crowninshield's vacant seat was Joseph Story. He was a dark horse whose fidelity to the embargo and other trade restrictions was tepid at best. Most of the Democratic-Republican Party's apprehensions about him hinged on the fact that Story was a lawyer — a distrusted profession far removed from his predecessor's mercantile background. Crowninshield's supporters eyed Story suspiciously during his run against the late congressman's younger brother Benjamin, but Jacob Crowninshield had given Story high praises in written introductions to Madison and other members of the administration and he won the caucus. As many in the party feared, however, Story was not committed to commercial coercion. As a matter of fact he previously told Crowninshield that he would not have voted for the embargo, although he did believe that after it became the law of the land it deserved a chance to succeed. Along with his poor opinion of their restrictive system, Jeffersonians also disliked Story's influence over other New Englanders, primarily Ezekiel Bacon, who, though once an avid supporter of the embargo, would soon join Story's call for repeal. Jefferson would never forgive either man's defection and the party would not support Story after he completed Crowninshield's term.[91]

The second change that affected support for the embargo involved John Quincy Adams. By his own admission, since 1806 Adams's loyalties were no longer with the Federalist Party. He decided to support nonimportation and the embargo even though both went against his better judgment. Rumors circulated that he would be appointed to an embassy post in the Madison administration for supporting the embargo (few doubted that Madison would succeed Jefferson). The General Court reacted to Adams's change of heart by electing James Lloyd to replace him in the Senate six months ahead of the scheduled election. When he heard the news, Adams resigned, realizing that that "the course I pursued has drawn upon me much obloquy." But he left the Senate with "a good conscience, and a firm belief that I have rendered essential service to my country."[92]

Federalists disagreed, and just as Story's colleagues would berate him for helping to defeat the embargo, Federalists reacted similarly toward Adams for supporting it. "Of what consequence is it ... that a man smiles in your face, holds out his hand, and declares himself the advocate of those political principles to which you are also attached, when you see him acting with your adversaries upon other principles?" asked one of Adams's critics.[93]

Losing Crowninshield and Adams deprived embargo supporters of important New England allies in the House and Senate, and as Samuel Taggart recognized, "It is the congressional elections which must determine the point and ... if the present embargo system continues and there is no prospect of anything else at present, the people must feel more severely than they do now."[94]

Even though he was no longer in Congress, Federalists also suffered a loss on July 4, 1808, when Fisher Ames died. After retiring from Congress he practiced law when he could, but as his illness progressed, Ames wrote letters and published essays from home. He communicated ideas and advice to congressional Federalists that included sharp criticism of the Haitian and Nonintercourse acts. He also admonished Federalists to agitate during congressional debates. At the end of 1807 Josiah Quincy asked Ames if Federalists should "make motions and speeches, or should wait in silence for the effect of the civil wars" inside of the Democratic-Republican Party. Ames provided an emphatic no. "A party out of action is out of existence." Federalists should not only continue to vote in Congress they should endeavor to sway public opinion. Even though the party would never recapture its former glory, "federalism checks, though it cannot govern.... [and] It is better to suffer the fatigue of pumping, than to sit sullen till the ship sinks." He promised Quincy, "There will be times when" the people "will hear you ... There will yet be many new organizations of party, [and] many overwhelming changes." Ames supported the Federal Party until he could no longer rise from his sickbed.[95]

Following the tumultuous summer of 1807 and a year under the embargo, Federalists understood that repeal was not forthcoming. Voters would be making a decision between congressional candidates who promised to save New England's economy or those who placed the region's future in the hands of "a southern aristocracy, hostile to the commerce and prosperity of your commonwealth." Sending Federalists to Congress was the best way to repeal the embargo.[96]

As the election approached, New Englanders publically praised Pickering, Quincy, Gardenier, and other opponents of the embargo. They were the champions of commerce who had boldly challenged trade restrictions and the "blind confidence" that embargo supporters placed in Jefferson. Campaigning as the "Peace Party," Federalists reminded voters that "Mr. Gardenier was shot for echoing [anti-embargo] sentiments in Congress." Electing Federalists would amplify the voices of those who regularly confronted the majority and called for repeal.[97] Voters agreed.

Federalists gained four new seats in Massachusetts, raising their number in that state's delegation to ten out of seventeen. Some were elected to represent Maine districts and Essex County South voters elected Benjamin Pickman to fill the seat previously held by Jacob Crowninshield. Pickman's election was the first time in six years that voters elected a Federalist to represent that district. Because they knew that he leaned toward repealing the embargo, Democratic-Republicans rejected Story and nominated Dr. Daniel Kilham as their candidate. Like William Bentley, the party's leaders determined that their "suffering is from the young lawyer Story whose duplicity has been very injurious to us."[98] They were still in the minority party, but Federalists picked up close to twenty-five seats in the House and a couple in the Senate.

Ironically, instead of looking honestly at problems caused by the embargo, Jeffersonians held Story responsible for losing an election in which he was not a candidate. But during their campaign, Federalists admonished voters, "Choose Dr. *Kilham* for your Representative and you in effect choose the embargo, and will have it. Choose Mr. *Pickman*, and you at least give a vote *against* the Embargo." On the other hand, Democratic-Republicans promoted Kilham as the representative of "Free Trade or an Embargo and Peace."[99]

Voters understandably rejected the oddly worded idea that a perpetual embargo fostered free trade. This confusing message likely contributed to why the number of Federalists in the Massachusetts delegation outnumbered Democratic-Republicans for the first time in nearly a decade. Federalists lost a seat in June 1809, after Democratic-Republicans contested the Plymouth District election. As a result, Federalist William Baylies lost his seat to Jeffersonian Charles Turner, but Federalists still held a majority of the Bay State's seats in the Eleventh Congress (1809–1811).

The pro-embargo coalition in the Tenth Congress, which convened for its last session from November 1808 to March 1809, began to unravel—though not soon enough. New England's Democratic-Republicans, including Orchard Cook, had begun to waver. In general Cook voted with his party on key issues, but for some time Federalists found Cook's reluctance to support commercial restrictions intriguing. He had been hanging onto his party's restrictive system by a thread since 1805, and Samuel Taggart observed that of all the Democratic-Republicans representing Massachusetts, "Cook . . . except [for] the name and nominal attachment to Thomas Jefferson, is little distinguishable from federalists."[100] Ezekiel Bacon and Joseph Story also voiced support for some type of relief for merchants and mariners. It was because of this turnabout that Jefferson characterized the lame duck Story as a Machiavellian who enthralled Bacon and led him down the path of anti-embargo treachery. In spite of his previous record of support, Bacon would never regain Jefferson's favor.[101]

Federalists made gains in Congress but failed to capture the presidency. The Federalists' presidential nominating committee flirted with the idea of supporting Vice President George Clinton, who was part of a schism that divided New York's Democratic-Republican Party. They abandoned the plan because it would make them appear disingenuous and opportunistic. The candidates they did nominate were Charles Cotesworth Pinckney of South Carolina for president and Rufus King of New York for vice president. As it turned out, neither the Clinton faction nor the Pinckney-King ticket posed a serious threat to Madison in 1808. He became the nation's fourth president.[102] Although success in each of New England's congressional elections except New Hampshire revealed growing dissatisfaction with the embargo, Federalists would still not have enough votes to unilaterally repeal the embargo should it last until the next Congress. However, they did not intend to let five months pass before calling for repeal—again.[103]

On November 10, shortly after the session began, Vermont Federalist Martin Chittenden entered a motion to repeal the embargo. Other Federalists recommended that the House investigate the constitutionality of the supplemental acts. For the first time since late 1807, several northern Jeffersonians supported a Federalist's motion. Cook and Richard Cutts urged "immediate consideration of the subject, because of its importance to the mercantile interests in Maine."[104]

Chittenden was "disappointed" that the policy was still in effect and "felt it a duty which he owed to his constituents and the nation . . . to relieve" them from the embargo. Vermonters were especially distressed because they had the "extreme mortification of being declared in a state of insurrection" by the president in his proclamation of April 19, 1808. Jefferson targeted Lake Champlain's merchants for violating the embargo by trading overland with British Canadians.[105]

Smilie of Pennsylvania, who previously insisted that Americans should have abandoned foreign commercial endeavors after the revolution, asked Chittenden if it was his plan to repeal the embargo without replacing it with comparable legislation. If so, Chittenden should admit forthrightly "that he and his constituents are willing to . . . surrender the independence of their country." Following Smilie's objections, Willis Alston of North Carolina attempted to discredit Vermont and the rest of New England by asking the House to consider from "what quarter and from whom the opposition to the execution of the measure had arisen and the desire for its removal now proceeded."[106]

Samuel Dana came to Vermont's defense and said that Chittenden was perfectly able to explain the object of his proposal without help from Alston. Furthermore, if he wanted to know anything about the "the spirit of Vermont," he need only look at the history of the Revolutionary War to see if "any other state gave the enemy more bloody battles." James Elliot requested documentation from Treasury Secretary Gallatin so that the House could investigate whether the methods used to enforce the embargo were constitutional. Elliot said he trembled "not for the character of Vermont." Even though most Vermonters were hostile to the embargo they "manifested a degree of patriotism that had not been exceeded by any." He rejected claims that the nation's only choices were "the embargo or war" and concluded that neither he nor any of the other representatives who had opposed the policy from the beginning were under "obligation to propose the substitute." Moreover, if they provided a replacement for the embargo it "would not have been adopted" anyway. Chittenden's motion for repeal was defeated 71–42 on November 21, and this was not the Federalists' first attempt.[107]

By December 1808 New Englanders had endured the embargo for one year. Within those twelve months resistance in the region escalated in town after town. According to one Federalist newspaper, the region was undergoing "distress, privations, and injuries . . . from the gross violations of our dearest rights by that scourge of our country the embargo." Federalists considered the law a "plot which our rulers have devised," that could only lead to "shocking tragedy." Congressional Federalists began to attend town meetings. By participating in these gatherings they demonstrated solidarity with the people in their districts and state who refused to tolerate the embargo any longer. They also helped to organize protests and support demands to lift the embargo.[108]

New Englanders had spoken through their votes, and now they hoped that Democratic-Republican legislators would finally listen. If they failed to repeal the embargo, seamen, merchants, and others affected by the policy would take actions more perilous than those already adopted. By January 1809, one county considered "Dissolution of the Union" as a justifiable reaction to the protracted embargo.[109] Congress needed to make a decision. Would the majority, even lame ducks see the recent congressional elections as a reason to repeal the embargo, or would they continue to defend a failed policy and deny that it was contributing to serious problems in New England? As their Federalist representatives continued to sponsor motions for repeal, mariners would soon know the answer.

NOTES

1. Fisher Ames, *Works of Fisher Ames: With a Selection from His Speeches and Correspondence*, ed. Seth Ames, 2 vols. (New York: Da Capo Press, 1969), 1:390, 392; 2:293.
2. Richard Buel Jr., *America on the Brink: How the Political Struggle over the War of 1812 Almost Destroyed the Young Republic* (New York: Palgrave Macmillan, 2005), 31.
3. U.S. Congress, *American State Papers, 1789–1838: Documents, Legislative and Executive, of the Congress of the United States*, 38 vols. (Washington, DC: Gales and Seaton, 1832–1861), 1, *Foreign Relations* 2:503, 504.
4. Ibid.
5. Donald R. Hickey, "The Monroe-Pinkney Treaty of 1806: A Reappraisal," in *William and Mary Quarterly* 3rd ser., 44, no. 1 (January 1987): 86; Madison to Messrs. Monroe and Pinkney, May 20, 1807 in U.S. Congress, *American State Papers, Foreign Relations* 1, 3:166–73; Josiah Quincy, "Journals, 1801–1829," Quincy, Wendell, Holmes, and Upham Family Papers, MHS.
6. *Statues at Large* "Appendix Proclamations," Proclamation No. 11, 11: 759–60; Robert E. Cray, Jr., "Remembering the USS Chesapeake: The Politics of Maritime Death and Impressment," in *Journal of the Early Republic*, vol. 25, no. 3 (Fall, 2005): 454–57; Samuel Flagg Bemis, *A Diplomatic History of the United States*, 5th ed. (New York: Henry Holt and Company, 1965), 145–46; Burton Spivak, *Jefferson's English Crisis: Commerce, Embargo, and the Republican Revolution* (Charlottesville: University of Virginia Press, 1979), 70–72; James Fulton Zimmerman, *Impressment of American Seamen* (New York: Longmans, Green and Co., 1925), 135, 136; c.f. Louis M. Sears, *Jefferson and the Embargo* (Durham: Duke University Press, 1966 [1927]), 28, 52; *Salem* (MA) *Gazette*, July 10 and 14, 1807.
7. Quoted in Merrill D. Peterson, *Thomas Jefferson and the New Nation: A Biography* (New York: Oxford University Press, 1970), 876.
8. See *Salem* (MA) *Gazette*, July 21, 1807; John Quincy Adams, *The Diary of John Quincy Adams, 1794–1845*, ed. Allan Nevins (New York: Longmans & Co., [1928]), 46.
9. *Salem* (MA) *Gazette*, August 4, 1807.
10. *Salem* (MA) *Gazette*, August 4, 1807 (emphasis in original).
11. *Annals of Congress*, 10th Cong., 1st sess., 9–18. For an interpretation regarding restraints to war that are inherent in the federal system of government, see, Scott A. Silverstone, *Divided Union: The Politics of War in the Early American Republic* (Ithaca, NY: Cornell University Press, 2004), 69–83, 253.
12. *Annals of Congress*, 10th Cong., 1st sess., 795.
13. Ibid., 796.
14. Ibid., 797–98.
15. Ibid., 806–7.
16. Ames, *Works of Fisher Ames*, 1 896; *Annals of Congress*, 10th Cong., 1st sess., 809–11.
17. *Annals of Congress*, 10th Cong., 1st sess., 811–15.
18. *National Intelligencer* (Washington, DC), November 9, 1807 (emphasis added).
19. *Annals of Congress*, 10th Cong., 1st sess., 923–25.
20. Ibid., 926–27.
21. See Spivak, *Jefferson's English Crisis*, 137–38; Sears, *Jefferson and the Embargo*, 153, 156; Robert A. McCaughey, *Josiah Quincy, 1772–1864: The Last Federalist* (Cambridge, MA: Harvard University Press, 1974), 51–53; see also Barnabus Bidwell to Jacob Crowninshield, December 27, 1807, Mss 4, Box 3, Folder 10, Crowninshield Family Papers, PEM.
22. *Annals of Congress*, 10th Cong., 1st sess., 1172–76.
23. *Newburyport* (MA) *Herald*, December 25, 1807.
24. McCaughey, *Josiah Quincy*, 41, 43, 51–53.
25. John Quincy Adams, *Memoirs of John Quincy Adams, Comprising Portions of His Diary from 1795 to 1848*, ed. Charles Francis Adams, 12 vols. (Philadelphia: J. B. Lippincott and Co., 1874), 1:488–89.

26. See Robert R. Thompson, "John Quincy Adams, Apostate: From 'Outrageous Federalist' to 'Republican Exile,' 1801–1809," in *Journal of the Early Republic* 11, no. 2 (Summer 1991): 167; McCaughey, *Josiah Quincy*, 35.
27. *Annals of Congress*, 10th Cong., 1st sess., 50, 51, 1216–1219; Buel, *America on the Brink*, 33, 34.
28. *Annals of Congress*, 10th Cong., 1st sess., 50, 51, 1216; Embargo on all Ships in U.S. Ports Act of 1807, Pub. L. No. 9–5, 2 Stat. 451 (1807).
29. Adams, *Memoirs*, 1:288–89, 471–73.
30. Pickering to Thomas Fitzsimons, Esq., December 4, 1807 and to Timothy Williams December 21, 1807, Timothy Pickering Papers, MHS; cf. Adams, *Memoirs* 1:490–492.
31. *Annals of Congress*, 10th Cong., 1st sess., 1218, 2815–17; *Statutes at Large of the United States* (1845): 2:451–54.
32. Pickering to Timothy Williams, December 21, 1807, Timothy Pickering Papers, MHS.
33. Spivak, *Jefferson's English Crisis*, x; Clifford L. Egan, *Neither Peace nor War: Franco-American Relations, 1803–1812* (Baton Rouge: Louisiana State University Press, 1983), 74–78; Robert W. Tucker and David C. Hendrickson, *Empire of Liberty: The Statecraft of Thomas Jefferson* (New York: Oxford University Press, 1990), 206–213; Garry Wills, *"Negro President": Jefferson and the Slave Power* (Boston: Houghton Mifflin, 2003), 147–149; *Annals of Congress*, 10th Cong., 1st sess., 1710.
34. *Annals of Congress*, 10th Cong., 1st sess., 1272.
35. *Annals of Congress*, 10th Cong., 1st sess., 1273–1276.
36. Supplementary to the Embargo Act of 1808, Pub. L. No. 10–7, 2 Stat. 453 (1808).
37. *Annals of Congress*, 10th Cong., 1st sess., 1649–1650.
38. *Annals of Congress*, 10th Cong., 1st sess., 1652–1653.
39. *Annals of Congress*, 10th Cong., 1st sess, 1653–1657.
40. Ibid., 1653–1658.
41. Buel, *America on the Brink*, 64; Peterson, *Thomas Jefferson and the New Nation*, 896; Friends of Peace, *To All the Electors of Massachusetts of Whatever Political Party They May Be* . . . March 28, 1808 (Boston, 1808), Broadsides, AAS.
42. Additional Supplement to the Embargo Act of 1808, Pub. L. No. 10–33, 2 Stat. 473 (1808); Douglas Lamar Jones, "'The Caprice of Juries': The Enforcement of the Jeffersonian Embargo in Massachusetts," in *American Journal of Legal History* 24, no. 4 (October 1980): 311, 312.
43. Quoted in Thorp Lanier Wolford, "Democratic-Republican Reaction in Massachusetts to the Embargo of 1807," in *New England Quarterly* 15, no. 1 (March 1942): 44–45.
44. Jeffrey L. Pasley et al., eds., *Beyond the Founders: New Approaches to the Political History of the Early American Republic* (Chapel Hill: University of North Carolina Press, 2004), 113–15.
45. Paul A. Gilje, ed. *Wages of Independence: Capitalism in the Early American Republic* (Lanham, MD: Rowman & Littlefield, 2006), 6; Benjamin Woods Labaree, "The Making of an Empire: Boston and Essex County, 1790–1850," in *Entrepreneurs: The Boston Business Community, 1700–1850*, ed. Conrad E. Wright and Katheryn P. Viens (Boston: MHS/Northeastern University Press, 1997), 344–48, 350; McCaughey, *Josiah Quincy*, 17; and Benjamin Woods Labaree, *Patriots and Partisans: The Merchants of Newburyport, 1764–1815* (Cambridge, MA: Harvard University Press, 1962), 152–54; Samuel Eliot Morison, *The Maritime History of Massachusetts, 1783–1860* (Boston: Houghton Mifflin, 1921), 191.
46. Leonard W. Levy, *Jefferson and Civil Liberties: The Darker Side* (Chicago: Ivan R. Dee, 1989), 106–7; cf. Morison, *Maritime History of Massachusetts*, 189–91.
47. *A Political Sermon Addressed to the Electors of Middlesex* (Boston, 1808), 36 (emphasis in original), Books and Pamphlets Collection, AAS.
48. *New-England Palladium* (Boston, MA), May 3, 1808; Phillips, *Salem and the Indies*, 280; John H. Reinoehl, "Post-Embargo Trade and Merchant Prosperity: Experiences of

"Squabbles in Madam Liberty's Family"   115

the Crowninshield Family, 1809–1812," in *Mississippi Valley Historical Review* 42, no. 2 (September 1955): 230.

49. Dinah Mayo-Bobee, "Understanding the Essex Junto: Fear, Dissent, and Propaganda in the Early Republic," in *New England Quarterly* 88, no. 4 (December 2015): 623–46; Morison, *Maritime History of Massachusetts*, 190; *Newburyport* (MA) *Herald*, March 15, 1808; Quote from Labaree, *Patriots and Partisans*, 155.

50. Daniel Webster, *Considerations of the Embargo Laws* (Boston, 1808), A2, 4–6, Collection of the BA.

51. Albert Gallatin to Jacob Crowninshield (n.d.), Crowninshield Family Papers, MSS 4, Box 3, Folder 10, Crowninshield Family Papers, PEM; Albert Gallatin, *The Writings of Albert Gallatin*, ed. Henry Adams (New York: Antiquarian Press, 1960), 427 (italics in original).

52. *Annals of Congress*, 5th Cong., 2nd sess., 961–962; 10th Cong., 1st sess., 1695–702; Sean Wilentz, *Rise of American Democracy: Jefferson to Lincoln* (New York: W. W. Norton and Company, 2005), 80.

53. *Annals of Cong.* 10th Cong. 1 sess., 1711–1712.

54. Ibid., 1711–12, 1850–1854.

55. *Salem* (MA) *Gazette*, May 24, 1808.

56. *Annals of Congress*, 10th Cong., 2nd sess., 580, 581; Thomas Jefferson to Albert Gallatin, April 19, 1808, *Jefferson Papers*, LC. Also see Levy, *Jefferson and Civil Liberties*, 107, 108.

57. Addition to the Embargo and Supplements Act of 1808, Pub. L. No. 10–66, 2 Stat. 499 (1808).

58. Jacob Nagle, *A Diary of the Life of Jacob Nagle, Sailor, From the Year 1775–1841*, ed. John C. Dann (New York: Weidenfield and Nicolson, 1988), 294; Egan, *Neither Peace nor War*, 90–91.

59. *Annals of Congress*, 10th Cong., 1st sess., 1665.

60. *Hampshire Gazette* (Northampton, MA), February 10, 1808.

61. See Steven G. Calabresi and Christopher S. Yoo, *The Unitary Executive: Presidential Power from Washington to Bush* (New Haven, CT: Yale University Press, 2008), 69–71, 74; Mark A. Graber, "Establishing Judicial Review? *Schooner Peggy* and the Early Marshall Court," in *Political Research Quarterly* 51, no. 1 (March 1998): 223, 232; Gerald T. Dunne, "Joseph Story: The Germinal Years," in *Harvard Law Review* 75, no. 4 (February 1962): 740–42; Labaree, *Patriots and Partisans*, 162; Levy, *Jefferson and Civil Liberties*, 133, 134; Jones, "'Caprice of Juries,'" 319–24; Orchard Cook to Unknown Party, November 22, 1807, David M. Rubenstein, Rare Book & Manuscript Library, Duke University.

62. John Marshal to Timothy Pickering, December 19, 1808, in John Marshall, *The Papers of John Marshall: Correspondence, Papers, and Selected Judicial Opinions*, 12 vols. (Chapel Hill: University of North Carolina Press, 1993), 7:188; *United States v. Burr* 25 F. Cas. 30 (No. 14,692d) C.C.D. Va 1807.

63. Labaree, *Patriots and Partisans*, 159–161; Authorization for the President to Suspend Embargo Act of 1808, Pub. L. No. 10–52, 2 Stat. 490 (1808).

64. Pickering to Gore, January 8, 1809, in Henry Adams, ed. *Documents Relating to New-England Federalism, 1800–1815* (Boston: Little, Brown, and Company, 1877), 376.

65. James M. Banner, *To the Hartford Convention: The Federalists and the Origins of Party Politics in Massachusetts, 1789–1815* (New York: Alfred A. Knopf, 1970), 298, 299n2; see also Sears, *Jefferson and the Embargo*, 152, 153.

66. *Hampshire Gazette* (Northampton, MA), November 9, 1808; cf. Banner, *Hartford Convention*, 51; Labaree, *Patriots and Partisans*, 158–68; Buel, *America on the Brink*, 74; Hervey Putnam Prentiss, *Timothy Pickering as the Leader of New England Federalism, 1800–1815* (New York: Da Capo Press, 1972), 64; *Annals of Congress*, 10th Cong., 2nd sess., 991.

67. Leonard L. Richards, *Slave Power: The Free North and Southern Domination, 1780–1860* (Baton Rouge: Louisiana State University Press, 2000), 65–68.

68. See Sears, *Jefferson and the Embargo*, 153; Siegel "'Steady Habits' under Siege," 199–200; Stanley Elkins and Eric McKitrick, *The Age of Federalism: The Early American Republic, 1788–1800* (New York: Oxford University Press, 1993), 623–26; David Hackett Fischer, *The Revolution of American Conservatism: The Federalist Party in the Era of Jeffersonian Democracy* (New York: Harper & Row, 1965), 175, 255. Cf. Wills, "*Negro President*," 127–139; Kevin M. Gannon, "Escaping 'Mr. Jefferson's Plan of Destruction': New England Federalists and the Idea of a Northern Confederacy, 1803–1804," in *Journal of the Early Republic* 21, no. 3 (Autumn 2001): 413–416; Forrest McDonald, *States' Rights and the Union: Imperium in Imperio, 1776–1876* (Lawrence: University Press of Kansas, 2000), 60–62; and Banner, *Hartford Convention*, 43.

69. Timothy Pickering to George Cabot, February 3, 1804, Timothy Pickering Papers, MHS. See also Mayo-Bobee, "Understanding the Essex Junto," 632–39; Elizabeth R. Varon, *Disunion! The Coming of the American Civil War, 1789–1859* (Chapel Hill: University of North Carolina Press, 2008), 37.

70. Thomas Green Fessenden, *Democracy Unveiled; or Tyranny Stripped of the Garb of Patriotism* (Boston: D. Carlisle, 1805), 107 (italics in original), American Culture Series, Reel 412.1, SCUA; Paul Finkelman, "The Problem of Slavery in the Age of Federalism," in Doron Ben-Atar and Barbara B. Oberg, eds., *Federalists Reconsidered* (Charlottesville: University of Virginia Press, 1998), 145; Fischer, *Revolution of American Conservatism*, 159; James Sidbury, "Thomas Jefferson in Gabriel's Virginia," in *The Revolution of 1800: Democracy, Race, and the New Republic*, ed. James Horn et al. (Charlottesville: University of Virginia Press, 2002), 199–204; Banner, *Hartford Convention*, 101–4.

71. Pickering to Jefferson, February 24, 1806; Pickering to Thomas Fitzsimons, December 3, 1807, Timothy Pickering Papers, MHS.

72. John Cushing to Pickering, September 2, 1808, Israel Thorndike to Pickering, February 2, 1809, Timothy Pickering Papers, MHS.

73. Federal Party, Massachusetts, *Salem Federal Meeting. Salem, Friday, March 25, 1808* (Salem, 1808), Broadsides, AAS.

74. *Post-boy and Vermont & New-Hampshire Federal Courier* (Windsor, VT), "Mr. Elliot to His Constituents Letter IX," June 11, 1805; Daniel Webster, *An Appeal to the Old Whigs of New-Hampshire* (United States, s.n., 1805), 13, 16, Books and Pamphlets Collection, AAS.

75. *Hampshire Gazette* (Northampton, MA), March 23, 1808.

76. *Columbian Centinel* (Boston, MA), March 30, 1808.

77. Robert E. Moody, ed., *The Saltonstall Papers, 1607–1815*, 3 vols. (Boston: Massachusetts Historic Society, 1974), 2:438.

78. *Newburyport* (MA) *Herald*, February 7, 1809.

79. *Salem* (MA) *Gazette*, March 11, 1808; and *Columbian Centinel* (Boston), March 30, 1808; *To the Merchants, Seamen, and Mechanicks of All Parties* (Salem, 1808), PEM.

80. *Salem* (MA) *Gazette*, March 11, 1807.

81. Sears, *Jefferson and the Embargo*, 314; Egan, *Neither Peace nor War*, 97.

82. *American Commerce in Flames!: Americans! See the execution of Bonaparte's orders to burn, sink, and destroy your ships! . . . and then vote for Sullivan, or any other Partizan of France, if you can!!* (Boston, 1808), Rare Book Collection, New York Public Library. Astor, Lenox, Tilden Foundations; Friends of Peace, *To All the Electors of Massachusetts of Whatever Political Party They May Be . . . March 28, 1808* (Boston, 1808), Broadsides, AAS.

83. John Adams to Josiah Quincy, November 25, 1808, Quincy, Wendell, Holmes, and Upham Family Papers, MHS.

84. John Adams to Josiah Quincy, December 23, 1808, Quincy, Wendell, Holmes, and Upham Family Papers, MHS.

85. William Bentley, The *Diary of William Bentley D.D.: Pastor of the East Church Salem, Massachusetts*, 4 vols. (Salem: Essex Institute, 1905–14), 3:391, 405.

86. John Park, *An Address to the Citizens of Massachusetts on the Causes and Remedy of Our National Distresses by A Fellow Sufferer* (Boston: Repertory Office, 1808), 4–11 (emphasis in original), Books and Pamphlets Collection, AAS.

87. Cf. Egan, *Neither Peace nor War*, 92–96.
88. Moody, *Saltonstall Papers*, 2:427–428; *Hampshire Gazette* (Northampton, MA), May 18, 1808 and September 7, 1808.
89. Finkelman, "The Problem of Slavery," 148. See also W. Jeffrey Bolster, *Black Jacks: African American Seamen in the Age of Sail* (Cambridge, MA: Harvard University Press, 1997), 154; and Bolster, "'To Feel Like a Man': Black Seamen in the Northern States, 1800–1860," in *Journal of American History* 76, no. 4 (March 1990): 1173–99; Ira Dye, "Early American Merchant Seafarers," in *Proceedings of the American Philosophical Society* 120, no. 5 (October 15, 1976): 348–53.
90. Samuel Taggart to John Taylor, January 27, 1808 and February 4, 1808, Samuel Taggart Letterbook, AAS; John Quincy Adams, *Memoirs of John Quincy Adams, Comprising Portions of His Diary from 1795 to 1848.*, ed. Charles Francis Adams, 12 vols. (Philadelphia: J. B. Lippincott and Co., 1874), 1:531.
91. Dunne, "Joseph Story," 727, 737–39; Buel, *America on the Brink*, 69
92. Adams, *Memoirs*, 1:535–36; Thompson, "John Quincy Adams," 180.
93. Quoted in Dunne, "Joseph Story," 714.
94. Samuel Taggart to John Taylor, March 21, 1808, Samuel Taggart Letterbook, AAS.
95. Ames to Josiah Quincy, November 19, 1807, in Ames, *Works of Fisher Ames*, 1:399–403; Winfred E. A. Bernhard, *Fisher Ames: Federalist and Statesman, 1758–1808* (Chapel Hill: University of North Carolina Press, 1965), 347–51.
96. *A Political Sermon*, 35, 37, Books and Pamphlets Collection, AAS.
97. Friends of Peace, *The Friends of Peace, To All the Electors of Massachusetts of Whatever Political Party They May Be . . . March 28, 1808* (Boston, 1808), Broadsides, AAS.
98. Bentley, *Diary*, 3:395.
99. *To Electors of Essex South District* (Massachusetts, 1808), 1, 8 (emphasis in original), Books and Pamphlets Collection, AAS; *No Tribute to England—No President for Life—No Topsfield Delegates . . .* (Salem, 1808), PEM.
100. Dunne, "Joseph Story," 739; Paul Goodman, *The Democratic-Republicans of Massachusetts: Politics in a Young Republic* (Cambridge, MA: Harvard University Press, 1964), 192; Sears, *Jefferson and the Embargo*, 159; Taggart to John Taylor, February 8, 1807, Taggart Letterbook, AAS.
101. Dunne, "Joseph Story," 744, 751.
102. Peterson, *Thomas Jefferson and the New Nation*, 890, 897; Banner, *Hartford Convention*, 295–297; "Massachusetts 1808 State Election for Governor," in Philip J. Lampi, First Democracy Project, AAS; Egan, *Neither Peace nor War*, 90.
103. Cf. Egan, *Neither Peace Nor War*, 20.
104. *Annals of Congress*, 10th Cong., 2nd sess., 474, 476–478.
105. *Ibid.*, 474, 580, 581; "Proclamation of April 19, 1808," Jefferson Papers, LC; Levy, *Jefferson and Civil Liberties*, 107, 108.
106. *Annals of Congress*, 10th Cong., 2nd sess., 475.
107. *Ibid.*, 476–78, 512–13.
108. *Hampshire Gazette* (Northampton, MA), November 6 and December 7, 1808; Bentley, *Diary*, 3:389.
109. *Hampshire Gazette* (Northampton, MA), January 1809.

John Quincy Adams (1767–1848). Artist: Pieter Van Huffel, 1815. Oil on canvas. National Portrait Gallery, Simthsonian Institution; gift of Mary Louisa Adams Clement in memory of her mother, Louisa Catherine Adams Clement. Adams broke away from the Federalist Party over the Embargo of 1807 and was replaced by the Massachusetts Legislature before the end of his Senate term. He joined the Democratic-Republicans, was appointed ambassador to Russia by James Madison and served as James Monroe's secretary of state. In 1835, he became the nation's sixth president, but served only one term. Adams was elected to the House of Representatives in 1831 and became an avid opponent of slavery. A few years before his death in 1848, Adams forced repeal of the House gag rule prohibiting debates on slavery, successfully defended the illegally imported Africans from the schooner *L'Amistad* before the Supreme Court, and fought the annexation of Texas and the Mexican War as machinations to increase the power of slave states by extending slavery.

Fisher Ames (1758–1808). Artist: Gilbert Stuart, c. 1807. Oil on wood. National Portrait Gallery, Smithsonian Institution; gift of George Cabot Lodge. Contemporaries viewed Ames as a leading voice in the Federalist Party and most historians agree. Ames championed ratification of the Constitution and was largely a nationalist until he saw the need to reject anti–New England commercial policies. He said little to oppose slavery, but after retiring from Congress, Ames praised France's former slaves and defended their right to declare independence and rule over the conquered territory that they established as Haiti in 1804. After denouncing U.S. policy toward Haiti, he published essays opposing what he saw as the Jefferson administration's Francophile, anti–New England policies, Ames urged Federalists to vigorously oppose Democratic-Republicans and their restrictive maritime policies. His sometimes mercurial writings can most likely be attributed to his long battle with the respiratory illness that ended his career and claimed his life at a young age.

Rufus King (1755–1827). Artist: Gilbert Stuart, 1819–1820. Oil on panel. National Portrait Gallery, Smithsonian Institution; this acquisition was made possible by a generous contribution from the James Smithson Society. King was able to keep slavery out of the Northwest in the Ordinance of 1787. Yet he supported the three-fifths clause and moratorium on ending the slave trade at the Massachusetts Ratifying Convention in 1788. King served as a diplomat and was the last Federalist to run for president. He lost handily to James Monroe in 1816. By the mid 1820s, he was a major opponent of slavery in Missouri, but also advocated compensated emancipation and the colonization of freed African Americans outside of the United States.

Timothy Pickering (1745–1829). Artist: Walter M. Brackett, c. 1872. Oil on canvas. Commissioned by Secretary of War William W. Belknap when assembling a War Department Gallery, the Army acquired the portrait of Secretary Pickering by Walter M. Brackett, 1873; reproduction of a painting by Gilbert Stuart, donated to the United States Military Academy. Courtesy of the Army Art Collection, U.S. Army Center of Military History. George Washington appointed Pickering Postmaster General, Secretary of War, and Secretary of State. Pickering opposed the spread of slavery into the Northwest Territories, and after Jefferson's reelection in 1804, hatched a stillborn plan for a Northern Confederacy because of the three-fifths clause. In the Senate, he opposed commercial restrictions and criticized Democratic-Republicans for their racist policy toward Haiti. They would later consider Pickering's opposition to Jefferson's Embargo of 1807 a central cause of the policy's failure.

Josiah Quincy (1772–1864). Reproduction of a painting by Gilbert Stuart, c. 1898. Courtesy of the Library of Congress Prints and Photographs Division, Washington, D.C. Quincy entered Congress as debates over the Haitian trade began. In Congress, he extolled the superiority of the North's free labor force, threatened disunion, and later opposed the entry of slavery into Missouri along with Daniel Webster. Quincy opposed the separation of Maine from Massachusetts but remained active in state and local politics. He became mayor of Boston and president of Harvard University. While he refused to formally join abolitionists, Quincy criticized former allies for compromising over slavery. He lived long enough to congratulate Abraham Lincoln for issuing the Emancipation Proclamation and compared it to the efforts of leading Federalists, such as Pickering and Rufus King.

Daniel Webster (1782–1852). Artist: Frances Alexander, 1800–1880 (Black Dan, Class of 1801, 1835). Oil on canvas. Courtesy of the Hood Museum of Art, Dartmouth College, Hanover, New Hampshire. Gift of Dr. George Shattuck, Class of 1803. Early in his career, Webster was an ardent opponent of the Embargo (1807–1809), spole against the South's growing power through slave representation, and publically condemned the spread of slavery into Missouri. Later in his career, Webster became a Whig. He was appointed secretary of state by three presidents and later supported compromises over the spread of slavery, which invoked the consternation of New Englanders and former Federalist colleagues such as Josiah Quincy.

FOUR

"O Grab Me!"

The Justification for Disunion (1808–1809)

On December 23, 1808, the people of Newburyport, Massachusetts, assembled for a somber event. At sunrise, noon, and four in the evening bells tolled, flags flew at half-mast, and townspeople discharged guns and cannons as sailors wearing black armbands marched slowly through the streets to a steady drumbeat. Following closely behind the marchers was a float containing a dismantled ship with the phrases "*Death to Commerce*" and "O-grab-me" inscribed on its bow. When the procession arrived at the local customhouse, it stopped. Then beneath a flag picturing a terrapin (turtle) with its head retracted, one of the mariners delivered an address from aboard the float. Some in the audience described the oration as so stirring that it "*reached the heart*." Recognizing the symbolism and agreeing with the sentiments expressed, spectators honored the pageant and speaker with thunderous applause.[1]

The occasion for this gloomy parade was the first anniversary of the federal government's embargo on all shipping. Towns throughout New England designated the day for mourning, and staged events similar to the ceremony described above to lament the death of commerce.[2] For New Englanders "O-Grab-Me," the inversion of the word "embargo," characterized the effect of the Jefferson administration's restrictive system. The term had become a metaphor for what protestors considered the apathetic and sometimes openly hostile treatment they received from the president and Democratic-Republicans in Congress. Each melancholy procession revealed that the political and economic climate in the region was deteriorating because of the embargo, which helped to drive individual apprehensions over the policy into a more collective opposition throughout the region.

Voters in the region already demonstrated that for many of them support for Jefferson had been a terrible mistake. At the end of 1808, New Englanders elected more Federalists to Congress than they had in years. But their representatives were still the minority and could not repeal the embargo without help from Democratic-Republicans or by winning the presidency.[3] Because of the political landscape they could accomplish neither. James Madison, Jefferson's secretary of state and close friend, became president and beginning in March 1809, New England's economic future again rested with a Virginia slaveholder.

Democratic-Republicans were understandably pleased with Madison's election. Unfortunately, they placed more emphasis on the election's outcome than it merited. In the face of calls to repeal the embargo, Democratic-Republicans used the victory as a reason to continue the policy. During the weeks between the election and Madison's inauguration they defiantly ignored public outcries in New England and did so until the law threatened national security and survival of the Union. Within this brief period several congressmen demonstrated a disconnection from or indifference to the economic plight of New England's mariners.

When New Englanders read apathetic or belligerent statements from their own congressmen or representatives from southern states in response to their petitions, their sense of isolation grew more acute. The idea that the central government would legislatively discriminate against loyal citizens and throw them into economic turmoil compelled more than a few New Englanders to continue to beg Congress for repeal, before demanding that state governments nullify the embargo or begin the process of seceding from the Union.[4] This discussion analyzes events that occurred between 1808 and early 1809 in conjunction with the conduct of representatives and senators who almost irreparably damaged New England's relationship with the central government. The anger and lack of trust that had been in the making since the restrictive system began in 1805 would push several states in the region closer to disunion than at any other time during the crisis over commerce. At the same time, the growth of southern power and its relationship to Democratic-Republican hegemony came into focus as Federalists assessed the region's susceptibility to conditions dictated by the nation's agricultural sector.

During the embargo, which went into effect in December 1807, growing numbers of New England voters lost faith in their congressional representatives as they saw partisan loyalties outweigh their economic concerns. Federalists motioned for repeal and organized resistance in Congress and their states to undermine the embargo whenever they could. Months of partisan bickering, inflammatory rhetoric, and the Jefferson administration's determination to doggedly prolong and enforce the controversial policy, evoked challenges to federal authority. A considerable number of New Englanders openly doubted that the Union was worth saving. Much of their resentment was aimed at slaveholders' political power and manipulation of Free State economies.

For these and other reasons, the wisest choice that Congress could make involved repealing the embargo after it had been in effect for a year. First, although majority members denied reports of widespread privation, the policy was having a negative impact on New Englanders in every socioeconomic level. Second, harsh and prejudicial enforcement of the embargo fostered an air of defiance that only increased violations and violent protests. Prolonging the embargo or passing new enforcement laws would only exasperate an already angry populace. Third, by the end of 1808, the policy's supporters in Congress had to grope for plausible reasons to justify prolonging the embargo and rejecting Federalist proposals for repeal.

Congressional embargo proponents engaged in hyperbolic accusations or digressions that included haranguing Federalists for fabricating accounts of suffering, inciting riots, and sabotaging the government's efforts to end French and British violations of U.S. sovereignty. Furthermore, even though petitions for repeal or relief flowed into Congress on a regular basis, Democratic-Republicans generally responded apathetically toward or expressed distrust of the merchants and seamen who petitioned for relief. A number of their imprudent speeches appeared in newspapers. Rhetoric insulting and dismissive of New England's residents, along with economic deprivations, increased the numbers of those who felt abandoned by the central government and infuriated that Congress channeled their requests for protection into excuses to deprive them of their livelihoods.[5]

Most important was the fact that Federalists had correctly estimated the consequences of extending the embargo. By the end of 1808, whenever they charged southern Democratic-Republicans with attempting to subdue maritime activities in order to subject New England and the rest of the North to the machinations of southern agriculturalists, Federalists sounded credible. Nevertheless, New England's Jeffersonians continued to reject repeal, claiming that Madison's election had been a national mandate in support of the embargo. In reality, even though losses in the recent congressional elections demonstrated that the policy had damaged them politically, northern Democratic-Republicans still chose to disregard the voters' message.[6]

In fact, Madison's election was far from substantiating claims that support for the embargo was nationwide. In 1804 Jefferson won every New England state but Connecticut, and with the exception of Delaware and Maryland, took every electoral vote in the South, Mid-Atlantic, and West. In 1808, however, the only New England state to cast electoral votes for Madison was Vermont and he failed to receive a single vote from other states in the region. Like Jefferson, Madison carried Kentucky, Tennessee, and Ohio, and again Delaware and Maryland were divided.

One of the most important changes in the electoral map took place in New York, where Democratic-Republicans did not solidly back Madison as they had Jefferson. North Carolina even provided support for the Federalist ticket, which was noteworthy because by this time Federalists had become generally unwelcomed in southern political circles and were hastening toward extinction throughout the South. Notably, even in the face of poor organization and dwindling numbers North Carolina's Federalists put three of their state's fourteen electoral votes in the Federalist column.[7]

The geographic contours of the electoral map in 1808 provided Federalists with proof that southerners were alienating New Englanders from the rest of the nation through their crushing commercial restrictions and description of the region as unpatriotic.[8] Regardless of the fact that the embargo also affected the South's economy, it had little if any impact in the interior where yeomen farmers could take or leave a policy that affected mariners.[9] Though concerned with the sale of cash crops and surplus produce, planters shared and supported Jefferson's agrarian philosophy. Throughout the period that the embargo was in effect, many opted to endure losses, while others, although their congressional representatives claimed otherwise, engaged in smuggling just as much if not more than New Englanders.[10]

Some of the embargo's supporters compared the policy with trade restrictions that they imposed on themselves during the Revolution, and saw their compliance as a patriotic duty. Of course, opponents argued that there was no comparison. Federalists rejoined that unlike the self-imposed policies during the War for Independence, the embargo indiscriminately prohibited trade with every foreign nation, not just one. In addition, they consistently complained that the policy had no expiration date, and questioned additions to the original law that kept the domestic trade bogged down in excessive bonds, oath swearing, time limits, and even gunboat fire. Nor did it help that every time repeal was suggested embargo proponents postponed or defeated the motions. When the southern leadership of the Democratic-Republican Party countered calls for repeal with hastily drafted laws imposing stricter enforcement, they seemed vindictive. Actions of this type reinforced Federalists' claims that, from the beginning, southerners promoted trade restrictions to destroy New England's maritime economy, not protect it. By the end of 1808, Josiah Quincy's conclusion that the federal government was "touched with madness" no doubt exposed a sentiment already ubiquitous in New England.[11]

As the embargo dragged on it escalated anxieties, deepened sectional hostilities, and fostered mistrust of the policy's supporters in Washington. Federalists cited several reasons to oppose the policy. Besides its damage to New England the law enforced Napoleon's Continental System by depriving Great Britain of U.S. and West Indian goods that were usually transported in American ships. Furthermore, through the Bayonne Decree, which allegedly enforced the embargo, France increased its attacks on the nation's merchant marine. The French began to seize, sell, or destroy Americans' ships and property at an alarming rate. Their agents even harassed and delayed U.S. government vessels with unnecessary searches and quarantines.[12]

Jefferson attempted to deal with the crisis early in 1808, by instructing diplomats in England and France to offer each nation an olive branch. The United States would favor whichever nation dropped its "obnoxious decrees" first, but the chief envoys assigned to these nations encountered problems.[13] John Armstrong, U.S. minister to France, originally supported the embargo but was disturbed by France's aggression and sent Napoleon several messages of disapproval. Because the emperor disliked Armstrong, he never responded to the correspondence. Finally, after several frustrated attempts to communicate Jefferson's proposal, Armstrong advocated repeal.[14] William Pinkney fared no better in Britain, but the outcome differed. Throughout the summer of 1808 Foreign Secretary George Canning toyed with Pinkney and wasted his time, first needling Pinkney and then asking him to write down Jefferson's proposition. Finally, he aloofly dropped hints that Britain was not interested in making a deal. This experience led Pinkney, who had previously opposed the embargo, to endorse it.[15]

If either of the warring nations wanted the United States as an ally, Jefferson provided the perfect opportunity. Secretary of State Madison made it clear that the administration was appealing directly to the belligerents' desire to "produce collisions between the United States and its adversary." But neither France nor Britain took the bait.[16] The overture might possibly have worked earlier in Jefferson's presidency, but by 1808 neither belligerent appeared to respect the United States. France seized some 390 U.S. vessels between 1803 and 1807, but Napoleon had nothing to fear from the U.S. Representative John G. Jackson, a Democratic-Republican from Virginia who supported the embargo, enumerated France's offenses. "How is it when we cross over the water and look at France? We find by the proclamation of General Ferrand, an attempt made to regulate our trade to St. Domingo [Haiti] inconsistent with our rights . . . [and the] burning of our vessels . . . for which no apology has been attempted."[17]

Jackson also criticized Federalists, however, for turning New Englanders against the embargo and threatening disunion. He acknowledged the severity of France's atrocities but made it clear that Britain's aggressions overshadowed any assault that Napoleon ever orchestrated against U.S. merchants and their property. In similar speeches other representatives informed Federalists that as long as Democratic-Republicans were at the helm, any war involving the United States would be against Britain, no matter how badly France behaved. The British charged Jefferson with demanding outrageous concessions to settle the nations' differences and then contributed to the crisis by seizing more than 500 merchantmen and impressing hundreds of U.S. citizens.[18]

Jefferson's olive branch appears to have failed because of what both nations perceived as his administration's partiality toward France. Armstrong endured unwarranted hostility from France's uncooperative emperor, whom the United States bent over backward to accommodate. Pinckney suffered abuse and condescension from Britain's authorities when engaging in negotiations because he could not satisfactorily answer questions about America's seemingly Francophile foreign policy.[19] Since neither belligerent discontinued its attacks or rescinded laws that violated U.S. neutrality, it took little effort for Federalists to conclude that the embargo failed to accomplish its objectives abroad. This meant that the restrictions were only hurting U.S. citizens.

In America and Europe events unfolded just as Federalists predicted: the administration had painted itself into a corner.[20] The *Hampshire Gazette* reported that, "Commerce, ships, seamen, [are] all wiped from the face of our country—not by England, or even France, but by our own rulers—those who got into power under assurances of protecting the interest of trade and commerce, and the rights and privileges of seamen."[21]

Between April and September of 1808 Federalists in Massachusetts organized a petition campaign urging repeal. At least seventy towns and several counties forwarded resolutions and memorials to Congress.[22] When their petitions were unanswered by November, the people of Essex County passed a resolution repudiating the federal government. The county's residents insisted that those with power in the federal government no longer protected or represented them. President Jefferson, they complained, was unaccommodating and Congress refused to take their "earnest supplications" seriously. Essex County could only "rely for relief on the wisdom and patriotism of our state government whom the people have placed as centinels [sic] to guard our rights and privileges from whatever quarter they may be invaded."[23]

Though the federal government ignored their pleas, the Massachusetts General Court was immediately responsive to residents' grievances. On November 15, 1808, the newly elected Federalist majority in the legislature passed a resolution instructing the state's delegates in Congress to "use their most strenuous exertions to procure an immediate repeal" of the embargo. Deeming it inappropriate for the state government to officially disapprove of a federal statute, Democratic-Republicans joined Benjamin Crowninshield's attempt to present resolutions swearing loyalty to the government and support for the embargo, but his motion was defeated.[24] Crowninshield, a future Secretary of the Navy (1815–1818) and younger brother of the late congressman Jacob Crowninshield, tried, but now found it difficult to embarrass opponents of the embargo.

In Washington, Federalists attempted to comply with the legislature's request. Pickering motioned to read the state's resolution in the Senate, but Joseph Anderson, a Jeffersonian from Tennessee, objected and the Senate postponed the reading indefinitely.[25] The efforts to repeal the policy did not end at this time however. Federalists continued to sponsor proposals for full or partial repeal.

On November 11 Senator James Hillhouse of Connecticut entered a motion for repeal and James Lloyd from Massachusetts requested a detailed account of the vessels that had traveled oversees under executive permit between December 1807 and September 1808. Lloyd wanted to demonstrate that the warring nations had not endangered commerce to the extent that embargo supporters claimed. Wasting no time and anticipating the Federalists' strategy, Democratic-Republicans ordered two hundred copies of the memorials that Congress received from merchants in Boston, Salem, New York, and elsewhere printed and distributed through Congress. Their plan was to use merchants' cries for help as a defense for the embargo.[26]

When deliberations over Hillhouse's motion began on November 21, Federalists argued that prolonging the embargo beyond a year could permanently close countless foreign markets to U.S. merchants. Hillhouse noted that while the embargo had no effect on foreign nations, Connecticut's corn meal and cattle export markets would soon collapse. In reply to assertions that lifting the embargo would lead to war with France, Hillhouse asked the law's proponents to explain how Napoleon could do more than "burn our ships and sequester our property?" If repeal meant war with France, "Let it come" he said, because unless the real purpose was to destroy commerce to help agriculturalists and manufacturers realize their financial ambitions, the embargo had failed anyway. Should armed conflict with France follow repeal, Lloyd added that the United States would be fighting a nation that was already waging a war against it.[27]

Kentuckian John Pope chided Federalists for displaying so much bravado after suffering a humiliating loss in the presidential election. If the embargo incited revolt against the federal government perhaps "foreign commerce should cease,"[28] he said. Pope was neither the first nor the last Jeffersonian to recommend permanently ending foreign trade, which only deepened sectional opposition to the embargo. The Columbian Centinel reported that, "Southern leaders who have no affection for commerce" had targeted the foreign and domestic trades for annihilation. The paper agreed with the General Court that Congress had become a "theatre of base contention and sanguinary threats." Frequent, bitter exchanges during congressional debates were merely reflections of the sectional divisions exposed in the presidential election returns.[29]

It did not take long for the Senate majority to postpone further consideration of the Hillhouse motion. After Pope's comments, James Lloyd of

Massachusetts complained that Federalists had already delayed discussing repeal "with as much civility as possible." In his opinion, no political event since ratification of the Constitution was as important as deciding the future of commerce. The restrictive system was an utter failure and neither France nor England had stopped seizing or destroying citizens' property. Worst of all, the law was dividing the nation. Congress had not conveyed an "urgent public necessity requiring" the embargo, which might unnecessarily "create great discontent and uneasiness" and "rebellion." For this reason alone it should be repealed, or at the very least, "if we cannot trade with France and England" interjected Lloyd, Congress should reopen trade with other nations and only restrict commercial interaction with France and Britain.[30]

To counter the Federalists' attempts to gain support for repeal, Democratic-Republicans presented dozens of memorials that mariners had sent to Congress. They then claimed that the pleas contained in the petitions proved that the embargo was the best way to safeguard commerce and was also what the petitioners wanted. Virginian Andrew More said he was convinced that that the only reason the embargo failed was that Federalists had not allowed it to operate as planned. Another Virginian asserted that critics like the people of Essex County disgraced the nation. Violations of the law in New England, he and others complained, was the handiwork of Federalists who seduced otherwise loyal Americans into committing treasonous acts. To them, this explained why the most recent petitions from New England, and Boston in particular, contradicted the merchants' earlier cries for help.[31]

Federalists shot back that there were no inconsistencies in the merchants' petitions. According to Lloyd, Bostonians originally asked the government to do something to protect them from British impressments and seizures, and it was only after the government failed to protect their property and crews from the French that these same merchants turned against the embargo. France deserved the same "promptitude and amplitude of redress" the government demanded from Great Britain, but no apologies were requested or forthcoming from that nation. Everyone, not just merchants, questioned the administration's failure to request restitution from the French government even though that nation wantonly seized, burned, or sold their property.[32] After a year of hardship, it was apparent that the embargo had not improved foreign relations, and New England's merchants would rather risk uncertain dangers at sea than face certain bankruptcy sitting at home, asserted Lloyd.

These arguments annoyed William Branch Giles of Virginia. In his opinion the Senate had already been excessively accommodating to northern merchants, especially those from New England. Senators had taken steps to protect them, he charged, but instead of appreciating their help the mariners behaved like ingrates, violating the embargo, making accusations about its constitutionality, and complaining that Congress had abused its power. He believed that the source of the problem was a few sanctimonious New Englanders, who after forcing the Constitution on the South in 1787, now tried to "absolve themselves from its sacred obligations." Lloyd called Giles' assertions "hogwash" and retorted that it was not the northern states that had needed help with slaves ("internal enemies") or "enemies on their frontiers, against whom they cannot protect themselves," but the South. To the contrary, the North entered the Union at a disadvantage because of the three-fifths clause. Furthermore, concluded Lloyd, the way that Democratic-Republicans were now interpreting it the Constitution was actually inimical to New England.[33]

Timothy Pickering turned the debate back to the topic of repeal. He estimated that 80 percent of over 140 vessels that sailed out of Boston, Salem, and Beverly, had returned to U.S. ports unharmed. This was evidence that neither France's decrees nor Britain's orders in council had significantly increased the dangers associated with the foreign trade. Reiterating an argument that he publicized through an anti-embargo letter to Massachusetts Governor James Sullivan, Pickering said that insurance prices would have soared if the risk of property loss had increased. Instead, the rates stabilized, confirming underwriters' confidence that merchantmen could traverse the seas safely.[34]

Opponents of repeal remained unconvinced. Giles repeated his charge that the policy would have worked were it not for the malcontents in New England spurred on by Federalists. Pickering sensed that Giles's ire was really directed at him, and replied that no one should be surprised that protests emanated out of Massachusetts. It was the birthplace of the Revolution, the place where Americans first revolted against England, and did so for the same reasons they were now resisting the embargo. Similar to Britain's policies, the embargo was an attempt to end New England's trade "with all parts of the world." Joseph Anderson of Tennessee attacked Pickering directly and claimed that the former secretary of state had singlehandedly eviscerated the embargo before it could take effect. It was his letter to Sullivan that encouraged "immoral, dissolute, and disorderly" New Englanders to break the law. According to Anderson, Pickering completely "destroyed" any chance for the legislation to succeed.[35]

Democratic-Republicans' fixation on what the Federalists had done or were doing diverted attention away from the fact that the embargo had itself created conditions conducive to lawbreaking. To be sure, Federalists undermined the law however and whenever they could, but the embargo deprived foreign markets of U.S. goods, which inflated prices and increased the profitability of smuggling. For example, the prices of West Indian flour, salt, tobacco, and other commodities rose to astonishing levels. Once profits exceeded penalties, smuggling was worth the risk. Merchants from Cape Cod engaged heavily in black-market trading in the West Indies and Canada through Passamaquoddy Bay and vexed the administration in the Lake Champlain region. In addition, ports in Pennsylvania, New York, Baltimore, and seaports south of Maryland were the scenes, though less frequently than in New England, of riots and mob action. Treasury Secretary Albert Gallatin proposed using the military to enforce the embargo, but because Jeffersonians had downsized the army and navy, the government had neither the manpower nor the resources to patrol or police every rebellious port.[36]

Actually, smuggling and rioting were symptoms of a larger problem. Violations increased in New England by the end of 1808 because of the toll that the embargo had taken on people's lives. When it began in December 1807, many in the business community anticipated tightening their belts for only few months. But as early as January 1808, laborers, shopkeepers, mechanics, and merchants saw dramatic decreases in their incomes along with declines in their standard of living. In the next few months shop owners began asking landlords to reduce their rents, and landlords found it difficult to lease vacant properties. New Englanders like Nathaniel Saltonstall Jr., scion of a prominent family from Haverhill and Salem, was forced to migrate southward to find work or establish new businesses. Some, such as former shipmaster John Greene, of the firm David Greene & Son in Boston, lost entire fortunes. Because of the diminished prospects in New England Greene trekked to Washington, DC to obtain a military appointment. At year's end, others found themselves in the same predicament as George Davis of Salem, who could no longer afford to pay for his room and board.[37]

While they tried to support the government's restrictive system without complaining, some of New England's Democratic-Republicans were concerned about the hardships that developed. A few months before Jacob Crowninshield's death in 1808, a constituent told him that over thirty businesses had failed as a result of the embargo. He feared that there would be many more bankruptcies and asked Crowninshield how long the embargo would continue, or if the law might be revised and restrictions "limited to the Belligerents." Another correspondent suggested that the government reopen trade with China, Russia, and other countries that did not violate U.S. sovereignty. He also disliked the fact that foreign merchants were coming into the country to "accumulate immense wealth which otherwise would fall into the hand of Americans." Another frustrated New Englander told Crowninshield that it might help if he could get to share his personal views on commerce with Secretary of State Madison in person.[38]

By December 1808, it had become obvious that Democratic-Republicans had ignored the problems in New England at their peril. To the disappointment of those who thought that Congress would repeal the embargo after one year, except for recycling old arguments, as did the writer "Hancock," who blamed the problem on Federalists and "a fleet of crazy merchant vessels," the pro-embargo majority would not budge.[39] It seemed that nothing could convince Democratic-Republicans to reexamine the policy or its socioeconomic impact. Even former president John Adams was perplexed that Jeffersonians had "taken an untenable position . . . which they are loath to yield."[40] By defeating the Hillhouse motion the Senate let New Englanders know that petitioning them was futile.[41]

As soon as the House began to debate repeal, any hope that New England's representatives might form a bipartisan coalition disappeared. When the time came to respond to the Massachusetts General Court's resolutions, the state's Democratic-Republicans issued a lengthy rebuttal flatly rejecting the request. They rebuked and insulted members of the state government as uninformed and bewildered when it came to foreign affairs. The General Court had provided a comprehensive history of political and diplomatic developments from the time that Napoleon issued his decrees and Britain its Orders in Council, to the *Chesapeake* affair. Nevertheless, Democratic-Republicans refuted the state's arguments point by point and stipulated that neither the *Chesapeake* nor impressments had anything to do with the embargo. The British Orders in Council, they concluded, were the only obstacles to lifting the embargo. If and when Britain revoked its laws commerce would resume.[42] The rebuttal also claimed that the state misrepresented the will of the people and had neither the right nor the authority to advise Congress on the proper course of action. Not only did they find the attempt to influence them humiliating, the indignant congressmen repeated the claim that Madison's election sanctioned the policy. His victory, they added, was their primary reason for rejecting efforts to repeal the embargo.[43]

All but two of Massachusetts's Democratic-Republican representatives signed the document. Neither Joseph Story nor John Chandler was available to endorse the rejoinder nor did either run for reelection. Of those who did sign, Josiah Dean, Daniel Ilsley, and Isaiah Green had already lost their seats to Federalists in the recent election, and Joseph Barker resigned. The signatories were therefore well aware, or would be, that voters had just rejected them because of the embargo, and those who were reelected won by slim margins.[44] At any rate, in spite of the bravado displayed in their refusal to comply with their state governments' wishes, it was soon apparent that these same representatives also knew that they needed to advocate repeal or lose whatever support they still had in New England.[45]

On November 16 Orchard Cook submitted a proposal containing provisions to repeal the embargo and replace it with a nonintercourse act that only prohibited trade with France and Britain. Cook's bill also included the use of armed merchant vessels to protect American ships from any "French and British cruisers, who may molest them" as they traded with other nations. The next day Federalist Edward St. Loe Livermore, who had made an unsuccessful motion for repeal during the previous session, presented petitions with over five thousand signatures, representing several Massachusetts towns "praying for a repeal of the embargo laws."[46] It finally seemed that New England's Federalists and Democratic-Republicans were on the same page, but as events would bear out they were not necessarily on the same side.

The House Committee on Foreign Relations considered the Massachusetts petitions and recommended continuing the embargo. The committee also rejected Cook's motion, concluding that arming merchant vessels would precipitate war with both France and Britain, and the implementation a policy of nonintercourse would lead to war with at least one of those nations. Nonintercourse was particularly unacceptable to Democratic-Republicans who felt that Great Britain might somehow profit directly or indirectly. A sectional disagreement then surfaced among Jeffersonians following New Yorker Gurdon Mumford's expression of doubts that a war would result from nonintercourse, followed by his assurance that armed conflict would have national support if it took place because Congress lifted the embargo. Instead of fearing the unknown or being concerned with whether France or Britain might profit, he admonished the House to concentrate on relieving the suffering taking place inside of the U.S. The president had sent fifty ships to Cuba, and all fifty had returned fully loaded and unharmed. Therefore, calculated Mumford, it was safe to reopen ports not compromised by the European conflict. This included Haiti, which he reminded the House had once accounted for half of the revenue that the country earned from the French West Indian trade.[47]

A few other New Yorkers defended commerce as indigenous to their region and necessary for their survival and cultural identity. "Commerce is blended with our customs and manners and is our right," observed Josiah Masters. He asked, can "industry, can wealth, can civilization, increase among the great bulk of the people without commerce?" Congress had to repeal the embargo because it stirred sectionalism, threatened national unity and, along with other "ill-timed measures," was driving "citizens to madness." Voters would reject another Democratic-Republican administration if Madison allowed Jefferson's policies to continue. The restrictive system had already forced merchants to submit to "insults, aggressions, and indignities," while the federal government did nothing but issue proclamations. When Masters finished, the Speaker of the House had to repeatedly call James Elliot of Vermont to order because he was shouting regrets about previously voting to implement any of the Democratic-Republicans' restrictive policies.[48]

In private correspondence with John Quincy Adams, Massachusetts' Democratic-Republicans began planning their retreat from the embargo. John Chandler worried that the administration had not adequately responded to Federalist charges pertaining to the real motives for the policy. In a letter to Richard Cutts he advocated devising a strategy "to counteract the exertions of the Federal members in Congress," who were "effecting considerable change in the mind of the people in spite of every exertion to prevent it."[49]

Adams, who had severed ties with Federalists over restricting commerce, also lost confidence that the policy could work, and suggested replacing it with nonintercourse. He figured that merchants would ultimately vindicate the administration by breaking the law and exposing themselves to French and British attacks anyway.[50] Cook, Bacon, Story, and Bidwell then put the administration and their party's southern leadership on notice that they would not support the embargo after Madison's inauguration. Similar statements came from various New York, New Jersey, and Maryland representatives. Given this turnabout Democratic-Republicans could have joined Federalists, or taken the initiative themselves to repeal the embargo as early as January 1, 1809. However, one of the problems was that their southern colleagues were not ready to admit the policy's failure. As a result, northern Jeffersonians decided to hold out until March.[51]

As Federalists continued to motion for immediate repeal, Josiah Quincy assailed southerners for promoting a perpetual embargo. Southern agriculturalists, he complained, only sacrificed surplus produce, but New Englanders were losing everything and being forced to choose between bankruptcy and violating a law that deprived them of their basic right to earn a living. Quincy invited embargo supporters to locate the page in the Constitution that gave Congress authority to lay a permanent embargo. He said they would not find that provision because the judiciary, not the Constitution, had granted that power. He then added that legislation as catastrophic as the embargo should have "no flaw" in its foundation or be based on exceptionally broad interpretations of the Constitution. His state had been the "cradle of liberty," but an unending embargo "was never cradled in Massachusetts."[52]

Ezekiel Bacon, a member of the Foreign Relations Committee and one of the Jeffersonians combating the embargo from behind the scenes, contradicted Quincy. Bacon claimed to have personally witnessed "much occupation and pretty general employment of some sort or other" in Massachusetts. Trouble only surfaced when Federalists like Quincy stirred it up. Bacon then challenged Quincy "and his friends" to come up with a better policy or stop criticizing the legislation Congress had already adopted. Of course Bacon discounted the fact that for some time Federalists had been calling for repeal, relaxation of the law, or partial repeal with nonintercourse with the belligerents (France and Britain). But as Chandler admitted, if Democratic-Republicans did not control repealing the unpopular law, Federalists would "take credit of it themselves" and then brag that repeal resulted from their "spirited and patriotic conduct."[53]

At the same time that partisans swapped insults in the House, Senate leaders were busy drafting another supplement that would intensify enforcement. The House majority delayed a vote on repeal to give the Senate time to draft and vote on their newest enforcement bill. Congressmen rambled on so excessively that the House stenographer sometimes only recorded the length of time that a particular representative spoke.[54] It became obvious that the House would not take a final vote on repeal before the enforcement bill arrived. Giles introduced the bill in the Senate just six days after defeating Hillhouse's motion for repeal. He was chair of the Senate's Foreign Relations Committee and sought advice from Treasury Secretary Gallatin on devising more effective ways to enforce the embargo. Gallatin proposed policies so imperious even he feared that they would alienate much of the country. Making only minor changes to Gallatin's original proposal, Giles's presented a bill outlining the most stringent enforcement measures to date.[55]

A major problem the administration sought to address was local courts' inability or unwillingness to uphold the embargo. In Massachusetts judges adjudicated cases involving property (i.e., vessels and cargo seized by customs agents), while juries usually decided proceedings against individual merchants and ship owners. Acquittals outpaced convictions in both venues, but judges decided in the government's favor and enforced the embargo more often than juries. Merchants also circumvented the law by challenging customs officials in court.[56] This form of legal intimidation, which first became popular in Massachusetts, obliged the government on several occasions to find replacements for beleaguered collectors—a difficult task in areas where armed mobs repeatedly harassed government agents. Collector Joseph Otis of Barnstable, for instance, was the defendant in at least three court cases and the Jefferson administration even found it difficult to convince district attorneys to argue cases on the government's behalf.[57]

Under the new act, plaintiffs in such cases were required to pay fees up to triple the amount of court costs if a case was decided in a collector's favor. To assist agents in the execution of their duties and to suppress mobs and rioters, the law gave the president authority to unilaterally take control of and deploy state militia. Jefferson no longer needed to issue a declaration of insurrection, a lesson learned in the Lake Champlain region of Vermont, after militia arrived too late to catch lawbreakers.[58] The enhanced embargo also gave the president discretionary powers that allowed him to override anti-embargo governors and direct the prosecution of related court cases.[59]

Jefferson and Gallatin were shocked by the growth of "fraud & open opposition by force" taking place in various seaport locales, so they augmented certain restrictions to curtail smuggling.[60] The law increased bonds on coasting vessels to six times the value of a ship and its cargo. Violators risked losing their vessels, could be fined quadruple the value of cargo, and forfeited any bonds that they paid at the beginning of a voyage. Bonds alone could run into tens of thousands. To keep Americans from interacting with foreign ships waiting just outside U.S. waters, or traveling to black-market emporiums in the Caribbean, the new policy reduced the time period that coastal vessels would have to complete voyages. Finally, to gather better intelligence on smugglers or potential smugglers, the law increased informants' pay to half the amount of the government's fines, which could also add up to thousands.[61]

These were some of the more contentious provisions in the final supplement known as the Enforcement or Force Act, which skated on the edges of the Constitution and blurred the lines between federal and state authority. During debates over these stringent provisions James Lloyd noted that the commerce clause in Article I, section 8, gave Congress the power to regulate international and interstate commerce. But the new act interfered with trade within a state, which Federalists decried as unconstitutional. He estimated that a Massachusetts ship owner would need to pay a bond of fifteen thousand dollars to transport lumber to Maine, which was in the same state. Intrastate trade was not stipulated in any category of commerce under congressional authority in the Constitution. Lloyd said that the government had so grossly overreached its authority in the Enforcement Act he doubted that the administration could find a judge to prosecute lawbreakers or uphold the legislation.[62]

Pickering asked fellow senators to consider whether obtaining better or even perfect enforcement of the embargo would be good for the country or "promote the public welfare." Far from being "a wild and intemperate performance filled with slanderous reproaches," as described in one study, Pickering's speech was an appeal to cool heads and sound judgment.[63] He cited a recent record of safe voyages to demonstrate that commerce would not be "swept from the ocean" by lifting the embargo. Majority leaders should consider "the situation as it really is," devoid of imagined dangers. Unfortunately, the Senate majority was not open to any option that Pickering outlined and Giles said he wished he could do something, but New England's problems were "among the least" of all those facing the nation. Giles's supplement passed the Senate 20–7.[64]

The bill's rapid progress through the Senate stymied Federalists such as Pickering who was chagrined that "just and reasonable claims" were blindly and quickly "defeated." He and others also regretted that the majority would successfully push the bill through both houses with as little debate as possible.[65] When Giles' bill reached the House, Virginian Thomas Newton motioned to move it out of the Committee of the Whole so that the "amendments wished by its friends" could be made without interruption. Frazzled by the maneuver, James Sloan, a Democratic-Republican from New Jersey, completing his final term in Congress, commented cynically, "If a majority of the House is determined to keep the people in their present state of suffering [in] suspense until spring, the least they can do during the dreary scenes of winter, will be to continue diverting them with eloquent speeches, of all sorts and sizes, from fifteen minutes to four hours long."[66]

As Sloan suggested, embargo supporters did engage in verbose oration. That is, until a Democratic-Republican proposed ending U.S. participation in the British license trade and calling all vessels back to the United States. The license trade required neutral traders to pay a fee and obtain a license before conducting business in specified European ports. Bacon, who on more than one occasion proclaimed that the embargo was not a financial burden on the people of his state, was the first to object. He disliked waiting for every vessel to come home because that would extend the embargo longer "than he wished to contemplate." Joseph Story concurred. It could take at least eighteen months for ships that had sailed beyond the Cape of Good Hope to return to the United States and the public would think that the embargo was going to last at least that much longer. Story had no problem ending the license trade but could not sanction another year and a half of the embargo. Other Democratic-Republicans agreed with Bacon and Story, and Sloan said he was so sick of the policy he would reject any future legislation connected with it.[67]

Despondent over the squabbling, Virginian John Wayles Eppes attacked Federalists, particularly Pickering, for disseminating false information about the economic damage and duration of the embargo. Quincy shot back, that if the embargo had a date of expiration, not even Democratic-Republicans would renew it for another year; but the law had no expiration date, so neither Pickering nor any other Federalist had lied. He then added that the nation's biggest problem was that northern Jeffersonians were spineless sycophants. Several of them wanted to repeal the embargo, but not one of them would oppose the president or Senate majority. What they would do, he predicted correctly, was support the enforcement bill despite the consequences.[68]

Jackson demanded that Quincy name the men to whom he was referring. Quincy, not about to be sucked into a duel, paused to reply that those men know who they are, and then continued to rail against the Federalists' opponents who could not stand "to hear the truth elucidated." Jackson objected again; Quincy's disorder had gone on too long. Then, in a move that probably surprised everyone, Speaker Joseph Varnum, Democratic-Republican from Massachusetts, told Jackson "to put down in writing the words to which he objected." At that point Jackson begged off and Varnum ruled that everyone had taken latitude; but "excluding personal matter," Quincy was certainly "in order" and could resume his response to Eppes.[69]

It was perhaps part of an effort to repair their damaged images back home that compelled New England's Democratic-Republicans to challenge their southern colleagues. In response to accusations that evasions of the embargo occurred exclusively in Massachusetts, Varnum replied that Americans from every part of the Union violated the law. Even the hardliner Bacon inserted calls for partial repeal into the debate on several occasions. But their bravura was temporary. When the time came to cast a final vote on the bill that became the Enforcement Act, most fell into line and voted to pass the measure while Federalists voted to defeat it. A few northern Jeffersonians, like Orchard Cook, did not cast a favorable vote, but neither did they vote against Giles's bill. On January 6, 1809, the measure passed the House by thirty-nine votes.[70]

When the Enforcement or Force Act went into effect, the reaction in New England was predictable and swift. In one Massachusetts town after another, citizens formally rejected federal authority. The town of Newburyport resolved that anyone helping to enforce the embargo violated the Constitution. Over two hundred townsmen formed the "Silver Greys," an armed group that vowed to oppose enforcement agents and detain any ships that attempted to sail via a government permit. The town had been battling trade restrictions for a while, and on several occasions armed mobs kept customs agents from enforcing the embargo. After a year of failed petitions and the federal government's indifference, explains Benjamin W. Labaree in his study of Newburyport, residents' "patience snapped." Prior to passage of the Enforcement Act, the town merely wanted the federal government to repeal the embargo; now they saw themselves combating a hostile administration waging war on their community. The only constitutional authority Newburyporters now acknowledged was their state government.[71]

The scene was similar in western Massachusetts. Beneath the illustration of a coffin the *Hampshire Gazette* denounced the Enforcement Act as the end of civil liberties, which only the "rising Sun of Federalism" could restore. Hampshire County's citizens met at the courthouse in Northampton and drafted resolutions similar to the Newburyport declarations. Attendees at the meeting denounced the law's provision allowing the president to deploy militias without state authority. The county then unanimously supported resolutions that condemned the Enforcement Act, renounced the federal government, and threw their full support behind the Massachusetts legislature.[72]

In the Maine districts of Massachusetts, where voters clung to Democratic-Republicanism more tenaciously than their downstate neighbors, a few municipalities also rejected federal authority. The anti-embargo residents of Bath passed a declaration citing "oppression and arbitrary laws" as the source of their "suffering and calamity." Portlanders repudiated the embargo as unconstitutional and denounced the Enforcement Act as legalized oppression. In a move reminiscent of Revolutionary Era organization, Portland called for the creation of a "Committee of Public Safety" to devise a plan to protect the city's merchants from callous treatment at the hands of government agents. Several towns ousted Democratic-

Republican selectmen (members of a board chosen annually to manage community affairs), and other local officials from office.[73] In the event that the General Court's overtures to the federal government were unsuccessful, these New Englanders were preparing to fight the U.S. military and even neighbors who might try to enforce the embargo.

Calls for disunion began to appear in print and in speeches with more frequency. According to newspaper headlines, "dissolution of the Union" was imminent. A Boston *Repertory* writer considered secession a last resort, but forewarned politicians who continued to deny the hardships in New England caused by the embargo, that they were making the same "fatal mistake" that the British made before the Revolution. If Congress refused to repeal the embargo and continued to ignore their resolutions and petitions, it bore sole responsibility for the consequences.[74]

John Lowell, writing under the pseudonym "A Yankee Farmer," argued that New Englanders were under attack because they were a *"commercial people"* and did not have "one million slaves to labor for their support." Other Federalists concurred, and reiterated that southerners in Congress were destroying commerce and trying to divert public attention away from their assault on New England. They also charged Democratic-Republicans with instigating a war with Britain instead of negotiating because reaching a "settlement of our differences with England would have benefited commerce." It was up to Americans "Whose farms are on the Ocean and whose Harvests are gathered in every sea" to take action. New Englanders could not passively allow agriculturalists to destroy commerce, for "with your commerce goes your freedom."[75]

By secretively arranging to leave the embargo in place until Madison's inauguration while openly supporting the Enforcement Act, northern Democratic-Republicans exacerbated an already volatile situation. Aggravating New Englanders who were already antagonistic toward the federal government and feeling betrayed by their own representatives was a political disaster. Federalists appeared to be the only representatives defending New England's interests in Washington. "In the present Congress, this state is represented by six federalists and eleven Tories. In the Congress elected, we have ten federalists, but seven Tories. We believe sincerely a general election at this time, would not leave a spot [of Jeffersonianism] in the character of our state," reported the *Newburyport Herald*. New England's "apostate representatives," as Harrison Gray Otis called them, were entirely responsible for the recent catastrophe.[76]

The unrest that erupted had a chilling effect on New Englanders in Congress who either supported the Enforcement Act or failed to oppose it. From his seat in the House of Representatives, Massachusetts Federalist Samuel Taggart provided vivid descriptions of the effect that grassroots activism and protests had on several of his state's Democratic-Republicans. Bacon displayed "considerable shrinking and shivering" from a nervousness that seemed uncontrollable and annoying to other members of his party. One of Taggart's favorite Jeffersonians, Orchard Cook, looked worried and appeared confused over what he should do next. Support for the embargo may have caused Joseph Barker to become ill and miss several sessions, while Daniel Ilsley looked taken aback by all of the commotion. Speaker Varnum, who recently refused to side with a southerner against Quincy, seemed "full of fear and trembling."[77]

Relations between New Englanders and the federal government deteriorated further after the Massachusetts General Court declared the Enforcement Act "unjust, oppressive and unconstitutional" and therefore "not legally binding on the citizens" of Massachusetts. By February 1809 Governor Sullivan had been dead for over a month and Lieutenant Governor Levi Lincoln, in cooperation with the Jefferson administration, activated militia to enforce the law. Instead of using the legal rosters, Lincoln handpicked officers loyal to the administration. The General Court criticized Lincoln's conduct and announced that the Enforcement Act violated Massachusetts' constitution by giving the federal government authority over the state's militia—a power reserved for the governor. Democratic-Republicans feared that those following the Federalists' lead might spill blood, even if they could not convince the New England states to secede.[78]

Connecticut's state government rejected the entire embargo along with the Enforcement Act. That body deemed provisions under the original embargo and every supplement "oppressive, arbitrary, and unconstitutional." The state also found it inconsistent that the majority in Congress assumed that the constitutional authority to regulate commerce "implies [the] power to *annihilate* it." Even though Connecticut refused to cooperate with enforcement, state leaders sought to avert violence by seeking "none but constitutional relief" from the throes of the embargo. Rhode Island's militiamen refused to enforce the embargo, and the town of Providence petitioned the state government to find some way to repeal the "oppressive restraints upon our trade."[79] In the midst of the region's state governments nullifying or refusing to enforce a federal law, Massachusetts resolved to establish a confederation of New England states authorized Harrison Gray Otis and Timothy Bigelow, leading officers of the state senate and house respectively, to invite representatives from New England's commercial states to a convention in Hartford, Connecticut, which Otis had suggested in 1808.[80]

Democratic-Republicans needed to avoid a proliferation of nullification resolutions and possible armed conflict between the government and rioters or paramilitary groups. To diffuse a menacing situation quickly, less than a month after the Enforcement Act went into effect, news that Congress was about to repeal the embargo began to circulate. Interestingly, the previous November William Eustis condescendingly related his amusement upon hearing "rumors of repeal," but now he along with others welcomed the scuttlebutt as lifesaving. Then, on February 8, 1809,

Giles, one of the embargo's staunchest proponents in the Senate and sponsor of the Enforcement Act, submitted a motion for partial repeal. He proposed lifting the embargo and replacing it with nonintercourse, just as Federalists had been recommending for months. When Giles presented his bill in its entirety however, it differed in key areas from the legislation previously advocated by Federalists. As worded, the Giles bill presented repeal as a precursor to war with Great Britain.[81]

Hillhouse and Lloyd objected. Lifting the embargo should encourage the preservation of peace and inform the belligerents that the United States would pursue a more "rigorous course of conduct" should they refuse to rescind their orders and decrees. Instead, Giles drafted a scenario for repeal that anticipated war as the inevitable consequence of lifting the embargo. Another problem that Federalists had with the bellicose spirit of Giles's bill was that Congress had slashed military appropriations, reduced the naval fleet, and done little to strengthen coastal fortifications. Hence, the nation was not prepared to fight one of the world's most powerful empires. But, the Senate ignored Lloyd's warning that instigating a war without a "rational prospect of success" was hazardous. On February 21, the Senate passed Giles's bill 21–12.[82]

In the House, neither Federalists nor Democratic-Republicans were eager to sanction repeal as a prelude to war. Varnum was convinced that France and Britain would pull the U.S. into their war no matter how hard Congress tried to avoid it. Still, he agreed that full repeal should precede nonintercourse, which the House needed to consider as a separate bill. Cook supported repeal and continued to propose arming commercial vessels if Congress wanted to save the Union and "reunite a divided people." This time his motion for armed protection of commerce failed by only five votes (50–45).[83]

Federalists wanted to repeal the law without caveats, and insisted that the embargo would be unenforceable after Madison's inauguration anyway. Quincy pressed disunion as the consequence should the legislation spark an Anglo-American war. He motioned that the House print and distribute a Massachusetts memorial declaring the embargo unconstitutional. Newton of Virginia objected on the grounds that the resolutions were hypocritical. He pointed out that in 1798 when the Virginia Resolutions challenged the Federalists' Alien and Sedition Acts, the Massachusetts legislature issued a proclamation stating that no state had the right to declare federal laws unconstitutional. He aimed to "show how the sentiments of a Federal Legislature then were warped . . . to answer party purposes." If Quincy's motion passed, Newton threatened to juxtapose the contradicting resolutions to show Massachusetts "castigating" itself. Ezekiel Bacon joined the dispute to brandish his protean loyalties and oppose Quincy's motion "without the least fear of being accused of disrespect for the state that he represented." Bacon insisted again that only a limited number of people in his state agreed with the legislature's efforts to repeal the embargo. Quincy pressed the issue because the "memorial contained the opinion of a large commercial state," but his motion was defeated.[84]

Newton's reference to Massachusetts's inconsistency is important because it speaks to changes in the Federalists' political philosophy and constitutionalism. A strong sense of order and the need for federal supremacy compelled Federalists to promote ratification, even with its controversial provisions safeguarding slavery. Federalists now embraced the idea that the Constitution was a conditional compact among independent sovereign states. Entering this agreement gave states the right to "interpose" themselves between the people and the federal government. Based on their newly adopted interpretation of state powers, whenever it deemed a federal statute in violation of the compact, a state retained the right to nullify that law, which was not an act of treason. The General Court had publically rejected the Kentucky and Virginia Resolutions but was now adopting the same theoretical justification for nullifying the Enforcement Act. During the debates over reading his state's resolutions, Livermore explained that Massachusetts "only supported the rights of the States, strengthening instead of weakening" the Union by "preserving a part in its proper operation." It was also out of character for Federalists to portray the central government as a hostile entity in order to condone disunion. Though they were cautious to not overtly sanction violence, Federalists no longer responded to civil disorder with the same foreboding that they conveyed after Shays Rebellion (1786–1787).[85]

Yet, the Federalist Party was essentially confined to New England where protests over the embargo sometimes turned violent. Democratic-Republican officials in the Mid-Atlantic and Upper South worked hard to avoid similar riots in their seacoast towns. To keep large gatherings from turning into nasty mobs, local political leaders maintained the peace by promising to give unemployed mariners financial assistance. In Philadelphia, Baltimore, and New York, where large crowds grew potentially dangerous, for example in response to provocations such as the deaths of Americans when the *Chesapeake* was attacked, officials were on hand to sympathize with would-be rioters. Historian Paul Gilje explains that mayors and other city officials collaborated with newspapers to calm potentially violent assemblies of mariners. When one Philadelphia mayor could not prevent a mass meeting from taking place, he decided to talk to the unemployed sailors and listen to their complaints. After the discussion he made "vague promise[s] of assistance" and "the crowd peacefully dispersed."[86]

Placating distraught seamen was a way that shrewd politicians avoided the violent outbursts that were commonplace in New England.[87] In some Mid-Atlantic and southern seaport towns, mariners took out their anger on foreigners. Foreign crews—especially if they were British and had engaged in impressments or taken some other action against

Americans—were frequently the recipients of violence. Attacks occurred in Virginia and Charleston, South Carolina, as revenge for the *Chesapeake*, and New Yorkers responded violently after the British ship *Leander* fired on a U.S. vessel and killed a sailor in the city's harbor.[88] Not only did mob action against the British steer anger away from the federal government, it also alienated New England's protesters from the rest of the nation.

As repeal drew closer, southerners still denied that the embargo caused anyone financial hardships and argued that war was the inevitable consequence of repeal. Northern representatives from both parties supported repeal, but as the House prepared to vote on Giles's bill, a few Jeffersonians were apprehensive. Cook called the measure the better "choice of evils" but refrained from voting. Story left Washington before the final vote was taken, and Sloan admitted that he was about to vote for a bill that he disliked, primarily because he was sick of the embargo. Once the embargo was repealed, Sloan said he prayed that "it would be *dead, dead, dead*," and never resurrected. The bill's flaws did not burden Federalists with indecision, however. They opposed language predicting an Anglo-American war and voted against the bill. As usual, Democratic-Republicans fell in line and the House passed Giles's partial repeal 81–40, on February 27.[89]

Congress had acted in time to calm the unrest in New England, and on March 1, 1809, Jefferson hesitatingly signed the bill.[90] As soon as the embargo was lifted, New Englanders began taking to the seas to recover whatever they could after more than two years of commercial restrictions. The embargo had thrown thousands in the maritime industry out of work and it would not be easy to rebuild commercial economies, or for some Americans to reconstruct their lives. Trade with England and France was banned, and slavery was still protected through an extended prohibition on the Haitian trade. Nevertheless, for most mariners, partial repeal was better than no engagement in commerce at all. The crisis was over for now, and scores of brigs, schooners, and other seaworthy vessels cleared for voyages to Indonesia, the Baltic, China, the Mediterranean, the Azores, the West Indies, Portugal, and other ports.[91]

Repeal coincided with Jefferson's retirement from the presidency. For the most part, New Englanders seemed happy that both were out of their lives, and the feeling was mutual. During the remainder of his life, Jefferson defended the embargo and vilified Massachusetts Federalists and a few of that state's Democratic-Republicans for undoing his policy. Over time, writes one biographer, "Jefferson transferred the blame of failure from himself and his policy to the party that opposed both."[92]

In his final annual message to Congress Jefferson planned to extol the growth of manufacturing to justify nearly eviscerating New England's maritime economy. Gallatin asked the president to reconsider. As written, the speech would substantiate every accusation that the Federalists made against his administration and surely win them more converts in New England. Jefferson edited his address and only briefly mentioned that the suspension of commerce had promoted the redistribution of capital into "manufactures and improvements," a change he welcomed as permanent.[93]

Curiously, Democratic-Republicans usually receive credit for lifting the embargo and in some instances scholars laud Story and Bacon for their backroom maneuverings but malign Federalists for contributing to the same effort publically. At the time that Congress repealed the embargo, Story, whom Jefferson called a "pseudo-Republican," was more than happy to take credit for engineering repeal.[94] Naturally, many studies omit the fact that northern Jeffersonians could and should have supported repeal by late 1808 to avoid the riots, nullification resolutions, and disunionism that threatened national unity. Indeed, for the most part, historical accounts depicting Federalists as unreliable, insular obstructionists with a dim view of humanity are merely repeating the Democratic-Republicans' descriptions of their political opponents. Opposition to the embargo became a major criticism against Federalists in the years leading to the War of 1812.[95] Yet since Jefferson and his party had personal axes to grind, controversial policies to justify, and political careers to salvage, perhaps this interpretation is worth revisiting and revising. But the question of whether or not it is unfair to suggest that Democratic-Republicans bear a lion's share of responsibility for the crisis of 1808–1809 should also be discussed.

Federalists certainly fanned the flames of sectionalism, yet Jeffersonians formed the congressional majority and could pass or repeal legislation with or without Federalist votes. In addition, some Democratic-Republicans steadily provided hostile rhetoric and articulated insensitive rationales for the controversial legislation. Each week, mariners and others waylaid by the embargo read newspapers full of insults that southerners such as Randolph and Eppes of Virginia, Williams of South Carolina, and others regularly hurled at New Englanders and their constituents during congressional debates.[96] As a response, disunionism became a palatable option.

Partisan papers were not above exaggerating or parsing the opposing party's statements, but embargo supporters suggested more than once that disgruntled mariners needed to stop whining and "take to the spade." A few held those engaged in foreign trade responsible for the "eternal quarrels with foreign nations" that precipitated the crisis and proposed abolishing New England's maritime culture altogether.[97] Because these views were available in print, Federalists had little trouble validating their accusation that southerners, beginning with the president, were opposed to commerce. Indeed, they could explain that southerners consistently attacked the wartime carrying trade because it thrived independently of the South's agriculture.

It is also useful to look at whether Federalists opposed the embargo and other commercial restrictions to stifle industrialization and economic progress. Historians have often considered the growth of large-scale manufacturing in New England a positive by-product of the embargo. They argue that transforming the region's economy from its maritime focus to manufacturing helped to bring New England and the rest of the nation into the industrial revolution and the modern age. On the other side of this interpretation is the assertion that Federalists had developed an aversion to manufacturing, which after 1800 was a sign of the retrograde conservatism that drove their opposition to the embargo.[98]

It was really no secret that restricting overseas trade and the importation of manufactured goods would generate domestic manufacturing. When rumors circulated that the Nonimportation Act would achieve this end, one opponent of the policy predicted that investors would withdraw funds from commerce and invest in manufacturing, but "It is hardly contended that" the policy was "brought forward for that purpose." Sarah Thatcher, wife of Massachusetts Congressman George Thatcher, said that Jefferson would make a "prudent housewife but I very much doubt his political economy" if he was sacrificing commerce "to raise the value of our own manufactures." She considered this course of action unwise because the duties on imports helped to support the federal government. In fact, when confronted with manufacturing as a possible motive for restricting commerce, embargo supporters denied that industrialization had anything to do with it. Hillhouse once hinted that the embargo was laid to assist the agriculture and manufacturing interests at the expense of the maritime industry. Kentuckian John Pope refuted that notion and replied that the Jefferson administration was too interested in paying down the national debt "to pursue a system which cuts off our only source of revenue." Hillhouse's "conjecture" was just "too improbable to require serious refutation" concluded Pope.[99]

If the Jefferson administration restricted trade to surreptitiously bolster manufacturing, the Federalists' opposition was justified and not merely a conservative opposition to change. Destroying commerce to achieve an unstated end would more than justify the Federalists' actions. However, the proponents of the restrictive system always insisted that nonimportation, the embargo, and other measures were enacted to protect commerce. Like Pope, most Democratic-Republicans denied even casual suggestions that their legislation served any other purpose.[100]

Federalists explained regularly that they opposed the restrictive system to preserve their region's political and economic freedom.[101] It is true that under Washington and Adams, Federalists fought protective tariffs on British imports and stifled the growth of manufacturing in New England. Yet since the early eighteenth century maritime pursuits dominated the region's economy and provided a large share of the nation's revenue from tonnage, the fishing fleet, and the coasting trade. In most cases the public works, improvements, and manufacturing that did exist came about because of maritime commerce.[102]

Right or wrong, when the restrictive system began Federalists argued that New England's maritime culture had developed organically, but they never reached a consensus that manufacturing was undesirable. Their literature and speeches largely forecasted calamity for all of the major economic interests—including agriculture and manufacturing—should commerce be destroyed. What they undeniably feared most was that the agrarian South would benefit after destroying commerce "at the point of a bayonet," as Newburyporters feared.[103]

There was much to protest. Wealthy merchants were not the only ones affected by the embargo. Business owners without large amounts of capital to reinvest in manufacturing ventures or large tracts of land were among those most vulnerable to financial ruin due to trade restrictions. Shipbuilders, chain smiths, and anchor shops were a few of the small-scale manufacturers facing what might be permanent economic ruin. In fact, the Beverly Cotton Manufactory, founded by the Federalist Cabot family, had to shut down during the embargo.[104]

Thomas Jefferson had certainly amended the philosophy he espoused, which depicted yeoman farmers as the "chosen people of God." By the time that he imposed the embargo, domestic manufacturing had become essential to Jefferson's vision of a self-contained economy weaned from its dependency on British goods.[105] Once peace in Europe and amicable trade relations with France and Britain resumed, Federalists realized that southerners would prosper from exporting agricultural staples to foreign markets and the burgeoning manufacturing establishments in the North. Jefferson definitely understood the potential benefits of a national economy built upon northern manufacturing, southern agriculture, and westward expansion, even though his supporters in Congress denied these as motives for their restrictive system.[106]

With Britain's manufacturing monopoly broken, southerners stood to reap the greatest benefits from the development of large-scale factories in the North. These industries would require raw materials that would be readily available from domestic providers.[107] Madison shared this vision of an interdependent, intersectional economy. In the aftermath of trade restrictions under Jefferson and then Madison because of the War of 1812, New England's old commercial economy was irreparable. Understanding the changes wrought by the restrictive system and war related embargoes, Madison confirmed that the only "profitable intercourse for New England . . . lies through the Wheat, the Cotton & the Tobacco fields, of her Southern & Western confederates."[108]

Federalist fears that commercial restrictions would lead to economic dependency on the Slave South were not farfetched. It was for this reason that they combined the fight to repeal the three-fifths clause along with their opposition to commercial restrictions. In the short run they lost both fights. Based on one estimate, the number of cotton mills in the nation grew from 15 to 85 between 1808 and 1809, and small factories sprang up throughout New England.[109]

After the War of 1812, foreign and domestic markets for cotton facilitated the expansion of slavery, and in conjunction, the three-fifths clause disproportionately increased the South's influence in national politics. By the 1840s the United States led the world in the use of slave labor and the production and export of cotton. Within two decades southern states would provide the global economy with 80 percent of its cotton and eventually become the major supplier of cotton for foreign manufacturers and New England factories.[110] New England had been forced through legislative engineering to relinquish its maritime economy for this to take place.

Both Jefferson and Madison knew that it was possible to achieve economic reforms and objectives that favored agriculture through trade restrictions. Shortly after leaving office, Jefferson suggested to Madison that the spread of manufacturing was a valid "reason to check imports." Uniting the older regions of the nation with the expanding west was likely one of the reasons that both Virginians wavered over ending slavery after the War of 1812.[111] If either ever encouraged emancipation, judging from correspondence with Edward Coles, they had abandoned such high ideals.

The young Virginian Edward Coles lived near Jefferson and was one of Madison's in-laws as well as his private secretary. In 1814 Coles informed Jefferson that he had decided to free his slaves and asked for advice on how to proceed. After explaining that he was himself too old and the business of freeing slaves was for "for the young," Jefferson said that freed persons were "pests in society by their idleness and depredations" and that racial amalgamation produced "degradation . . . to which no lover of his country . . . [can] innocently consent." He then advised Coles not to free his slaves. Coles responded that he never considered age "an obstacle to the undertaking." In fact, Benjamin Franklin, "to whom by the way, Pennsylvania owes her early riddance of the evils of slavery, was as actively and as usefully employed" in the effort to end slavery "after he had passed your age" replied Coles. Coles did manumit his slaves in 1819. He took them to Illinois, which as part of the territory organized under the Northwest Ordinance of 1787 entered the Union as a free state. Madison expressed similar sentiments and informed Coles that freed persons "instead of deriving advantage from the partial benevolence of their masters, furnish arguments against the general efforts in their behalf." He said it would have been much better if Coles could change "their color as well as their legal condition [because] . . . without this they seem destined to a privation" and a type of freedom that had little value.[112]

Neither Jefferson nor Madison lived long enough to reap the benefits of owning slaves in the cotton belt nor did they endorse abolition. Moreover, westward expansion and other developments during their presidencies ensured that slavery was not about to end. It was therefore reasonable for New Englanders who opposed slavery for any number of reasons and in varying degrees, to resist becoming economically dependent on the Slave South. Indeed, the expansion of slavery prompted Vermonter James Elliot to caution northerners in 1805, that the free states of the North were losing political ground to the Slave South.[113]

After the embargo was repealed, according to one historian, Federalists "having been so long an opposition party," looked for something else to protest instead of celebrating.[114] However, instead of crediting Democratic-Republicans with ending the embargo, New Englanders expressed their appreciation to Federalists for their efforts. At public celebrations, crowds revered Timothy Pickering, James Lloyd, Josiah Quincy, and others in Congress who helped to defeat the embargo. Writers immortalized them in poetry and song, towns held dinners and receptions in their honor, and local officials praised "the minority in Congress" for their "manly eloquence and sound reasoning in defense of correct principles." In most cases, the honorees were present to celebrate with their supporters.[115]

Of course, due to partisanship and pro-southern sentiment, opposition to the embargo was never unanimous in New England. For opposing commercial restrictions and raising the specter of disunion, Jeffersonians condemned Federalists as traitors. The *National Aegis* assured readers that despite riots in Newburyport and Bath, there would never be a civil war because Federalists could not incite disunion statewide.[116] For example, William Gray of Salem, Massachusetts, who was possibly the wealthiest man in America at the time, ended his association with the Federalist Party and like John Quincy Adams, supported the embargo.[117] Hence, the same way that opponents of the embargo praised the likes of Pickering and Quincy, pro-embargo New Englanders such as "A Democratic-Republican of Massachusetts" cheered the loyalties of Adams and Gray while extolling the embargo.[118]

Another important point involves whether or not Federalists could have successfully orchestrated disunion. Most historians recognize the seriousness of the threat and admit that northern secession was more likely to occur between 1808 and 1809 than at any other time. Had Congress failed to repeal the embargo, some Federalists were brash enough to put a plan into action. As their past actions revealed Pickering and Hillhouse were predisposed to creating a northern confederacy.[119]

Democratic-Republicans certainly feared that New England might be permanently alienated or severed from the rest of the nation. They spoke of the Federalists' "Hellish disposition . . . to pave the way for a separation of the states" even though they doubted that such schemes could ever succeed. Pickering had already devised a plan for secession and Quincy regularly waved the flag of disunion in Congress. Planning this involved governors, state legislatures, and a great deal of public support before even one state would formally secede. This did not mean that it was impossible or improbable for maritime New England states by late 1808. As it turned out, however, just as the colonies took their time and made conciliatory gestures before declaring independence, the New England states proceeded cautiously and pursued legislative solutions first. Anti-embargo resolutions from Massachusetts, Connecticut, and Providence, Rhode Island, adopted moderate tones, but nullifying the Enforcement Act and refusing to enforce the embargo was a step in the direction of taking more drastic measures. Even Federalist newspapers stressed proceeding *"temperately,"* but without submitting to "the grasp of arbitrary power" that the federal government seized from 1805 through 1809.[120]

The embargo crisis did present a unique opportunity for secessionists to put plans into motion. And in the absence of repeal, the sailors who marched in mock funerals, juries that acquitted embargo violators, mobs that intimidated or attacked collectors, and townspeople who signed resolutions calling for nullification sought passionate politicians who cared about protecting their financial security. Even after a period of frustration and economic hardship that lasted longer than expected, along with the fact that slave representation never ceased to offend a good number of New Englanders, many would need much more prodding to support disunion as an alternative to a permanent embargo.

Federalist Senator James A. Bayard of Delaware certainly believed that the embargo had produced a climate in New England conducive to disunion. He took issue with Giles' treatment of nonintercourse as a precursor to war. Giles confirmed brusquely that repealing the embargo was a "concession" to New England when Bayard shot back, "I rejoiced to hear this sentiment of forbearance. Such sentiments give hopes that the Union may still be preserved. We have been led to the brink of a tremendous precipice—another false step and we shall be lost in the abyss. Our safety is in treading back our steps."[121]

Of course, it will never be possible to say what would have happened or gauge the extent of disunionist sentiment in New England had the embargo remained in effect. Once the crisis passed, disunion evaporated as a threat, but not because Federalists lacked sincerity. At the height of tensions a *Repertory* writer warned, "Were even our state government to unite with that of the nation, in an attempt to carry the embargo laws into effect, the attempt would be in vain."[122] Yet, even though the embargo revived the Federalist Party, after its repeal as John Adams and Fisher Ames predicted, many of the disgruntled voters lost interest in political affairs and went about their daily business.[123]

Besides "o-grab-me," by 1809 New England Federalists had given substance to the anagrammatic variables derived from the word "embargo," including "go-bar-em," and "mob-rage." But more to the point, at the same time Federalists revised their assessment of civic engagement and broadened their opinion of proper public deportment to include protests, nullification, and the possibility of disunion.[124]

The onetime champions of federal authority under the Constitution also adopted the theory of interposition, which altered their view of federal supremacy in the government's compact with the states. Closely related was the Federalists' call for the New England states to "speak with one voice." They hoped to create a united North that could ward off future encroachments on its social, cultural, and economic institutions and successfully combat the slave power in government. Regional unity would help keep the South from diminishing the northern states' political and economic importance in the Union even further.[125] In the end, the embargo put a large number of Federalists on a course that deviated greatly from their historical path. They began to question the federal government's constitutional boundaries, justify disunion, and attempt to mold New England into a regional polity, powerful enough to check the federal government when its interests were threatened. For members of the party associated with creating a strong central government under the Constitution, these were radical steps.

NOTES

1. *Hampshire Gazette* (Northampton, MA), January 11, 1809 (emphasis in original).

2. For other examples, see the *Gazette* (Portland, ME), January 2, 1809, and *Litchfield* (CT) *Gazette*, January 4, 1809; for comments, see *Vermont Gazette* (Burlington), January 27, 1809; *Providence* (RI) *Gazette*, January 21, 1809; Compare David Hackett Fischer, *The Revolution of American Conservatism: The Federalist Party in the Era of Jeffersonian Democracy* (New York: Harper and Row, 1965), 105.

3. Richard Buel Jr., *America on the Brink: How the Political Struggle over the War of 1812 Almost Destroyed the Young Republic* (New York: Palgrave Macmillan, 2005), 58, 59; James M. Banner, *To the Hartford Convention: Federalists and the Origins of Party Politics in Massachusetts, 1789–1815* (New York: Alfred A. Knopf, 1970), 296–99.

4. Fischer, *Revolution of American Conservatism*, 175–77; Banner, *Hartford Convention*, 52, 299–303; Jeffrey L. Pasley, *"The Tyranny of Printers": Newspaper Politics in the Early American Republic* (Charlottesville: University of Virginia Press, 2001), 255; Lawrence A. Peskin, "How the Republicans Learned to Love Manufacturing: The First Parties and the 'New Economy,'" in *Journal of the Early Republic* 22, no. 2 (Summer 2002): 244–48; Banner, *Hartford Convention*, 51.

5. See Federal Party, *Massachusetts, Fifth of November, Federalists of Danvers, with Poem* (Salem, 1808), Broadsides, AAS.

6. Peter Onuf and Leonard J. Sadosky, *Jeffersonian America* (Malden: Blackwell, 2002), 28.

7. See *Annals of Congress*, 10th Cong., 2nd sess., 344.

8. *Boston Gazette*, March 9, 1809.

9. Onuf and Sadosky, *Jeffersonian America*, 28, 29; James H. Broussard, *Southern Federalists, 1800–1816* (Baton Rouge: Louisiana State University Press, 1978), 95–109.

10. Banner, *Hartford Convention*, 51–52; Hickey, *War of 1812*, 21; Broussard, *Southern Federalists*, 95, 96, 102–9; *Annals of Congress*, 10th Cong., 2nd sess., 285–86.

11. Josiah Quincy to John Eliot, November 18, 1808, and John Adams, December 14, 1808, Quincy, Wendell, Holmes, and Upham Family Papers, MHS.

12. Samuel Flagg Bemis, *A Diplomatic History of the United States*, 5th ed. (New York: Henry Holt and Company, 1965), 139, 152; Burton Spivak, *Jefferson's English Crisis: Commerce, Embargo, and the Republican Revolution* (Charlottesville: University of Virginia Press, 1979), 135; Clifford L. Egan, *Neither Peace nor War: Franco-American Relations, 1803–1812* (Baton Rouge: Louisiana State University Press, 1983), 29–31, 97.

13. Jefferson to Madison, March 11, 1808, *Jefferson Papers* LC. Also quoted in Robert W. Tucker and David C. Hendrickson, *Empire of Liberty: The Statecraft of Thomas Jefferson* (New York: Oxford University Press, 1990), 211.

14. Egan, *Neither Peace nor War*, 97, 98; Bemis, *Diplomatic History*, 149–52.

15. Spivak, *Jefferson's English Crisis*, 124–30.

16. James Madison to General Armstrong, May 2, 1808, in T. B. Wait, ed., *State Papers and Publick Documents of the United States from the Accession of Thomas Jefferson to the Presidency, Exhibiting a Complete View of Our Foreign Relations Since That Time*. 3 vols. (Boston: T. B. Wait and Sons, 1814–1815), 3:235.

17. Donald R. Adams Jr., "American Neutrality and Prosperity, 1793–1808: A Reconsolidation," in *Journal of Economic History* 40, no. 4 (December 1980): 733; *Annals of Congress*, 10th Cong., 2nd sess., 79, 637; Madison to Armstrong, July 21 and 22, 1808, and extracts of Armstrong's correspondence from November 12, 1807, through August 6, 1808, in Wait, *State Papers and Publick Documents*, 3:238–58.

18. See Lucia Stanton, "Looking for Liberty: Thomas Jefferson and the British Lions," in *Eighteenth-Century Studies* 26, no. 4 (Summer 1993): 649–55; Marilyn K. Parr, "Chronicle of a British Diplomat: The First Year in the 'Washington Wilderness,'" in *Washington History* 12, no. 1 (Spring/Summer 2000): 82; Charles O. Paullin, "Early British Diplomats in Washington," in *Records of the Columbia Historical Society* 44/45 (1942/1943): 247, 248; Dumas Malone, "Mr. Jefferson and the Traditions of Virginia," in *Virginia Magazine of History and Biography* 75, no. 2 (April 1967): 135; Cynthia D. Earman, "Remembering the Ladies: Women, Etiquette, and Diversions in Washington City, 1800–1814," in *Washington History* 12, no. 1 (Spring/Summer 2000): 109–11; Anthony Steel, "Anthony Merry and the Anglo-American Dispute about Impressment, 1803–1806," in *Cambridge Historical Journal* 9, no. 3 (1949): 334; Adams, "American Neutrality and Prosperity," 733.

19. Spivak, *Jefferson's English Crisis*, 128; cf. Bemis, *Diplomatic History*, 143.

20. Adams, "American Neutrality and Prosperity," 733; Adam Seybert, *Statistical Annals, Embracing Views of the Population, Commerce, Navigation, Fisheries, Public Lands, Post-Office Establishment, Revenues, Mint, Military and Naval Establishments, Expenditures, Public Debt, and Sinking Fund of the United States of America . . . 1789–1818* (1818; New York: Burt Franklin, 1969), 143; Thomas C. Cochran, ed., *The New American State Papers* [1789–1860], Social Policy, 47 vols. (Wilmington, DE: Scholarly Resources, 1972–1973), 3:29, 40; William M. Fowler Jr., "Marine Insurance in Boston: The Early Years of the Boston Marine Insurance Company, 1799–1870," in Conrad E. Wright and Katheryn P. Viens, eds., *Entrepreneurs: The Boston Business Community, 1700–1850*, ed. (Boston: MHS/Northeastern University Press, 1997), 172n32.

21. *Hampshire Gazette* (Northampton, MA), October 26, 1808; Adams, "American Neutrality and Prosperity," 733.

22. Banner, *Hartford Convention*, 298, 299 fn. 2; see also Sears, *Jefferson and the Embargo*, 152, 153.

23. *Northampton Hampshire Gazette*, November 9, 1808; cf. Banner, *Hartford Convention*, 51; Benjamin Woods Labaree, *Patriots and Partisans: The Merchants of Newburyport, 1764–1815* (Cambridge, MA: Harvard University Press, 1975), 158–68; see Hervey Putnam Prentiss, *Timothy Pickering as the Leader of New England Federalism, 1800–1815* (New York: Da Capo Press, 1972), 64.

24. Massachusetts General Court, *Commonwealth of Massachusetts, In the House of Representatives, Nov. 15, 1808: The Committee Appointed to Consider "Whether It will be Expedient for this Legislature to Adopt any Measures with a View to Procure a Repeal of the Laws of the United States . . .* (Boston, 1808), Broadsides, AAS; Massachusetts General Court, *Mr. Crowninshield's Resolutions. Commonwealth of Massachusetts. In the House of Representatives, November 16th 1808* (Boston, 1809), 1, 5, 6, 7, 9, Broadsides, AAS.
25. *Annals of Congress*, 10th Cong., 2nd sess., 127–31.
26. *Annals of Congress*, 10th Cong., 2nd sess., 16–20.
27. Ibid., 20–27, 30.
28. Ibid., 28–34.
29. *Columbian Centinel* (Boston), March 30, 1808; *Boston Gazette*, March 9, 1809.
30. *Annals of Congress*, 10th Cong., 2nd sess., 28–35.
31. Ibid., 28, 47–48, 64, 66, 69, 71, 93.
32. Ibid., 127–28, 132–35.
33. Ibid., 118, 136.
34. *Annals of Congress*, 10th Cong., 2nd sess., 175–83; also Timothy Pickering, *A Letter from the Hon. Timothy Pickering, a Senator of the United States from the State of Massachusetts, Exhibiting to His Constituents a View of the Imminent Danger of an Unnecessary and Ruinous War. Addressed to His Excellency James Sullivan, Governor of the Said State* (Portsmouth, MA: William Treadwell, 1808), 5; Buel, *America on the Brink*, 41–44.
35. *Annals of Congress*, 10th Cong., 2nd sess., 185–94, 200–12; Lawrence Peskin, "Conspiratorial Anglophobia and the War of 1812," in *The Journal of American History*, 98 no. 3 (December 2011), 657.
36. Ibid., 94; Spivak, *Jefferson's English Crisis*, 166–70; Gallatin to Jefferson, August 9 and 17, 1808; September 2, 1808, in Thomas Jefferson, *Writings*, ed. Merrill D. Peterson (New York: Literary Classics of the United States, 1984), 403–7, 413.
37. Nathaniel Saltonstall Jr. to Leverett Saltonstall, December 21, 1807; Nathaniel Saltonstall Jr. to Nathaniel Saltonstall, January 1, 1808; Samuel May to Nathaniel Saltonstall, March 7, 1808; Nathaniel Saltonstall Jr. to Nathaniel Saltonstall, June 5, 1808; George Badger to Nathaniel Saltonstall, November 9, 1808; Leverett Saltonstall to Nathaniel Saltonstall, January 6, 1809, in Robert E. Moody, ed., *The Saltonstall Papers, 1607–1815*, 3 vols. (Boston: Massachusetts Historical Society, 1974), 2:412, 417, 434, 444, 450, 454. See also Henry Lee to Peter Remsen, January 13, 1808; Lee to Benjamin Pickman, February 9, 1808; Lee to Remsen, February 10, 1808, in *The Jacksons and the Lees: Two Generations of Massachusetts Merchants, 1765–1844*, ed. Kenneth Wiggins Porter (Cambridge, MA: Harvard University Press, 1937), 827–29.
38. Elijah Boardman to Jacob Crowninshield, January 27, 1808; Benjamin Bailey to Jacob Crowninshield, January 30, 1808; Elisha Tracy to Jacob Crowninshield, January 31, 1808, Crowninshield Family Papers, MSS 4, Box 3, Folder 10, PEM.
39. For examples, see Republican of Massachusetts, *A Review of Political Affairs During the Last Half Year* (Boston: Adams and Rhoades, 1808), 1–12, Books and Pamphlets Collection, AAS; and Jonathan Russell [Hancock, pseud.], *The Whole Truth; or, The Essex Junto Exposed. Addressed to the Freemen of New England* (New York: Advertiser Office, 1809), 20–36, Books and Pamphlets Collection, AAS.
40. John Adams to Josiah Quincy, December 23, 1808, Quincy, Wendell, Holmes, and Upham Family Papers, MHS
41. *Annals of Congress*, 10th Cong., 2nd sess., 230.
42. Joseph Varnum et al., *The Reply of the Majority of the Representatives from the State of Massachusetts, In Congress and the Resolutions and Instructions of the Legislature of that State, on the Subject of the Embargo Laws* (Salem, MA: Pool and Palfray, 1808), 9–12, Books and Pamphlets Collection, AAS.
43. Varnum et al., *Reply of the Majority*, 12, 14–16, Books and Pamphlets Collection, AAS.
44. Jeffersonians who signed the response won in 1808 by fewer votes than in the previous (1806) election in the Berkshire, Middlesex, Norfolk, Lincoln, and York districts, Lampi, First Democracy Project, AAS.

45. Paul Goodman, *The Democratic-Republicans of Massachusetts: Politics in a Young Republic* (Cambridge, MA: Harvard University Press, 1964), 193, 195, 196.
46. *Ibid.*, 495, 496.
47. *Ibid.*, 514–19, 532–34.
48. *Annals of Congress*, 10th Cong., 2nd sess., 991, 992, 994.
49. John Chandler to Richard Cutts, February 4, 1809, Richard Cutts Papers, 1753–1886, Accession #10029-e, Special Collections, UVA.
50. See Andrew C. Lenner, *The Federal Principle in American Politics, 1790–1833* (Lantham: Rowman & Littlefield, 2001), 100, 101; Lance Banning, *The Jeffersonian Persuasion: Evolution of a Party Ideology* (Ithaca, NY: Cornell University Press, 1978), 293; Spivak, *Jefferson's English Crisis*, 183–84.
51. See Spivak, *Jefferson's English Crisis*, 180–97.
52. *Annals of Congress*, 10th Cong., 2nd sess., 521, 537, 538, 540, 542, 545.
53. See Egan, *Neither Peace nor War*, 98–99, and Goodman, *Democratic-Republicans of Massachusetts*, 195; *Annals of Congress*, 10th Cong., 2nd sess., 550, 568–71, 857–61; John Chandler to Richard Cutts, February 4, 1809, Richard Cutts Papers, 1753–1886, Accession #10029-e, Special Collections, UVA.
54. For examples see *Annals of Congress*, 10th Cong., 2nd sess., 856, 861, 862.
55. Spivak, *Jefferson's English Crisis*, 156, 157; Douglas Lamar Jones, "'The Caprice of Juries': The Enforcement of the Jefferson Embargo in Massachusetts," in *American Journal of Legal History* 24, no. 4 (October 1980): 313.
56. See Jones, "'Caprice of Juries,'" 314, 315, 325–29.
57. See also Gallatin to Jefferson, July 29, 1808; August 9 and 17, 1808; September 2, 1808; November 8, 1808, in Albert Gallatin, *The Writings of Albert Gallatin*, ed. Henry Adams (New York: Antiquarian Press, 1960), 396, 402, 405, 413, 427.
58. Forrest McDonald, *States' Rights and the Union: Imperium in Imperio, 1776–1876* (Lawrence: University Press of Kansas, 2000), 63, 64; Leonard W. Levy, *Jefferson and Civil Liberties: The Darker Side* (Chicago: Ivan R. Dee, 1989), 107, 108.
59. Steven G. Calabresi and Christopher S. Yoo, *Unitary Executive: Presidential Power from Washington to Bush* (New Haven, CT: Yale University Press, 2008), 72–74.
60. Jefferson to Gallatin, August 11, 1808, in Jefferson, Papers, LC.
61. Gallatin to Jefferson, November 8, 1808; Gallatin to Giles, November 24, 1808, in Gallatin, *Writings*, 427–435; Jones, "'Caprice of Juries,'" 313, 314; Spivak, *Jefferson's English Crisis*, 172–77.
62. *Annals of Congress*, 10th Cong., 2nd sess., 250–55.
63. *Ibid.*, 276–81; Gerard H. Clarfield, *Timothy Pickering and the American Republic* (Pittsburgh, PA: University of Pittsburgh Press, 1980), 249.
64. *Annals of Congress*, 10th Cong., 2nd sess., 298; Enforcement of the Embargo Act of 1809, Pub. L. No. 10–5, 2 Stat. 506 (1809).
65. Timothy Pickering to Rev. Doc. John Mason, January 4, 1809, Timothy Pickering Papers, MHS.
66. *Annals of Congress*, 10th Cong., 2nd sess., 910, 911, 915.
67. *Ibid.*, 941–43.
68. *Ibid.*, 950–61; Buel, *America on the Brink*, 68, 71.
69. *Annals of Congress*, 10th Cong., 2nd sess., 960–68.
70. *Ibid.*, 979, 1024; Enforcement of the Embargo Act of 1809, Pub. L. No. 10–5, 2 Stat. 506 (1809).
71. Labaree, *Patriots and Partisans*, 166, 167; Gallatin to Jefferson, August 9, 1808, in Gallatin, *Writings*, 406.
72. *Hampshire Gazette* (Northampton, MA), January 25 and 18, 1809.
73. *Gazette* (Portland, ME), January 2, 1809; *New England Palladium* (Boston), January 27, 1809; Federal Party (Mass), Portland, March 23, 1809. *Sir, The Committee of Public Safety and Correspondence, Chosen by the Town of Portland, Seriously Impressed with the Necessity of Exertion on the Part of the Federalists at the Approaching Election for Governor, Lieut. Governor and Senators, Cannot Neglect the Solemn Duty Which Urges Them to Ad-*

dress You at This Time (Portland, 1809), facsimile researched at the AAS; Wolford, "Democratic-Republican Reaction," 53; Buel, *America on the Brink*, 84, 85.

74. *Hampshire Gazette* (Northampton, MA), January 18, 1809; *National Aegis* (Worcester, MA), January 11, 1809; *Repertory* (Boston), January 31, 1809.

75. *American Commerce in Flames!* Friends of Peace, *To All the Electors of Massachusetts of Whatever Political Party They May Be . . . March 28, 1808* (Boston, 1808), Rare Book Collection, New York Public Library, Astor, Lenox, Tilden Foundations; *Let Every Federalist Do His Duty and Massachusetts May Yet Be Saved!!! Federal Republicans! Boston, April 1811. You Have Lost the Election of Governor. You Have Elected but Nineteen Federal Senators . . .* (Boston,1811), Broadsides, AAS.

76. *Newburyport* (MA) *Herald*, January 27, 1809; Harrison G. Otis to Josiah Quincy, December 15, 1808, Quincy, Wendell, Holmes, and Upham Family Papers, MHS.

77. Taggart to John Taylor, January 7, 1809, Taggart Letterbook, AAS.

78. Massachusetts General Court, *Report of a Committee of the House of Representatives Respecting Certain Military Orders Issued by His Honour Levi Lincoln, Lieutenant Governor . . . with the Documents* (Boston, 1809), 1–8, Books and Pamphlets Collection, AAS; John Chandler to Richard Cutts, February 4, 1809, Richard Cutts Papers, 1753–1886, Accession #10029-e, Special Collections, UVA.

79. Connecticut General Assembly, *At a Special Session of the General Assembly of the State of Connecticut, held at Hartford, on the Twenty Third day of February, A.D. 1809* (Hartford, 1809), 1, 2, 5, American Tracts Collection, BLYU; Providence, RI, *Proceeding of the Town of Providence* (Providence: Carter, 1809), ASU; Buel, *America on the Brink*, 84.

80. Banner, *To the Hartford Convention*, 303–6.

81. William Eustis to Richard Cutts, November 18, 1808, Richard Cutts Papers, 1753–1886, Accession #10029-e, Special Collections, UVA; *Annals of Congress*, 10th Cong., 2nd sess., 353–87; also see Buel, *America on the Brink*, 74, 75.

82. *Annals of Congress*, 10th Cong., 2nd sess., 414–23, 424, 436, 444–50; Donald R. Hickey, "Federalist Defense Policy in the Age of Jefferson, 1801–1812," in *Military Affairs* 45, no. 2 (April 1981): 63–70; Hickey, *War of 1812*, 8, 9.

83. *Annals of Congress*, 10th Cong., 2nd sess., 460, 1461, 1516, 1517.

84. Ibid., 1538–1539.

85. *Annals of Congress*, 10th Cong., 2nd sess., 1538; McDonald, *States' Rights and the Union*, 107, 108.

86. Paul A. Gilje, *Liberty on the Waterfront: American Maritime Culture in the Age of Revolution* (Philadelphia: University of Pennsylvania Press, 2004), 146–50.

87. See *Annals of Congress*, 10th Cong., 2nd sess., 428, 429.

88. Robert E. Cray Jr., "Remembering the USS *Chesapeake*: The Politics of Maritime Death and Impressment," in *Journal of the Early Republic* 25 (Fall 2005): 445, 454–455; Gilje, *Liberty on the Waterfront*, 146.

89. *Annals of Congress*, 10th Cong., 2nd sess., 1541 (emphasis in original).

90. Partial Repeal of Embargo with Nonintercourse, Pub. L. No. 10–24, 2 Stat. 528 (1809).

91. James Duncan Phillips, "Jefferson's 'Wicked Tyrannical Embargo,'" *New England Quarterly* 18, no. 4 (December 1945): 476, 478.

92. Peterson, *Thomas Jefferson and the New Nation*, 898, 917, 918; Thomas Jefferson to Thomas Mann Randolph, February 7, 1809, *Jefferson Papers* LC.

93. Tucker and Hendrickson, *Empire of Liberty*, 212.

94. Buel, *America on the Brink*, 68, 70; Spivak, *Jefferson's English Crisis*, 180–97; Louis M. Sears, *Jefferson and the Embargo* (1927; Durham: Duke University Press, 1966), 140–42, 150, 158–62; Egan, *Neither Peace nor War*, 91, 94; Wolford, "Democratic-Republican Reaction," 54; Samuel Eliot Morrison, *The Maritime History of Massachusetts, 1783–1860* (Boston: Houghton Mifflin, 1921), 192; Goodman, *Democratic-Republicans of Massachusetts*, 195; Phillips, "Jefferson's 'Wicked Tyrannical Embargo,'" 474–76. See also Jeffrey A. Frankel, "The 1807–1809 Embargo Against Great Britain," in *Journal of Economic History* 42, no. 2 (June 1982): 308; James Duncan Phillips, *Salem and the Indies: The Story of the Great Commercial Era of the City* (Boston: Houghton Mifflin, 1947), 278.

152   *Chapter 4*

95. Dinah Mayo-Bobee, "Understanding the Essex Junto: Fear, Dissent, and Propaganda in the Early Republic," in *New England Quarterly* 88, no. 4 (December 2015): 635, 637–41; Hickey, "Federalist Policy in the Age of Jefferson," 63, 64.

96. Mayo-Bobee, "Understanding the Essex Junto," 645; Pasley, *"Tyranny of Printers,"* 236, 254; and Fischer, *Revolution of American Conservatism*, 175–77. Such remarks were frequent, but a few samples are seen in *Annals of Congress*, 9th Cong., 1st sess., 644, 706; 10th Cong., 1st sess., 2137; 9th Cong., 2nd sess., 71, 185.

97. *Salem* (MA) *Gazette*, March 11, 1808; *Columbian Centinel* (Boston), March 30, 1808; *Hampshire Gazette* (Northampton, MA), May 30, 1804; *Repertory* (Boston), April 4 and 8, 1806.

98. Peskin, "How the Republicans Learned to Love Manufacturing," 235–62; Egan, *Neither Peace nor War*, 95, 96; Robert A. East, "Economic Development and New England Federalism, 1803–1814," *New England Quarterly* 10, no. 3 (September 1937): 430–46.

99. Sarah S. Thatcher to Judge Thacher, December 28, 1806, George Thacher Papers, MSS 313, Box 1, Folder 2, PEM.

100. *Annals of Congress*, 9th Cong., 1st sess., 576, 581; 10th Cong., 2nd sess., 49, 66.

101. Morison, *Maritime History of Massachusetts*, 37, 38; and Doron S. Ben-Atar, "Alexander Hamilton's Alternative: Technology Piracy and the Report on Manufactures," in Doron Ben-Atar and Barbara Oberg, eds., *Federalists Reconsidered*, (Charlottesville: University of Virginia Press, 1998), 45; Peter Onuf and Leonard J. Sadosky, *Jeffersonian America* (Malden, MA: Blackwell, 2002), 126, 127; Joyce Appleby, *Inheriting the Revolution: The First Generation of Americans* (Cambridge, MA: Belknap Press of Harvard University Press, 2000), 80; John R. Commons et al., *History of Labour in the United States*, 2 vols. (reprint; New York: Macmillan, 1966); Christopher L. Tomlins and Andrew J. King, eds., *Labor Law in America: Historical and Critical Essays* (Baltimore: Johns Hopkins University Press, 1992).

102. Peskin, "How the Republicans Learned to Love Manufacturing," 240, 241; Morison, *Maritime History of Massachusetts*, 188, Peterson, *Thomas Jefferson and the New Nation*, 893; Wright and Viens, *Entrepreneurs*, 344–350; Oscar Handlin and Mary Flug Handlin, *Commonwealth: A Study of the Role of Government in the American Economy: Massachusetts, 1774–1861*, rev. ed. (Cambridge, MA: Harvard University Press, 1969), 122.

103. Newburyport, Massachusetts Town Meeting, *Newburyport Resolutions at a Legal Meeting of the Inhabitants . . . Holden at the Court-House on Thursday, the 12th of January 1809, the Following Resolutions Were Passed and Adopted. . . .* (Newburyport: E. W. Allen, 1809), 11, 14, Books and Pamphlets Collection, AAS.

104. Phillips, "Jefferson's 'Wicked Tyrannical Embargo,'" 470; Walter Wilson Jennings, *The American Embargo, 1807–1809: With Particular Reference to Its Effect on Industry* (Iowa City: University of Iowa, 1921), 175; Robert W. Lovett, "The Beverly Cotton Manufactory: Or Some New Light on an Early Cotton Mill," in *Bulletin of the Business Historical Society* 26, no. 4 (December 1952): 235.

105. Jefferson, "Query XIX," in Jefferson, *Writings*, 290.

106. Jefferson to Jean Baptiste Say, February 1, 1804, in Jefferson, *Writings*, 1144; *Annals of Congress* 10th Cong., 2nd sess., 66.

107. Jefferson to Abraham Bishop, January 20, 1809, also Jefferson to A. Bishop, November 13, 1808; Jefferson to William Short, June 18, 1813; and Jefferson to Thomas Leiper, June 12, 1815, in *Jefferson Papers* LC.

108. Rogers M. Smith, "Constructing American National Identity: Strategies of the Federalists," and Paul Finkelman, "The Problem of Slavery in the Age of Federalism," in Ben-Atar and Oberg, *Federalists Reconsidered*, 24, 135–56; James Madison to David Humphreys, March 23, 1813, in Madison, *The Writings of James Madison*, ed. Gaillard Hunt, 9 vols. (New York: Knickerbocker Press, 1908), 8:241.

109. Gordon S. Wood, *Empire of Liberty*, 702.

110. Seymour Drescher, *Abolition: A History of Slavery and Antislavery* (New York: Cambridge University Press, 2009), 297–99; Peskin, "Conspiratorial Anglophobia and

the War of 1812," 668–69. Also see Nicole Eustice, *1812: War and the Passions of Patriotism* (Philadelphia: University of Pennsylvania Press, 2012), 25

111. Jefferson to William Short, June 18, 1813, *Jefferson Papers* LC.

112. Thomas Jefferson to Edward Coles, August 25, 1814; Edward Coles to Thomas Jefferson, September 26, 1814, *Jefferson Papers* LC; James Madison to Edward Coles, September 3, 1819, Richard Cutts Collection of the James and Dolley Madison Papers, LC; Paul Finkelman, *Slavery and the Founders: Race and Liberty in the Age of Jefferson*, 2nd ed. (Armonk, NY: M. E. Sharpe, 2001), 159, 195–96; Peterson, *Thomas Jefferson and the New Nation*, 999–1001.

113. *Boston Gazette*, March 9, 1809; *Post-Boy and Vermont & New-Hampshire Federal Courier* (Windsor, VT), June 11, 1805.

114. Wolford, "Democratic-Republican Reaction," 53–55; Goodman, *Democratic-Republicans in Massachusetts*, 195; Spivak, *Jefferson's English Crisis*, 181–86.

115. *Hampshire Gazette* (Northampton, MA), January 11, 1809 and March 15, 1809; *New-England Palladium* (Boston), March 31, 1809; Labaree, *Patriots and Partisans*, 162, 173; Phillips, "Jefferson's 'Wicked Tyrannical Embargo," 473; Prentiss, *Timothy Pickering*, 61–64; Miles Standish Jr. [pseud.], *The Times: A Poem, Addressed to the Inhabitants of New-England, and the State of New-York* . . . (Plymouth, MA: Printed for the Author, 1809); Books and Pamphlets Collection, AAS; Phillips, *Salem and the Indies*, 270.

116. *Boston Patriot*, July 22, 1809; *National Aegis* (Worcester, MA), January 11, 1809.

117. Banner, *Hartford Convention*, 182; Phillips, *Salem and the Indies*, 280.

118. Republican of Massachusetts, *Review of Political Affairs*, 4, 5, AAS.

119. Mayo-Bobee, "Understanding the Essex Junto," 632–45 passim; Fischer, *Revolution of American Conservatism*, 176–78; Banner, *Hartford Convention*, 109, 112, 117–19.

120. John Chandler to Richard Cutts, February 4, 1809, Richard Cutts Papers, 1753–1886, Accession #10029-e, Special Collections, UVA; *Palladium*, quoted in Buel, *America on the Brink*, 73, 74 (emphasis in original).

121. *Annals of Congress*, 10th Cong., 2nd sess., 354, 357, 409; also James Asherton Bayard, *Mr. Bayard's Speech upon His Motion to Amend the Resolution Offered by Mr. Giles, By Striking Out that Part Which Is in Italics, Delivered in the Senate of the United States Tuesday, February 13, 1809* (Portland: Shirley, 1809), 1, 17, Books and Pamphlets Collection, AAS.

122. *Repertory* (Boston), January 1, 1809.

123. Nathaniel Saltonstall Jr. to Nathaniel Saltonstall, June 5, 1808, in Moody, *Saltonstall Papers*, 445.

124. Robert W. T. Martin, *Government by Dissent* (New York: New York University Press, 2013), 91, 194; Gilje, *Liberty on the Waterfront*, 147, 148.

125. *Boston Gazette*, March 9, 1809; *Annals of Congress*, 10th Cong., 2nd sess., 444–48.

FIVE

"Sincere Neutrality"

War, Moderates, and the Federalist Party's Decline (1810–1820)

On March 4, 1809, president elect James Madison appeared before the "six years' class" of the Senate to take the oath of office and deliver his first inaugural address. His speech painted an idyllic portrait of the United States as a country with a thriving economy which balanced agriculture, commerce, and manufacturing. As a result, the nation enjoyed domestic tranquility and peaceful relations with the rest of the world. Madison lastly invoked "that Almighty Being whose power regulates the destiny of nations," to guide his administration, as he relied on the "intelligence and virtue" of the American people, and the wisdom of their representatives, to offset his personal shortcomings.[1]

The timing of Madison's speech was serendipitous. Just as his presidency began the embargo of 1807 ended. Lifting the ban on all exports except to Britain and France defused the clamor for disunion that had been escalating in New England. Democratic-Republicans had held onto the presidency and most of Congress in elections in states south and west of New York. But Madison's idealism and electoral victory were deceptive. The wars in Europe raged on and the problems involving French and British depredations on America's merchant fleet resulted in infringements on the nation's sovereignty that remained immediately challenged Madison's success as president.

Even though repeal diminished the threat of northern secession and armed civil unrest, Federalists did not regard Madison's election as an indication that the entire nation embraced Democratic-Republican trade restrictions. The electoral map furnished evidence that Federalists were correct, they were becoming isolated and needed to place more emphasis on northern unity to combat the growth of southern political power. The need for a united North became even more apparent for Federalists after, as far as they were concerned, Congress needlessly plunged the nation into war with Britain. Like the embargo, they considered the War of 1812 another scheme of mendacious politicians to pursue hostilities toward New England. Based on events from 1809 through 1815, a good many New Englanders shared this belief and opposed the conflict, feeling that the war was largely at their expense and should be waged without their assistance.

New Englanders such as Vermont Representative James Elliot had been advocating the idea of "a union of the people in the northern states" since Jefferson's reelection in 1804. In the Union that Elliot proposed representation would be equitably distributed throughout the states. If "the northern states [were] as well united as the southern we should not be so unreasonable to desire more than our due degree of political weight," observed Elliot.[2] The *New-England Palladium* agreed, "New-England . . . while united, may always defend her freedom against foreign and domestic foes."[3] Others surmised that even a united New England would be subjugated to the Slave South and Southwestern states if the region remained in the Union. New England, it seemed, was at a permanent disadvantage. According to Daniel Webster of New Hampshire, the elimination of that "excessive inequality caused by the counting of three-fifths of the Southern slaves" had to occur, or New England could never exert the political power to which it was entitled.[4]

A Northern Confederacy may have been what "radical," or "extreme" Federalists such as Timothy Pickering supported, partly because they were a powerless minority in Congress, which was evident during their battle against commercial restrictions between 1805 and 1809. As the nation drew closer to a second war with Great Britain Federalists surpassed their previous protests. Along with their opposition to Madison's diplomacy and the War of 1812, the radicals' fading role in their party reveals changes in and outside of Federalist politics that would lead to the party's demise while heightening New Englanders' concern over their place in the expanding nation. Many developed a determination to make a lasting impression on the evolving country's culture.

Their last efforts to assert New England's national status and influence public policy exposed the Federalists' limitations at the same time that it validated the need for Northern unity. A substantial number of northerners would eventually rally against southern power in the federal government, and some would even form formidable abolitionist organizations. The type of unity envisioned would not develop before the Federal party's demise. The following study demonstrates how the radicals kept the Federalist Party afloat and made a lasting impression on the course of U.S. politics and history, when the party failed.

After Congress lifted the embargo the number of American ships seized or destroyed by the French and British began to increase steadily. Merchants regained access to hundreds of ports not directly involved in Europe's war, but France, Britain, and their wartime allies resumed their frequent interference with U.S. commerce.[5] Madison was beginning to face the same problems that led to the embargo, but he looked for alternatives.

For most of his political career Madison endorsed commercial coercion as a diplomatic tool, primarily to influence Great Britain. Barely a month after the Nonintercourse Act (1809) went into effect, it appeared that the restrictive system had finally worked. The British minister in Washington, David M. Erskine, contacted Secretary of State Robert Smith with news that Britain was willing to suspend its Orders in Council, pay reparations for the 1807 attack on the frigate *Chesapeake*, draft a new Anglo-American treaty, and reopen trade with the United States as early as June 1809. The reason for Britain's olive branch, according to Erskine, was the impartiality of the Nonintercourse Act, which unlike the embargo, had "produced a state of equality in the relations of the two belligerent powers with respect to the United States."[6] By treating France and Britain equally it appeared that the United States was really neutral.

Madison accepted the terms outlined by Erskine and issued a proclamation to reopen trade with Great Britain in June. When the newly assembled Eleventh Congress (1809–1811) received Madison's message, both parties and their respective media approved of the Erskine accord.[7] Although a few of them complained that the end of nonintercourse posed a threat to the nation's burgeoning manufacturing sector, Democratic-Republicans accepted the Erskine agreement as proof that their restrictive system had successfully protected commerce, saved the nation from war, and restored the republic's image abroad.[8]

Federalists also took credit for the Erskine agreement, claiming that their victories in the congressional elections of 1808 had helped to initiate the settlement. They believed that persistent opposition during the embargo forced Madison to acknowledge that New England would not tolerate unending trade restrictions. To avoid the protests and threats of disunion that began to emanate out of New England over the embargo, Federalists were sure that Madison needed to cooperate with the British to "save the remnants of his sinking party."[9]

As a result of his proclamation, hundreds of vessels cleared U.S. ports for British markets before Madison learned that Erskine failed to follow his official instructions from Britain's Foreign Secretary George Canning. Canning had only authorized Erskine to offer repeal of the Orders in Council of January and November 1807 if the United States agreed to continue the nonintercourse policy against France after lifting the law against Britain, respected the Rule of 1756 barring neutrals from trading in areas prohibited to them in peacetime, and consented to British enforcement of U.S. sanctions against France. The last point would allow the British to intercept and seize U.S. ships that attempted to trade with the French.[10] Erskine did not reveal the range of Canning's instructions to Smith until July. Once he became aware of Britain's actual terms, Smith said that relating those instructions in their entirety would have made it "impossible for the President to have perceived in its conditions, or in its spirit, that conciliatory disposition . . . which, it was hoped, had really existed" with the British.[11]

Erskine claimed that he had fully divulged all of his government's terms to Treasury Secretary Albert Gallatin at an unofficial meeting. Based on the alleged conversation with Gallatin, Erskine felt confident that the administration would accept all of the terms. Gallatin, on the other hand, denied that he ever conveyed that idea to Erskine and said he would never have conceded to the Rule of 1756 under any circumstances. That rule, he noted, would hamstring the West Indian trade and leave the United States at a disadvantage. Britain, Gallatin stipulated, would first need to address and settle "all the points in dispute and particularly that of impressments," or there could never be an amicable settlement. Now that the administration knew that he never fully revealed his instructions, all that Erskine could do was insist that there had been no misunderstandings during his conversation with Gallatin.[12] In August Erskine finally confessed to Smith that he had edited Canning's dispatch. His reason for suppressing the truth was fear that the official terms could never win the necessary concessions from Madison.[13]

Federalists defended Madison's decision to rescind nonintercourse against Britain without verification. They attributed the haste with which the president accepted Erskine's terms to the anti-British majority in Congress. Madison chose "this method to raise the embargo [and] open a door for trade" to avoid the obstructionists in his own party. Expecting Erskine's replacement, Francis James Jackson, to settle matters, Federalists decided to wait before passing further judgment.[14]

Madison still seemed to be in a conciliatory mood when Jackson arrived in Washington, but his good humor was about to end. Instead of presenting Britain's terms upon arrival, Jackson expected and waited for the Madison administration to approach him. When talks did begin, Jackson and Secretary Smith clashed over every point negotiated and expressed mutual distrust after spending a great deal of time and energy arguing over such trivial matters as whether to conduct their exchanges in writing or verbally. At first Smith repeatedly reiterated the president's willingness to negotiate, but finally found it impossible to deal with Jackson. In November Madison broke off the negotiations and ordered Jackson recalled.[15] Even after he needlessly alienated his hosts, Jackson asked for a transfer to New York. He informed the administration that he feared for his family's safety because newspapers were stirring up anti-British rage and people in the capital were insulting British officers in the streets.[16]

Papers around the country published the Smith-Jackson correspondence. The letters showed that Democratic-Republicans demanded an agreement with terms identical to those made by Erskine. When this failed they castigated Jackson for insulting the United States.[17] It defied logic to expect the same terms from Jackson that had forced Britain to recall his predecessor but, according to the Jeffersonian *Independent Chronicle*, "It matters not whether Erskine exceeded his instructions or not, if he did it proves he was not instructed to do justice . . . what he agreed to . . . we have a strict right to demand."[18]

Of course, the Federalist press adopted a different interpretation. Their newspapers attacked the administration and facetiously offered a reward to anyone who could locate the insults in Jackson's letters.[19] Various editorials contended that a diplomatic solution was still possible, but not under Erskine's terms. They deemed Madison's termination of Jackson a disgrace and stretched the facts by alleging that Jackson had attempted to reach "an accommodation and sacrifice every punctilio, except where the . . . dignity of his government was concerned." Federalists alleged, erroneously, that the administration knew of Erskine's official orders and orchestrated a fiasco to dupe Britain into accepting a one-sided agreement.[20]

Regardless of the partisan spin, there was some truth in both interpretations. Jackson, who entered the United States in a snit, played a foolhardy game of cat-and-mouse and completely mishandled an extremely important assignment. But even though he had no apparent talent for finesse, Jackson was not solely responsible for botching the parley. From the outset, even though he already knew the answer, Smith focused on extracting an explanation for Britain's refusal to honor Erskine's agreement. He also ignored Jackson's offer of reparations for the *Chesapeake*, and refused to compromise over British enforcement of U.S. sanctions against France.[21]

Diplomacy ultimately failed because of both men. Jackson lacked tact and resorted to abrasive doublespeak, while Smith remained inflexible and demanded that Britain, in the middle of a war with France, drop its Orders in Council and stand idly by as American ships transported provisions to their enemy and its allies. On this point Madison's response appeared to convey the same pro-French bias displayed by Jefferson. British seizures were the nation's key source of anxiety while the United States expressed few complaints about French spoliations.[22]

The failure of diplomatic efforts with Britain left Madison in a quandary. The Nonintercourse Act that repealed the embargo would expire when the Eleventh Congress' first session ended in May 1810, and the administration had no plans in place to keep the French or British from preying on the nation's merchant marine, nor had they devised any policy to protect Americans from seizures and impressment.[23] Neither the Madison administration nor Congress could refute Federalist charges that the federal government appeared incapable of protecting commerce. Democratic-Republicans, they asserted, would not allow merchants to protect themselves, refused to deploy the navy as protective escorts, and could not devise a way to solve the problem without obliterating commerce.

As the expiration of the Nonintercourse Act drew closer, Nathaniel Macon of North Carolina proposed a solution known as Macon's Bill No. 2. The act banned French and British war vessels from U.S. ports until Britain, France, or both rescinded laws that violated U.S. neutrality. If only one of these nations repealed orders or decrees that interfered with U.S. commerce, within three months sanctions would be imposed on the other nation if it did not also comply.[24] This meant that the United States would openly trade exclusively with the other nation's enemies. The United States was essentially announcing the end of its neutrality.

For Britain compliance would entail repealing the Orders in Council of January 7, 1807, which prohibited neutral trade between enemy ports, and November 11, 1807, that declared all enemy nations and colonies under blockade and off limits. France would need to rescind its Berlin Decree (1806), which prohibited all trade with the British Isles, as well as the Milan Decree (1807) under which the French deemed that any ships searched by the British or paying a duty to that nation was subject to seizure.[25]

France apparently took advantage of the provisions under Macon's Bill No. 2. In a letter dated August 5, 1810, from French minister Jean-Baptiste Champagny, the Duke of Cadore informed the U.S. minister to France, John Armstrong, that Napoleon planned to annul his decrees after November 1, if Britain revoked its policies, or the United States "shall cause their rights to be respected by the English."[26] Cadore's letter repeated the demands that French officials had been making of the United States for some time, but Madison accepted the communiqué as evidence that France was willing to comply with U.S. terms. Madison then gave Britain three months to repeal its 1807 Orders in Council.[27]

In practical terms, accepting the Cadore letter ended the diplomatic stalemate with Britain—a favorable outcome if both nations acted honorably. It was now up to the British to settle matters with the United States. If Napoleon's overture was earnest, Britain should also revoke its orders in council. If France complied and the British refused to change their policies, further sanctions were justified. This is not what Federalists anticipated. They suspected that the French would not abide by Madison's interpretation of the Cadore letter, but that the administration would still be holding Britain responsible based on France's promises. Federalists expected Democratic-Republicans in Congress, along with Madison, to levy sanctions against Great Britain whether or not France lived up to

U.S. terms. Short of an outright attack on American soil they were convinced that Jeffersonians would never consider armed conflict against France. Either scenario jibed with the Federalists' earlier predictions that federal policies since Jefferson were positioning the nation for another war with Great Britain.

The nation would soon know Britain's response. The French continued to seize, sell, and destroy U.S. merchant vessels but the Madison administration appeared reluctant to challenge Napoleon.[28] Federalists attempted to refocus the public's attention on the differences between the government's treatment of Britain after the Erskine agreement and its responses to France when it became evident that they had not repealed their decrees. Federalists pointed out that there were no displays of outrage from Congress or the president comparable to their condemnations of Britain. France was still subjecting the nation's merchant marine to quarantines, searches, and seizures. For piddling reasons the French even delayed diplomatic vessels as they entered or departed French-controlled harbors. Anglophobia was steering the nation into a war that could be avoided if only Democratic-Republicans were capable of an unbiased approach.

When the Madison administration addressed the ongoing attacks, French officials said that seizures were retaliation for French vessels taken by the United States. On March 23, 1810, Napoleon had issued another decree at Rambouillet sanctioning the seizure, sale, or destruction of vessels without notifying the United States. By September the administration was pressing Napoleon to relinquish money he received for the sale of citizens' property, but he refused and continued to harass the traders. The excuse that "the principles of reprisal" validated the seizures, preceded Cadore's repeated assurance that, "His majesty loves the Americans."[29]

Shortly after he became president, leading Federalists argued that Madison was "possessed of more profound knowledge for a useful citizen and magistrate than Jefferson," but within a short period they had begun to castigate Madison for extending Jefferson's policies. As he had been Jefferson's secretary of state, the similarities should not have shocked anyone, but "A Former Madisonian" held the "French influence with which the Jefferson cabinet was so manifestly disgraced" responsible for the current problems plaguing commerce and foreign relations.[30] In a similar vein Federalist Samuel Taggart complained, "France burns our ships, confiscates our property, and imprisons our seamen," but the government vents its wrath against Great Britain because it would not "accede to such terms" as the United States was now "pleased to dictate."[31]

France was not acting in good faith, according to Federalists, and the president's proclamation provided no proof that Napoleon had repealed his decrees. As the House debated sanctions against Britain, a few Democratic-Republicans were reluctant to penalize the British without confirmation of France's compliance with the terms of Macon's Bill No. 2. Massachusetts representative Edward St. Loe Livermore called it "contrary to reason as well as precedent" to accept the president's flimsy assurances pertaining to France. Josiah Quincy, maintained that Madison had been deceived, suggested that Congress repeal all commercial restrictions, and concluded that the nation should go to war with both nations. The United States owed "nothing to France . . . [or] Great Britain."[32]

The Federalists' arguments were moot, however, because the administration implemented the next phase of Macon's Bill No. 2 despite evidence that France failed to respond satisfactorily to U.S. terms. So much commotion accompanied the final vote over nonintercourse against Britain that New Yorker Peter B. Porter called the debate a "disreputable" scene. Representatives' speeches were so vulgar that the House recorder added a special note explaining the need to omit much of the language. When the House was ready to take the final vote several representatives disappeared, but the bill passed, 65–12. In the Senate a Federalist proposed reinstating nonintercourse against France if Napoleon did not demonstrate that his decrees were no longer in operation. The proposal for possible action against France was defeated shortly before the sanction against Britain passed, 20–7. The Nonintercourse Act against Britain, unless they "cease to violate the neutral commerce of the United States," was scheduled to go into effect on the final day of the Eleventh Congress, March 3, 1811.[33]

Besides confirming Federalists' suspicions, the problem associated with France eroded unity in the Democratic-Republican Party. Secretary of State Smith became increasingly hostile to the president, and the U.S. envoy to France John Armstrong resigned. To escape further dissent, Congress classified any information that contradicted the president's proclamation concerning France. This included new accounts of seizures and destruction of U.S. property.[34] But the gag did not keep Americans or the British from recognizing the facts. This prompted British diplomat Augustus J. Foster to conclude that Napoleon's decrees were still in operation and noted that the French were even engaged in the British license system, which for a fee, gave them permission to trade in specific ports controlled by Great Britain.[35]

By 1812, France's claims, Federalist opposition, and intraparty disharmony jeopardized Madison's chances for reelection. Further complicating matters was a schism that developed involving Secretary of State Smith and former diplomat Armstrong. Both opposed Madison's leniency toward France and conspired with the administration's enemies within the party, notably the Clinton faction in New York, to make a run for the presidency. In retaliation for publicly criticizing him, Madison dismissed Smith and appointed James Monroe secretary of state.[36]

In spite of turmoil within the president's party, it was difficult for Federalists to capitalize on the situation or exploit Madison's vulnerabilities.[37] In the months after Congress repealed the embargo, the Democratic-Republican press pummeled New England Federalists without letup. While Federalist newspapers celebrated the triumphs that Quincy, Pickering, and Taggart had in defeating the embargo, opponents called for their removal from office. The House seat won by William Baylies of Massachusetts in 1808 was lost to Democratic-Republican Charles Turner Jr. following a contentious ousting and special election in 1809, which took place because of different presentations of Turner's name on ballots.[38]

Adding to this was a redistricting attempt to keep Federalists from making greater progress in Massachusetts. Governor Elbridge Gerry, a Democratic-Republican, realigned the voting districts to favor his party. Because one of the districts looked like a salamander, the term "gerrymandering" was applied to the process and has been used every since. The redrawn districts deprived Federalists of several congressional seats until 1812 and gave Democratic-Republicans more seats in the General Court.[39]

Federalists also lost a powerful ally in the Senate. Timothy Pickering, who had been more influential through published polemics against the majority's policies than his votes in the Senate, lost his seat in 1812. Democratic-Republicans considered his opposition to the embargo so damaging that they dubbed his anti-embargo jeremiads "Pickering's panic."[40] Congress and the press looked for every imperfection or abnormality they could find to silence Pickering, including his military record during the War for Independence to his son's foreign connections. While under the microscope Pickering could not afford a misstep. But while delivering a speech opposing U.S. occupation of West Florida in January 1811, Pickering read a letter in front of gallery spectators that had been classified confidential. After discussing the matter, the Senate censured Pickering for a breach of confidence 20–7. Unlike the public's election of representatives today, before the 17th Amendment was ratified in 1913, state legislatures elected senators. As a result of the gerrymandered districts, Democratic-Republicans controlled the Massachusetts legislature, and in 1812 elected Joseph Varnum to replace Pickering in the Twelfth Congress.[41]

Federalists fared the same or slightly better in other New England states. Connecticut's congressional delegation remained entirely Federalist until 1817 and Rhode Island continued to elect Federalists to Congress until 1821. Both parties were elected in Vermont, but in 1812 that state's Democratic-Republican–controlled legislature changed the congressional elections into a statewide format in order to keep Federalists out of office. The maneuver worked until 1815 when Vermont voters sent a Federalist majority to Congress, and continued to do so until the Federalist Party disbanded in the 1820s. New Hampshire also continued to elect representatives from both parties to Congress, but Federalists formed a majority of the state's delegation until 1819.[42] Thus, with the help of Democratic-Republican majorities in the state legislatures of Vermont and New Hampshire, the distribution of Federalists in the Senate was paltry and fluctuated little until Federalists gained control during the War of 1812. Even after that time, some state legislatures continued to elect one senator from each party.

Before the War of 1812, with the exception of Josiah Quincy and doubtless a few others, Federalists argued that besides diminishing New England's economy, an Anglo-American war was the underlying objective for the Democratic-Republicans' string of trade restrictions. Quincy fervently maintained that using the threat of war to excuse commercial restrictions was a ruse to divert attention away from Democratic-Republicans' true objective—the destruction of New England's maritime economic culture. Among his reasons for doubting that they would declare war was the fact that Jeffersonians had decimated the military and refused to impose taxes to rebuild it.[43] Quincy also felt that the congressional majority was incapable of making policy decisions besides an "embargo without limit," their "universal panacea." He told former President John Adams that Jeffersonians would do nothing but pay lip service to war. Others, including John Lowell, a Federalist caucus organizer in Massachusetts, charged Madison and Napoleon with planning the Erskine fiasco to turn public opinion against Britain to justify a war.[44]

Once war was imminent, Federalists knew that they could do nothing to stop it. They did maintain that the congressional majority used war as a ploy to sidetrack and divide New Englanders. Focusing on war would divert attention away from southerners' growing power in the Union. The broadside *Let Every Federalist Do His Duty* (1811) explained, "War is coming upon you! Because . . . the North would bear the brunt of the calamity . . . [and] the planters of the South own slaves but no ships." Both the federal government's policies and southern slaveholders' power, the broadside argued, had conspired to make sure that "the manly spirit of Freedom and Independence which once dwelt in New England is already dead!!!"[45]

Federalists needed a strategy and response to a declaration of war or another embargo. Yet they could not unite over a single course of action. John Adams mentioned this problem to Quincy after praising him for a speech dealing with maritime protections. Adams was "puzzled and confounded . . . that not one member from New England has been found to second or support you." He was equally astonished that Federalists from New York and Pennsylvania remained silent. The dearth of leadership and solidarity meant that Federalists still needed to rely on their opponents' failures instead of their own innovations for political success. In the short term this might help them regain congressional seats, but the situation did not bode well for ambitious Federalists aiming for the presidency or planning to make an impact during a lifelong career in national politics.

As events began to unfold, Democratic-Republicans saw war as the only way to unite their splintering party and keep Madison in office. While Federalists were still in the minority, Madison needed to silence the radicals who might undermine his plans, mobilize New Englanders against his administration, and threaten his bid for reelection. A solution to the Federalist problem surfaced in March 1812 when the president announced that a report from a spy named John Henry proved that New England Federalists had conspired with the British to undermine the government and destroy the Union during the embargo.[46]

Henry was an Irishman who migrated first to the United States and then to Canada. He was more of a mercenary than a government operative, but during a business trip to New England in 1808, Henry witnessed anti-embargo protests and received $900 from the British for sending reports to their officials in Canada. Not deeming that payment adequate, in February 1812 Henry sold the information to Madison for $50,000, which was the entire fund available to the president for intelligence. Madison, without verifying Henry's credentials or the intelligence, presented documents to Congress as evidence that a British "secret agent" was employed in certain states and especially in the "Government in Massachusetts" to foment disunion and form an alliance between New England and Great Britain.[47]

Scholarly discussions of the Henry plot often highlight Democratic-Republicans' observations that congressional Federalists "began to kick and *squirm*" as the plot was exposed.[48] But on the other side of the aisle, Federalists expressed relief that a conspiracy of that sort, if it existed, had been uncovered. Based on the content of his papers Henry produced nothing to prove his case and the documents mentioned no specific names. Henry left before he could be interviewed by Congress, but after questioning his accomplice, a French con man named Paul Emile Soubiran (Count Edward De Crillon), the House Foreign Relations Committee determined that Britain had indeed attempted to incite disunion and civil war during the embargo. But with the evidence they possessed Congress could do nothing more.[49]

William Reed, a representative from Massachusetts, was sure that the administration had hatched a fake plot as an excuse to continue their "ruinous commercial restrictions."[50] Madison also sent several copies of Henry's papers to Governor Gerry with permission to "make whatever use of the episode he chose in the forthcoming state elections." Not coincidentally, pamphlets linking Federalists to the British began to surface throughout Massachusetts. As a countermeasure, Federalists distributed copies of their "Boston Resolutions" by the thousands.[51] Largely the work of Harrison Gray Otis, Edward St. Loe Livermore, and William Sullivan, vice president of Boston's Washington Benevolent Society, the

Boston Resolutions expressed resentment over the government's circulation of unfounded accusations and enumerated the Federalists' position on pertinent political issues. With slight variations, Federalist candidates used most of the Resolution's points during the campaigns of 1812.[52]

Anglophobia was not as pervasive, especially in New England, on the eve of the War of 1812 as is generally thought. This was why Madison saw the need to use public funds to uncover an espionage plot to silence his critics and raise support for the upcoming war.[53] Federalists emerged from the Henry controversy with no new scars, but in spite of its many inconsistencies, the scandal worked against Federalists in other parts of the country. Partisan newspapers controlled the flow of information, which is why southerners and westerners considered New England Federalists unprincipled advocates of disunion.[54] Explaining Federalist opposition to trade restrictions and the war as proof that radicals were conspiring with Britain also helped to galvanize support for the war and for Madison.

The Henry Plot lost some momentum when another scandal surfaced involving an American agent in Florida, George Mathews. Mathews was a former congressman and governor from Georgia who became a covert operative in 1811 to help force the annexation of East Florida. Madison sanctioned Matthews' mission to seize East Florida through the organization of revolts in the Spanish Territory. Mathews captured St. Augustine, but could not spark a popular revolution by March 1812 without more funds and further exposure. Some in the North already opposed such early filibustering attempts to spread slavery into new territories. To avert even more problems at a time that required as much public support as he could get for a declaration of war, Madison recalled Mathews that April. The move alienated southerners who wanted to annex Florida and the combination of intrigues caused Madison to lose appeal as a presidential candidate.[55]

Throughout 1812 relations with Britain continued to deteriorate and in May Foster demanded proof that Napoleon had repealed his decrees and stopped attacking U.S. ships. It was "impossible for Great Britain to rescind her Orders in Council whilst the French decrees are officially declared to remain in force." But because no such evidence existed it could not be produced. Madison had Monroe contact Foster to let him know that the United States would discuss the matter with Britain no further.[56] Foster never had a chance to address impressments or Indian uprisings in the West because Monroe's letter arrived after the president sent his message to Congress that led to the declaration of war.[57]

With scandals and dissent threatening his reelection, Madison proceeded with a strategy to neutralize Federalists, heal ruptures in his party, and secure the nomination and reelection. In April he recommended that Congress pass an embargo to stop exports and give merchants time to return to the United States before Congress declared war.[58] News of another embargo ignited protests in New England. Quincy was still arguing that there would be no war, because in his opinion the purpose of this new round of commercial restrictions was still the destruction of New England. But if war did occur another embargo was "self-slaughter" and insufficient preparation for war.[59]

As the House prepared to debate imposing another embargo, Democratic-Republicans defeated Quincy's motion for a one-day postponement. Silas Stow, a Democratic-Republican from New York, was alarmed and worried that the "country was wholly unprepared" to enter into a war within the time frame that had been outlined. Taking the opposite position, Hugh Nelson from Virginia complained that war was inevitable and "ought not to be delayed." The Senate did extend the length of the embargo to ninety days but some senators were so eager to begin the process for war they agreed to suspend the rule specifying a full reading, on three separate days. After it passed both houses in a combined vote of 90–54, a ninety-day embargo went into effect on April 4, 1812.[60]

On the first day of June, Madison sent Congress a confidential message recommending action against Great Britain. His reasons included the Orders in Council, impressments, and Britain's instigation of wars with Indians in the West. At the very end of his message the president acknowledged that France "since the revocation of her decrees . . . has authorized illegal captures by its privateers and public ships; and that other outrages have been practised [sic] on our vessels and our citizens." For the time being he opposed taking any "definitive measures." Congress needed to take immediate action against Great Britain alone. Over Federalists' objections, on June 17 and 18 Congress responded to the spirit of Madison's message by declaring the United States at war with Great Britain, 79–49 in the House and 19–13 in the Senate. The nation's first formal declaration of war went into effect on June 18, 1812.[61]

The U.S. had legitimate grievances against Great Britain, but the case against France was equally compelling. In an interesting twist, Britain repealed its Orders in Council on June 23, before receiving news of the declaration of war. Given this development, the decision to proceed with the conflict provoked doubts about the reasons for the War of 1812 and Federalists began raising questions.[62] In their "Minority Report on the War," Federalists criticized the nation's military unpreparedness. They also addressed the problems inherent in one-party rule: "Power is assumed by the majority to deny the privilege of speech, at any state, and under any circumstances of debate."[63] Putting it even more succinctly, Taggart called war "a great evil" that should be entered into with exactitude, and not "enlarging upon and aggravating every subject of difference."[64] This is what Federalists thought was happening once again, but this time it was not a prohibition on trade but armed conflict with a stronger nation that was already engaging in an international conflict.

Federalists denounced the war as having little if anything to do with attacks on commerce, which they explained was why the southern and western regions of the Union supported the conflict and maritime New England did not. To Federalists, support from regions whose representatives seemed generally hostile toward maritime New England confirmed that the Democratic-Republicans' promotion of trade restrictions to protect commerce had been a diversion from the start. Speaker of the House Henry Clay of Kentucky seemed to confirm this view. In an attempt to humiliate New Englanders for their opposition, he announced that the southern and western states "were united for war."[65] Federalist claims that expansion had shifted the balance of power to the South and the West also intensified. Quincy and others confirmed that "the safety of every state depends upon its proportion of political power," and this power was quickly slipping away from New England.[66]

According to Federalists, the War of 1812, like the Haitian policy, nonimportation, and the embargo, was never about commerce or impressments, and all pretenses to those claims were exposed after Britain repealed its Orders in Council. The *Berkshire Reporter* agreed with Federalists who argued that war with France "would be much more just and proper than a war with England." While it is easy to conclude that they forgave Britain gratuitously, Federalists did correctly argue that Britain had been more straightforward than France and that both nations were guilty of the same infractions. More than one Federalist supported war with both France and Britain or no war at all, but most realized that the United States was unprepared for war in either case.[67]

News of the ninety-day embargo forced commercial state mariners to rush resolutions into Congress, begging for a postponement and a way to avoid the war altogether.[68] At an Essex County meeting led by Timothy Pickering, Federalists denounced the gerrymandering tactic that allowed Democratic-Republicans to defy "the voice of the people" and concluded that because of the restrictive system and declaration of war, New Englanders' rights had been "more injured, oppressed, and endangered, by the doings of our own national government than they were when in 1775, we took arms to protect and defend them against" Great Britain. To counter the Federalists' memorials, Democratic-Republicans also sent resolutions to Congress pledging their support for the war.[69]

Violence among those who disagreed over the war was unavoidable in this supercharged political climate. In July 1812, after Baltimore's *Federal Republican* published antiwar comments, rioters attacked the newspaper's staff. City officials stood by as a small group of ruffians grew into a mob estimated at about twenty-five hundred. Many of the same politicians who had carefully avoided riots over the embargo made no effort to prevent several nights of violence that culminated in the vicious beating and deaths of several Federalists associated with the paper. Boston Federalists allegedly attempted to avenge deaths from the Baltimore riots by attacking Charles Turner, the Democratic-Republican who had unseated Federalist William Baylies in 1809 after the congressional majority rejected the results of a Plymouth District election. One unforeseen consequence of the violence was Federalist Party victories in Maryland, New Jersey, New York, and throughout New England in 1812.[70]

Outside of Congress Federalists opposed the war for a variety of reasons. They cited its immorality, the nation's vulnerability to slave insurrections, and the fear of divine retribution for waging an unjust war. Congressional Federalists mainly opposed the war because they considered it to be the wrong war. A majority would certainly have concurred with those who preferred war with France instead of Britain.[71] They correctly noted that Britain had been willing to make some accommodations with the United States, while France had been duplicitous and backbiting. It is difficult to envision Federalists opposing a war against France or both France and England. Their antiwar resistance was therefore neither inordinately moralistic nor highhandedly pacific.

By the end of 1812, national elections demonstrated that Federalists no longer commanded support nationally and could not win the presidency. Instead of focusing on their own candidate, a number of Federalists supported the Democratic-Republican candidate, DeWitt Clinton of New York. Clinton was leader of a New York faction that broke away from the Virginia leadership of the Democratic-Republican Party during the embargo. With strong Federalist support he posed a formidable challenge to the incumbent. As the "Peace Party" candidate Clinton advocated immediately ending diplomatic hostilities with Great Britain, which was attractive to New England and Mid-Atlantic voters. But as many Democratic-Republicans calculated, the declaration of war helped to solidify Madison's base and increase his popularity. Federalists even alleged that Congress actually declared war to help reelect the president. Madison won reelection with 128 electoral votes to Clinton's 89, but once again the Electoral College exposed sectional divisions within the Democratic-Republican Party and the nation. Madison received no support from New England except Vermont; while New York, New Jersey, and Delaware cast votes for Clinton.[72]

The congressional elections exposed greater public support for Federalists. Peace candidates won large majorities in the Massachusetts legislature despite the gerrymandered districts.[73] The state's voters even elected the most infamous fomenter of disunion, Timothy Pickering, to the U.S. House of Representatives. As a result of their victories, Federalists, though still in the minority, had enough strength in the Thirteenth Congress (1813–1815) to initiate an investigation into the circumstances that resulted in the declaration of war. The inquiry examined the administration's policy toward France in addition to the evidence that justified sanctions and further actions against Britain.

Federalists participating in the congressional investigation attempted to indict the administration over whether or not France repealed its decrees. A coalition led by Federalist Daniel Webster looked into the administration's reasons for declaring war. A reexamination of Madison's diplomacy suggested that neither the revocation of the French decrees nor impressment were legitimate reasons to go to war.[74] Webster questioned the administration's reasons for levying sanctions against Britain based on the Cadore letter. At this time Webster, who would go on to have an illustrious career as a senator from Massachusetts, orator, and secretary of state in 1841, 1845, and 1850, had bipartisan support for his motion to review all related diplomatic correspondence.[75]

Monroe had to justify the case he made for war, especially since documents such as the fraudulent St. Cloud Decree provided further proof that France had manipulated the United States and facilitated the administration's hasty pursuit of war. The St. Cloud Decree was an attempt by the French to show that an official announcement repealing Napoleon's decrees was made on April 28, 1811, and became effective on November 1, 1811, before Congress passed the Nonintercourse Act against Britain. Many believed that the St. Cloud Decree was created much later than its authors claimed. However, Monroe stood behind his report and the declaration of war, and actually confirmed Federalist allegations that the administration based its arguments for war for reasons contradicted by the facts.[76]

The documents that Monroe provided in July 1813 separated the administration's actions against Britain and the declaration of war from the St. Cloud decree. His report then criticized Britain for questioning Napoleon's compliance under Macon's Bill No. 2 and insisted that France had made an "advance toward complete accommodation." The report intentionally discounted the fact that France and its allies continued to seize and destroy American ships after the decrees were supposedly repealed. Monroe concluded that the war was necessary because of impressments, but his report left several questions unanswered. Motions to continue the investigation were defeated on July 20. For what it was worth, Federalists proved their point but the matter died in committee and the war raged on.[77]

In opposition to the war, the Federalist governors of Massachusetts, Connecticut, and Rhode Island refused to muster state militia to comply with federal conscription quotas.[78] Massachusetts was unwilling to contribute to the war effort, and when the British seized eastern Maine, the federal government declined to send aid. British forces occupied parts of Maine until the war ended, but in the meantime residents there had the option of leaving the region or vowing to keep the peace. Those who took an oath of allegiance to King George III received the commercial privileges of British subjects.[79]

Federalist Martin Chittenden, a former congressman whose calls to repeal the embargo met harassment from southern representatives in the Tenth Congress, had become governor of Vermont. In 1813–1814 Chittenden issued an order for Vermont militiamen serving under federal authority in New York to come home. The order prompted a challenge to Chittenden's authority from the field and a resolution in Congress. Democratic-Republican-leaning militia officers sent the governor a letter refusing to obey his orders, but several troops returned home anyway. Kentucky Representative Solomon P. Sharp motioned for the U.S. attorney general to prosecute Chittenden for enticing soldiers to leave their posts. However, James Fisk of Vermont argued that the entire Vermont delegation was against the resolution and claimed that only a few people in the state agreed with the governor. Sharp backed down and agreed to table the motion. Vermont proclaimed that its militia would serve, but only under state officers.[80]

Following the British occupation of Washington, DC in 1814 and the invasion of New Orleans in 1815, some of the old radicals considered striking a separate peace, believing that the British would seize New Orleans. Pickering expected "the severance of the Union." If this should happen, he welcomed a scenario under which the "western states and territories will necessarily go off" and leave the original thirteen states independent and intact.[81] The expansion of slavery and slave representation would end along with commercial restrictions and New England's servility to the South.

Discussions about a New England confederation and convention in Hartford, Connecticut, circulated outward from Massachusetts during the embargo, but repeal truncated any interest among the other states. The situation changed by December 1813, when a more debilitating embargo enacted to end smuggling disrupted all commerce, including the coasting trade. Outraged over the imposition of yet another embargo imposed by a government whose long arm appeared to do everything but protect them, the citizens of South Hadley, Massachusetts, assembled a town meeting that mushroomed into new calls for a convention of the New England states to address grievances.[82]

Federalists in western Massachusetts were historically suspicious of the state's leadership in Boston and objected to the legislature's restrained tone after the embargo of 1813. Afterward, the interior had become extreme in its opposition to the war and demanded Madison's resignation or threatened disunion. Bostonians were more hesitant when it came to organizing a convention of New England states, which led to a power shift in the General Assembly. Memorials from the West streamed into the state government and the uproar ended the conservatives' dithering. Federalists controlled the state government and even those adverse to radical measures realized that they had to appease the agitated and potentially violent residents.[83]

The legislature assigned the business of assembling delegates to a committee chaired by Harrison Gray Otis. The committee proposed a convention without input from the state's Democratic-Republican minority, which had earlier walked out in protest and then published its opposition to the proposed convention.[84] The legislature selected delegates who, according to Josiah Quincy, were "of known moderation of views and tried discretion of conduct." As a precaution Timothy Bigelow, perhaps the most radical of the delegates, was not given an important role in the convention.[85] The other New England states willingly joined Massachusetts to address some of their common grievances. After delegates were selected the convention was under way.

Among their demands, attendees of the Hartford Convention called for repeal of the three-fifths clause, a regional check on federal commercial policies, stronger defenses for New England's coasts, and changes in presidential nominating procedures to prevent successive elections of candidates from the same state.[86] Twelve representatives from Massachusetts, seven from Connecticut, four from Rhode Island, two from New Hampshire, and one from Vermont attended the convention which lasted from December 15, 1814, to January 5, 1815.[87] Missing from the convention were Josiah Quincy, Timothy Pickering, James Lloyd, and other radicals responsible for capturing popular support after the onset of the restrictive system. Although the radicals influenced the content of the Convention's resolutions, the hardliners were deemed too provocative to physically participate in the Convention or present New England's demands to the president.

While he could not openly participate, Pickering worked closely with the convention and framed a majority of its demands. Nevertheless, in a letter to John Lowell, Pickering deduced that the Convention would take place too late to influence the course of the war or the federal government. Along with Lowell who found Otis "naturally timid and frequently wavering," and the other delegates unprepared "to *act*," Pickering feared that they would not present New England's demands as forcefully as they should.[88] Quincy, who had battled Democratic-Republicans toe-to-toe in Congress, also despaired that the delegates lacked the drive and intensity required to bring about constitutional reform.[89]

Indeed, the delegate's reticence and moderation had already delayed the Convention. Furthermore, as Pickering surmised during his flirtation with disunion, any confederation of northern states must include New York to have even a modicum of success. As it was, the Convention's delegation barely represented all of New England. Low attendance and the delegates' tepid disposition eased any fears Madison may have had about New England seceding from the Union. He always doubted that it would happen, but increased security at the Springfield Armory in Massachusetts nonetheless. Then too, when they arrived in Washington Madison refused to legitimize the Convention by meeting with the delegates.[90]

In reality, the Hartford Convention did little more than give Democratic-Republicans more material with which to discredit Federalists and kept the participants from earning political appointments. Nor did the convention meet the expectations of New Englanders who wanted to send a strong message to the federal government and possibly bring about changes. Their disappointment was articulated by one dissatisfied Bay State Federalist who said he regretted that Hartford Convention participants "certainly [had] not done as much as was expected of them by the great Body of the people of the State." The delegates had proven "much more temperate" than many desired. Newburyporters were outraged that the Hartford delegates had done nothing to protect them from an imposing central government dominated by westerners and southerners. They sent a petition to the General Court demanding that New England strike a separate peace with Britain or take steps to secede from the Union. And they did not let the issue die until the war was over.[91]

Activies in Hartford were overshadowed by U.S. negotiations of a peace treaty with Britain in Ghent, Belgium, that began in December 1814, as well as Andrew Jackson's victory at New Orleans in January 1815. Otis later confessed that the Convention's true purpose was to calm Massachusetts' more radical citizens. No matter the motive the attitude expressed by Otis contributed to making the Hartford Convention anticlimactic. The more charismatic Federalists were reduced to consultants, and along the end of hostilities between the United States and Britain, Democratic-Republicans like William Bentley were gratified that, "The Hartford convention . . . did not give much anticipation."[92]

After the war, it was clear that the conflict sparked a boost in national morale, even though its cause was never concretely defined for Federalists. Because Britain repealed its Orders in Council, impressment was touted as the primary reason for the war. This was shrewd in the face of the Federalists' opposition because impressing U.S. citizens was one of the few infractions that France and Britain did not commit with equal frequency. Federalists rightly recalled that Democratic-Republicans never rallied behind impressments as a cause for war. Many held merchants responsible for impressments. In fact they did not even see the practice as a reason to restrict British imports. They may have forgotten or found it inconvenient to admit it after war was declared in 1812, but southern Jeffersonians made this exact argument during debates over nonimportation in 1806.[93]

One of southern congressmen's objections to interfering with British imports as a response to impressments stemmed from the fact that U.S. merchants hired British subjects while seamen counterfeited and sold government certificates originally issued for their protection. Providing "protections" to British deserters had nullified the documents' ability to protect U.S. citizens. Southerners also worried in 1806 that Britain, the largest consumer of U.S. cotton, tobacco, and other raw materials, would place prohibitions on their exports if Congress imposed a strong ban on that nation's imports. They were reluctant to pass nonimportation and certainly did not agree to sacrifice southern markets over impressments. Few southerners at that time believed that the U.S. would or should go to war for a problem caused by greedy merchants and mariners.[94] Yet their perspective regarding impressment changed to justify the war.

Another rationale for continuing the war after repeal of the Orders in Council was Britain's precipitation of wars with Native Americans in the West. In addition to decelerating settlement, slaveholders lost their human property to Native Americans and the British who either kidnapped slaves or assisted runaways. This problem added to the resentment that southerners already harbored toward the British for neither returning nor remitting compensation for thousands of slaves carried away at the end of the Revolution. Madison mentioned the frontier problem in his war message. New Englanders felt that problems in the West, instead of the orders in council or impressments, were really behind the declaration of war.[95] They resented what they saw as the actual causes of the war, which for these Federalists had nothing to do with depredations on maritime commerce.

When the war ended in 1815 Federalists continued to influence New England politics and the region's voters elected Federalist Party governors and congressmen. Soon, however, the Party began to dissolve. The three-fifths clause cost Federalists the presidency and Congress in 1800. Were it not for slave representation, New England would not have suffered under commercial restrictions, and the nation would not have been drawn into a war that it was unprepared to fight. All of this, they reasoned, had taken place because the party in power was under the direction of southern slaveholders.[96] These assertions were based in reality, but the Federalist Party's demise was more complicated.

Election victories should have been more gratifying, but most of the Federalists elected between 1812 and 1815 eschewed the uncompromising attitudes displayed by Thatcher, Elliot, Hillhouse, Quincy, and Pickering, whose straightforward attacks and denunciations helped to repeal the embargo and bring the inequities associated with the three-fifths clause to light. The party's new, more reasonable and inoffensive leadership contributed to Quincy's decision not to seek reelection to the Thirteenth Congress. He remained a champion of New England's economic independence and political influence but saw the situation becoming hopeless for Federalists at the national level. It became increasingly apparent, Quincy would later observe, that the northern states lacked solidarity. Appearing somewhat disheartened, he wrote Pickering, "As I mean to keep my temper, I will keep myself on my farm. Should I say a word on politics I know not where this letter would end."[97] The radicals were supplanted by less zealous Federalists. As the unifying message of the radicals diminished, the electorate fragmented and the Federalist Party began to die.

Moderate Federalists were unhappy with southern domination of the federal government, but not inclined to threaten disunion or repeatedly call for an amendment to eliminate slave representation. Many wanted long careers and hoped to escape the stigma of disloyalty that was attached to Federalism since the embargo. Some of them repudiated the extreme rhetoric that had energized New Englanders before the war. Harrison Gray Otis had agreed to participate in the Hartford Convention, but intended to restore the Federalist Party to its former greatness or at least reestablish a national coalition. Some unrealistically hoped to capture enough seats in Congress to eliminate the three-fifths clause while compromising with southerners and westerners whenever possible.[98]

After the party disbanded in the 1820s, a few former Federalists continued to work toward repealing the three-fifths clause. Similar to what free-soil advocates would argue before the Civil War, Samuel Taggart said that Federalists would tolerate slavery where it was already established, but opposed its expansion into new territories. They also promoted northern unity as the only way to preserve New England's political power and economic liberties. The pamphlet *Awake! O Spirit of the North*, published in 1812, expanded on the Federalists' call for a united North. The "slave country" had insisted on the three-fifths ratio at the Constitutional Convention in order to "gain and preserve an undue ascendancy in both branches of the national government." In the midst of what Federalists considered an unjust war and years of "repeated injuries and . . . galling oppressions," Boreas, god of the north wind from Greek mythology, was calling on northerners to excise that "rotten part" of the Constitution.[99]

The ideas expressed in the pamphlets, speeches, and other Federalist writings reflected the very early stages of the free-soil movement, including racial divisions and regional protectionism. For example, the pamphlet *Slave Representation by Boreas* contrasted the "genial climate and a friendly soil" of the Free States and territories with the oppressive "Slave country," which had grown dangerously powerful with only a few white inhabitants. At the beginning of the pamphlet he says, "*Free Blacks* . . . are placed on the same footing with *Whites*" in northern states and appears satisfied that this is just, although there were civil rights and segregation in the northern states. As the essay continues Dwight then combines all African Americans into a broader rejection of "Black Representation," adding an unfortunate racist element to his condemnation of the slave power.[100]

The free soil concept had been around for several decades and had roots in British law. *Somerset v. Stewart* (1772) created a legal and theoretical basis for barring slavery from specific locations and freeing slaves that entered those locations regardless of their residence and status in areas where slavery was upheld. The original decision that a slave could not be removed from England where slavery did not exist and returned to where it was practiced sparked freedom lawsuits in Europe and the United States. The idea of freeing slaves on the basis of their birth, entry, or residence in free-soil areas affected comity among the states and federal fugitive slave laws. This problem affected sectional relations as early as 1794 when first fugitive slave law was enacted in response to a dispute between Pennsylvania and Virginia.[101] Eventually, the number of Americans fighting to keep slavery out of newly acquired territories and states would expand to include Democrats (formerly Democratic-Republicans), abolitionists, immigrants, and former Federalists.

Though there are connections between the free soil movement and the Federalists' fight to keep slavery out of new territories and repeal the three-fifths clause, the Federalists' relationship to antislavery politics continues to spark debate among historians. Several argue that Federalists actively promoted the abolition of slavery, while others maintain that they "never upheld a moral or political opposition to slavery itself." This encapsulates a broader interpretation that sees overt concern for the plight of slaves as a litmus test for antislavery sentiment. Thus, the absence of this form of humanitarianism in Federalist rhetoric delegitimizes any other rhetoric regarding slavery.[102] An enduring argument maintains that Federalists had no interest in slavery and only wanted to end slave representation for political purposes. This depiction which mirrors Democratic-Republicans criticisms has survived into the twenty-first century.[103]

Political enemies first endeavored to discredit the Federalist calls to eliminate the three-fifths clause as an insincere, partisan scheme. In an address to New Englanders attacking both maritime commerce and "the pygmy scraps of land . . . which calls itself the state of Rhode Island," publisher Mathew Carey defended slave representation and disparaged Quincy, Lloyd, and Pickering for opposing it. Carey praised the South and marveled at southerners' ability to drain New England of its population and ruin the region's economy. Other writers insisted that Federalists only came close to mentioning the abolition of slavery as a ploy to promote disunion.[104]

An important reason for Democratic-Republicans to edit the history of New England was the support that Federalists received from black voters. African American contributions to Federalist victories in 1812, in addition to the Federalist Party's opposition to slave representation, moved an *Eastern Argus* correspondent to complain that in the South, "5 Negroes are equal in taxation to 3 white men, but in Massachusetts the vote of any old stupid Negro is equal to the election of a Governor."[105] Other efforts to disparage the Federalist Party's support among black voters could be found in portrayals of Federalists as ardently proslavery.[106]

Of course, southerners would benefit if the government repealed slave representation and counted all of the South's inhabitants, including slaves, as whole persons for congressional representation. Federalists understood this but condemned slavery as immoral and unchristian nonetheless. Many promoted repealing the three-fifths clause to restore a balance of regional power in national politics. The Federalists objections to slave representation did not emerge solely from political expediency. Antislavery sentiment had a long history in New England that produced over a century of antislavery propaganda reaffirmed by natural rights philosophies.[107] The early republic also produced antislavery writers and many of these were Federalists or Federalist leaning. From the 1790s onward, explains historian Rachel Hope Cleves, newly published literature disseminated antislavery arguments to broad audiences throughout New England. She shows that like their political counterparts, these antislavery writers linked commercial restrictions and the War of 1812 to the violence of slavery and the interests of slaveholders. Lemuel Haynes, an African-American abolitionist, added slavery to the Federalists' list of reasons for opposing to the war.[108]

Without a doubt, more than a few Federalists were apathetic toward slavery, but African Americans provide an important and frequently overlooked perspective of the party. The oration before the Wilberforce Philanthropic Association of New York mentioned at the start of this book praised Federalists for opposing the spread of slavery and supporting African American rights. The organization also criticized Democratic-Republicans for perpetuating slavery. At a Boston Sons of Africa meeting, the speaker commended Massachusetts in general and the town of Salem in particular for their "partiality to freedom and likewise for their particular benevolence to the Africans."[109] Black Americans expressed their appreciation and approval for the stances that Federalists took on their behalf. Adopting the Democratic-Republican perspective obscures the fact that African Americans supported the Federalist Party even if some were indifferent or proslavery. Black voters did not differentiate between calls to abolish slavery or limit its extension depending on whether they were based on political motives, moral arguments, or humanitarian concerns.

Race relations were tense in nineteenth-century New England and free African Americans battled discrimination in northern states as much as they did elsewhere in the Union. For example, whites in Salem, Massachusetts, refused to send their children to school with black children, and in 1810 a stage company in that town demanded that a black minister ride outside with the driver instead of in the cab with other passengers. According to William Bentley the minister "angrily refused" to ride outside, which demonstrates the need for African Americans to confront problems related to racial discrimination and the exercise of civil rights, even in the absence of slavery.[110]

Yet it was obvious that black men and women preferred the troubled freedom they had in New England and other northern free states to slavery. Many conveyed appreciation to individuals and towns that built schools for black children, whites who attended churches with black ministers and those who called for the abolition of slavery and fought to preserve their voting rights. Despite arguments against Federalists attempts to revoke the three-fifths clause or arrest the spread of slavery, efforts to limit the voting rights of African Americans in northern states by the 1820s was related more to racism within the Democratic-Republican Party than the Federalist Party, which had begun to disband by this time.[111]

Federalist opposition to the three-fifths clause often demonstrated personal abhorrence of slavery. Leverett Saltonstall refused to help a friend capture a runaway slave. When discussing ways to keep slavery out of western territories ceded by the states in 1785, Pickering called slavery "inhuman" and "iniquitous in itself." Commenting on Congress' reluctance to ban slavery from the Northwest, Pickering noted that "After the admission of *Slavery*" members of the legislature should "say nothing of *Christianity*." He concluded that expanding slavery was inconsistent in a nation that advocated "*liberty*, and the *pursuit of happiness*."[112] Federalist newspapers also condemned slavery as immoral and unchristian, often dramatizing the horrors of the slave trade and the mistreatment of slaves in the South.[113]

It was because of their attempts to restrict the westward spread of slavery that political writers called the Federalist Party the "father of *Abolitionism*." In the 1840s, pundits were still criticizing former Federalists for "tampering with the abolitionists of the North" by insisting that Congress repeal the three-fifths clause.[114] Even more significant, however, was the abolitionists' view of the Federalist Party. In a May 1848 speech commemorating the anniversary of the American Antislavery Society, Wendell Phillips bemoaned the erosion of rights for African Americans, including disenfranchisement in many northern states. He recalled Pickering's motion to repeal the three-fifths clause, as well as the antislavery proposals made by Rufus King and asked, "Where are . . . the successors of these men [and] their anti-slavery sentiments?"[115]

The failed Hartford Convention and War of 1812 left the three-fifths clause intact and the Federalist Party on its last leg. "What luck attends our wicked rulers," wrote Leverett Saltonstall. Just when the situation seemed hopeless for Democratic-Republicans, "Peace comes to their aid . . . to close the war with Glory."[116]

During the war, Democratic-Republicans saw the need to adopt many of the Federalists' defense and tax policies.[117] But for resisting the war and trying to end southern power they continued to accuse Federalists of "stoking the animosity and hatred" in New England by calling Jefferson and Madison "the enemies of commerce and . . . the cause of our commercial embarrassments!" In 1813 Josiah Quincy predicted that Democratic-Republicans would continue to discredit Federalists to keep them out of power. He was correct.[118] Outside of New England, most Americans accepted the Democratic-Republican interpretation of events and participated in denunciations of Federalists long after its demise.[119]

As Quincy had predetermined, years of trade restrictions transformed New England's economy. The emphasis on maritime activities gave way to manufacturing. Peace did not heal the wounds caused by the commercial restrictions. One New England merchant complained in 1815 that money was scarce and "the prospect of our foreign trade becomes less & less. . . Commerce will need all the assistance which can consistently be afforded it by the government." Though a supporter of Democratic-Republican policies, he opposed "bestow[ing] too much upon the *manufacturing* at the expense of the *commercial* interests," but it was too late.[120]

The War of 1812 combined solutions for problems in the West with an uncertain future for maritime commerce. Federalists maintained that putting an end to the Indian attacks and slave seizures provoked by the British was more important to the war's supporters than solving the problems involving maritime trade. For example, Democratic-Republican Nathaniel Silsbee of Massachusetts was satisfied that the war would force the British to end their "system" of "stealing Negroes." By settling problems on the frontier and restricting commerce for a decade, the war put manufacturing on surer footing and created the potential for new domestic markets for the expanding Slave South.[121]

Already under way during the embargo, manufacturing experienced unrestricted development in postwar New England.[122] Slavery had become inconsequential to the region's economy long before the War of 1812, and merchants developed a measure of independence from the slaveholding states through the wartime carrying trade. For these reasons Federalists charged Jefferson and Madison with destroying commerce to restrict New Englanders' economic and political freedom. Manufacturing changed the culture of labor and fewer mariners enjoyed the "lives of activity, of enterprise" that once separated them from agriculturalists. The new economy required wage laborers to toil in factories, or as one commentator assessed it, "There must be white slaves or black ones, or more properly there must be laborers! The Negroes are the laborers of the South and West, the whites of the East." The change that Federalists despised most had come to pass. Manufacturing allowed the "purse proud negro-drivers" to benefit from trade restrictions to both dominate and "stigmatize" the North's labor force.[123]

New Englanders who could, reinvested capital in such enterprises as the American Cotton Factory, the Boston and Springfield Manufacturing Company, paper mills, and shoe factories. Patrick Jackson and Benjamin

Crowninshield were among many merchants who abandoned maritime activities for manufacturing. Jackson established the Boston Manufacturing Company at Waltham, Massachusetts, and immediately after announcing the end of the war, Benjamin Crowninshield, who was appointed secretary of the navy in the Madison administration and the most successful heir of his family's shipping fortune, advised his father and brothers to "sell off all ships" and leave the trading business.[124] Even Hartford Convention participant Harrison Gray Otis had an interest in manufacturing corporations and interstate commerce.[125]

While they remained influential in New England after the war, the Federalist Party's moderate leadership eschewed the audacity of the radicals or extremists that attracted voters to the party from 1808 to 1814. The radicals seemed to understand something that moderates failed to comprehend: southerners would never compromise to favor New England's interests over their own. For all of their cautious rhetoric, delegates to the Hartford Convention spent the rest of their careers defending themselves against charges of sedition.[126] Rebuilding the Federalist Party nationally was out of the question. Although there were still Federalists in the South, their numbers were dwindling and even before the war, many no longer called themselves Federalists due to the party's unpopularity in the region. Another barrier to saving the Federalist Party was their opposition to slave representation. As historian James Broussard notes, "Southern Federalist leaders were still southerners, and none of them took nearly so advanced a position on the slavery issue as some of their northern colleagues."[127]

Josiah Quincy, who had opposed statehood for Louisiana, warned that divisions of the vast Louisiana Purchase territory into new slave states would "shift the balance of power still farther to the South and West." When the crisis over slavery in Missouri began in 1819, Quincy joined forces with Daniel Webster to write and publish a memorial to Congress supporting congressional authority to prohibit slavery in any new states. Identifying themselves as part of "a Christian community" compelled by the "dictates of religion and humanity," they called slavery "a moral evil . . . in violation of the fundamental laws of nature." Slavery should have been abolished after the revolution they insisted, but since it had not been, it was up to Congress to keep it out of Missouri. If it gave up its constitutional obligation to decide the status of slavery in new territories and states, Congress was beginning a trend that would eventually force slavery into the northern states where it was abolished and perpetuate the "inequality of representation, which already exists in regard to the original states."[128]

Missourians had also drafted a state constitution barring free African Americans from entering the state. "[I]f I were a member of the Legislature of one of the free States [sic]," wrote John Quincy Adams, "I would move for a declaratory act, that so long as the article in the Constitution of Missouri depriving the colored citizens of the State, say of Massachusetts, of their rights as citizens of the United States" Missouri's "white citizens" should be "held as aliens within the Commonwealth of Massachusetts," and receive the same discriminatory treatment they mete out to African Americans. Adams went even further and said that he would keep Missourians from claiming "the property or possession of a human being as a slave." He argued that the Framers had made "a dishonorable compromise with slavery," and that its expansion would increase the South's political power. Little more than a decade would pass between the Missouri crisis and Adams's election to the House of Representatives, but Congress did demand that Missouri amend its constitution and remove clauses that infringed on the rights of any U.S. citizen before granting statehood.[129]

In February 1819 New Yorker James Tallmadge, a Democratic-Republican, introduced an amendment barring slavery from Missouri as a condition for statehood. Even though Tallmadge's amendment passed the House several times, the Senate rejected it repeatedly. For a while southerners tried unsuccessfully to use the admission of Maine as a free state to offset the entry of Missouri with slavery. Finally Jesse B. Thomas from Illinois proposed what became the Missouri Compromise of 1820, by suggesting that Congress admit Missouri as a slave state but prohibit slavery in other parts of the Louisiana Purchase territories north of 36° 30'.[130]

During debates over Missouri, Federalists organized antislavery demonstrations. Harrison Gray Otis voted with the South however. Otis did not side with Federalists until Rufus King pointed out that the slave states already had twenty more representatives and electoral votes than they would have without the three-fifths clause and Missouri would unfairly increase that number. At King's urging northerners backed the Tallmadge amendment. Otis then joined others from north in their fight to restrict slavery, who remained firm until southerners threatened to secede from the Union. Several representatives from the North backed down and accepted the compromise. In the final vote, fourteen northerners voted along with southerners to allow slavery in Missouri. John Randolph of Virginia then sniped, "They were scared at their own dough faces—yes, *they were scared at their own dough faces!*—we had *them*, and if we wanted *three* more, we could have them . . . the men, *whose conscience, and morality, and religion, extend to 'thirty-six degrees and thirty minutes north latitude.'*"[131]

Quincy coined a different phrase for northern politicians who not only sided with the South, but also did so against their own constituents' interests. He called them "six-dollar-a-day patriots" who were willing to "barter away our birth rights on the floor of Congress, for offices, contracts, appointments, and every mess of pottage corrupt men can proffer." Until northerners recognized the need to consolidate their efforts, he reasoned, the North would remain powerless. Quincy was not the only one to mention the problem of northern voters sending politicians of this ilk to Congress, where they "blind and cheat their Northern friends."[132] As long as northern voters tolerated pro-southern representatives, no antislavery politician could check the spread of slavery.

Federalists then proposed that the Constitution's three-fifths ratio only apply to the original thirteen states. Although the North was more populous, the three-fifths clause gave southerners disproportionate access to government appointments, which allowed them to control of their party. Southerners held chairmanships, cabinet posts, and other high federal offices in the federal government. Many were proslavery zealots, Leonard Richard points out, such as John C. Calhoun of South Carolina, who from 1817 to 1850 was secretary of war, vice president, secretary of state, and senator, and Georgian John Forsyth, who served as a representative, senator, diplomat, and secretary of state. However, it was only with northern support that southerners could pass proslavery legislation from the Missouri Compromise of 1820 through and the Kansas-Nebraska Act (1854).[133]

Along with the propaganda that kept them from holding national offices, internal divisions decimated the Federalist Party even further. Otis and other Federalists supported statehood for Maine in an effort to eliminate the Democratic-Republican districts to the north and strengthen the Federalist base in Massachusetts proper. Quincy, now a member of the state legislature, believed that separation would be unfair to Maine's Federalists. Quincy opposed proposals for separation in 1816 and 1819, earning him criticism from some members of his party.[134] Maine finally acquired statehood in 1820, and as Quincy figured, the separation did little to preserve the Federalist Party.

From the late 1790s onward Federalists had fought unsuccessfully to maintain a sectional balance of power in the federal government. They lost battle after battle in Congress when trying to stem the tide of southern and southwestern power. Their opposition to southern power was defeated largely because northern Democratic-Republicans and Federalists such as Otis were either apathetic or sympathetic when it came to stopping the spread of slavery or repealing the three-fifths clause.[135] By the time conflict erupted over Missouri, several important advocates for the North, such as Elliot, Thatcher, Pickering, Quincy, and Hillhouse, were no longer in Congress. Northern delegations continued to form a numerical majority in Congress, but instead of siding with Federalists, they earned the epithet "doughfaces" for their acquiescence to southerners' demands. The results of the controversy notwithstanding, northern legislators initially displayed an embryonic unity over the spread of slavery during the conflict over Missouri. Federalists may not have realized it at the time but some northern onlookers began to recognize the wisdom in presenting a united front against southern power. Opposition to slavery in Missouri failed and it was an important moment for abolitionism in the North, but not the Federalist Party.[136]

So long as they opposed the three-fifths clause and westward spread of slavery, Federalists could never reestablish a national coalition. When in 1797 they supported the petitions of freed African Americans who asked Congress to help them maintain their freedom, southerners treated the case as they did every petition regarding slavery, but George Thatcher and others insisted that Congress make amendments to fugitive slave laws. Instead the House decided to return the slaves to North Carolina for "justice."[137]

Interregional harmony among Federalists slowly eroded because of proposals attacking slavery, such as when Thatcher motioned to check the spread of slavery into the Mississippi Territory in 1798. Thatcher's support for government intervention on behalf of freed persons who petitioned Congress to help them avoid enslavement in North Carolina earned him the praise of African Americans such as the Philadelphia-based abolitionist James Forten, but taking this and similar stands alienated New England Federalists from their southern counterparts. South Carolina Federalist John Rutledge warned that "the discussion of such questions" was damaging the party and costing it support in "certain parts of the Union." Rutledge considered himself a Federalist to the end, but correctly cautioned New Englanders that southerners would reject any political association with politicians who attacked slavery.[138]

Intraparty divisions also played an important role in the Federalist Party's collapse. After 1815 Federalists aspiring to public office at the state and national levels had no reason to tolerate backbiting from members of a dying party. Complaints and criticisms over their support of the compensation bill of 1816, which raised congressional representatives' salaries, forced some Federalists out of the party. Some of them ran for office as Democratic-Republicans. Others, such as Otis, attempted to curry favor with President James Monroe, but patronage remained a partisan reward offered only to members of the president's party and Otis could not wash away the taint from his involvement in the Hartford Convention. For opposing the war, future Vermont congressman Orasmus C. Merrill said the government should classify all Federalists as public enemies.[139]

Jefferson's sweep of Federalists from public offices, including judgeships and state agencies, also contributed to the Federalist Party's eventual demise, but more important was the constant barrage of anti-Federalist propaganda that exploited fears of secret cabals and plots to destroy the republic. Propaganda was an effective way to eliminate or at least diminish the influence of a threatening political adversary.[140]

Steering newly arriving immigrants away from the Federalist Party also helped. Immigrant aid societies informed newly arriving persons that Federalists would keep them from exercising political rights and that

New England's culture fostered intemperance. On the other hand, new arrivals in the country were steered toward the vast and fertile lands of the untamed West, which offered agricultural opportunities and the American virtues that they should embrace. Therefore, settling the West became a more inviting prospect than stopping, even temporarily, in New England.[141]

Mathew Carey attacked New England's Federalist past in *An Examination of the Pretenses of New England to Commercial Pre-Eminence* in 1814. In response to charges of sectional bias in federal policy, Carey upbraided all New Englanders for their "arrogant and unfounded pretensions." He specifically targeted Massachusetts, which "since the close of the reign of Federalism" had been "the seat of discontent, complaint, and turbulence." Carey took issue with New Englanders for opposing slavery, especially after they had profited from the slave trade. He insulted the region's below-average politicians and unscrupulous merchants who cheated customers and harassed the federal government "more than all the rest of the union together." Because of the state's consistent carping after 1800, Carey opined that the rest of the nation should vote to expel Massachusetts from the Union, as an exercise of justice.[142]

In other parts of the country Federalists found it increasingly difficult to elect candidates to public office and some began to float the idea of disbanding the party.[143] In the Massachusetts gubernatorial race of 1824 Harrison Gray Otis ran with support from Daniel Webster and a young, optimistic William Lloyd Garrison. But Federalists were not solidly behind Otis and the Democratic-Republican candidate William Eustis won the election. Following Otis's defeat, no other Federalist ran for the governorship in Massachusetts.[144]

For ambitious politicians the burdens of Federalism—disunionism, antiwar activism, and constitutional reform to nullify the three-fifths clause—proved too powerful to overcome. Like Otis, several tried to distance themselves from their party's record and attempted to create an amalgamation party with Democratic-Republicans. Amalgamation did not succeed because Democratic-Republicans were always suspicious of former Federalists. Some believed that Federalists could only survive in national politics, as Jacob Crowninshield said in 1803, by "throwing themselves into our ranks, changing their old name, and . . . incorporating their party into a union with the Republicans." An amalgamation party was deemed "a great evil" and most Democratic-Republicans maintained that the parties should remain distinct to avoid a Federalist infiltration and takeover. Defections from Federalism became common anyway and the dividing lines of the First Party System began to blur. Fewer politicians ran for office as Federalists, and some state elections became chaotic such as in 1826, when more than eight hundred candidates received votes to represent one city in the Massachusetts General Court. The Federalist Party had essentially died by 1824.[145]

Controversies that surfaced in antebellum politics over the extension of slavery reanimated condemnations of the Federalist Party. Though few leading Democratic-Republicans really thought that Federalists could divide the Union, it damaged antislavery opponents when newspapers and pamphlets suggested that voting for them was a vote against the republic's survival. So, even after the Federalist Party's demise, Democratic-Republicans looked over their shoulders to make sure that former Federalists did not reappear under a new name or resurface as part of another party or movement unchecked. In fact, Federalists did join the National Republican Party, which began about 1828 with John Quincy Adams. The old radical Timothy Pickering became a Jacksonian Democrat around the same time.[146]

After Henry Clay lost to Andrew Jackson in 1832, National Republicans, anti-Jackson Democratic-Republicans, and former Federalists formed the Whig Party. The Whigs gave former Federalists a national party that was able to elect William H. Harrison and Zachary Taylor to the presidency. But their past continued to follow Federalists wherever they went. In 1840 Charles G. Greene tracked down the whereabouts of former Federalists and connected them to Whigs in an attempt to defeat William Henry Harrison. To drive voters away from Harrison, Greene revived controversies involving Federalists from the Jay Treaty through the Hartford Convention. These devious men, Greene warned, were hatching yet another scheme to return Federalists to the White House. Once there, they would abolish slavery using a slaveholder and the military hero Harrison to dupe the unsuspecting.[147]

Fear of a Federalist resurgence and the benefits of patronage kept northern Democratic-Republicans in line with the southern wing of their party. Some of them deplored the brashness of southerners who were only in Congress because of "slave votes," but still went along with pro-southern policies or refused to cast dissenting votes. While they were loath to convey their hostilities in public, private correspondence was different. In 1808 Orchard Cook told John Quincy Adams that he and others were "hurt" that New England was being degraded and oppressed by "that part of the country . . . kept by Negro votes." New Yorker DeWitt Clinton and his supporters broke away from their party's southern leadership before the War of 1812. And Clinton, who contributed to emancipation efforts in his state, ran for president to oust the Virginia dynasty. Eventually, more northern Democrats would crack under the weight of southern dominance of the party, but this would not happen until shortly before the civil war.[148]

Before then it would take decades but eventually as Federalists had urged, northerners began to confront their diminishing status in the Union. The idea of creating a "Universal Yankee Nation" surfaced around 1822 to encourage the cultivation of regional ideals and culture. New Englanders spread Yankee culture to new territories and states as they migrated west.[149] Soon debates over slavery in new territories differed only slightly from the earlier contests between Democratic-Republicans and Federalists. Some of the radicals who gave Jefferson and his congressional allies the most trouble were still a threat. In 1833, as it appeared to one reporter that the "intention of the Federal party in the North and East, to interfere with slavery" had been "disclaimed . . . except by a few such fanatics as abolitionist William Lloyd Garrison." Unwittingly, this correspondent, though attempting to diminish antislavery sentiment in the North, had identified the Federalist lasting influence in New Englanders' fight against slavery. As that movement intensified, the lessons taught by the extreme Federalists had far-reaching consequences for the nation they so desperately wanted to mold. As one historian concludes, "The New England Federalist idiom was Garrison's native tongue, and he employed it in challenging Yankees to combat slavery." Thus, despite efforts to mar their memory and keep them from regaining power in government, the causes championed by radical Federalists and their methods to achieve those ends remained energetic and spirited.[150]

NOTES

1. *Annals of Congress*, 10th Cong., 2nd sess., 462–66. For Jefferson's inaugural addresses, see T. B. Wait, ed., *State Papers and Publick Documents of the United States from the Accession of Thomas Jefferson to the Presidency, Exhibiting a Complete View of Our Foreign Relations since That Time*, 3 vols. (Boston: T. B. Wait and Sons, 1814–1815), 1:9–13, 253–59; and Thomas Jefferson, The President's Speech Register Office, March 14, 1801 (Salem: Printed by William Carlton, 1801), 11, 13.

2. "Mr. Elliot to His Constituents, Letter VIII," *Rutland (VT) Herald*, June 8, 1805.

3. *New-England Palladium* (Boston), September 9, 1808.

4. Daniel Webster, *An Appeal to the Old Whigs of New-Hampshire* (United States, s.n., 1805), 16, Books and Pamphlets Collection, AAS.

5. *Salem (MA) Gazette*, March 14, 17, and 21, 1809; *Newburyport (MA) Herald*, June 20, 1809; James Duncan Phillips, "Jefferson's 'Wicked Tyrannical Embargo,'" in *New England Quarterly* 18, no. 4 (December 1945): 476, 478.

6. See Letters of Erskine to Smith April 17, 18, and 19, 1809; and Smith to Erskine, April 17, 18, and 19, 1809, in Wait, ed., *State Papers and Publick Documents*, 461–66. See also Hickey, *The War of 1812: A Forgotten Conflict* (Urbana: University of Illinois Press, 1989), 22; and Richard Buel Jr., *America on the Brink: How the Political Struggle over the War of 1812 Almost Destroyed the Young Republic* (New York: Palgrave Macmillan, 2005), 90.

7. *Annals of Congress*, 11th Cong., 1st sess., 11–12; *Columbian Detector* (Boston), April 25, 1809; *Hampshire Gazette* (Northampton, MA), May 3, 1809; John C. A. Stagg, *Mr. Madison's War: Politics, Diplomacy, and Warfare in the Early American Republic, 1783–1830* (Princeton, NJ: Princeton University Press, 1983), 24, 25; Hickey, *War of 1812*, 22.

8. *Columbia Detector* (Boston), April 25, 1809; *Democrat* (Boston), April 1, 1809.

9. *Massachusetts Spy, or Worcester Gazette*, April 26, 1809.

10. Secretary Canning to D. M. Erskine, January 23, 1809, in *Annals of Congress*, 11th Cong., 1st and 2nd sess., 2066–68; Buel, *America on the Brink*, 90; Hickey, *War of 1812*, 22; Roger H. Brown, *The Republic in Peril: 1812* (New York: Columbia University Press, 1964), 21–22; Stagg, *Mr. Madison's War*, 25; Peter Onuf and Leonard J. Sadosky, *Jefferso-*

nian America (Malden, MA: Blackwell, 2002), 209; Samuel Flagg Bemis, *A Diplomatic History of the United States*, 5th ed. (New York: Henry Holt and Company, 1965), 39n2, 153–52.

11. Erskine to Smith, July 13, 1809, and Secretary of State to Erskine, August 9, 1809, in Wait, *State Papers and Publick Documents*, 3:498–501; and *Annals of Congress*, 11th Cong., 1st and 2nd sess., 2069, 2076.

12. Gallatin to D. M. Erskine, August 13, 1809, in Albert Gallatin, *The Writings of Albert Gallatin*, ed. Henry Adams (New York: Antiquarian Press, 1960), 458–461; *Annals of Congress*, 11th Cong., 1st and 2nd sess., Appendix, 2069, 2076–2085; Wait, ed., *State Papers and Publick Documents*, 501–2.

13. Erskine to Smith, July 13, 1809; August 14, 1809, in *Annals of Congress*, 11th Cong., 1st and 2nd sess., 2103.

14. *Massachusetts Spy, or Worcester Gazette*, August 2, 1809.

15. Smith to Jackson, October 9 and 19, 1809; November 1, 1809; Jackson to Smith, October 11, 23, and 27, 1809, and November 4 and 8, 1809; Circular, November 13, 1809, in *Annals of Congress*, 11th Cong., 1st and 2nd sess., 2085–2113, 2123–2124; Buel, *America on the Brink*, 92, 93; Stagg, *Mr. Madison's War*, 26; Brown, *Republic in Peril*, 22; Bemis, *Diplomatic History*, 153.

16. Oakley to Smith, November 11 and 13, 1809, in *Annals of Congress*, 11th Cong., 1st and 2nd sess., 2113–2115.

17. *Essex Register* (Salem, MA), November 4, 1809; *Boston Patriot*, December 13, 1809.

18. *Independent Chronicle* (Boston), November 2, 1809.

19. *New-England Palladium* (Boston), December 5, 1809; *Repertory* (Boston), November 24, 1809; *Massachusetts Spy, and Worcester Gazette*, December 13, 1809; *Boston Gazette*, December 14, 1809.

20. *Massachusetts Spy, or Worcester Gazette*, August 2, 1809; *Boston Gazette*, December 14, 1809.

21. See Smith to Jackson, October 27, 1809, and Smith to Jackson, November 1, 1809, in *Annals of Congress*, 11th Cong., 1st and 2nd sess., 2107–2109.

22. Wait, *State Papers and Publick Documents*, 3:400–1; Bemis, *Diplomatic History*, 152; Clifford L. Egan, *Neither Peace nor War: Franco-American Relations, 1803–1812* (Baton Rouge: Louisiana State University Press, 1983), 97–98.

23. The special session lasted from May 22 to June 28, 1809, and although it appears as the first session, the official first session of the Eleventh Congress began on November 27, 1809, and ended on May 1, 1810. Technically, because of the extra session, the Nonintercourse Act ended at the end of the second session of Congress (which ended up counting as three sessions) and not the first. See *Statutes at Large of the United States* 2 (1845): 533.

24. *Annals of Congress*, 11th Cong., 3rd sess., 1248, 1338; Hickey, *War of 1812*, 22; Stagg, *Mr. Madison's War*, 28, 29; Brown, *Republic in Peril*, 22; Onuf and Sadosky, *Jeffersonian America*, 209; Bemis, *Diplomatic History*, 154; Buel, *America on the Brink*, 100–1, 108–9.

25. Samuel Flagg Bemis, *A Diplomatic History of the United States* (New York: Henry Holt and Company, 1942), 148–50; Egan, *Neither Peace nor War*, 28, 30.

26. Cadore to Armstrong, August 5, 1810, in *Annals of Congress*, 11th Cong., 3rd sess., 1235–36; Hickey, *War of 1812*, 22; Buel, *America on the Brink*, 110; Egan, *Neither Peace nor War*, 120–24; Stagg, *Mr. Madison's War*, 55; Brown, *Republic in Peril*, 23–25; Bemis, *Diplomatic History*, 154. Jean-Baptist Nompere, comte de Champagny became the first duc de Cadore (Duke of Cadore) in 1809.

27. *Annals of Congress*, 11th Cong., 3rd sess., 1248–1249; Egan, *Neither Peace nor War*, 122–124; Brown, *Republic in Peril*, 23.

28. John Lowell, *The Impartial Inquirer, Being a Candid Examination of the Conduct of the President of the United States in Execution of the Powers Vested in Him, By the Act of Congress of May 1, 1810: To Which Is Added, Some Reflections upon the Invasion of the Spanish Territory of West-Florida . . . By a Citizens of Massachusetts* (Boston: Russell and Cutler, 1811), 20, AAS.

29. Armstrong to Smith, January 28, 1810; April 16, 1810; May 24, 1810; September 10, 1810; Armstrong to Duke of Cadore, March 10, 1810; September 7, 1810; Champagny, Duke of Cadore to Armstrong, February 14, 1810; September 7 and 12, 1810, in *Annals of Congress*, 11th Cong., 3rd sess., 1220–1240. See also Samuel Taggart, *An Address to the Independent Electors of Hampshire North District* (Greenfield, MA: J. Denio, Printer, 1811), 6–10, AAS.

30. Notation of July 28, 1823, Timothy Pickering Papers, MHS; *Boston Gazette*, December 14, 1809.

31. Taggart to John Taylor, April 27, 1810, Taggart Letterbook, AAS.

32. *Annals of Congress*, 11th Cong., 3rd sess., 863–94, 909–27, 998, 1016–1025. See also Josiah Quincy, *Speech of the Hon. Josiah Quincy In The House of Representatives of the U. States, February 25, 1811, on the Amendment Offered by Mr. Eppes to the Bill . . . Which Proposed to Revive and Enforce the Nonintercourse Law Against Great Britain*, (Alexandria, VA: S. Snowden, 1811), 10–16, AAS.

33. *Annals of Congress*, 11th Cong., 3rd sess., 360–61, 1094, 1095, 1338–39; Hickey, *War of 1812*, 24; Stagg, *Mr. Madison's War*, 56; Bemis, *Diplomatic History*, 154–55.

34. Stagg, *Mr. Madison's War*, 56–57; Bemis, *Diplomatic History*, 154–55; Hickey, *War of 1812*, 22.

35. Brown, *Republic in Peril*, 26–28; Hickey, *War of 1812*, 22, 24; Stagg, *Mr. Madison's War*, 75–76; Egan, *Neither Peace nor War*, 121–22; John Quincy Adams to Robert Smith, May 19, 1810, in John Quincy Adams, *Writings of John Quincy Adams*, ed. Chauncey Ford Worthington, 7 vols. (New York: Macmillan, 1913–17), 3:439–41; Bemis, *Diplomatic History*, 151.

36. Stagg, *Mr. Madison's War*, 57–67, 71–74.

37. Federal Party, Massachusetts, *Federal Proceedings in Salem, Friday Evening, March 30, 1810* (Salem, MA., 1810), Broadside Collection, AAS.

38. Banner, *To the Hartford Convention*, 362, 363; Paul Goodman, *The Democratic-Republicans of Massachusetts: Politics in a Young Republic* (Cambridge, MA: Harvard University Press, 1964), 144–45; See Massachusetts 1810 State Election for Governor in Lampi, First Democracy Project, AAS; William Bentley, *The Diary of William Bentley D.D.: Pastor of the East Church Salem, Massachusetts*, 4 vols. (Salem, MA: Essex Institute, 1905–1914), 4:92.

39. *Annals of Congress*, 11th Cong., 1st sess., 61, 238–39, 266–67, 361–63, 417–18, 461–62. A detailed account of events can be found in William Baylies, *A View of the Proceedings of the House of Representatives of the United States in the Case of the Plymouth Election. Addressed to the Electors of Plymouth District* (Boston: Greenough and Stebbins, 1809), AAS.

40. *Massachusetts Spy, or Worcester Gazette*, July 12, 1809.

41. *Annals of Congress*, 11th Cong., 3rd sess., 65, 66, 67–83; Gerard Clarfield, *Timothy Pickering and the American Republic* (Pittsburgh, PA: University of Pittsburgh Press, 1980), 246, 247; Hervey Putnam Prentiss, *Timothy Pickering as the Leader of New England Federalism, 1800–1815* (New York: Da Capo Press, 1972), 62, 78n5; *Salem (MA) Gazette*, June 12, 1810; *Repertory* (Boston, MA), July 18, 1810; *Massachusetts Spy, or Worcester Gazette*, July 12, 1809.

42. *Washingtonian* (Windsor, VT), November 9, 1812; Lampi, First Democracy Project, AAS; Buel, *America on the Brink*, 56, 94.

43. Josiah Quincy, Congress. House of Representatives Debate on Extra Session Thursday, January 19, Speech of Mr. Quincy (Baltimore: Federal Republican Office for Hanson & Wagner, 1809), 11; Stagg, *Mr. Madison's War*, 59–61.

44. Josiah Quincy to John Adams, January 17, 1809, Adams Papers, Microfilm Edition, 608 Reels, Reel 36, MHS; Donald Hickey sees Federalists as consistent in their support of a strong military, which explains their support of appropriations for the military in the congressional votes leading to the War of 1812. See Hickey, "Federalist Defense Policy in the Age of Jefferson, 1801–1812," in *Military Affairs* 45, no. 2 (April 1981): 63–70, and Hickey, *War of 1812*, 5–6, 45. For the conventional interpretation, see Stagg, *Mr. Madison's War*, 90–91; Brown, *Republic in Peril*, 106; Matthew H. Crocker,

The Magic of the Many: Josiah Quincy and the Rise of Mass Politics in Boston, 1800–1830 (Amherst: University of Massachusetts Press, 1999), 11; John Lowell, *Interesting Political Discussion: The Diplomatic Policy of Mr. Madison Unveiled: In a Series of Essays Containing Strictures upon the Late Correspondence between Mr. Smith and Mr. Jackson* (Boston, 1810), 3, 16, 29, AAS; Fischer, *Revolution of American Conservatism*, 268.

45. Federal Party, Massachusetts, Let Every Federalist Do His Duty and Massachusetts May Yet Be Saved!!! Federal Republicans! Boston, April 1811. You Have Lost the Election of Governor. You Have Elected but Nineteen Federal Senators. . . . (Boston, 1811), Broadside, AAS.

46. Stagg, *Mr. Madison's War*, 93; Hickey, *War of 1812*, 37; Brown, *Republic in Peril*, 92; Egan, *Neither Peace nor War*, 171; Lawrence A. Peskin, "Conspiratorial Anglophobia and the War of 1812," in *The Journal of American History*, vol. 98, no. 3 (December 2011), 667.

47. *Annals of Congress*, 12th Cong., 1st sess., 1162; Henry's documents appear on 1163–81; Stagg, *Mr. Madison's War*, 93; Hickey, *War of 1812*, 37; Brown, *Republic in Peril*, 92; Egan, *Neither Peace nor War*, 171, 172.

48. Quoted in Hickey, *War of 1812*, 38 (emphasis in original); also see Egan, *Neither Peace nor War*, 172.

49. *Annals of Congress*, 12th Cong., 1st sess., 1220–1224; Hickey, *War of 1812*, 37–39; Stagg, *Mr. Madison's War*, 93–95; Peskin, "Conspiratorial Anglophobia and the War of 1812," 658–63.

50. William Reed to Pickering, March 11, 1812, Timothy Pickering Papers; *Salem (MA) Gazette*, March 20, 1812; *New Bedford Mercury*, March 27, 1812; *Weekly Messenger* (Boston), March 20, 1812; Fischer, *Revolution of American Conservatism*, 274; "Henry Plot," Timothy Pickering Papers, MHS; *Salem (MA) Gazette*, March 20, 1812.

51. Quoted in Stagg, *Mr. Madison's War*, 94; John Henry, *The Essex Junto and the British Spy; or, Treason Detected* (Salem, 1812), 2; Josiah Quincy to Harrison Gray Otis, March 19, 1812, Quincy Family Papers, MHS.

52. Federal Party, Massachusetts, *Let Every Federalist Do His Duty*, Broadsides AAS; *Columbian Centinel* (Boston), March 25, 1812; *Salem (MA) Gazette*, March 31, 1812. For criticism of the Boston Resolutions, see *The Yankee* (Boston), March 27, 1812. For more on William Sullivan, see Fischer, *Revolution of American Conservatism*, 275–76.

53. Also, see Hickey, *War of 1812*, 39.

54. For examples, see *The Star* (Raleigh, NC), February 9, 1809; *Charleston City Gazette and Commercial Daily Advertiser*, August 28, 1812; and *The Enquirer* (Richmond, VA), November 27, 1812; Stagg, *Mr. Madison's War*, 94–95; Peskin, "Conspiratorial Anglophobia and the War of 1812," 666–67.

55. Joseph A. Fry, *Dixie Looks Abroad: The South and U.S. Foreign Relations, 1789–1973* (Baton Rouge: Louisiana State University Press, 2002), 30; Stagg, *Mr. Madison's War*, 97–99; also see *The Star* (Raleigh, NC), April 24, 1812; *Alexandria (Va.) Daily Gazette*, April 10, 1812, and George Mathews to James Madison, April 16, 1812, *James Madison Papers*, LC.

56. Foster to Monroe, May 30 and June 4, 1812; Monroe to Foster, June 6 and 13, 1812; and related correspondence in *Annals of Congress*, 12th Cong., 1st sess., 1829–933. See also Hickey, *War of 1812*, 24; Stagg, *Mr. Madison's War*, 100; Brown, *Republic in Peril*, 27–29.

57. Foster to Monroe, June 1, 1812 and Monroe to Foster, June 8 and 10, 1812; in *Annals of Congress*, 12th Cong., 1st sess., 1843–1845, 1854–1856. Correspondence on Indian hostilities in *Annals of Congress*, 12th Cong., 1st sess., 1856–1862.

58. *Annals of Congress*, 12th Cong., 1st sess., 2262–2264; Hickey, *War of 1812*, 39, 40; Stagg, *Mr. Madison's War*, 102.

59. *Annals of Congress*, 12th Cong., 1st sess., 1601–1606.

60. Ibid., 187–189, 1595–1598; also see Stagg, *Mr. Madison's War*, 101–3.

61. *Annals of Congress*, 12th Cong., 1st sess., 1624–1629, 1637, 1682, 2322, 2323.

62. Stagg, *Mr. Madison's War*, 108; Brown, *Republic in Peril*, 28, 33; 39, 40; Hickey, *War of 1812*, 43.

63. *Annals of Congress*, 12th Cong., 1st sess., 2196–2223; also see "Minority Report on the War," June 23, 1812, Quincy, Holmes and Upham Family Papers, MHS.
64. *Annals of Congress*, 12th Cong., 1st sess., 1638–1679.
65. Ibid., 1596.
66. Reginald Horsman, "The Dimensions of an 'Empire for Liberty': Expansion and Republicanism, 1775–1825," in *Journal of the Early Republic* 9, no. 1 (Spring 1989): 4; Essex County Convention, *Declaration of the County of Essex, in the Commonwealth of Massachusetts . . . at Ipswich* (Salem, MA: Thomas C. Cushing, 1812), 3–5, 13–16, Books and Pamphlets Collection, AAS; Josiah Quincy, *An Oration Delivered before the Washington Benevolent Society of Massachusetts on the Thirtieth Day of April 1813: Being the Anniversary of the First Inauguration of President Washington* (Boston: William S. and Henry Spear, 1813), 9–10, Collection of the BA; Rothman, *Slave Country*, 24.
67. *Annals of Congress*, 12th Cong., 1st sess., 1624–29, 1637, 1682, 2196–221, 2322, 2323; also see "Minority Report on the War," Quincy, Holmes and Upham Family Papers, MHS; *Berkshire Reporter*, May 4, 1811. See Lawrence Delbert Cress, "'Cool and Serious Reflection': Federalist Attitudes toward War in 1812," in *Journal of Early Republic* 7 (Summer 1987): 123–45. Cress argues that Federalists opposed the war because it disregarded "Christian values," sparked military mobilization, which was immoral, and "would invoke divine displeasure with the nation" (143).
68. *Annals of Congress*, 12th Cong., 1st sess., 1489, 1562, 1570.
69. *New-England Palladium* (Boston), July 31, 1812; *Annals of Congress*, 12th Cong., 1st sess., 1510.
70. Wood, *Empire of Liberty*, 683; Banner, *Hartford Convention*, 308; Hickey, *War of 1812*, 52–72; Rachel Hope Cleves, *The Reign of Terror in America: Visions of Violence from Anti-Jacobinism to Antislavery* (New York: Cambridge University Press, 2009), 169–71.
71. Cress, "'Cool and Serious Reflection'"; Cleves, *Reign of Terror in America*, 154, 162–66; *Berkshire Reporter* (MA), May 4, 1811.
72. *Annals of Congress*, 12th Cong., 2nd sess., 1021; W. P. Preble to Richard Cutts, November 23, 1812, Richard Cutts Papers, 1753–1886, Accession #10029-e, Special Collections, UVA; *New-England Palladium* (Boston), July 31, 1812; Steven Edwin Siry, "Sectional Politics of 'Practical Republicanism': De Witt Clinton's Presidential Bid, 1810–1812," in *Journal of the Early Republic* 5 (Winter 1985): 441–62.
73. *Newburyport* (MA) *Herald*, November 10, 1812; Cleves, *Reign of Terror in America*, 156.
74. Fisher, *Revolution of American Conservatism*, 238; Stagg, *Mr. Madison's War*, 305–9.
75. *Annals of Congress*, 12th Cong., 1st sess., 2043–2046; Stagg, *Mr. Madison's War*, 305–9. The St. Cloud decree was first mentioned on July 5, 1810, but was dated April 28, 1811, when published in May 1812; Fisher, *Revolution of American Conservatism*, 238.
76. Egan, *Neither Peace Nor War*, 169; Bemis, *Diplomatic History*, 155; Stagg, *Mr. Madison's War*, 309.
77. *Annals of Congress* 12th Cong., 1st sess., 2043–2046.
78. Prentiss, *Timothy Pickering*, 91, 92, 94, 98; Stagg, *Mr. Madison's War*, 258–61.
79. Hickey, *War of 1812*, 194–95, 215; Stagg, *Mr. Madison's War*, 469–70.
80. *Annals of Congress*, 13th Cong., 2nd sess., 859, 860; Buel, *America on the Brink*, 194; Hickey, *War of 1812*, 267.
81. Pickering to Caleb Strong, January 9, 1815, Caleb Strong Papers, MHS; and Pickering to Cutter (n.d.), Timothy Pickering Papers, MHS; Hickey, *War of 1812*, 269.
82. Hickey, *War of 1812*, 173, 270.
83. Banner, *Hartford Convention*, 313–325; Hickey, *War of 1812*, 270–73.
84. Massachusetts General Court, Senate, *Protest of the Minority of the Senate of Massachusetts, Against the Report of the Joint Committee of the Legislature, on the Governor's Message* (Boston: Yankee-Office, 1814), American Tracts Collection, American Tracts Collection, BLYU.
85. Quoted in Banner, *Hartford Convention*, 326 n313. See also Theodore Dwight, *History of the Hartford Convention: With a Review of the Policy of the United States Govern-*

ment , Which Led to the War of 1812 (New York: N & J White, 1833), 379; Hickey, War of 1812, 275–77.

86. Prentiss, *Timothy Pickering*, 115–16.

87. Banner, *Hartford Convention*, 323–29; Dwight, *History of the Hartford Convention*, 379, 383.

88. Pickering to Lowell, November 7 and 28, 1814; Lowell to Pickering, December 3, 1814, in Henry Adams, ed., *Documents Relating to New-England Federalism, 1800–1815* (Boston: Little, Brown, and Company, 1877), 404, 407, 410–12; Prentiss, *Timothy Pickering*, 111; Banner, *Hartford Convention*, 310n8 (emphasis in original).

89. McCaughey, *Josiah Quincy*, 82, 83; Buel, *America on the Brink*, 218.

90. Stagg, *Mr. Madison's War*, 478–82; Hickey, *War of 1812*, 277–78; Banner, *Hartford Convention*, 329, 338–49.

91. Benjamin Woods Labaree, *Patriots and Partisans: The Merchants of Newburyport, 1764–1815* (Cambridge, MA: Harvard University Press, 1962), 197–99; Morison, *Harrison Gray Otis*, 381; Banner, *Hartford Convention*, 345; Nathaniel Saltonstall Jr. to Leverett Saltonstall, February 23, 1815, in Robert E. Moody, ed., *The Saltonstall Papers, 1607–1815*, 3 vols. (Boston: Massachusetts Historical Society, 1974), 2:369.

92. Bentley, *Diary*, 4:313; Elizabeth R. Varon, *Disunion! The Coming of the American Civil War, 1789–1859* (Chapel Hill: University of North Carolina Press, 2008), 37, 38.

93. *Annals of Congress* 9th Cong., 1st sess., 624–25, 750–60; Declaration of War with Great Britain, Pub. L. No. 12–102, 2 Stat. 755 (1812).

94. Burton Spivak, *Jefferson's English Crisis: Commerce, Embargo, and the Republican Revolution* (Charlottesville: University of Virginia Press, 1979), 41.

95. Don E. Fehrenbacher, *The Slaveholding Republic: An Account of the United States Government's Relations to Slavery* (New York: Oxford University Press, 2001), 91–96.

96. *Philadelphia Gazette*, January 28, 1801; Federal Party, Massachusetts, *Let Every Federalist Do His Duty*, Broadsides, AAS.

97. Robert A. McCaughey, *Josiah Quincy, 1772–1864: The Last Federalist* (Cambridge, MA: Harvard University Press, 1974), 50, 71–76, 83–84; Quincy to Pickering, June 20, 1811, "Oration," 21–23, Quincy, Holmes and Upham Family Papers, MHS.

98. Samuel Eliot Morison, *Harrison Gray Otis, 1765–1848: The Urbane Federalist* (Boston: Houghton Mifflin, 1969), 307, 377; Banner, *To the Hartford Convention*, 339.

99. [Sereno Edwards Dwight], *Slave Representation by Boreas, Awake! O Spirit of the North* (New Haven, 1812), 1, 3, 4, Antislavery Collection, 1725–1911 (RB 003), SCUA

100. Leonard L. Richards, *The Slave Power: The Free North and Southern Domination, 1780–1860* (Baton Rouge: Louisiana State University Press, 2000), 116–30; Joshua Michael Zeitz, "The Missouri Compromise Reconsidered, Antislavery Rhetoric and the Emergence of the Free Labor Synthesis," in *Journal of the Early Republic*, 20, no. 3 (August 2000): 468–70; Eric Foner, *Free Soil, Free Labor, Free Men: The Ideology of the Republican Party before the Civil War* (New York: Oxford University Press, 1995), 296, 297; Dwight, *Slave Representation by Boreas*, 4–7, 19–22, SCUA. About Dwight and the Pennsylvania Colonization Society in the 1830s see Matthew Mason, "Federalists, Abolitionists, and the Problem of Influence," in *American Nineteenth Century History*, 10, no. 1, (March 2009):12.

101. Seymour Drescher, *Abolition: A History of Slavery and Antislavery* (New York: Cambridge University Press, 2009), 100–5, 132–34.

102. Samuel Eliot Morison, *The Life and Letters of Harrison Gray Otis, Federalist, 1765–1848*, 2 vols. (New York: Houghton Mifflin Co., 1913), 2:223; Banner, *Hartford Convention*, 103–9; Rogers M. Smith, "Constructing American National Identity: Strategies of the Federalists," in *Federalists Reconsidered*, Doron Ben-Atar and Barbara Oberg, eds., (Charlottesville: University of Virginia Press, 1998), 24–25; Matthew E. Mason, "'Nothing Is Better Calculated to Excite Divisions': Federalist Agitation against Slave Representation during the War of 1812," in *New England Quarterly* 75, no. 4 (December 2002): 531–61.

103. See Linda Kerber, *Federalist in Dissent*, 23–66; Paul Finkelman, "The Problem of Slavery in the Age of Federalism," 135–56; Andrew Siegel, "'Steady Habits' under

Siege: The Defense of Federalism in Jeffersonian Connecticut," in Ben-Atar and Oberg, *Federalists Reconsidered*, 137–49, 216–18.

104. Mathew Carey, *A Calm Address to the People of the Eastern States on the Subject of the Representation of Slaves, Representation in the Senate, and the Hostility to Commerce Ascribed to the Southern States. By the Author of the Olive Branch* (Boston: Rowe and Hooper, 1814), 9, 13–19, 23–29, 44–48, Books and Pamphlets Collection, AAS; *Pittsfield (MA) Sun*, September 17, 1840; *New-York Dailey Advertiser*, September 17, 1840.

105. *Eastern Argus* (Portland, ME), January 21, 1813; Eustice, *1812: War and the Passions of Patriotism*, 190; Fischer, *Revolution of American Conservatism*, 166.

106. For example, see *Edes' Kennebec Gazette* (Augusta, ME), October 9, 1801; *New-Hampshire Gazette* (Portsmouth), July 30, 1833.

107. Antislavery literature on the inhumanity and unchristian nature of slavery include Samuel Sewall, *The Selling of Joseph: A Memorial* (Boston: Bartholomew Green and John Allen, 1700); Elihu Coleman, *A Testimony against that Antichristian Practice of Making Slaves of Men. Wherein I Shewed It to Be Contrary to the Dispensation of the Law and Time of the Gospel, and Very Opposite Both to Grace and Nature* (Boston: 1733); Benjamin Rush, *An Address to the Inhabitants of the British Settlements in America, Upon Slave-Keeping* (Philadelphia: Printed by John Dunlap, 1773); Theodore Parsons, *A Forensic Dispute on the Legality of Enslaving the Africans Held at Public Commencement in Cambridge, New-England, July 21st 1773, By Two Candidates for the Bachelor's Degree* (Boston: John Byle for Thomas Leverette, 1773); Warner Mifflin, *A Serious Expostulation With the Members of the House of Representatives of the United States* (New Bedford, MA: J. Spooner, 1793).

108. See Cleves, *Reign of Terror in America*, 104–72; Eustice, *1812: War and the Passion of Patriotism*, 192–93.

109. Member of the African Society, *The Sons of Africans: An Essay on Freedom, with Observations on the Origin of Slavery* (Boston, 1808), 14, 17, Collection of the BA; Joseph Sidney, *An Oration Commemorative of the Abolition of the Slave Trade: Delivered before the Wilberforce Philanthropic Association, in the City of New York on the Second of January, 1809* (New York: J. Seymour, 1809), 6, 13–15, Collection of the BA.

110. Bentley, *Diary*, 3:490.

111. Thomas Gray, *A Sermon Delivered in Boston before the African Society, on the 14th Day of July 1818, The Anniversary of the Abolition of the Slave Trade* (Boston: Seymour, 1818), 9, 13, Collection of the BA; Bentley, *Diary*, 3:273, 294, 296, 301, 453, 456, 500, Collection of the BA. Concerning Jeffersonian and Democratic Party racism, see Richards, *Slave Power*, 116–19.

112. Charles W. Green to Leverett Saltonstall, January 9 and 23, 1804, in Moody, *Saltonstall Papers*, 180, 182; Timothy Pickering to Rufus King, March 8, 1785, Timothy Pickering Papers, MHS (emphasis in original).

113. For examples, see *American Advocate* (Hallowell, ME), April 17, 1811; September 29, 1812; *Newburyport (MA) Herald*, September 25, 1812; *Berkshire (MA) Reporter*, December 5, 1810; February 9, 1811.

114. Charles G. Greene and Benjamin Franklin Hallet, *The Identity of the Old Hartford Convention Federalists with the Modern Whig, Harrison Party: Carefully Illustrated by Living Specimens and Dedicated to the Young Men of the Union* (Boston: 1840), 1, 9 (emphasis in original) Collection of the BA.

115. *Pennsylvania Freeman* (Philadelphia), June 1, 1848.

116. Leverett Saltonstall to Nathaniel Saltonstall, February 18, 1815, in Moody, *Saltonstall Papers*, 569–70.

117. Shaw Livermore, *The Twilight of Federalism: The Disintegration of the Federalist Party, 1815–1830* (Princeton: Princeton University Press, 1962), 14, 15, 262; *Newburyport (MA) Herald*, May 19, 1812.

118. *Annals of Congress*, 12th Cong., 2nd sess., 553.

119. *Independent Chronicle* (Boston), March 4, 1911.

120. Nathaniel Silsbee to Benjamin Crowninshield, November 26, 1815, MSS 4, Box 8 Folder 1, Crowninshield Family Papers, PEM.

121. Rothman, *Slave Country*, 120; Nathaniel Silsbee to Benjamin Crowninshield, February 5, 1815, MSS 4, Box 8, Folder 1A, Crowninshield Family Papers, PEM.

122. Robert W. Tucker and David C. Hendrickson, *Empire of Liberty: The Statecraft of Thomas Jefferson* (New York: Oxford University Press, 1990), 239–48; Banner, *To the Hartford Convention*, 110–12.

123. *Annals of Congress*, 9th Cong., 1st sess., 1033, 1037, 1039–1041; *Salem (MA) Gazette*, May 28, 1813; Federal Party, Massachusetts, *Let Every Federalist Do His Duty*, Broadsides, AAS.

124. Benjamin Crowninshield to Mary Crowninshield, July 15, 1815, MSS 4, Box, 9, Folder 1, Crowninshield Family Papers, PEM.

125. Samuel Eliot Morison, *The Maritime History of Massachusetts, 1783–1860* (Boston: Houghton Mifflin, 1921), 213, 214; Oscar Handlin and Mary Flug Handlin, *Commonwealth: A Study of the Role of Government in the American Economy: Massachusetts, 1774–1861*, rev. ed. (Cambridge, MA: Harvard University Press, 1969), 184; Kenneth W. Porter, *The Jacksons and the Lees: Two Generations of Massachusetts Merchants, 1765–1844*, 2 vols. (New York: Russell and Russell, 1969), 1:766, 764; 2:1166; Victor S. Clark, *History of Manufactures in the United States, vol. 1, 1607–1860* (1929; New York: Carnegie Institution of Washington / Peter Smith, 1949), 1:336; Banner, *Hartford Convention*, 343.

126. Mayo-Bobee, "Understanding the Essex Junto," 645–53; Banner, *Hartford Convention*, 330–33, 344; Dwight, *History of the Hartford Convention*, 401–6; Greene and Hallet, *Identity of the Old Hartford Convention Federalists*, Collection of the BA; Fischer, *Revolution of American Conservatism*, 181, 268; Banner, *Hartford Convention*, 299.

127. See "Minority Report on the War," June 23, 1812, Quincy Papers, MHS. Although twenty-five congressmen from New England and the Mid-Atlantic states signed the report, there were only nine representing the South: three from Maryland, four from Virginia, and two from North Carolina. See also James H. Broussard, *The Southern Federalists, 1800–1816* (Baton Rouge: Louisiana State University Press, 1978), 320.

128. Josiah Quincy, *An Oration Delivered before the Washington Benevolent Society of Massachusetts on the Thirtieth Day of April 1813: Being the Anniversary of the First Inauguration of President Washington* (Boston: William S. and Henry Spear), 16, 29, Collection of the BA; Boston (MA) Citizens, [Daniel Webster, Josiah Quincy, et al.], *A Memorial to the Congress of the United States, on the Subject of Restraining the Increase of Slavery in New States to Be Admitted into the Union, Prepared in Pursuance of a Vote of the Inhabitants of Boston and Its Vicinity, Assembled at the State House, on the Third of December, A.D. 1819* (Boston: Sewell Phelps, Printer, 1819), 3, 4, 6–9, 13–21, Antislavery Collection, 1725–1911 (RB 003), SCUA; Van Cleve, *A Slaveholders' Union*, 217.

129. John Quincy Adams, *Diary of John Quincy Adams, 1794–1845*, ed. Allan Nevins (New York: Scribner's, 1951), 246; Adams quoted in, Charles N. Edel, *Nation Builder: John Quincy Adams and the Grand Strategy of the Republic* (Cambridge, MA: Harvard University Press, 2014), 250–52; Richards, *Slave Power*, 78–79.

130. Varon, *Disunion!* 39; Daniel Walker Howe, *What Hath God Wrought: The Transformation of America, 1815–1848* (New York: Oxford University Press, 2007), 151–55; John Craig Hammond, *Slavery, Freedom, and Expansion in the Early American West* (Charlottesville: University of Virginia Press, 2007), 154–56; Glover Moore, *The Missouri Controversy, 1819–1821* (Gloucester, MA: P. Smith, 1967), 33–47; Livermore, *Twilight of Federalism*, 89; Rothman, *Slave Country*, 210–16; Fehrenbacher, *Slaveholding Republic*, 265.

131. Quoted in Richards, *Slave Power*, 85, 88 (emphasis in original); Howe, *What Hath God Wrought*, 151.

132. Josiah Quincy, *Oration Delivered before the Washington Benevolent Society of Massachusetts*, 19, 29, Collection of BA; Federal Party, Massachusetts, *Let Every Federalist Do His Duty*, Broadsides, AAS.

133. C. Edward Skeen, *1816: America Rising* (Lexington: University Press of Kentucky, 2003), 40; Richards, *Slave Power*, 8, 9, 57, 61–68, 92–94, 102–17.

134. McCaughey, *Josiah Quincy*, 84, 85; Buel, *America on the Brink*, 232; Skeen, *1816*, 156–60.

135. Morison, *Harrison Gray Otis*, 425–27.

136. Richards, *Slave Power*, 69, 70, 84–86. Also see Zeitz, "The Missouri Compromise Reconsidered," 450.

137. Donald L. Robinson, *Slavery in the Structure of American Politics, 1765–1820* (New York: Harcourt Brace Jovanovich, 1971), 288, 290.

138. *Annals of Congress*, 5th Cong., 2nd sess., 1307–1308; Jeffrey L. Pasley et al., eds. *Beyond the Founders: New Approaches to the Political History of the Early American Republic* (Chapel Hill: University of North Carolina Press, 2004), 187; Richard Newman, "Not the Only Story in 'Amistad': The Fictional Joadson and the Real James Forten," in *Pennsylvania History* 67, no. 2 (Spring 2000): 224; Rutledge partially quoted in Morison, *Harrison Gray Otis*, 425; Broussard, *Southern Federalists*, 16, 18, 259–62, 291.

139. Morison, *Harrison Gray Otis*, 403–6; Livermore, *Twilight of Federalism*, 36–41, 52, 53; Skeen, *1816*, 20.

140. Mayo-Bobee, "Understanding the Essex Junto," 632.

141. Livermore, *Twilight of Federalism*, 61, 68; Skeen, *1816*, 30, 31.

142. Mathew Carey, *Examination of the Pretensions of New England to Commercial Pre-Eminence* (Philadelphia: Printed for M. Carey, 1814), B, vii, 2, 3, 45, 61, 63, 66, Collection of the BA; Livermore, *Twilight of Federalism*, 34, 61; Skeen, *1816*, 21.

143. Livermore, *Twilight of Federalism*, 78–87.

144. Ronald P. Formisano, *The Transformation of Political Culture: Massachusetts Parties, 1790s–1840s* (New York: Oxford University Press, 1983), 80, 120–25; Matthew Mason, "Federalists, Abolitionists, and the Problem of Influence," 7, 14.

145. Jacob Crowninshield to George W. Prescott, November 15, 1803, Crowninshield Family Papers, MH 15, Box 2, Folder 9, PEM; Morison, *Harrison Gray Otis*, 440–46; Livermore, *Twilight of Federalism*, 197–222.

146. Howe, *What Hath God Wrought*, 95; Clarfield, *Timothy Pickering*, 267–68.

147. Greene and Hallet, *Identity of the Old Hartford Convention Federalists*, 3–7, Collection of the BA; Mayo-Bobee, "Understanding the Essex Junto: Fear, Dissent, and Propaganda in the Early Republic," in *New England Quarterly* (Winter, 2015): 651; Howe, *What Hath God Wrought*, 95.

148. Adams, *Diary*, 53; Howe, *What Hath God Wrought*, 147, 155; Richards, *Slave Power*, 64–70, 144, 145.

149. Livermore, *Twilight of Federalism*, 95–96.

150. *New-Hampshire Gazette* (Portsmouth), July 30, 1833; Matthew Mason, *Slavery & Politics in the Early American Republic* (Chapel Hill: University of North Carolina Press, 2006), 231.

Epilogue

Old Romans—Federalist Activism and Their Antislavery Legacy (1820–1865)

On a winter evening in 1821 Eliza Susan Quincy, the twenty-three-year-old daughter of former Massachusetts representative Josiah Quincy, recorded her experiences and impressions from the day in her diary. At the start of her entry Eliza described the physical appearance of an aging patriot and ex-politician whom she had seen earlier that day. "Col. Pickering" she wrote, "looks like an old Roman." To the young woman, the seventy-six-year-old Federalist displayed "nothing of the weakness of an old man about him." Eliza insisted that the old firebrand and "radical" or "high" Federalist was "as spirited . . . as a young man."[1] Given the turbulence in his life and career, it was astonishing that Pickering showed no outward signs of an extremely stressful public career filled with political intrigue and controversy.

Within a short time after the Federalist Party's demise, New Englanders and other northerners of Eliza's generation developed an appreciation for members of the defunct party. This included the Pennsylvania petitioners who argued against extending the three-fifths clause to new states during the Missouri Crisis in 1820, Vermonters who opposed applying the ratio to Texas in 1845, and those who later created the Liberty Party. Along with their opposition to increasing the number of states that could count slaves toward representation, many actively embraced the Federalists' opposition to the growth of southern power as well as the westward spread of slavery.[2] Even though favorable interpretations of their politics did not follow Federalists into the twentieth or twenty-first centuries, many antebellum Americans, whether apathetic or opposed to the westward spread of slavery, associated Federalists with changes in northern politics and a culture that initiated the development of a serious antislavery movement.

Timothy Pickering, who was a high-ranking Federalist supported efforts to arrest the spread of slavery as early as 1785. By the time Eliza Quincy praised his countenance and stature, Pickering had been in public service for over half a century. He had participated in colonial politics and served as quartermaster in the Continental Army. At the end of the war Pickering moved to Pennsylvania became a merchant and partner in the firm Pickering and Hodgdon, which failed in the postwar economy. Pickering was also a member of the Pennsylvania Assembly, participated in that state's constitutional convention, and served as government agent to Indian nations. Following ratification of the Constitution, George Washington appointed Pickering secretary of war, postmaster general, and secretary of state. In 1800, in the wake of clashes over policy and his dealings with Alexander Hamilton, Pickering was fired by President Adams.[3]

Pickering returned to Salem Massachusetts in 1802, where he lost a congressional election to Democratic-Republican Jacob Crowninshield and successfully sued the editor of the Democratic-Republican *Impartial Register* for printing libelous articles about him during the campaign. That same year the Massachusetts legislature elected Pickering and John Quincy Adams to the U.S. Senate (Adams also lost a congressional election in 1802). During Pickering's time in the Senate, Federalists attempted to eliminate the three-fifths clause and keep slavery out of the Southwest but failed. When Federalists lost a second presidential election to Jefferson in 1804, Pickering drafted plans for a northern confederacy. The plan failed, but Pickering earned a reputation for disunionism and for more than three decades, political enemies lampooned or castigated Pickering in the partisan press. When Pickering lost his seat in the Senate, Massachusetts voters elected him to the U.S. House of Representatives, where he served from 1813 to 1817. Near the end of his life and career, neither his contentious years in national politics nor many personal political battles appear to have dampened Pickering's spirit or dulled his outward appearance.

While in the House of Representatives, Pickering sat on the House Committee on the African Slave Trade with fellow Massachusetts Federalist Samuel Taggart. The committee attempted to protect commerce and punish illegal slave traders. Pickering also presented petitions to end the interstate slave trade and introduced a joint resolution outlining the diplomatic process for colonizing free African Americans in Africa. The resolution stated that leaving them in western territories would result in the harm or abuse of freed persons of color at the hands of white settlers.[4]

In retirement Pickering continued to participate in antislavery organizations such as the Society for the Suppression of Slavery, where he joined other Federalists such as Daniel Webster. He also continued to support the American Colonization Society until he realized that the colonization of more free African Americans than slaves was strengthening instead of weakening slavery. In a letter to Chief Justice John Marshall written in 1826, Pickering said slavery would tear the Union apart and called the Colonization Society ineffective because each time it transported "one freedman, a thousand slaves are born." He was full of "gloomy foreboding" that slavery was expanding and suggested that the institution might end if "the Negro population, in the slave-holding states . . . mingle their blood with the Whites." Here, however, he agreed with Jefferson that racism would most likely prevent attempts to render interracial unions "permanent." Marshall, who was a Virginian, concurred and admitted that slavery was rife with calamity and mischief, but southerners "cherish the evil . . . with immovable prejudice & dislike every thing [sic] which may tend to diminish it."[5]

On January 4, 1829, Pickering died at age eighty-three following a long illness. His intellectual energy did not forsake him until the end. Pickering's final words to a friend were from a favorite poem that ends, "All fear, none aid you, and few understand."[6] Throughout his public life Pickering often made rash decisions and did not always display the discipline and levelheadedness that others felt should have governed the conduct of a man of his stature and experience. Nevertheless, friends and enemies alike always knew where Pickering stood. Because of his regionalism, disdain for the three-fifths clause, and willingness to go to extremes, Pickering challenged the irresolute and disingenuous, earning him the praises of abolitionist William Lloyd Garrison, who called Pickering "one of the greatest minds of the country."[7]

In 1819, Federalist Elias Boudinot from New Jersey asked Pickering to help him organize citizens in an antislavery organization to oppose "the numerous and appalling evils that must result from extending and perpetuating slavery among us." Boudinot had served in the nation's first three congresses, from 1789 to 1795, and was later an ally of the New Jersey antislavery society. Beginning in 1773, he worked with the New Jersey legislature to pass bills ending slavery, but petitioners killed efforts at that time. Boudinot became involved in the abolition movement after the War of 1812 ended in 1815.[8] Though some historians may disagree, endorsements from Garrison and Boudinot give us a clearer picture of Pickering's interactions with abolitionists and the impression he made on his own generation and the next.

Rufus King, a member of the Continental Congress, delegate to the Constitutional Convention in 1787, and signer of the Constitution, served several years in the U.S. Senate, and was twice appointed minister to Great Britain, turned out to be the Federalist Party's last presidential candidate in 1816. King was originally from Massachusetts and moved to New York in 1788, where he was part of the New York assembly. He attempted to keep slavery out of western territories and eventually new states. As early as 1785, King consulted Pickering and others for their insights on the topic. Following an unsuccessful attempt to ban slavery in the Ordinance of 1785, King participated in the Constitutional Convention of 1787, where he issued a warning that northerners would object to the three-fifths clause and the twenty-year moratorium on prohibiting the foreign slave trade. Even though he supported the three-fifths clause when advocating ratification, King called "the provision of the Constitution on this subject . . . one of its greatest blemishes." Before the Constitution went into effect in 1788, King was able to include the ban of slavery in the Northwest Ordinance of 1787. Later, he attempted to keep slavery out of the Louisiana Purchase territory, recognizing that the treaty under which the territory was ceded allowed for its exclusion. Had the opponents of slavery "foreseen that we could raise revenue to the extent we have done, from indirect taxes," King finally admitted, "the Representation of Slaves wd. never have been admitted."[9]

During the crisis over Missouri, King led the fight to ban slavery from the state. Just as political enemies would infer of other Federalists, King was charged with taking the position for self-promotion. King was "deeply mortified at the issues," and was also "resentful," according to John Quincy Adams, "at the imputations of the slave-holders, that his motives on this occasion have merely of personal aggrandizement." Adams admitted that this type of political attack "is one of the most envenomed weapons of political and indeed of every sort of controversy." Adams then praised King for his "integrity" and said there was no man "purer."[10]

Before leaving Congress in 1824, King proposed using funds from the sale of public lands to purchase and emancipate slaves, but also planned to relocate free people of color to a location outside the United States. Some antislavery Americans advocated ejecting persons of color out of the country as a practical way to end slavery. Whenever the idea of abolishing slavery became serious, slaveholders and many non-slaveholding whites complained that they could not live in a biracial society and accepted colonization as a solution. Yet only free African Americans were selected for colonization, which actually strengthened and protected slavery and ensured its perpetuation. Abolitionists and antislavery politicians immediately saw the predicament posed by colonization and agreed that the emancipation of slaves, not the relocation or colonization of freed persons, was the only way to end slavery.[11]

Some outspoken Federalists later abandoned the radicalism of the Jeffersonian era—the most outstanding of these being Daniel Webster. As a young orator and representative from New Hampshire, Webster kept pace with Josiah Quincy and Pickering, publishing pamphlets that protested the embargo, the growth of southern power because of the three-fifths clause, the War of 1812, and the entry of slavery into newly formed territories and states. Webster moved to Massachusetts in 1816, eventually joined the Whig Party, and earned renown as secretary of state and U.S. senator during the most contentious years of the republic. As he aged, Webster became conciliatory on the subject of slavery and supported such controversial legislation as the Fugitive Slave Act, which was part of the Compromise of 1850. Webster's willingness to compromise with southerners created problems for the Whigs and earned criticism from former supporters and colleagues. Webster the onetime "champion of the north and the assailant of the south" wrote one northerner now stooped to emphasizing "the wrongs of the former" and "the apologist of the latter."[12]

Webster's transformation was stark. During the controversy over slavery in Missouri, he headed a committee that drafted a resolution urging Congress to keep slavery out of Missouri and other new states and territories. In the resolution Webster called "any toleration of Slavery" an injustice. Allowing new slave states into the Union could only "tarnish the proud fame of the country."[13] He was one of the Whig Party's candidates for president in 1836, but was unable to escape his Federalist past and new milquetoast perspective regarding the spread of slavery. The only electoral votes that Webster received were from Massachusetts his home state.[14]

In a speech to the Senate in 1850, Webster attacked abolitionists and the North in general for antagonizing southerners and provoking pro-slavery extremists in the South. When he publically sided with the South, Webster fell out of favor with former friends like Josiah Quincy who refuted Webster's claims that both northerners and southerners considered slavery evil when ratifying the Constitution. Quincy set out to correct Webster's revision of history with accounts from his personal observations and experiences. Resistance to slavery after ratification was not a political ploy, as Webster claimed. New Englanders had begun to attack slavery as early as the 1770s because of the "incompatibility of that institution with the principles of the American Revolution." Furthermore, in 1811 and 1819 Webster had agreed with him that neither Louisiana nor Missouri should enter the Union with slavery, but since then Webster had disavowed his past in a speech that was "neither that of a statesman or a patriot."[15]

Another Federalist who rejected the platform of the more extremist, sectionalist wing of his party from the beginning was Harrison Gray Otis. Otis served several years in the U.S. House of Representatives before entering the U.S. Senate in 1817. Through most of his career, when it came to slavery Otis was more apathetic and even more racist than most of his New England colleagues. There were occasions when Otis could have voted against the spread of slavery but did not.[16]

In 1800 the House considered petitions from former slaves who had been legally manumitted under a North Carolina law. They had moved to Pennsylvania, but North Carolinians repealed the law and the freed persons faced extradition proceedings to return them to slavery. When these African Americans appealed to the House, Otis objected to taking up the issue. He argued that the former slaves were "incapable of writing their names, or of reading the petition, and, *a fortiori*, of digesting the principles of it." To Otis, the question of whether persons legally manumitted and now living in a free state were entitled to keep their freedom was inconsequential. For him the real issue was that white persons were responsible for writing the petition and teaching these black people "the art of assembling together, debating, and the like." If encouraged by Congress and allowed to continue, such conduct might "extend from one part of the Union to the other."[17] Even considering the petition was dangerous in his estimate because other freed persons might ask Congress to protect their rights. Otis supported proslavery southerners in that case and in many others for reasons obviously more distasteful than simple respect for property rights.

After his last term in Congress, Otis became mayor of Boston (1829–1831) and never returned to national politics. Before his death on October 28, 1848, at age eighty-three, he commented publicly on Whig defectors to the Free Soil Party and published a letter titled "To the People of Massachusetts," in which he warned of the dangers that abolitionists and Free Soilers posed to the Union. Even though his views had not evolved like many of his contemporaries, well into his eighties Otis's mind remained sharp and alert until he slipped into a coma and died twenty-six days later.[18]

Ironically, onetime Federalist John Quincy Adams who had parted ways with his party over the embargo in 1808 and publicly rebuked their opposition with a widely publicized pamphlet, pursued a political course opposite to those of Webster and Otis. Adams already had an enviable career by the time he entered the U.S. Senate as a Federalist in 1802. After leaving the Federalist Party he joined Democratic-Republicans and received a diplomatic appointment to Russia from President Madison. From this point forward Adams navigated the seas of national politics shrewdly and in dramatic fashion ended one of the most distinguished careers in U.S. political history fighting the spread of slavery.[19]

Adams helped to negotiate the Treaty of Ghent that ended the War of 1812, served as diplomat to Britain, and became a highly successful secretary of state in the Monroe administration. He helped annex Florida, settled territorial boundary lines, and is believed to have authored the Monroe Doctrine. In 1824 he became president after winning a contest against the wildly popular war hero, Andrew Jackson of Tennessee. Although few studies describe the presidential election of 1824 as sectional, it should be noted that every New England state voted for Adams, and he received no votes from the Deep South. Jackson finished with ninety-nine votes and Adams came in second with eighty-four votes, but because there were four major candidates and no one won a majority, choosing the president fell to the House of Representatives. Federalists were barely visible by this time, but Democratic-Republicans in New England were still worried that sectional divisions might irreparably rupture the party. "If Jackson and Calhoun and their friends are friendly to a union of the *Republican Party* and wish to defeat the intrigues and efforts of the radicals, they must no longer stand against Mr. Adams but join . . . [the] cause of the North to have the honor & best interests of the nation at heart," wrote one Massachusetts Jeffersonian.[20]

When the selection process reached the House, Speaker Henry Clay of Kentucky, a onetime candidate in the race, threw his support behind Adams. The endorsement from Clay sealed the victory for Adams, who defeated Jackson in a 13–7 vote. Of those pleased with the outcome, African Americans in the Washington were reportedly "the only persons who expressed their joy by Hurras [sic]."[21] In office Adams attempted to rise above partisan politics and pursued a nationalist agenda, but his reluctance to mobilize support in Congress resulted in a failed presidency. His nationalist agenda included a naval academy, a national university and an observatory, which reflected Adams's interest in science. When his plans failed in Congress, Adams attributed the defeat to "the slave oligarchy" that "systematically struggle[d] to suppress all public patronage or countenance to the progress of the mind, especially scientific knowledge." Southerners dismissed much of Adams's nationalist agenda as part of a plot to "benefit the manufacturers of the North . . . and . . . fan wider the flame of sectional prejudice."[22]

Also contributing to his failures as president was Andrew Jackson's ability to build a base of support in Congress in preparation for the 1828 election. Jackson recruited members of Adams's administration to join his coalition, including Vice President John C. Calhoun. During the campaign, political foes also raised suspicions over Adams's former association with Federalists, including his choice of Rufus King for minister to Great Britain. Critics seized upon the relationship with King to connect Adams and his policies to the Federalists' anti-southern posture and schemes to dismantle the Union.[23]

Jackson handily defeated Adams in 1828. The electoral difference was 178 to 83, but Jackson won without New England's support. Once again the Federalists' former states overwhelmingly supported Adams but he received no votes from the Deep South or West. Some New Englanders opposed Jackson's rejection of internal improvements, which had been part of Adams's agenda for roads and canals. Massachusetts congressman Henry Dearborn complained, "The northern states are the last to object to measures of internal improvement for in the *North*, the people will make roads and canals, while in the less wealthy portions of the union they can never be established but by the *general government*." Dearborn believed that Jackson threatened national unity and suggested that northerners had no respect for Jackson as a president or as a person.[24]

As president he did nothing to affect slavery, but in 1831 Massachusetts voters sent Adams to the U.S. House of Representatives. In Congress Adams became an uncompromising opponent of expanding slavery, regularly introduced antislavery petitions, and campaigned on an almost daily basis for the abolition of slavery. Slavery "is absorbing all my faculties," he wrote in 1837, and in 1841 Adams argued a highly publicized case before the U.S. Supreme Court, winning exoneration and freedom for a group of illegally enslaved Africans who staged a revolt and killed all but two of their captors before they were imported into the United States on the schooner *L'Amistad*. The case ended in one of the most important Supreme Court decisions slavery-related before *Dred Scott v. Sanford* (1856–1857). During a two-day argument Adams excoriated southerners for participating in the illegal slave trade and President Martin Van Buren for his complicity. Because of his antislavery stance in Congress, Adams also became popular among abolitionists and African Americans who turned to him for help. In 1841 John Davies found a sympathetic ear when he sought Adams's advice and help regarding his stepson, who was the victim of an illegal sale that enslaved him in Arkansas.[25]

From 1836 to 1848 Adams also fought and finally defeated the House gag rule, which banned discussions of slavery. Congress imposed a gag because northerners submitted antislavery petitions numbering in the hundreds of thousands to legislators. This was the same tactic used by southerners and likeminded northerners in 1807, who attempted to impose a gag on discussions of the embargo raised by New Englanders' petitions and resolutions. The gag did not work then but the contours of the nation and southern power had grown. Adams challenged the rule as unconstitutional and continued to read petitions in Congress despite the gag. After he read a petition calling for the dissolution of the Union because of slavery, the Senate held hearings to censure Adams. When the attempt failed, Kentucky representative Thomas Frances Marshall expressed his frustrations and reasons for opposing Adams: "If he could be removed from the councils of the nation, or silenced upon the exasperating subject . . . [of slavery] none other, I believe, could be found hardy enough or bad enough to fill his place."[26]

Adams continued to frustrate the South's representatives by entering antislavery petitions until he defeated the gag rule. He also vigorously denounced the annexation of Texas (1845) and opposed the Mexican War (1846–1848) as conspiracies to expand slavery. He gave lengthy anti–Mexican War speeches in the House, asserting that the government's chief objective for sacrificing American and Mexican lives was imposing slavery into territories where it had already been abolished. Adams was preparing to vote against appropriations for tributes to Mexican War officers when on February 21, 1848, he gripped his desk and collapsed. Adams had suffered a cerebral stroke and died two days later in the Capitol. Through speeches in the House and consistent criticisms that federal policy was proslavery, the eighty-year-old Adams perfected a pattern of political protest that antislavery politicians would emulate until the Civil War.[27]

During Adams's years in the House, northern voters began to nominate and elect politicians who rejected southern domination of the federal government and legislation. They formed the Liberty Party in 1839, the Free Soil Party in 1848, and then founded the Republican Party in 1854.

As in Jefferson's day, the bias in federal legislation initiated calls for northern unity. Antislavery sentiment also mounted with the passage of each proslavery policy or congressional compromise that facilitated slavery's expansion. In an 1856 pamphlet, Josiah Quincy advised northerners to "send men to Congress who have no particular interests in common with slaveholders."[28] As pro-northern and antislavery politicians entered state and national governments, many emulated a previous generation's methods of opposing proslavery legislation.

It is perhaps fitting that Josiah Quincy lived to witness the northern states unite against the slave power and elect a presidential candidate from a strictly northern political party. After retiring from Congress and the Massachusetts General Court, Quincy became mayor of Boston, president of Harvard College, and editor of John Quincy Adams's memoirs. He also conducted agricultural experiments on his farm and became one of Boston's largest landowners, which brought him wealth and supported his family long after his demise. Yet he kept up with political events and the growing political controversies over slavery. As early as 1819 Quincy attended an antislavery meeting with other Federalists and in 1836 praised John Quincy Adams for fighting slavery's entry into new territories and states. But Quincy was skittish about the abolitionist movement. He said, "Northern men owe it to their character as well as to that of their country, to meet every attempt to extend the evil to new states with the most decided opposition."[29]

By the 1850s Quincy resumed his public opposition to southern power by joining the antislavery movement and criticizing the Compromise of 1850 and the Kansas-Nebraska Act (1854). Just as he had berated northern Democratic-Republicans for voting with the South during the embargo, Quincy attacked "Cotton Whigs," northern members of the Whig Party who supported proslavery legislation, for the same reason.[30] As earlier noted, one target for Quincy's harshest criticism was Daniel Webster. Webster had been an ally forty years earlier and joined the Federalist opposition to the three-fifths clause, the embargo, and the War of 1812. He also worked with Quincy on the petition opposing slavery in Missouri. But Quincy referred to Webster as part of the "Northern Wing of the Slave Power" who began to vote with the South and support legislation that facilitated the spread of slavery. He became another "six dollar-a-day-patriot."[31]

In his old age Quincy entered a new chapter in U.S. political history. A younger generation of politicians from the North and Northwest schooled in the Federalist tradition of opposition formed the type of regional alliance that once eluded the Federalists. At every turn federal legislation deepened sectional hostilities, but the political leaders that northern voters elected to federal and state offices boldly brandished their antislavery credentials and separated themselves from northerners who supported the South.[32] Quincy also saw the implementation of the free-soil, free-labor movement committed to banning slavery in new states and territories.

When slavery finally did tear the Union apart in December 1860, Quincy celebrated northern unity and efforts to preserve the Union without slavery. He said, "I have anticipated such an event for more than sixty years. I am only disappointed and regret that it has not come before." He did live long enough to see his sons Edmund and Josiah Jr. become abolitionists and his grandson, Samuel Miller Quincy, fight with the Second Massachusetts Infantry, where he received wounds at Cedar Mountain and Chancellorsville. For the remainder of the war, Samuel served as a staff officer with the Seventy-Third U.S. Colored Infantry.[33]

Until he died on July 1, 1864, at age ninety-two, Quincy remained proud of his Federalist past. In a letter to President Lincoln, Quincy praised the Emancipation Proclamation and added that the possibility of emancipation had been a subject "of my thought more than seventy years; being first introduced to it by the debates in the Convention of Massachusetts for adopting the Constitution in 1788, which I attended. I had subsequent opportunities of knowing the views, on that subject . . . of such men as Hamilton, King, Jay & Pickering" and never personally encountered an individual "who did not express a detestation" of slavery and the "desire & disposition to get rid of it."[34]

For years Quincy had maintained that more than partisanship fueled Federalists' calls for constitutional reform to end slave representation, protect New England, and restore a modicum of political equality in the federal government. Federalists failed to achieve their objectives for several reasons, but most of all because they had become a regional party before northerners were willing or able to sustain it. Federalists were generally disorganized, and perhaps as ambitious young men, individual Federalists—including Pickering, Adams, and Quincy—did not fully grasp the significance of their opposition to the three-fifths clause or commercial restrictions.

It was Quincy who realized decades earlier that only a North united against the spread of slavery could maintain a sectional balance in national politics. For the most part, however, it was the long fight over the protection of maritime commerce and an economy independent of southern slavery that demonstrated to Federalists the need for a consolidated effort in the North. Unlike the next generation of New Englanders, Federalists lacked the political strength to protect their way of life as long as the Constitution apportioned representation based on the possession of slaves. Extreme or radical opposition to policies they deemed harmful to their economic culture and antithetical to their participation in the democratic process many deemed this their only available course of action after 1805. Ironically, this became the most enduring part of the Federalists' legacy.

NOTES

1. "Diary of Eliza Susan Quincy, entries September 16, 1814–September 30, 1821," Quincy, Wendell, Holmes, and Upham Family Papers, MHS.
2. *U.S. Senate Journal*, 16th Cong., 2nd sess., January 5, 1820, 79; *U.S. House Journal*, 28th Cong., 2nd sess., January 25, 1845, 259; Liberty Party, *The Slave Power. Political Tracts, No. 1.* (Hartford: Christian Freeman, c. 1844), 2–4, SCUA.
3. Gerald H. Clarfield, *Timothy Pickering and the American Republic* (Pittsburgh, PA: University of Pittsburgh Press, 1980), 211–13.
4. *Annals of Congress*, 14th Cong., 2nd sess., 939–41; *House Journal*, 1817, 14th Cong., 1st sess., 449; *Poulson's American Daily Advertiser* (Philadelphia), August 5, 1817; *Boston Recorder*, January 7, 1817.
5. *Salem* (MA) *Gazette*, October 18, 1822; *New Bedford* (MA) *Mercury*, October 30, 1829; Pickering to John Marshall, January 17, 1826, Timothy Pickering Papers, MHS; Marshall to Pickering, March 20, 1826, in John Marshall, *The Papers of John Marshall*, ed. Herbert A. Hobson, 12 vols. (Chapel Hill: University of North Carolina Press, 2000), 10:277; Clarfield, *Timothy Pickering*, 264.
6. Quoted in Clarfield, *Timothy Pickering*, 264–69.
7. *Pennsylvania Freeman* (Philadelphia), March 25, 1847.
8. Elias Boudinot to Pickering, November 5, 1819, Timothy Pickering Papers, MHS; David Hackett Fischer, *The Revolution of American Conservatism: The Federalist Party in the Era of Jeffersonian Democracy* (New York: Harper and Row, 1965), 322; *New-Bedford* (MA) *Mercury*, November 12, 1819; *Hallowell (ME) Gazette*, November 17, 1819; George William Van Cleve, *A Slaveholders' Union: Slavery, Politics, and the Constitution in the Early American Republic,* (Chicago: The University of Chicago Press, 2010), 39.
9. Rufus King to Timothy Pickering, April 15, 1785, in *Letters to Delegates to Congress, 1774–1789*, ed. Paul H. Smith et al., 26 vols. (Washington, DC: U.S. Government Printing Office, 1979), 22:342; Rufus King to Colonel (Timothy) Pickering, November 4, 1803, in Max Farrand, ed., *The Records of the Federal Convention of 1787*, 3 vols. (New Haven, CT: Yale University Press, 1966), 3:399, 401.
10. John Quincy Adams, *The Diary of John Quincy Adams, 1794–1845: American Diplomacy, and Political, Social, and Intellectual Life, From Washington to Polk*, ed. Allan Nevins (New York: Charles Scribner's Sons, NY, 1951), 232.
11. See U.S. Congress, *Senate Journal* (18th Cong., 1st. sess.), February 18, 1825, 171; *The American* (Jamaica, NY), November 22, 1819; *Hallowell (ME) Gazette*, April 13, 1825.
12. D. Hammond, *A Letter to the Hon. Daniel Webster [Dated March 20, 1850, on Slavery]* (Cherry Valley, NY, 1850), 4, 6–8 (unsigned, typed copy) Martin Van Buren Papers, LC; Dinah Mayo-Bobee, "Understanding the Essex Junto: Fear, Dissent, and Propaganda in the Early Republic, *New England Quarterly* (Winter, 2015): 648; Elizabeth R. Varon, *Disunion! The Coming of the American Civil War, 1789–1859* (Chapel Hill: University of North Carolina Press, 2008), 8, 217–20; Leonard L. Richards, *Slave Power: The Free North and Southern Domination, 1780–1860* (Baton Rouge: Louisiana State University Press, 2000), 110–12; Fischer, *Revolution of American Conservatism*, 238–39; Jabez.
13. Boston (MA) Citizens, [Daniel Webster, Josiah Quincy, et al.], A Memorial to the Congress of the United States, on the Subject of Restraining the Increase of Slavery in New States to Be Admitted into the Union, Boston: Sewell Phelps, Printer, 1819), 21, Antislavery Collection, 1725–1911 (RB 003, SCUA).
14. Dinah Mayo-Bobee, "Understanding the Essex Junto," 648.
15. Josiah Quincy, *Whig Policy Analyzed and Illustrated* (Boston: Phillips, Sampson and Company, 1856), 9–12, Collection of the BA; Varon, *Disunion!* 217–20.
16. Samuel Eliot Morison, *Harrison Gray Otis, 1765–1848: The Urbane Federalist* (Boston: Houghton Mifflin, 1969), 425–26.
17. *Annals of Congress*, 6th Cong., 1st sess., 231; also partially quoted in Donald L. Robinson, *Slavery in the Structure of American Politics, 1765–1820* (New York: Harcourt Brace Jovanovich, 1971), 515n44.

18. Morison, *Harrison Gray Otis*, 454, 508–9; Mathew Mason, "Federalists, Abolitionists, and the Problem of Influence," in *American Nineteenth Century History*, 10, no. 1 (March 2009): 14.

19. Richmond (VA) Enquirer, August 15, 1828; see Joseph Wheelan, *Mr. Adams's Last Crusade: John Quincy Adams's Extraordinary Post-Presidential Life in Congress* (New York: PublicAffairs, 2008), 1–65.

20. John Quincy Adams, *The Diary of John Quincy Adams, 1794–1845*, ed. Allan Nevins (New York: Longmans & Co., [1928]), 559; Cochran (?) to Benjamin W. Crowninshield, July 17, 1824; H. Dearborn to Benjamin W. Crowninshield, January 2, 1828, and December 19, 1830, Crowninshield Family Papers, PEM.

21. *Register of Debates*, 18th Cong., 2nd sess., 525–27; Adams, *Diary*, 335–36; Quote from Charles N. Edels, *Nation Builder: John Quincy Adams and thee Grade Strategy of the Republic*, (Cambridge, MA: Harvard University Press, 2014), 205.

22. Adams, *Diary*, 344; *New-Hampshire Patriot & State Gazette* (Concord), September 8, 1828; Edel, *Nation Builder*, 214.

23. Mayo-Bobee, "Understanding the Essex Junto," 651; Edel, *Nation Builder*, 210; Daniel Walker Howe, *What Hath God Wrought: The Transformation of America, 1815–1848* (New York: Oxford University Press, 2007), 246; Shaw Livermore, *The Twilight of Federalism: The Disintegration of the Federalist Party, 1815–1830* (Princeton, NJ: Princeton University Press, 1962), 136; See also W. Lee to Benjamin W. Crowninshield July 13, 1824, Crowninshield Family Papers, PEM.

24. *U.S. House Journal*, 1829, 20th Cong., 2nd sess., 273.

25. Adams, Diary, 477, 545; Adams, *Argument of John Quincy Adams before the Supreme Court of the United States in the Case of the United States, Appellants, vs. Cinque, and Others, Africans Captured in the Schooner Amistad, by Lieut. Grundy, Delivered on the 24th of February and 1st of March 1841: With a Review of the Case of the Antelope, Reported in the 10th, 11th, and 12th Volumes of Wheaton's Reports* (New York: S. W. Benedict, 1841), Rare Books, E441.A1 no. 4, SCUA; *United States v. Libellants & Claimants of the Schooner Amistad*, 40 U.S. 518; 10 L. Ed. 826. 1841 U.S. exis 279, March 9, 1841, Decided.

26. Thomas Frances Marshall, *On the Resolutions to Censure John Q. Adams. Delivered in the House of Representatives of the U.S.*, January 25, 26, and 28, 1842 (Washington, DC, 1842), 3, 5, Pamphlets in American History, 594 B 10, SCUA; Wheelan, *Mr. Adams' Last Crusade*, 91–251; Richards, *Slave Power*, 136–41 and *The Life and Times of Congressman John Quincy Adams* (New York: Oxford University Press, 1986).

27. Richards, *Life and Times*, 202–203; Wheelan, *Mr. Adams' Last Crusade*, 247–49.

28. Richards, *Slave Power*, 23–27; Quincy, *Whig Policy Analyzed and Illustrated*, 16, BA.

29. McCaughey, *Josiah Quincy*, 206.

30. Richards, *Slave Power*, 110–11; McCaughey, *Josiah Quincy*, 201.

31. Robert A. McCaughey, *Josiah Quincy, 1772–1864: The Last Federalist* (Cambridge, MA: Harvard University Press, 1974), 207–12; also see Webster, Quincy, et al., Memorial to the Congress of the United States; Josiah Quincy, *An Oration Delivered before the Washington Benevolent Society of Massachusetts on the Thirtieth Day of April 1813: Being the Anniversary of the First Inauguration of President Washington* (Boston: William S. and Henry Spear, 1813), Collection of the BA.

32. Jonathan Halperin Earle, *Jacksonian Antislavery and the Politics of Free Soil, 1824–1854* (Chapel Hill: University of North Carolina Press, 2004), 18, 78, 93, 102, 106.

33. McCaughey, *Josiah Quincy*, 196–97, 207–13.

34. Josiah Quincy to Abraham Lincoln, September 7, 1863, *Abraham Lincoln Papers*, LC.

Bibliography

ARCHIVAL COLLECTIONS

American Tracts Collection, Beinecke Rare Book & Manuscript Library, Yale University, New Haven, Connecticut.
Antislavery Tracts, 1725–1911. Special Collections and University Archives, University of Massachusetts Libraries, Amherst.
Books and Pamphlets Collection. American Antiquarian Society, Worcester, Massachusetts.
Broadsides. American Antiquarian Society, Worcester, Massachusetts.
Collection of the Boston Athenaeum. Boston, Massachusetts
Caleb Strong Papers. Massachusetts Historian Society, Boston.
Crowninshield Family Papers. Phillips Library, Peabody Essex Museum, Salem, Massachusetts.
George Thatcher Papers. Phillips Library, Peabody Essex Museum, Salem, Massachusetts.
James Cox Papers. Phillips Library, Peabody Essex Museum, Salem, Massachusetts.
James Madison Papers. Manuscript Division, Library of Congress.
Joseph Bowditch Papers. Phillips Library, Peabody Essex Museum, Salem, Massachusetts.
Josiah Quincy Jr. Diary. Massachusetts Historical Society, Boston.
Parsons Family Papers. Philips Library, Peabody Essex Museum, Salem, Massachusetts.
Philip J. Lampi, First Democracy Project. Lampi data now available at A New Nation Votes: American Election Returns, 1787–1824,http://elections.lib.tufts.edu. American Antiquarian Society, Worcester, Massachusetts.
Richard Cutts Collection of the James and Dolley Madison Papers, Library of Congress.
Richard Cutts Papers, 1753–1886. University of Virginia Library, Charlottesville.
Samuel Taggart Letterbook. American Antiquarian Society, Worcester, Massachusetts.
Thomas Handasyd Perkins Papers. Massachusetts Historical Society, Boston.
Thomas Jefferson Papers. Manuscript Division, Library of Congress.
Timothy Pickering Papers. Massachusetts Historical Society, Boston.
Wendell Holmes Quincy and Upham Family Papers. Massachusetts Historical Society, Boston.

NEWSPAPERS AND PERIODICALS

Albany (NY) *Central*
Albany (NY) *Register*
American (Jamaica, NY)
American Advocate (Hallowell, ME)
Bee (Hudson, NY)
Berkshire Reporter (MA)
Boston Gazette
Boston Patriot

Charleston City Gazette and Commercial Daily Advertiser (SC)
Columbia Detector (Boston)
Columbian Centinel (Boston)
Columbian Courier (New Bedford, MA)
Columbian Minerva (Dedham, MA)
Constitutional Telegraph (Boston)
Democrat (Boston)
Eastern Argus (Portland, ME)
Eastern Herald and Maine Gazette (Portland, ME)
Edes' Kennebec Gazette (Augusta, ME)
Enquirer (Richmond, VA)
Essex Register (Salem, MA)
Gazette (Portland, ME)
Green Mountain Patriot (Windsor, VT)
Hallowell (ME) *Gazette*
Hampshire Federalist (Springfield, MA)
Hampshire Gazette (Northampton, MA)
Independent Chronicle and the Universal Advertiser (Boston)
Independent Gazetteer (Philadelphia)
Litchfield (VT) *Gazette*
Massachusetts Spy or Worcester Gazette
National Aegis (Worcester, MA)
National Intelligencer (Washington, DC)
New Bedford (MA) *Mercury*
Newburyport (MA) *Herald*
New-England Palladium (Boston)
New Hampshire Patriot and State Gazette (Concord, NH)
New-York Dailey Advertiser
Pennsylvania Freeman
Pittsfield (MA) *Sun*
Poulson's American Daily Advertiser (Philadelphia)
Providence (RI) *Gazette*
Repertory (Boston)
Richmond (VA) *Enquirer*
Rutland (VT) *Herald*
Salem (MA) *Gazette*
Star (Raleigh, NC)
Telescope or American Herald (Leominster, MA)
Vermont Gazette (Bennington)
Weekly Messenger (Boston)
Weekly Wanderer (Randolph, VT)
Western Star (Stockbridge, MA)
Worcester (MA) *Magazine*
Yankee (Boston)

COURT CASES CITED

United States v. Burr 25 F. Cas. 30 (No. 14,692d) C.C.D. Va 1807.
United States v. Libellants & Claimants of the Schooner Amistad, 40 U.S. 518; 10 L. Ed. 826. 1841 U.S. Lexis 279, March 9, 1841, Decided.
United States v. The Penelope; Case No. 16,024 District Court, D. Pennsylvania 1806 U.S. Dist. Lexis 5; 27 F. Case 486; 2 Pet. Adm. 438.
United States v. The Schooner Betsey and Charlotte and Her Cargo 8 U.S. 443; 2 L. Ed. 673; U.S. Lexis 405; 4 Cranch 443 (1807);

Yeaton And Others, Claimants of The Schooner General Pinkney And Cargo, v. United States; 9 Sup. Ct. 281; 3 L. Ed. 101; (1809) U.S. Lexis 431; 5 Cranch 281 March 7, 1809, Decided;
Young et al. v. Tavel 18,175 S.C. (1806) U.S. Dist. Lexis 4; 30 F. Case 867, 1 Bee 228 (1806).

PUBLIC ACTS CITED

Defense of Merchant Vessels Act of 1798, Pub. L. No. 5–60, 1 Stat. 572 (1798).
Effectual Protection for Commerce and Coasts Act of 1798, Pub. L. No. 5–62, 1 Stat. 574 (1798).
Suspension of Trade with France Act of 1798, Pub. L. No. 5–88, 1 Stat. 611 (1798).
Suspension of Trade with St. Domingo (Haiti) Act of 1806, Pub L. 9–9, 2 Stat. 351 (1806).
Nonimportation of items from Britain Act of 1806, Pub. L. 9–29, 2 Stat. 379 (1806).
Fortification of Ports and Harbors Act of 1806, Pub. L. No. 9–47, 2 Stat. 402 (1806)
Prohibition on Slave Importations Act of 1807, Pub. L. No 9–22, 2 Stat. 426 (1807).
Embargo on all Ships in U.S. Ports Act of 1807, Pub. L. No. 10–5, 2 Stat. 451 (1807).
Fortification of Ports and Harbors Act of 1808, Pub. L. No. 10–7, 2 Stat. 453 (1808)
Supplementary to the Embargo Act of 1808, Pub. L. No. 10–7, 2 Stat. 453 (1808).
Additional Supplement to the Embargo Act of 1808, Pub. L. No. 10–33, 2 Stat. 473 (1808).
Authorization for the President to Suspend the Embargo Act of 1808, Pub. L. No. 10–52, 2 Stat. 490 (1808).
Addition to the Embargo and Supplements Act of 1808, Pub. L. No. 10–66, 2 Stat. 499 (1808).
Enforcement of the Embargo Act of 1809, Pub. L. No. 10–5, 2 Stat. 506 (1809)
Partial Repeal of Embargo with Nonintercourse, Pub. L. No. 10–24, 2 Stat. 528 (1809)
Declaration of War with Great Britain, Pub. L. No. 12–102, 2 Stat. 755 (1812).

BOOKS, BROADSIDES, AND PAMPHLETS

Adams, Donald R., Jr. "American Neutrality and Prosperity, 1793–1808: A Reconsideration." *Journal of Economic History* 40, no. 4 (December 1980): 713–37.
Adams, Henry, ed. *Documents Relating to New-England Federalism, 1800–1815.* Boston: Little, Brown, and Company, 1877.
Adams, Henry. *History of the United States during the Administrations of James Madison.* New York: Library of America, 1986.
Adams, Henry. *History of the United States during the Administrations of Thomas Jefferson.* 2 vols. New York: Literary Classics of the United States distributed by Viking Press, 1986.
Adams, John Quincy. *A Letter to the Hon. Harrison Gray Otis, a Member of the Senate of Massachusetts, on the Present State of Our National Affairs; with Remarks upon Mr. Pickering's Letter to the Governor of the Commonwealth.* Newburyport, MA: W. and J. Gilman, 1808.
Adams, John Quincy. *Argument of John Quincy Adams before the Supreme Court of the United States in the Case of the United States, Appellants, vs. Cinque, and Others, Africans Captured in the Schooner Amistad, by Lieut. Grundy, Delivered on the 24th of February and 1st of March 1841: With a Review of the Case of the Antelope, Reported in the 10th, 11th, and 12th Volumes of Wheaton's Reports.* New York: S. W. Benedict, 1841.
Adams, John Quincy. *Memoirs of John Quincy Adams, Comprising Portions of His Diary from 1795 to 1848.* Edited by Charles Francis Adams. 12 vols. Philadelphia: J. B. Lippincott and Co., 1874.
Adams, John Quincy. *The Diary of John Quincy Adams, 1794–1845.* Ed. Allan Nevins. New York: Scribner, [1951].

Adams, John Quincy. *Writings of John Quincy Adams*. Ed. Chauncey Ford Worthington. 7 vols. New York: Macmillan, 1913–1917.
Adams, John. *The Works of John Adams, Second President of the United States: With a Life of the Author*. Ed. Charles Francis Adams. Freeport, NY: Books for Libraries Press, 1969.
American Commerce in Flames! Boston, 1808.
Ames, Fisher. *The Works of Fisher Ames: With a Selection from His Speeches and Correspondence*. Ed. Seth Ames. 2 vols. New York: Da Capo Press, 1969.
Anti-Aristocrat, or Congressional Election for York District, Nov. 1806. Portland, 1806.
Appleby, Joyce. "A Different Kind of Independence: The Postwar Restructuring of the Historical Study of Early America." *William and Mary Quarterly* 3d ser., 50, no. 2 (April 1993): 245–67.
Appleby, Joyce. *Capitalism and a New Social Order: The Republican Vision of the 1790s*. New York: New York University Press, 1984.
Appleby, Joyce. *Inheriting the Revolution: The First Generation of Americans*. Cambridge, MA: Belknap Press of Harvard University Press, 2000.
Bailyn, Bernard. *The Ideological Origins of the American Revolution*. Cambridge, MA: Belknap Press/Harvard University Press, 1967.
Banner, James M. *To the Hartford Convention: The Federalists and the Origins of Party Politics in Massachusetts, 1789–1815*. New York: Alfred A. Knopf, 1970.
Banning, Lance. *The Jeffersonian Persuasion: Evolution of a Party Ideology*. Ithaca, NY: Cornell University Press, 1978.
Bayard, James Asherton. *Mr. Bayard's Speech upon His Motion to Amend the Resolution Offered by Mr. Giles, By Striking Out that Part Which Is in Italics, Delivered in the Senate of the United States Tuesday, February 13, 1809*. Portland, ME: Shirley, 1809.
Baylies, William. *A View of the Proceedings of the House of Representatives of the United States in the Case of the Plymouth Election: Addressed to the Electors of Plymouth District*. Boston: Greenbush and Stebbins, 1809.
Bemis, Samuel Flagg. *A Diplomatic History of the United States*. 5th ed. New York: Henry Holt and Company, 1965.
Ben-Atar, Doron and Barbara Oberg, eds. *Federalists Reconsidered*. Charlottesville: University of Virginia Press, 1998.
Ben-Atar, Doron. *The Origins of Jeffersonian Commercial Policy and Diplomacy*. New York: St. Martin's Press, 1993.
Bentley, William. *The Diary of William Bentley D.D.: Pastor of the East Church Salem, Massachusetts*. 4 vols. Salem, MA: Essex Institute, 1905–1914.
Bernhard, Winfred E. A. *Fisher Ames: Federalist and Statesman, 1758–1808*. Chapel Hill: University of North Carolina Press, 1965.
Blake, Francis. *An Examination of the Constitutionality of the Embargo Laws: Comprising a View of the Arguments on that Question before the Honorable John Davis, Esquire, Judge of the District Court for Massachusetts, in the Case of the United States vs. Brigantine William, Tried and Determined at Salem (Mass.) September Term, 1808: to Which Is Added, the Opinion Pronounced by the Court on the Constitutional Question, Arising in the Trial of the Case*. Worcester, MA: Goulding and Stow, 1808.
Bolster, W. Jeffrey. "'To Feel Like a Man': Black Seamen in the Northern States, 1800–1860." *Journal of American History* 76, no. 4 (March 1990): 1173–99.
Bolster, W. Jeffrey. *Black Jacks: African American Seamen in the Age of Sail*. Cambridge, MA: Harvard University Press, 1997.
Bowling, Kenneth R., and Donald R. Kennon, eds. *Neither Separate nor Equal: Congress in the 1790s*. Athens: Ohio University Press, 2000.
Broussard, James H. *The Southern Federalists, 1800–1816*. Baton Rouge: Louisiana State University Press, 1978.
Brown, Roger H. *Redeeming the Republic: Federalists, Taxation, and the Origins of the Constitution*. Baltimore: Johns Hopkins University Press, 1993.
Brown, Roger H. *The Republic in Peril: 1812*. New York: Columbia University Press, 1964.

Buel, Richard, Jr. *America on the Brink: How the Political Struggle over the War of 1812 Almost Destroyed the Young Republic*. New York: Palgrave Macmillan, 2005.
Calabresi, Steven G., and Christopher S. Yoo. *The Unitary Executive: Presidential Power from Washington to Bush*. New Haven, CT: Yale University Press, 2008.
Carey, Mathew. *Examination of the Pretensions of New England to Commercial Pre-Eminence*. Philadelphia: Printed for M. Carey, 1814.
Carnegie Endowment for International Peace, Division of International Law. *Arbitrations and Diplomatic Settlements of the United States*. Washington, DC: The Endowment, 1914.
Citizens of Boston, *A Memorial to the Congress of the United States on the Subject of Restraining the Increase of Slavery in New States to Be Admitted into the Union*. Boston: Sewell Phelps, Printer, 1819.
Clarfield, Gerard, "Postscript to the Jay Treaty: Timothy Pickering and Anglo-American Relations, 1795–1797." *William and Mary Quarterly* 3d ser., 23, no. 1 (January 1966): 106–20.
Clarfield, Gerard. *Timothy Pickering and the American Republic*. Pittsburgh, PA: University of Pittsburgh Press, 1980.
Clark, Victor S. *History of Manufactures in the United States, vol. 1, 1607–1860*. New York: Carnegie Institution of Washington / Peter Smith, 1949 [1929].
Cleves, Rachel Hope. *The Reign of Terror in America: Visions of Violence from Anti-Jacobinism to Antislavery*. New York: Cambridge University Press, 2009.
Cochran, Thomas C., ed. *The New American State Papers [1789–1860]; Social Policy*. 47 vols. Wilmington, DE: Scholarly Resources, 1972–1973.
Coleman, Elihu. *A Testimony against that Antichristian Practice of Making Slaves of Men. Wherein I Shewed It to Be Contrary to the Dispensation of the Law and Time of the Gospel, and Very Opposite Both to Grace and Nature*. Boston, 1733.
Commons, John R., et al. *History of Labour in the United States*. 2 vols. Reprint. New York: Macmillan, 1966.
Conley, Patrick T., and John P. Kaminski, eds. *The Constitution and the States: The Role of the Original Thirteen in the Framing and Adoption of the Federal Constitution*. Madison, WI: Madison House, 1988.
Connecticut General Assembly. *At a Special Session of the General Assembly of the State of Connecticut, Held at Hartford, on the Twenty Third Day of February, A.D. 1809*. Hartford, 1809.
Cray, Robert E., Jr. "Remembering the USS *Chesapeake*: The Politics of Maritime Death and Impressment." *Journal of the Early Republic* 25 no. 3 (Fall 2005), 445–74.
Cress, Lawrence Delbert. "'Cool and Serious Reflection': *Federalist Attitudes toward War in 1812*." *Journal of the Early Republic* 7, no. 2 (Summer 1987): 123–45.
Crocker, Matthew H. *The Magic of the Many: Josiah Quincy and the Rise of Mass Politics in Boston, 1800–1830*. Amherst: University of Massachusetts Press, 1999.
Cunningham, Noble E. "The Diary of Frances Few, 1808–1809." *Journal of Southern History* 29, no. 3 (August 1963): 345–61.
Cunningham, Noble E. *The Jeffersonian Republicans in Power*. Chapel Hill: University of North Carolina Press, 1963.
Davis, David Brion. "American Equality and Foreign Revolutions." *Journal of American History* 76, no. 3 (December 1989): 729–52.
Davis, David Brion. *The Problem of Slavery in the Age of Revolution, 1770–1823*. New edition. New York: Oxford University Press, 1999.
Davis, Joshua. *A Narrative of Joshua Davis, an American Citizen, Who Was Pressed and Served On Board Six Ships of the British Navy . . . The Whole Being an Interesting and Faithful Narrative of the Discipline, Various Practices and Treatment of Pressed Seamen in the British Navy, etc*. Boston: B. True, 1811.
Dawson, Mathew Q. *Partisanship and the Birth of America's Second Party, 1796–1800*. Westport, CT: Greenwood, 2000.

Declaration of the County of Essex, in the Commonwealth of Massachusetts, by Its Delegates, Assembled in Convention at Ipswich, on Tuesday, The 21st of July 1812. Salem, MA: Thomas C. Cushing, 1812.

Democratic Party, Massachusetts. *Sir, Agreeably to a Previous Notice a Convention of Delegates Was Held at Danvers . . . to Nominate a Republican Candidate for Essex South District, as a Member to the Eighth Congress . . . the Hon. Jacob Crowninshield Was Unanimously Chosen. . . .* Salem, MA, 1802.

Dorfman, Joseph. "The Economic Philosophy of Thomas Jefferson." *Political Science Quarterly* 55, no. 1 (March 1940): 98–121.

Douglass, Elisha P. "Fisher Ames, Spokesman for New England Federalism." *Proceedings of the American Philosophical Society* 103, no. 5 (October 15, 1959): 693–715.

Drescher, Seymour. *Abolition: A History of Slavery and Antislavery.* New York: Cambridge University Press, 2009.

Dunne, Gerald T. "Joseph Story: The Germinal Years." *Harvard Law Review* 75, no. 4 (February 1962): 707–54.

Durand, James R. *The Life and Adventure of James R. Durand, During a Period of Fifteen Years from 1801 to 1816: In Which Time He Was Impressed on Board the British Fleet and Held in Detestable Bondage for More than Seven Years.* Rochester, NY: E. Peck and Co., 1820.

[Dwight, Sereno Edwards]. *Slave Representation by Boreas, Awake! O Spirit of the North.* New Haven, CT, 1812.

Dwight, Theodore. *History of the Hartford Convention: With a Review of the Policy of the United States Government, Which Led to the War of 1812.* New York: N & J White, 1833.

Dye, Ira. "Early American Merchant Seafarers." *Proceedings of the American Philosophical Society* 120, no. 5 (October 15, 1976): 331–60.

Earle, Jonathan Halperin. *Jacksonian Antislavery and the Politics of Free Soil, 1824–1854.* Chapel Hill: University of North Carolina Press, 2004.

Earman, Cynthia D. "Remembering the Ladies: Women, Etiquette, and Diversions in Washington City, 1800–1814." *Washington History* 12, no. 1 (Spring/Summer 2000): 102–17.

East, Robert A. "Economic Development and New England Federalism, 1803–1814." *New England Quarterly* 10, no. 3 (September 1937): 430–46.

Edel, Charles N. *Nation Builder: John Quincy Adams and the Grand Strategy of the Republic.* Cambridge, MA: Harvard University Press, 2014.

Egan, Clifford L. "Franco-American Relations, 1803–1814." PhD dissertation, University of Colorado, 1969.

Egan, Clifford L. *Neither Peace nor War: Franco-American Relations, 1803–1812.* Baton Rouge: Louisiana State University Press, 1983.

Elkins, Stanley, and Eric McKitrick. *The Age of Federalism: The Early American Republic, 1788–1800.* New York: Oxford University Press, 1993.

Elliot, James. *The Poetical and Miscellaneous Works of James Elliot, Citizen of Guilford, Vermont, and Late a Noncommissioned Officer in the Legion of the United States, in Four Books [Thirteen Lines from Pope].* Greenfield, MA: Dickman, 1798.

Elliot, Jonathan, ed. *The Debates in the Several State Conventions, on the Adoption of the Federal Constitution, As Recommended by the General Convention at Philadelphia in 1787.* 5 vols. Philadelphia: J. B. Lippincott & Co., 1876.

Ennis, Daniel James. *Enter the Press-Gang: Naval Impressment in Eighteenth-Century British Literature.* Newark: University of Delaware Press, 2002.

Essex County, Massachusetts. *Declaration of the County of Essex, in the Commonwealth of Massachusetts, by Its Delegates, Assembled in Convention at Ipswich, on Tuesday, the 21st of July 1812.* Salem, MA: Thomas C. Cushing, 1812.

Estes, Todd. "Shaping the Politics of Public Opinion: Federalists and the Jay Treaty Debate." *Journal of the Early Republic* 20, no. 3 (Autumn 2000): 393–422.

Eustace, Nicole. *1812: War and the Passions of Patriotism.* Philadelphia: University of Pennsylvania Press, 2012.

Farrand, Max, ed. *The Records of the Federal Convention of 1787*. 3 vols. New Haven, CT: Yale University Press, 1966 [1911].
Federal Party, Massachusetts. *Central Committee. Boston, Feb. 1806: Sir, The Central Committee Have Taken Measures to Circulate Two Pamphlets, Calculated, as They Hope, to Produce a Favorable Effect at the Approaching Election.* Boston, 1806.
Federal Party, Massachusetts. *Fifth of November, Federalists of Danvers, with Poem.* Salem, MA, 1808.
Federal Party, Massachusetts. *Salem Federal Meeting. Salem, Friday, March 25, 1806.* Salem, MA, 1808.
Federal Party, Massachusetts. *Federal Proceedings in Salem. Friday Evening, March 30, 1810.* Salem, MA, 1810.
Federal Party, Massachusetts. *Let Every Federalist Do His Duty and Massachusetts May Yet Be Saved!!! Federal Republicans! Boston, April 1811. You Have Lost the Election of Governor. You Have Elected but Nineteen Federal Senators. . . .* Boston, 1811.
Fehrenbacher, Don E. *The Slaveholding Republic: An Account of the United States Government's Relations to Slavery.* New York: Oxford University Press, 2001.
Ferguson, E. James. "Public Finance and the Origins of Southern Sectionalism." *Journal of Southern History* 28, no. 4 (November 1962): 450–61.
Ferrer, Ada. "Haiti, Free Soil, and Antislavery in the Revolutionary Atlantic." *American Historical Review* 117, no. 1 (February 2012): 40–66.
Fessenden, Thomas Green. *Democracy Unveiled; or Tyranny Stripped of the Garb of Patriotism.* Boston: D. Carlisle, Printer, 1805.
Finkelman, Paul. "Slavery and the Northwest Ordinance: A Study in Ambiguity," *Journal of the Early Republic* 6, no.4 (Winter, 1986): 343–70.
Finkelman, Paul. *An Imperfect Union: Slavery, Federalism, and Comity.* Chapel Hill: University of North Carolina Press, 1981.
Finkelman, Paul. *Slavery and the Founders: Race and Liberty in the Age of Jefferson.* 2nd ed. Armonk, NY: M. E. Sharpe, 2001.
Fischer, David Hackett. "The Myth of the Essex Junto." *William and Mary Quarterly* 3d ser., 21, no. 4 (April 1964): 191–235.
Fischer, David Hackett. *The Revolution of American Conservatism: The Federalist Party in the Era of Jeffersonian Democracy.* New York: Harper and Row, 1965.
Foner, Eric. *Free Soil, Free Labor, Free Men: The Ideology of the Republican Party before the Civil War.* New York: Oxford University Press, 1995.
Formisano, Ronald P. *The Transformation of Political Culture: Massachusetts Parties, 1790s–1840s.* New York: Oxford University Press, 1983.
Frankel, Jeffrey A. "The 1807–1809 Embargo Against Great Britain." *Journal of Economic History* 42, no. 2 (June 1982): 291–308.
Friends of Peace. To All the Electors of Massachusetts of Whatever Political Party They May Be . . . March 28, 1808. Boston, 1808.
Fry, Joseph A. *Dixie Looks Abroad: The South and U.S. Foreign Relations, 1789–1973.* Baton Rouge: Louisiana State University Press, 2002.
Gallatin, Albert. *The Writings of Albert Gallatin.* Ed. Henry Adams. New York: Antiquarian Press, 1960.
Gannon, Kevin M. "Escaping 'Mr. Jefferson's Plan of Destruction': New England Federalists and the Idea of a Northern Confederacy, 1803–1804." *Journal of the Early Republic* 21, no. 3 (Autumn 2001): 413–43.
Gawalt, Gerard W. "Sources of Anti-Lawyer Sentiment in Massachusetts, 1740–1840." *American Journal of Legal History* 14, no. 4 (October 1970): 283–307.
Gilje, Paul A, ed. *Wages of Independence: Capitalism in the Early American Republic.* Lanham, MD: Rowman & Littlefield, 2006.
Gilje, Paul A. *Liberty on the Waterfront: American Maritime Culture in the Age of Revolution.* Philadelphia: University of Pennsylvania Press, 2004.
Goodman, Paul. *The Democratic-Republicans of Massachusetts: Politics in a Young Republic.* Cambridge, MA: Harvard University Press, 1964.

Gould, Eliga H. *Among The Powers of the Earth: The American Revolution and the Making of a New World Empire.* Cambridge, MA: Harvard University Press, 2012.
Graber, Mark A. "Establishing Judicial Review? *Schooner Peggy* and the Early Marshall Court." *Political Research Quarterly* 51, no. 1 (March 1998): 221-39.
Gray, Thomas. *A Sermon Delivered in Boston before the African Society on the 14th Day of July 1818, The Anniversary of the Abolition of the Slave Trade.* Boston: Seymour, 1818.
Greene, Charles G., and Benjamin Franklin Hallett. *The Identity of the Old Hartford Convention Federalists with the Modern Whig, Harrison Party: Carefully Illustrated by Living Specimens and Dedicated to the Young Men of the Union.* Boston, 1840.
Hamilton, Alexander. *Letter from Alexander Hamilton Concerning the Public Conduct and Character of John Adams, Esq. President of the United States.* New York: George F. Hopkins for John Lang, 1800.
Hamilton, Alexander. *The Papers of Alexander Hamilton.* 27 vols. Ed. Harold C. Syrett et al. New York: Columbia University Press, 1961-1987. *The President's Speech Register Office.*
Hamilton, Alexander. *Writings.* Ed. Merrill D. Peterson. New York: Literary Classics of the United States, 1984.
Hammond, Jabez D. *A Letter to the Hon. Daniel Webster [Dated March 20, 1850, on Slavery].* Cherry Valley, NY, 1850.
Hammond, John Craig and Matthew Mason, eds. *Contesting Slavery: The Politics of Bondage and Freedom in the New American Nation.* Charlottesville: University of Virginia Press, 2011.
Hammond, John Craig. *Slavery, Freedom, and Expansion in the Early American West.* Charlottesville: University of Virginia Press, 2007.
Handlin, Oscar, and Mary Flug Handlin. *Commonwealth: A Study of the Role of Government in the American Economy: Massachusetts, 1774-1861.* Rev. ed. Cambridge, MA: Harvard University Press, 1969.
Henry, John. *The Essex Junto and the British Spy; or, Treason Detected.* Salem, MA, 1812.
Herring, George C. *From Colony to Superpower: U.S. Foreign Relations since 1776.* New York: Oxford University Press, 2008.
Hickey, Donald R. "America's Response to the Slave Revolt in Haiti, 1791-1806." *Journal of the Early Republic* 2, no. 4 (Winter 1982): 361-79.
Hickey, Donald R. "American Trade during the War of 1812." *Journal of American History* 63, no. 3 (December 1981): 517-38.
Hickey, Donald R. "Federalist Defense Policy in the Age of Jefferson, 1801-1812." *Military Affairs* 45, no. 2 (April 1981): 63-70.
Hickey, Donald R. "The Monroe-Pinkney Treaty of 1806: A Reappraisal." *William and Mary Quarterly* 3rd ser., 44, no. 1 (January 1987): 65-88.
Hickey, Donald R. *The War of 1812: A Forgotten Conflict.* Urbana: University of Illinois Press, 1989.
Hoffman, Elizabeth Cobbs. *American Umpire.* Cambridge, MA: Harvard University Press, 2013.
Horn, James, Jan Ellen Lewis, and Peter S. Onuf. *The Revolution of 1800: Democracy, Race, and the New Republic.* Charlottesville: University of Virginia Press, 2002.
Horsman, Reginald. "The Dimensions of an 'Empire for Liberty': Expansion and Republicanism, 1775-1825." *Journal of the Early Republic* 9, no. 1 (Spring 1989): 1-20.
Howe, Daniel Walker. *What Hath God Wrought: The Transformation of America, 1815-1848.* New York: Oxford University Press, 2007.
Hoxie, Elizabeth F. "'Harriet Livermore': Vixen and Devotee." *New England Quarterly* 18, no. 1 (March 1945): 39-50.
Hunt, Alfred N. *Haiti's Influence on Antebellum America: Slumbering Volcano in the Caribbean.* Baton Rouge: Louisiana State University Press, 1988.
Huston, James L. "The Experiential Basis of the Northern Antislavery Impulse." *Journal of Southern History* 56, no. 4 (November 1990): 609-40.
Jefferson, Thomas., *March 14, 1801.* Salem, MA: Printed by William Carlton, 1801.

Jennings, Walter Wilson. *The American Embargo, 1807–1809: With Particular Reference to Its Effect on Industry*. Iowa City: The University, 1921.
Jones, Douglas Lamar. "'The Caprice of Juries': The Enforcement of the Jeffersonian Embargo in Massachusetts." *American Journal of Legal History* 24, no. 4 (October 1980): 307–30.
Kaplan, Catherine O'Donnell. *Men of Letters in the Early Republic: Cultivating Forums of Citizenship*. Chapel Hill: University of North Carolina Press, 2008.
Kaplan, Lawrence S. *Entangling Alliances with None: American Foreign Policy in the Age of Jefferson*. Kent, OH: Kent State University Press, 1987.
Kerber, Linda K. *Federalists in Dissent: Imagery and Ideology in Jeffersonian America*. Ithaca, NY: Cornell University Press, 1970.
Labaree, Benjamin Woods. *Patriots and Partisans: The Merchants of Newburyport, 1764–1815*. Cambridge, MA: Harvard University Press, 1962.
Lenner, Andrew C. *The Federal Principle in American Politics, 1790–1833*. Lanham, MD: Rowman & Littlefield, 2001.
"Letters to Caleb Strong, 1786, 1800." *American Historical Review* 4, no. 2 (January 1899): 328–30.
Levy, Leonard Williams. *Jefferson and Civil Liberties: The Darker Side*. Chicago: Ivan R. Dee, 1989.
Livermore, Edward St. Loe. *Mr. Livermore's Speech, in The House of Representatives, Friday Morning, January 6: on the Bill from the Senate, Making Further Provision for Enforcing the Embargo Law*. Washington, DC, 1809.
Livermore, Shaw. *The Twilight of Federalism: The Disintegration of the Federalist Party, 1815–1830*. Princeton: Princeton University Press, 1962.
Logan, Rayford W. *The Diplomatic Relations of the United States with Haiti, 1776–1891*. Chapel Hill: University of North Carolina Press, 1969.
Lovett, Robert W. "The Beverly Cotton Manufactory: Or Some New Light on an Early Cotton Mill." *Bulletin of the Business Historical Society* 26, no. 4 (December 1952): 218–42.
Lowell, John. *Interesting Political Discussion: The Diplomatic Policy of Mr. Madison Unveiled: In a Series of Essays Containing Strictures upon the Late Correspondence between Mr. Smith and Mr. Jackson*. Boston, 1810.
Lowell, John. *The Impartial Inquirer, Being a Candid Examination of the Conduct of the President of the United States in Execution of the Powers Vested in Him, By the Act of Congress of May 1, 1810: To Which Is Added, Some Reflections upon the Invasion of the Spanish Territory of West Florida . . . by a Citizen of Massachusetts*. Boston: Russell and Cutler, 1811.
Madison, James. *The Papers of James Madison: Secretary of State Series*. Volume 6, November 1, 1803–March 31, 1804. Ed. Mary A. Hackett et al. Charlottesville: University of Virginia Press, 2002.
Malone, Dumas. "Mr. Jefferson and the Traditions of Virginia." *Virginia Magazine of History and Biography* 75, no. 2 (April 1967): 131–42.
Malsberger, John W. "The Political Thought of Fisher Ames." *Journal of the Early Republic* 2, no. 1 (Spring 1982): 1–20.
Marshall, John. *The Papers of John Marshall: Correspondence, Papers, and Selected Judicial Opinions*. 12 vols. Chapel Hill: University of North Carolina Press, 1993.
Marshall, Thomas Frances, ed. *On the Resolutions to Censure John Q. Adams, Delivered in the House of Representatives of the U.S., January 25, 26, and 28, 1842*. Washington, DC, 1842.
Martin, Robert W. T. *Government by Dissent: Protest, Resistance, & Radical Democratic Thought in the Early American Republic*. New York: New York University Press, 2013.
Mason, Matthew E. "'Nothing Is Better Calculated to Excite Divisions': Federalist Agitation against Slave Representation during the War of 1812." *New England Quarterly* 75, no. 4 (December 2002): 531–61.
Mason, Matthew E. "Federalists, Abolitionists, and the Problem of Influence. *American Nineteenth Century History* 10, no. 1 (March 2009): 1–27.

Mason, Matthew E. *Slavery and Politics in the Early American Republic.* Chapel Hill: University of North Carolina Press, 2006.

Massachusetts Federal Party. *Portland, March 23, 1809. Sir, The Committee of Public Safety and Correspondence, Chosen by the Town of Portland, Seriously Impressed With the Necessity of Exertion on the Part of the Federalists at the Approaching Election for Governor, Lieut. Governor and Senators, Cannot Neglect the Solemn Duty Which Urges Them to Address You at This Time.* Portland, ME, 1809.

Massachusetts General Court. *Acts and Laws Passed by the General Court of Massachusetts at the Session Begun and Held at Boston, in the County of Suffolk, on Thursday the Thirteenth Day of January, Anno Domini, 1803.* Boston: Young and Minns, 1803.

Massachusetts General Court. *Commonwealth of Massachusetts. In the House of Representatives, Nov. 15, 1808: The Committee Appointed to Consider "Whether It will be Expedient for this Legislature to Adopt any Measures with a View to Procure a Repeal of the Laws of the United States, Interdicting to the Citizens all Foreign Commerce . . . Ask Leave to Report the Following Resolutions:—Resolved, that the Senators of this Commonwealth in Congress be Instructed, and the Representatives thereof Requested to use Their Most Strenuous Exertions to Procure an Immediate Repeal of the . . . Embargo . . ."* Boston, 1808.

Massachusetts General Court. *House of Representatives. Resolved, That the Senators of This Commonwealth in the Congress of the United States Be Instructed.* Boston, 1809.

Massachusetts General Court. *Mr. Crowninshield's Resolutions. Commonwealth of Massachusetts. In the House of Representatives, November 16th 1808.* Boston, 1809.

Massachusetts General Court. *Report of a Committee of the House of Representatives Respecting Certain Military Orders Issued by His Honour Levi Lincoln, Lieutenant-Governor . . . With the Documents.* Boston, 1809.

Massachusetts General Court. *Report on the Virginia Resolutions, Relative to the Alien and Sedition Laws, Passed by the Congress of the United States.* Boston: Young and Minns, 1799.

Massachusetts General Court. *The Alien and Sedition Laws. Virginia and Kentucky Resolutions. Published by Order of the Legislature of Massachusetts.* Boston: Young and Minns, 1798.

Massachusetts General Court. *Resolves of the General Court of the Commonwealth of Massachusetts, Together with the Governor's Communication to the Court, Begun and held at Boston in the County of Suffolk, on Wednesday, The Thirtieth Day of May, Anno Domini MDCCIV.* Boston: Young and Minns, 1804.

Massachusetts General Court. Senate. *Protest of the Minority of the Senate of Massachusetts, Against the Report of the Joint Committee of the Legislature, on the Governor's Message.* Boston: Yankee-Office, 1814.

Matthewson, Tim. "Jefferson and Haiti." *Journal of Southern History* 61, no. 2 (May 1995): 209–48.

Matthewson, Tim. "Jefferson and the Nonrecognition of Haiti." *Proceedings of the American Philosophical Society* 140, no. 1 (March 1996): 22–48.

Matthewson, Tim. *A Proslavery Foreign Policy: Haitian-American Relations during the Early Republic.* Westport, CT: Praeger, 2003.

Mayo-Bobee, Dinah. "Understanding the Essex Junto: Fear, Dissent, and Propaganda in the Early Republic." *New England Quarterly* 88, no. 4 (December 2015): 623–56.

McCaughey, Robert A. *Josiah Quincy, 1772–1864: The Last Federalist.* Cambridge, MA: Harvard University Press, 1974.

McCoy, Drew R. "Republicanism and American Foreign Policy: James Madison and the Political Economy of Commercial Discrimination, 1789 to 1794." *William and Mary Quarterly* 3d ser., 31, no. 4 (October 1974): 633–46.

McCoy, Drew R. *The Elusive Republic: Political Economy in Jeffersonian America.* Chapel Hill: University of North Carolina Press, 1980.

McDonald, Forrest. *States' Rights and the Union: Imperium in Imperio, 1776–1876.* Lawrence: University Press of Kansas, 2000.

Member of the African Society. *The Sons of Africans: An Essay on Freedom, with Observation on the Origin of Slavery.* Boston, 1808.

Mifflin, Warner. *A Serious Expostulation with the Members of the House of Representatives of the United States*. New Bedford, MA: J. Spooner, 1793.
Monroe, James. *Writings of James Monroe*. Ed. Stanislaus Murray Hamilton. New York: AMS Press, 1969.
Montague, Ludwell Lee. *Haiti and the United States, 1714–1938*. Durham, NC: Duke University Press, 1940.
Moody, Robert E., ed. *The Saltonstall Papers, 1607–1815*. 3 vols. Boston: Massachusetts Historical Society, 1974.
Morison, Samuel Eliot. *Harrison Gray Otis, 1765–1848: The Urbane Federalist*. Boston: Houghton Mifflin Co., 1969.
Morison, Samuel Eliot. *The Life and Letters of Harrison Gray Otis, Federalist, 1765–1848*. 2 vols. Boston: Houghton Mifflin Co., 1913.
Morison, Samuel Eliot. *The Maritime History of Massachusetts, 1783–1860*. Boston: Houghton Mifflin Co., 1921.
Nagle, Jacob. *A Diary of the Life of Jacob Nagle, Sailor, From the Year 1775–1841*. Ed. John C. Dann. New York: Weidenfield and Nicolson, 1988.
Newburyport, Massachusetts Town Meeting. *Newburyport Resolutions at a Legal Meeting of the Inhabitants . . . Holden at the Court-House on Thursday, the 12th of January 1809, the Following Resolutions Were Passed and Adopted . . . .* Newburyport, MA: E. W. Allen, 1809.
Newman, Richard. "Not the Only Story in 'Amistad': The Fictional Joadson and the Real James Forten." *Pennsylvania History* 67, no. 2 (Spring 2000): 218–39.
No Tribute to England—No President for Life—No Topsfield Delegates to the Inhabitants of Marblehead. As Some Noble Federalist Has Condescended to Address You, You Will Excuse a Republican in Exposing the Absurdity of the Tory Handbill. . . . Salem, 1808.
Onuf, Peter and Leonard J. Sadosky. *Jeffersonian America*. Malden, MA: Blackwell, 2002.
Palmer, Michael A. *Stoddert's War: Naval Operations during the Quasi-War with France, 1798–1801*. Columbia: University of South Carolina Press, 1987.
[Park, John]. *An Address to the Citizens of Massachusetts on the Causes and Remedy of Our National Distresses by a Fellow Sufferer*. Boston: Repertory Office, 1808.
Parr, Marilyn K. "Chronicle of a British Diplomat: The First Year in the 'Washington Wilderness.'" *Washington History* 12, no. 1 (Spring/Summer 2000): 78–89.
Parsons, Theodore. *A Forensic Dispute on the Legality of Enslaving the Africans Held at Public Commencement in Cambridge, New-England, July 21st, 1773. By Two Candidates for the Bachelor's Degree*. Boston: John Byle for Thomas Leverette, 1773.
Pasley, Jeffrey L., et al., eds. *Beyond the Founders: New Approaches to the Political History of the Early American Republic*. Chapel Hill: University of North Carolina Press, 2004.
Pasley, Jeffrey L. *"The Tyranny of Printers": Newspaper Politics in the Early American Republic*. Charlottesville: University of Virginia Press, 2001.
Paullin, Charles O. "Early British Diplomats in Washington." *Records of the Columbia Historical Society* 44/45 (1942/1943): 241–62.
Peskin, Lawrence A. "Conspiratorial Anglophobia and the War of 1812." *The Journal of American History*. 98, no. 3 (December 2011): 647–69.
Peskin, Lawrence A. "How the Republicans Learned to Love Manufacturing: The First Parties and the 'New Economy.'" *Journal of the Early Republic* 22, no. 2 (Summer 2002): 235–62.
Peterson, Merrill D. *Thomas Jefferson and the New Nation: A Biography*. New York: Oxford University Press, 1970.
Phillips, James Duncan. "Jefferson's 'Wicked Tyrannical Embargo.'" *New England Quarterly* 18, no. 4 (December 1945): 466–78.
Phillips, James Duncan. *Salem and the Indies: The Story of the Great Commercial Era of the City*. Boston: Houghton Mifflin, 1947.
Phillips, James. *Thoughts on the Slavery of the Negroes*. London: James Phillips George-Yard, Lombard-Street, 1784.

Pickering, Octavius, and Charles W. Upham. *The Life of Timothy Pickering*. 4 vols. Boston: Little, Brown, and Company, 1867–1873.

Pickering, Timothy. *A Letter from the Hon. Timothy Pickering, a Senator of the United States from the State of Massachusetts, Exhibiting to His Constituents a View of the Imminent Danger of an Unnecessary and Ruinous War. Addressed to His Excellency James Sullivan, Governor of the Said State*. Portsmouth, MA: William Treadwell, 1808.

Pickering, Timothy. *Mr. Pickering's Speech, in the Senate of the United States: On the Resolution Offered by Mr. Hillhouse to Repeal the Several Acts Laying an Embargo: November 30, 1808*. Hanover, NH: C. & W. S. Spear, 1808.

Pitkin, Timothy. *A Statistical View of the Commerce of the United States of America: Its Connection with Agriculture and Manufactures: And an Account of the Public Debt, Revenues, and Expenditures of the United States. With a Brief Review of the Trade, Agriculture, and Manufactures of the Colonies, Previous to Their Independence*. Hartford, CT: Charles Hosmer, 1816.

Plumer, William. *William Plumer's Memorandum of Proceedings in the United States Senate, 1803–1807*. Ed. Leverett Somerville Brown. New York: Macmillan, 1923.

A Political Sermon: Addressed to the Electors of Middlesex. Boston, 1808.

Porter, Kenneth Wiggins. *The Jacksons and the Lees: Two Generations of Massachusetts Merchants, 1765–1844*. 2 vols. Cambridge, MA: Harvard University Press, 1937.

Prentiss, Hervey Putnam. *Timothy Pickering as the Leader of New England Federalism, 1800–1815*. New York: Da Capo Press, 1972.

Prince, Carl E. "The Passing of the Aristocracy: Jefferson's Removal of the Federalists, 1801–1805." *Journal of American History* 57, no. 3 (December 1970): 563–75.

Quincy, Josiah. *An Oration Delivered before the Washington Benevolent Society of Massachusetts on the Thirtieth Day of April 1813: Being the Anniversary of the First Inauguration of President Washington*. Boston: William S. and Henry Spear, 1813.

Quincy, Josiah. *House of Representatives Debate on Extra Session Thursday, January 12, Speech of Mr. Quincy*. Baltimore: Federal Republican Office for Hanson & Wagner, 1809.

Quincy, Josiah. *Speech of the Hon. Josiah Quincy in The House of Representatives of the U. States, February 25, 1811, on the Amendment Offered by Mr. Eppes to the Bill. . . Which Proposed to Revive and Enforce the Nonintercourse Law Against Great Britain*. Alexandria, VA: S. Snowden, 1811.

Quincy, Josiah. *Whig Policy Analyzed and Illustrated*. Boston: Phillips, Sampson and Company, 1856.

Randolph, John. *Speech of the Hon. J. Randolph, on the Non-importation Resolution of Mr. Gregg*. New York, 1806.

Randolph, John. *The Speech of the Hon. J. Randolph: Representative for the State of Virginia, in the General Congress of America, on a Motion for the Non-importation of British Merchandize, Pending the Present Disputes between Great Britain and America; with an Introduction, by the Author of "War in Disguise."* London: J. Butterworth and J. Hatchard, 1806.

Reinoehl, John H. "Post-Embargo Trade and Merchant Prosperity: Experiences of the Crowninshield Family, 1809–1812." *Mississippi Valley Historical Review* 42, no. 2 (September 1955): 229–49.

Reinoehl, John H. "Some Remarks on the American Trade: Jacob Crowninshield to James Madison, 1806." *William and Mary Quarterly* 3d ser., 16, no. 1 (January 1959): 83–118.

Republican of Massachusetts. *A Review of Political Affairs during the Last Half Year*. Boston: Adams and Rhoades, 1808.

Richards, Leonard L. *The Life and Times of Congressman John Quincy Adams*. New York: Oxford University Press, 1986.

Richards, Leonard L. *The Slave Power: The Free North and Southern Domination, 1780–1860*. Baton Rouge: Louisiana State University Press, 2000.

Robinson, Donald L. *Slavery in the Structure of American Politics, 1765–1820*. New York: Harcourt Brace Jovanovich, 1971.

Roediger, David R. *The Wages of Whiteness: Race and the Making of the American Working Class*. Rev. ed. New York: Verso, 1991.
Rothman, Adam. *Slave Country: American Expansion and the Origins of the Deep South*. Cambridge, MA: Harvard University Press, 2005.
Rush, Benjamin. *An Address to the Inhabitants of the British Settlements in America, Upon Slave-Keeping*. Boston: Printed and Sold for John Dunlap, 1773.
Russell, Jonathan [Hancock, pseud.]. *The Whole Truth; or, The Essex Junto Exposed. Addressed to the Freemen of New England*. New York: Advertiser Office, 1809.
Sears, Louis M. *Jefferson and the Embargo*. Durham: Duke University Press, 1966 [1927].
Senex. *Letters under the Signatures of Senex and of a Farmer, Comprehending an Examination of the Conduct of Our Executive towards France and Great Britain, Out of Which the Present Crisis Has Arisen*. Baltimore: P. K. Wagner, 1809.
Sewall, Samuel. *The Selling of Joseph: A Memorial*. Boston: Bartholomew Green and John Allen, 1700.
Seybert, Adam. *Statistical Annals, Embracing Views of the Population, Commerce, Navigation, Fisheries, Public Lands, Post-Office Establishment, Revenues, Mint, Military and Naval Establishments, Expenditures, Public Debt, and Sinking Fund of the United States of America . . . 1789–1818*. New York: Burt Franklin, 1969 [1818].
Sheidley, Harlow W. *Sectional Nationalism: Massachusetts Conservative Leaders and the Transformation of America, 1815–1836*. Boston: Northeastern University Press, 1998.
Sidbury, James. "Saint Domingue in Virginia: Ideology, Local Meanings, and Resistance to Slavery 1790–1800." *Journal of Southern History* 63, no. 3 (August 1997): 531–53.
Sidney, Joseph. *An Oration of Slavery Commemorative of the Abolition of the Slave Trade: Delivered before the Wilberforce Philanthropic Association, in the City of New York on the Second of January, 1809*. New York: J. Seymour, 1809.
Silverstone, Scott A. *Divided Union: The Politics of War in the Early American Republic*. Ithaca, NY: Cornell University Press, 2004.
Skeen, C. Edward. *1816: America Rising*. Lexington: University Press of Kentucky, 2003.
Smith, James Morton, ed. *The Republic of Letters: The Correspondence between Thomas Jefferson and James Madison, 1776–1826*. New York: Norton, 1995.
Smith, Paul H., et al., eds. *Letters to Delegates to Congress, 1774–1789*. 26 vols. Washington, DC: U.S. Government Printing Office, 1979.
Smith, Robert W. *Keeping the Republic: Ideology and Early American Diplomacy*. De Kalb: Northern Illinois University Press, 2004.
Spivak, Burton. *Jefferson's English Crisis: Commerce, Embargo, and the Republican Revolution*. Charlottesville: University of Virginia Press, 1979.
Stagg, John C.A. *Mr. Madison's War: Politics, Diplomacy, and Warfare in the Early American Republic, 1783–1830*. Princeton, NJ: Princeton University Press, 1983.
Standish, Miles, Jr. [pseud.]. *The Times: A Poem, Addressed to the Inhabitants of New-England, and the State of New-York, Particularly on the Subject of the Present Anti-Commercial System of the National Administration*. Plymouth, MA, 1809.
Stanton, Lucia. "Looking for Liberty: Thomas Jefferson and the British Lions." *Eighteenth-Century Studies* 26, no. 4 (Summer 1993): 649–68.
Steel, Anthony. "Anthony Merry and the Anglo-American Dispute about Impressment, 1803–1806." *Cambridge Historical Journal* 9, no. 3 (1949): 331–51.
Stephen, James. *Observations on the Speech of the Hon. John Randolph, Representative for the State of Virginia, in the General Congress of America: On a Motion for the Non-Importation of British Merchandize, Pending the Present Dispute between Great-Britain and America*. New York: S. Gould, Printer, 1806.
Stephen, James. *War in Disguise, or, the Frauds of the Neutral Flags*. New York: Hopkins and Seymour, 1806.
Taggart, Samuel. *An Address to the Independent Electors of Hampshire North District*. Greenfield: J. Denio, Printer, 1811.

Tansill, Charles C. *The United States and Santo Domingo, 1790–1873: A Chapter in Caribbean Diplomacy*. Baltimore: Johns Hopkins University Press, 1938.
Thompson, Robert R. "John Quincy Adams, Apostate: From 'Outrageous Federalist' to 'Republican Exile,' 1801–1809." *Journal of the Early Republic* 11, no. 2 (Summer 1991): 161–83.
To Electors of Essex South District. United States, 1808.
To the Merchants, Seamen, and Mechanicks of All Parties. Salem, MA, 1808.
Tomlins, Christopher L., and Andrew J. King, eds. *Labor Law in America: Historical and Critical Essays*. Baltimore: Johns Hopkins University Press, 1992.
Tucker, Robert W., and David C. Hendrickson. *Empire of Liberty: The Statecraft of Thomas Jefferson*. New York: Oxford University Press, 1990.
U.S. Congress. *American State Papers, 1789–1838: Documents, Legislative and Executive, of the Congress of the United States*. 38 vols. Washington, DC: Gales and Seaton, 1832–1861.
U.S. Congress. *Journal of the Executive Proceedings of the Senate of the United States of America*. Washington, DC: Printed by order of the Senate of the United States, 1805.
U.S. Congress. *Journal of the House of Representatives of the United States, at the Second Session of the Fourth Congress. Anno M.DCC.XCVI. And of the Independence of the United States the Twenty-first*. Philadelphia: Printed by William Ross, 1796 [1797].
U.S. Congress. *Journal of the Senate of the United States of America Being the First Session of the Seventh Congress, Begun and Held at the City of Washington, December 7th, 1801: and in the Twenty-sixth Year of the Sovereignty of the Said United States*. Washington, DC: Printed by Way and Groff, 1801.
U.S. Congress. *Journals of the Continental Congress*. 34 vols. Chauncey Ford Worthington et al., eds. Washington, DC: Government Printing Office, 1896–1899.
U.S. Congress. *Letters to Delegates of Congress, 1774–1789*. Ed. Paul H. Smith et al. 26 vols. Washington, DC: U.S. Government Printing Office, 1979.
U.S. Congress. *Statutes at Large of the United States of America, 1789–1873*. 17 vols. Washington, DC: Government Printing Office, 1850–1873.
U.S. Congress. *The Debates and Proceedings in the Congress of the United States: With an Appendix Containing Important State Papers and Public Documents, and all the Laws of a Public Nature; With a Copious Index; Compiled from Authentic Materials*. 42 vols. Washington, DC: Gales and Seaton, 1834–1856.
Van Cleve, George William. *A Slaveholders' Union: Slavery, Politics, and the Constitution In the Early American Republic*. Chicago: The University of Chicago Press, 2010.
Varnum, Joseph, et al. *The Reply of the Majority of the Representatives from the State of Massachusetts, In Congress and the Resolutions and Instructions of the Legislature of that State, on the Subject of the Embargo Laws*. Salem: Pool and Palfray, 1808.
Varon, Elizabeth R. *Disunion! The Coming of the American Civil War, 1789–1859*. Chapel Hill: University of North Carolina Press, 2008.
Vermont Assembly. *Journals of the General Assembly of the State of Vermont at Their Session, Begun and Holden at Rutland, on Thursday, October 11, 1804*. Bennington: Haswell and Smead, 1805.
Vickers, Daniel. *Farmers and Fishermen: Two Centuries of Work in Essex County, Massachusetts, 1630–1850*. Chapel Hill: University of North Carolina Press, 1994.
Wait, T. B. editor, *United States. State Papers and Publick Documents of the United States from the Accession of Thomas Jefferson to the Presidency, Exhibiting a Complete View of Our Foreign Relations Since That Time*. 3 vols. Boston: T. B. Wait and Sons, 1814–1815.
Webster, Daniel. *An Appeal to the Old Whigs of New-Hampshire*. s.n., 1805.
Webster, Daniel. *Considerations of the Embargo Laws*. Boston, 1808.
Webster, Noah. *Effects of Slavery on Morals and Industry*. Hartford: Hudson and Goodwin, 1793.
Wheelan, Joseph. *Mr. Adams's Last Crusade: John Quincy Adams's Extraordinary Post-Presidential Life in Congress*. New York: Public Affairs, 2008.
White, Ashli. *Encountering Revolution: Haiti and the Making of the Early Republic*. Baltimore: The Johns Hopkins University Press, 2010.

White, Samuel. *Mr. White's Speech in the Senate of the United States, on the Bill Interdicting all Intercourse Between the United States and the Island of St. Domingo; February 20, 1806*. Washington, DC, c. 1806.
White, Samuel. *Mr. White's Speech in the Senate of the United States, on Mr. Hillhouse's Resolution to Repeal the Embargo Laws, November 22, 1808*. Washington, DC, 1808.
Whitehill, Walter M., ed. *Captain Joseph Peabody: East India Merchant of Salem (1757–1844): A Record of His Life Ships and of His Family Compiled by William Crowninshield Endicott with a Sketch of Joseph Peabody's Life*. Salem, MA: Peabody Essex Museum, 1962.
Wilentz, Sean. *The Rise of American Democracy: Jefferson to Lincoln*. New York: W. W. Norton & Company, 2005.
Wills, Garry. *"Negro President": Jefferson and the Slave Power*. Boston: Houghton Mifflin, 2003.
Wolford, Thorp Lanier. "Democratic-Republican Reaction in Massachusetts to the Embargo of 1807." *New England Quarterly* 15, no. 1 (March 1942): 35–61.
Wood, Gordon S. *Empire of Liberty: A History of the Early Republic, 1789–1815*. New York: Oxford University Press, 2009.
Wood, Gordon S. *The Radicalism of the American Revolution*. Reprint. New York: Vintage Books, 1993.
Worthington, Erastus. *An Oration on the Recent Measures of the American Government, Pronounced at Dedham, July 4th, 1809*. Boston: E. Oliver, c. 1809.
Wright, Conrad Edick, and Katheryn P. Viens, eds. *Entrepreneurs: The Boston Business Community, 1700–1850*. Boston: MHS/Northeastern University Press, 1997.
Young, Alfred F, and Joyce Appleby. *Inheriting the Revolution: The First Generation of Americans*. Cambridge, MA: Belknap Press of Harvard University Press, 2000.
Young, Alfred F. *The Democratic Republicans of New York*. Chapel Hill: University of North Carolina Press, 1967.
Zeitz, Joshua Michael. "The Missouri Compromise Reconsidered: Antislavery Rhetoric and the Emergence of the Free Labor Synthesis." *Journal of the Early Republic* 20 no. 3 (Autumn 2000): 447–85.
Zimmerman, James Fulton. *Impressment of American Seamen*. New York: Longmans, Green and Co., 1925.
Zuckerman, Michael. *Almost Chosen People: Oblique Biographies in the American Grain*. Los Angeles: University of California Press, 1993.

Index

Adams, Abigail, 9
Adams, Henry, 37
Adams, John: elections and, 7, 9; role of, 25, 129, 147, 164; slavery and, 1
Adams, John Quincy: Embargo of 1807 and, 106; legacy, ix, 200–204; maritime trade and, 26, 27–28, 28, 29, 33–34, 37; nonimportation and, 92; role of, ix, 72, 86–87, 90, 108–109; slavery and, 8, 201–202
Adams Clement, Louisa Catherine, ix
Adams Clement, Mary Louisa, ix
An Address to the Inhabitants of the British Settlements in America, Upon Slave-Keeping (Rush), 192n107
African Americans, 175; Negro Seamen's Act and, 59–60; with seamen as free laborers, 68, 107; Seventy-Third U.S. Colored Infantry and, 204; voters, 176–177, 177; Wilberforce Philanthropic Association and, 1, 177. *See also* slavery
Alston, Willis, 111, 112
American Colonization Society, 196
American Cotton Factory, 179
Ames, Fisher: elections and, 70; legacy, ix–x, 83, 109; nonimportation and, 64, 65, 67; role of, ix, 9, 36, 38, 70, 83–84
Amiens. *See* Treaty of Amiens
L'Amistad, ix, 202
Anderson, Joseph, 125
annexation: of Texas, ix, 202; of West Florida, 41, 69, 72, 166
antislavery literature, 192n107
Armstrong, John, 123, 124, 160, 162
Awake! O Spirit of the North (pamphlet), 175

Bacon, Ezekiel: Embargo of 1807 and, 108, 110–111, 131, 134, 135, 139, 141; role of, 95, 131
Barker, Joseph, 73, 129, 137
Barron, James, 86
Bartlett, Joseph, 71–72
Bayard, James A., 146
Baylies, William, 110, 163, 169
Bayonne Decree, 106, 123
Bentley, William, 39, 107, 110, 177
Berlin Decree (1806), 92, 160
Beverly Cotton Manufactory, 143
Bidwell, Barnabus: economy and, 43–44; role of, 56, 62; slavery and, 73–74
Bigelow, Timothy, 137, 172
Bonaparte, Napoleon: Bayonne Decree and, 106, 123; decrees of, 92, 116n82, 160, 161, 162, 170; influence of, 122; slavery and, 29, 38
Boston Manufacturing Company, 179–180
Boston Sons of Africa, 177
Boudinot, Elias, 197
Bradley, Stephen Row, 8
Breckinridge, John, 8
Britain: corruption with supporters of, 96; Embargo of 1807 and, 123; France and relations with, 5, 25, 29; with impressments and American citizenship, 55, 61; Jay Treaty and, 25, 26, 54; Macon's Bill No. 2 and, 160; maritime trade and, 23–24, 25, 30, 85, 88, 157–158; ship seizures by, 51, 53–54, 54, 56, 88, 157, 158; wartime carrying trade and, 54
Broussard, James, 180
Burr, Aaron, 7, 102

Cadore, Duke of. *See* Champagny, Jean-Baptiste
Calhoun, John C., 182, 201
Campbell, George W., 60, 96
Canada, 95, 96, 101, 127, 165
Canning, George, 123, 157–158
capitalism: development of, 68; economy and innovative forms of, 105; southerners and, 58
Carey, Mathew, 176, 184
Carter, James, 27
Champagny, Jean-Baptiste (Duke of Cadore), 160, 161
Chandler, John, 71, 129, 130, 131
Chittenden, Martin: Embargo of 1807 and, 111–112; militia and, 171; role of, 10
Christianity, 178; Exodus 21:16, 74–75; slavery and, 177, 180, 192n107; War of 1812 and values of, 190n67
citizenship, British impressments and, 55, 61
civil disobedience, 4. *See also* protests
Clay, Henry: elections and, 201; role of, 168, 185
Cleves, Rachel Hope, 177
Clinton, DeWitt, 103, 169, 185
Clinton, George, 103, 111, 162
Coleman, Elihu, 192n107
Coles, Edward, 144–145
colonization: American Colonization Society, 196; free slaves and, x, 196, 198; racism and, 198
Compromise of 1850, 198, 203
Cook, Orchard: elections and, 71; Embargo of 1807 and, 94, 99, 129, 135, 136–137, 140; nonimportation and, 65, 66; role of, 39, 44, 56–57, 102, 110; slavery and, 73, 185
corruption, 60; in elections, 71; Embargo of 1807 and, 97–98, 132; "six-dollar-a-day patriots" and, 181; with supporters of Britain, 96
cotton, 143, 145, 174; American Cotton Factory, 179; Beverly Cotton Manufactory, 143; economy, 58, 95, 143, 144; price of, 63; smuggling, 101
"Cotton Whigs," 203
Cress, Lawrence Delbert, 190n67

Crowninshield, Benjamin, 108, 124, 179–180
Crowninshield, Jacob, 8, 31, 35, 43, 57, 108; elections and, 70–71; Embargo of 1807 and, 97–98, 128; nonimportation and, 64–65, 66, 67; role of, 76, 90, 184; slavery and, 62
Crowninshield, Sarah, 67
Cuba, 23, 30, 54, 130
Cuffe, Paul, 59
Cutts, Richard, 10, 71–72, 111, 130

Dana, Samuel W., 89, 112
Davies, John, 202
Davis, George, 128
Davis, John, 101–102
Dean, Josiah, 129
Dearborn, Henry, 201
death penalty, 74–75
Democratic-Republican Party: in context, 2–3, 4; elections and, 70, 71, 72, 72–73; growth of, 4, 18
Dessalines, Jean Jacque, 29, 30
de Yrujo, Carlos Fernando Martinez, 30, 49n94
discrimination: education and, 177; race relations with, 16, 177–178; race relations without, 59
disunion: in context, 17, 141; Embargo of 1807 and, 146; media and, 136; support for, 145, 147
Dred Scott v. Sanford, 202
Dummer, Nathaniel, 39
Durand, James, 61
Dwight, Timothy, 42

Early, Peter, 35, 73
economy, 43–44; with capitalism, innovative forms of, 105; cotton, 58, 95, 143, 144; free labor ideology and, 68; slavery and, 16, 53, 57, 73, 84, 104, 143–144, 174, 179; southerners and, 69, 174
education, discrimination and, 177
Egerton, Douglas R., 53
elections: corruption in, 71; gerrymandering and, 163, 168, 169; influence of, 3, 129; role of, x, 7, 9, 17, 70–73, 84, 103, 120, 121–122,

149n44, 196, 201; voter disenchantment in, 71
Eleventh Congress (1809–1811), 110, 157, 159
Elliot, James, 10, 112, 130, 145; free laborers and, 63; role of, 156; slavery and, 11; three-fifths clause and, 69, 104
Ely, William: Embargo of 1807 and, 104–105; role of, 10, 11, 36, 74–75
Emancipation Proclamation, xi, 17, 204
Embargo of 1807, ix, x; in context, 2, 16, 85–86, 93, 94, 119, 120, 142; corruption and, 97–98, 132; disunion and, 146; enforcement of, 97, 121, 135–136, 137–139; influence of, 98, 108, 110–112, 122–123, 123, 126, 128, 131, 133, 134, 136–137, 140, 141, 142, 143, 145; militia and, 100, 137; opposition to, xi, 97, 99–101, 102–103, 104, 104–105, 106, 108, 109–110, 124, 125–127, 129–130, 131; protests and, 139; repeal of, 132, 140, 157, 159–160; supplemental acts, 94–95, 96, 100, 133; support for, 101, 122, 141–142; violations, 128
Eppes, John Wayles, 31, 32, 134
Erskine, David M., 157–158, 159
Eustis, William, 31, 138, 184
An Examination of the Pretenses of New England to Commercial Pre-Eminence (Carey), 184
Exodus 21:16, 75
extremism, Federalists and: in context, 84–85, 199; Northern Confederacy and, 156; voters attracted to, 180

Federalists, 164; civil disobedience and, 4; in context, 1–2, 5; elections and, 70, 72, 72–73, 84; fall, 2–3, 18, 83, 164, 180, 182, 184; slavery and, 5. *See also* extremism, Federalists and
Fessenden, Thomas, 103
Findley, William, 62
Fisk, James, 171
"flogging through the fleet," 63, 79n51
Florida, 166, 200; annexation of West, 41, 69, 72, 166; with smuggling, 101

A Forensic Dispute on the Legality of Enslaving the Africans Held at Public Commencement in Cambridge, New England, July 21st 1773, By Two Candidates for the Bachelor's Degree (Parsons), 192n107
Forsyth, John, 182
Forten, James, 183
Foster, Abiel, 10
Foster, Augustus J., 162, 166
France: Britain and relations with, 5, 25, 29; Embargo of 1807 and, 123; with Jay Treaty, 26; Macon's Bill No. 2 and, 160, 162; maritime trade and, 23–24, 25–26, 26, 27, 30, 32, 33, 157–158; role of, 84, 106, 107; ship seizures and, 54, 157, 161; St. Cloud Decree and, 170; Treaty of Môrtefontaine and, 29
Franklin, Benjamin, 53, 144
free laborers: seamen as, 52, 61, 63, 68, 107; slaves and, 52–53, 61, 63; support for, 68, 68–69
free labor ideology, 52, 53; economy and, 68; politics and, 69, 76; racism and, 68
free slaves: colonization and, x, 196, 198; maritime trade and, 59–60; slavery for, 199–200
free soil movement, 175–176
Free Soil Party, 200, 202
Fugitive Slave Act of 1793, 10, 43, 176, 198

gag rule, on slavery, 202
Gallatin, Albert: Embargo of 1807 and, 132, 140; on Haiti, 41; role of, 33, 98–99, 128, 158
Gardenier, Barent, 95
Garrison, William Lloyd, 186, 197
George III (King of England), 170
Gerry, Elbridge, 163
gerrymandering, 163, 168, 169
Ghent. *See* Treaty of Ghent
Giles, William Branch: Embargo of 1807 and, 138; role of, 126–127, 127, 132
Gilje, Paul, 139
Gore, Christopher, 87

Graves, Eleazer, 60
Gray, Vincent, 30
Gray, William, 145
Green, Isaiah, 129
Greene, Charles G., 185
Greene, John, 128
Gregg, Andrew, 57, 58, 61
Griswold, Roger, 99

Haiti: in context, ix, 54; racism and, x, 41
Haiti, trade with: barriers, 33, 34, 54; in context, 2, 16, 23–25; slavery and, 24, 28, 31, 35, 36–37, 38, 51–52
Haitian Act of 1806, 24, 35, 39
Hamilton, Alexander: role of, 196; slavery and, 5, 28
Harrison, William H., 185
Hartford Convention, 172, 173, 175, 178, 180, 183
Hastings, Seth, 72
Haynes, Lemuel, 177
Hemings, Sally, 103
Henry, John, 165, 166
Hickey, Donald, 188n44
Hillhouse, James: Embargo of 1807 and, 125, 138; role of, 7, 8, 34, 37
Hodge, Michael, 51
Humphrey, Salusbury Pryce, 86

Ilsley, Daniel, 129, 137
immigrants: politics and, 4, 183–184; role of, 176; Sedition Act and, 99
impeachment, of federal judges, 72
impressments, seamen and: citizenship and British, 55, 61; opposition to, 62, 63, 179; protection, 173–174; role of, 60–61, 87; as slavery, 62–63

Jackson, Andrew: elections and, 201; role of, 173, 185
Jackson, Francis James, 158–159
Jackson, John G., 34, 123
Jackson, Patrick, 179, 180
James Smithson Society, x
Jay Treaty, 25–26, 54
Jefferson, Thomas: criticism of, 87, 179; elections, 3; Embargo of 1807 and, x, 2, 85–86, 140, 143; maritime trade and, 30, 32, 33, 55; racism and, 41; role of, 38, 71, 75; slavery and, 29, 40–41, 42, 103, 144–145
Johnson, Ronald Angelo, 28–29
judges, impeachment of federal, 72

Kansas-Nebraska Act (1854), 182, 203
Kilham, Daniel, 110
King, Rufus: legacy, x, 197; role of, x, 85, 111, 178, 201; slavery and, 1, 5, 198

Labaree, Benjamin W., 135
laborers. *See* free laborers; seamen
Leclerc, Charles Victor Emmanuel, 29
Leland, Joseph, 71
Let Every Federalist Do His Duty, 164
Liberty Party, 12, 195, 202
Lincoln, Abraham, xi, 17, 204
Lincoln, Levi, 137
literature, antislavery, 192n107
Livermore, Edward St. Joe: Embargo of 1807 and, 99, 99–100, 129–130; role of, 72, 139, 162, 165
Livingston, Robert, 31, 41, 49n94
Lloyd, James: Embargo of 1807 and, 125–126, 127, 133; role of, 10, 108, 125, 172
Lodge, George Cabot, ix
Logan, George, 32, 33, 34
Logan's Act, 33, 34
Louisiana Purchase, 7, 29
Lowell, John, 136, 164
Lowndes, Thomas, 31
Lurney, John, 23
Lyon, Matthew, 99–100

Macon, Jeffersonian Nathaniel: impressments and, 63; role of, 56, 60
Macon's Bill No. 2, 160, 162, 170
Madison, James: administration of, 158–159, 166; criticism of, 179; elections and, 17, 103, 120, 121, 129; on Haiti, 41; maritime trade and, 31, 32, 40; role of, ix, 49n94, 71, 75, 85–86, 123, 143, 155, 162
manufacturing, 104, 144; growth of, 142, 143, 144, 179–180; nonimportation and, 57, 66, 85, 142;

role of, 13, 140
maritime trade: barriers to, 15, 23–24, 25–27, 31, 32, 33, 33–34, 37; dangers, 52; free laborers and, 52–53; free slaves and, 59–60; Jay Treaty and, 25–26, 54; Macon's Bill No. 2, 160, 170; nonimportation and, 57; protection of, 27, 28, 30, 31–32, 55, 69–70; Quasi War (1798–1800) and, 27–28, 29; role of, 26–27, 30, 37, 40, 85, 88–89, 90, 157; ship seizures and, 51, 53–54, 56, 88, 157, 158, 161. *See also* Embargo of 1807; seamen
Marshall, John, 29, 102, 196
Marshall, Thomas Frances, 202
Massachusetts: militia in, 86, 137, 170; Second Massachusetts Infantry, 204
Masters, Josiah, 130
Mathews, George, 166
media: disunion and, 136; politics in, 14; War of 1812 protests and, 168–169
Merrill, Orasmus C., 183
Merry, Anthony, 75, 86
Mexican War (1846–1848), ix, 202
Mifflin, Warner, 192n107
Milan Decree (1807), 160
militia: Embargo of 1807 and, 100, 137; in Massachusetts, 86, 137, 170; with protests, 132; in Rhode Island, 137, 170; role of, 11, 87, 135, 137; War of 1812 and, 171
Milnor, William, 94
Missouri Compromise of 1820, 181, 182
Mitchill, Samuel, 33, 34
Mobile Act of 1804, 41
Monroe, James: elections and, x; on Haiti, 41, 54; role of, ix, 40, 73, 85; War of 1812 and, 170
Monroe Doctrine, 200
Monroe-Pinkney Treaty, 85, 87
Moore, Thomas, 75
morality: of slavery, 177, 178, 180; of wartime carrying trade, 58
More, Andrew, 126
Morris, William, 51
Môrtefontaine. *See* Treaty of Môrtefontaine
Mumford, Gurdon, 130

Nagle, Jacob, 101
Napoleon Bonaparte. *See* Bonaparte, Napoleon
National Republican Party, 185
Native Americans, 68, 174
Negro Seamen's Act, 59–60
Nelson, Hugh, 167
Newton, Thomas, 64, 94, 133
Nicholson, Joseph, 61, 66
nonimportation: in context, 16; controversy, 57, 64–66, 91–92; manufacturing and, 57, 66, 85, 142; opposition to, 57–58, 59, 61; policies, 66–67; supporters of, 60
Nonimportation Act of 1806, 2, 73, 84, 85
Nonintercourse Act of 1809, 157, 159–160, 162, 170, 187n23
Northern Confederacy, plan for, x, 8, 10, 103, 145, 196
Northwest Ordinance of 1787, x, 5, 6, 144, 198
Notes on the State of Virginia (Jefferson), 41

Orders in Council, 100, 127, 129, 157, 160
Otis, Harrison Gray: Embargo of 1807 and, 137; on Hartford Convention, 173; legacy, 200; manufacturing and, 180; racism and, 199–200; role of, 6, 9, 86–87, 136, 165, 175; slavery and, 181
Otis, Joseph, 132

Parsons, Theodore, 192n107
Peabody, Joseph, 39
Perkins, James, 30
Perkins, Thomas H., 30
Phillips, James, 52–53
Phillips, Wendell, 178
Pickering, Timothy: disunion and, 145; elections and, 163, 169, 196; Embargo of 1807 and, 104, 127, 133; impressments and, 61; influence, 195; legacy, x, 10, 103, 197; maritime trade and, 26–27; nonimportation and, 65; with Northern Confederacy, plan for, x, 8, 10, 103,

145, 196; role of, x, 8, 83, 92–93, 98, 172; slavery and, 1, 5, 7–8, 28, 42, 104, 195–197; War of 1812 and, 171
Pickman, Benjamin, 110
Pinkney, William: Monroe-Pinkney Treaty and, 85, 87; role of, 73, 85, 111, 123
Pitkin, Timothy, 73
Plumer, William, 8, 52, 56
politics: free laborers and, 53; free labor ideology and, 69, 76; immigrants and, 4, 183–184; in media, 14; propaganda in, 183; slavery and, 185; Wilberforce Philanthropic Association and, 177
Pope, John, 125, 142
Porter, John, 94
Porter, Peter B., 162
propaganda, in politics, 183
protests: antislavery, 181; civil disobedience, 4; Embargo of 1807 and, 139; militia with, 132; War of 1812, 168–169, 171
Putnam, Samuel, 71

Quakers, 34
Quasi War (1798–1800), 27–28, 29, 60, 106
Quincy, Eliza Susan, 195
Quincy, Josiah: elections and, 70; Embargo of 1807 and, 131; free laborers and, 68–69, 69; legacy, x–xi, 91; maritime trade and, 88–89, 90; nonimportation and, 64, 65, 66, 67; role of, x, 10, 31, 36, 70, 83, 106, 122, 172, 179; sectionalism and, 67–68; slavery and, 73–74, 75, 180–181, 181–182, 199, 203
Quincy, Samuel Miller, 204

race relations: with discrimination, 16, 177–178; without discrimination, 59
racism, 175; colonization and, 198; free-labor ideology and, 68; Haiti and, x, 41; Jefferson and, 41; nonimportation and, 59; voters and, 199–200. *See also* slavery
Randolph, John: elections and, 70, 73; nonimportation and, 67; role of, 57–58, 60, 62, 181
Read, Nathan, 70
Reed, William, 165
remorse, of voters, 120
Republican Party, 200, 202. *See also* Democratic-Republican Party; National Republican Party
Rhode Island: Embargo of 1807 and, 145; Hartford Convention and, 172; militia in, 137, 170; role of, 163, 176
Richards, Leonard, 11, 43
"rights of man," 6, 74
Rule of 1756, 157, 158
Rush, Benjamin, 192n107
Rutledge, John, 43, 183

Saltonstall, Leverett, 7, 105, 107, 178
Saltonstall, Nathaniel, Jr., 128
Saverneau, John, 23
"scorched earth" policy, 84
seamen: advocates for, 63; "flogging through the fleet" and, 63, 79n51; as free laborers, 52, 61, 63, 68, 107; free slaves as, 59; Negro Seamen's Act, 59–60. *See also* impressments, seamen and
Second Massachusetts Infantry, 204
sectionalism: opponents, 67–68; role of, 14, 25, 84, 90, 130, 141; southerners and, 57, 58
Sedgwick, Theodore: role of, 9; slavery and, 5–6
Sedition Act, 99, 138
The Selling of Joseph: A Memorial (Sewall), 192n107
A Serious Expostulation With the Members of the House of Representatives of the United States (Mifflin), 192n107
Seventy-Third U.S. Colored Infantry, 204
Sewall, Samuel, 192n107
Sharp, Solomon P., 171
ship seizures: Britain and, 51, 53–54, 54, 56, 88, 157, 158; France and, 54, 157, 161
Shirley, William, 60
Silsbee, Nathaniel, 179
"six-dollar-a-day patriots," 181, 203

Index

Sixth Congress (1799–1801), 5
Slave Representation by Boreas (pamphlet), 175
slavery: Christianity and, 177, 180, 192n107; death penalty and, 75; economy and, 16, 53, 57, 73, 84, 104, 143–144, 174, 179; Emancipation Proclamation and, xi, 17, 204; end of, 73–75; for free slaves, 199–200; free soil movement and, 175–176; Fugitive Slave Act of 1793, 10, 43, 176, 198; gag rule on, 202; impressments as, 62–63; literature against, 192n107; morality of, 177, 178, 180; Northwest Ordinance of 1787 and, x; opposition to, ix, x, xi, 1, 5–6, 6, 7–8, 9–10, 11, 28, 42, 52–53, 59, 62, 67, 73–74, 75, 104, 156, 177, 178, 180–181, 181–182, 183, 195–199, 201–202, 203; politics and, 185; protests against, 181; support for, 5, 29, 38, 40–41, 42, 57, 75, 103, 144–145, 175, 176, 184; trade in Haiti and, 24, 28, 31, 35, 36–37, 38, 51–52; voters and, 182. *See also* three-fifths clause
slaves: free, x, 59–60, 196, 198, 199–200; free laborers and, 52–53, 61, 63
The Slave Power (Liberty Party), 12
Sloan, James: Embargo of 1807 and, 140; role of, 35, 133–134; slavery and, 73, 75
Smilie, John, 62–63, 75, 93, 111
Smith, John Cotton, 56
Smith, Robert, 157, 158, 158–159, 159
smuggling, 96, 101, 127
Society for the Suppression of Slavery, 196
Somerset v. Stewart, 175–176
Soubiran, Paul Emile, 165
southerners: capitalism and, 58; economy and, 69, 174; Madison with, 166; nonimportation and, 59; sectionalism and, 57, 58; wartime carrying trade and, 58, 60, 72. *See also* slavery
Springfield Armory, 172
St. Cloud Decree, 170
Stephen, James, 54

Stoddert, Benjamin, 27–28
Story, Joseph: Embargo of 1807 and, 134, 140, 141; role of, 36, 66, 102, 108, 109, 110
Stow, Silas, 167
Strong, Caleb, 6
Stuart, Gilbert, ix, x
Sullivan, James, 104, 116n82, 127, 137
Sullivan, William, 165

Taggart, Samuel: Embargo of 1807 and, 136; on France, 161; role of, 38, 64, 108, 109, 110; slavery and, 175
Talleyrand, Charles, 34
Tallmadge, Benjamin, 75
Tallmadge, James, 181
Taylor, John, 94
Taylor, Zachary, 185
A Testimony against that Antichristian Practice of Making Slaves of Men (Coleman), 192n107
Texas: annexation of, ix, 202; three-fifths clause and, 195
Thatcher, George, 71; Embargo of 1807 and, 142; slavery and, 6, 9–10, 183
Thatcher, Sarah, 142
Thirteenth Congress (1813–1815), 169
Thomas, Jesse B., 181
three-fifths clause: in context, 1, 5, 6–7, 8, 104, 195; criticism of, 69, 103; influence of, 182; opposition to, x, 2, 6, 7, 10, 11, 12, 105, 178; repeal of, 172, 176, 177, 178; support for, x, 5, 6, 197
Tichenor, Isaac, 10
tobacco, 174; exports, 58; prices, 63, 127
"To the People of Massachusetts" (Otis, H. G.), 200
trade. *See* Haiti, trade with; maritime trade; wartime carrying trade
Treaty of Amiens (1802), 29
Treaty of Ghent, 173, 200
Treaty of Môrtefontaine, 29
Turner, Charles, 110, 163, 169
Turreau, Louis, 34, 42

United States v. Aaron Burr, 102
United States v. The Penelope, 40

United States v. The Schooner Betsey and Charlotte and Her Cargo, 40
United States v. The William, 101–102
"Universal Yankee Nation," 185
Upham, Jabez, 72

Van Buren, Martin, 202
Van Huffel, Pieter, ix
Varnum, Joseph: Embargo of 1807 and, 138; role of, 56, 99, 134–135, 163; slavery and, 6
voters: African Americans, 176–177, 177; disenchantment of, 71; extremism attracting, 180; gerrymandering and, 163, 168, 169; racism and, 199–200; remorse, 120; slavery and, 182; undecided, 105. *See also* elections

Wadsworth, Peleg, 70
War of 1812, 156, 164, 167; Christian values and, 190n67; influence of, 171, 179; militia and, 171; opposition to, 168, 169, 170; protests, 168–169, 171; reasons for, 170, 174; Treaty of Ghent and, 173, 200
wartime carrying trade, 179; Britain and, 54; morality of, 58; opposition to, 13, 58, 60, 72, 142
Washington, George, 196
Washington Benevolent Society, 165
Webster, Daniel, xi; Embargo of 1807 and, 98; on free laborers, 69; legacy, xi; slavery and, 104, 156, 180, 196, 198–199; on War of 1812, 170
Webster, Noah, 52–53
Whig Party: in context, 17; "Cotton Whigs" and, 203; role of, 185, 198, 199, 200, 203
White, Samuel, 35
Wilberforce, William, 1
Wilberforce Philanthropic Association: politics and, 177; role of, 1
William, David R., 95
Williams, David Rogerson, 58

About the Author

Dr. **Dinah Mayo-Bobee** earned her PhD in history at the University of Massachusetts–Amherst and is currently assistant professor in the Department of History at East Tennessee State University. She specializes in early national politics and is the author of "Understanding the Essex Junto: Fear, Propaganda, and Dissent in Early American Politics," "Servile Discontents: Slavery and Resistance in Colonial New Hampshire, 1645–1785," and "The Patriot: Historic Memory, Cinematic Interpretation, and the Historian's Critique." While continuing her research, Dr. Mayo-Bobee teaches courses in early national history covering such topics as foreign relations, espionage and treason, U.S. Presidents, slavery in the Constitution, and early American history on film.